SCIENCE
TECHNOLOGY
AND
SOCIETY

A HISTORICAL PERSPECTIVE

MARTIN FICHMAN

KENDALL/HUNT PUBLISHING COMPANY
4050 Westmark Drive   Dubuque, Iowa 52002

For Ken

For Betty

Copyright © 1993 by Kendall/Hunt Publishing Company

ISBN 0-8403-8621-4

Printed in the United States of America
10 9 8 7 6 5 4 3 2

Library of Congress Cataloging-in-Publication Data

Fichman, Martin, 1944-
    Science, technology, and society: a historical perspective/
Martin Fichman.
        p.   cm.
    Includes bibliographical references and index.
    ISBN 0-8403-8621-4
    1. Technology—Social aspects—History. 2. Science—Social
aspects—History. I. Title.
T14.5.F46 1993
                                        93-24429
                                        CIP

Table of Contents

■ ■ ■

Preface

■ ■ ■

This book presents a historical introduction to the social context of modern science and technology. A number of books surveying the history of science and technology are already in print, many of them of excellent quality. Numerous fine books also exist which analyze various aspects of the current controversies concerning contemporary science, technology and the environment. There are, however, few studies which examine the crucial significance of the history of science and technology for assessing the current sociopolitical context of issues such as nuclear energy, computers, acid rain and biotechnology. A major theme of this work is that a complete understanding of current debates concerning issues as central as science/technology and ethics, science/technology and public policy, or science/technology and the economy, is impossible without some appreciation of the historical factors which have contributed to modern society's unique fascination with science and technology. Indeed, the extent and depth of the links between science, technology, and culture which characterize contemporary society are without precedent in human history.

After an introductory chapter outlining the cultural context of science and technology in the ancient and medieval periods, chapters Two and Three present a detailed examination of crucial episodes in the growing interaction between science, technology and society in the sixteenth, seventeenth, eighteenth, and nineteenth centuries. Chapters Four and Five examine the sociopolitical impact of major advances in science and technology in the twentieth century. The final two chapters assess some of the critical questions confronting science/technology policy at the national and international levels today.

For a book to be both introductory and comprehensive, the amount of space devoted to each of the significant issues must be limited. Therefore, I have chosen to concentrate on a few of the most representative topics in each historical period. In the sixteenth, seventeenth, and eighteenth centuries, for example, I examine in some depth the Copernican Revolution, the rise of modern chemistry, and the Enlightenment. In the nineteenth century, the focus is on the cultural impact of evolutionary theory, the professionalization of science, and the interaction between technology and industrial working and living conditions. In the twentieth century, I focus on the scientific revolutions in quantum physics, relativity theory, and molecular biology. Since the book is intended for both professional scholars as well as university and college students and the general reader, I have included a lengthy bibliography to facilitate further study in the specific areas covered.

Because a book of this breadth could not be written without the rich scholarly resources provided by historians of science and technology in the past several decades, I wish to acknowledge my debt to the authors listed in the bibliography. I owe a special obligation to Bernard Lightman, my colleague at York University. His comments on chapter three were particularly helpful.

Martin Fichman

Introduction 1

A. Themes and Objectives

■ ■ ■

Science, technology, and society are interwoven profoundly in the late twentieth century. The various impacts of scientific and technological developments—such as computers, processed foods, automobiles and nuclear weapons—are today obvious and pervasive. Quite literally, modern industrial societies are inconceivable without science and technology. It is, therefore, sometimes easy for us to forget how recent this interconnection is in terms of the long span of human history.

Of course, even the simplest human communities can hardly function without a certain level of technology. As soon as those early groups of food-gatherers began to form the first, primitive agricultural settlements, technology had come into service. These early human societies possessed the basic technical skills needed to build houses, to weave cloth, to make weapons and to manufacture domestic utensils (such as pots, ovens, and cutlery) and simple furniture. More sophisticated tools, weapons and transportation devices (from the invention of the wheel onwards) gradually followed. In this sense, the evolution of technology is practically synonymous with the history of civilization.

Science, also, has its origins deep in the human past. When those early peoples first began to attempt to comprehend the natural world in a certain orderly way, we may say that the scientific imagination began to stir (Worthen, 1991). We possess few records of these earliest approaches to scientific thinking in prehistoric times. We possess more evidence from the first great civilizations—Egypt, Mesopotamia, Phoenicia, Israel, and India—which, while still imbued primarily with magical and utilitarian concerns, made the first momentous approaches to scientific *reasoning*. The crucial point is that these cultures perceived (however tenuously) an intellectual link between the forces of nature and the practical activities of humanity. That is, they comprehended that human survival depended on the operation of natural forces. The primitive "doctor," for example, would apply herbal and animal remedies, coupled with charms and spells, to achieve some type of cure. In time, these primitive doctor-magicians would acquire an impressive body of rudimentary medical knowledge and methods of treatment. At some point in human history—much later than the first appearance of technology, however—the idea arose that humanity could better adjust to the forces of nature (rain, floods, the seasons) if it understood how those forces acted. Gradually, the concept emerged that humankind, by comprehending Nature in a certain orderly, logical manner, could gain some degree of influence over the natural world (Greene, 1992). The stage was set for the powerful belief that science might afford humans the power to modify, possibly control, nature.

This book aims to provide an overview of the history of the *social context* of science and technology. By necessity, certain selectivity is mandated. Thus, this first chapter will survey some of the basic stages—from earliest recorded history to the late Middle Ages—by which human society, or, rather, certain quite *specific* groups within that broader historical framework, developed the first technological and scientific outlooks. Chapters Two and Three will focus on certain major developments in two periods crucial to the rise of what is termed "modern science": the Renaissance and Scientific Revolution (roughly from the fifteenth to the seventeenth centuries) and the Industrial Revolution (of the eighteenth and nineteenth centuries). The remaining four chapters will analyze, in greater detail, the profound interaction between science, technology and modern civilization in the twentieth century. In so doing, the historical uniqueness of our modern fascination with science and technology—with its potential for benefits as well as catastrophe—will be made clear. ■

B. Origins of Technological Civilization

■ ■ ■

One of the characteristic features of the human species—though not its only one—is the ability to fashion tools, both material and intellectual, to alter the conditions of its existence. It will probably remain forever unknown when or where human technology first appeared. Humanity's earliest technological discovery was fire. Lumps of flint and pyrite struck together, for example, would give off sparks with which straw and other inflammable materials could be lit. Prehistoric humans used fire not only to warm their bodies, but also applied it to the preparation of food. This not only increased the range of foodstuffs enormously; fire also enabled humans, by drying meat and other foods, to create a supply that would last through the seasons. Thus, humans—almost uniquely among animal species—long ago began a continuous effort to transform their environment using the many natural materials (both organic and inorganic) that lay at hand. This process, which can be called the origins of technology and industry, has persisted—with increasing sophistication and consequence—to the present day. It should be noted that although the use of fire is ancient, the precise scientific understanding of its chemical and physical properties came about relatively recently, some two hundred years ago (see section 2b). The marriage of science and technology, so characteristic of the modern era, is a novel historical phenomenon.

Roughly speaking, from the period from 5000 to 1000 B.C., the regions of the Near East and the Eastern Mediterranean (including Mesopotamia [now the west and southwest of Iraq], Egypt, and Greece) were among the principal centers for the dissemination of technology. The wheel and plough appear to have been invented c. 3500 B.C. in Mesopotamia. About the same time, the sail was invented in Egypt. One of the most significant technological developments of this formative period was the beginning of copper metallurgy. While this was at first of very limited economic significance, metal came to play an increasingly important role as a raw material. The experience of copper working—for tools, weapons, and ornaments—led to a knowledge of the properties of other materials. The early urban communities of the third millennium had to develop ways of dealing with the large-scale production of copper from more complex ores, often combined with sulfur and iron. It was thus as a waste product to be removed that early smiths first encountered that metal—iron—which was later to supersede copper as the major metal for the tools and weapons of emerging technological civilization. Others regions also contributed to the rise of technological civilization. Southeastern Europe and Central Asia transmitted early metallurgical traditions to the Mediterranean peoples. From the dawn of history, industrial activity was also in evidence in eastern Asia, southern Africa and western Europe. More specifically, it was between 4000 and 3000 B.C. that Neolithic (or New Stone Age) culture became well established in Mesopotamia and Egypt (Lucas and Harris, 1989). Here, the first organized cities and states arose. Similar developments also took place in China, India, and the Americas.

The important point, then, is not precisely where or at what historical period the beginnings of technical civilization took root. In fact, the potential for technological invention and application—the use of machines, vehicles and domestic devices that would make certain work less fatiguing or more productive, for instance—exists throughout the human species and throughout much of its long history. What is crucial, is that certain peoples developed the knowledge and desire for technological *innovation*—while others did not. These curious peoples were not satisfied to rest when their essential biological needs were satisfied. There appeared the tendency to exploit mankind's creative urge to foster greater and greater technical inventiveness and more profound transformation of the natural environment (Cotterell and Kamminga, 1990). This technological "drive" is one of the characteristics of modern industrial civilization. When modern Westerners or Japanese or Koreans (or, indeed, members of any advanced industrial societies) encounter a people whose material culture has much less sophistication and diversity than their own, they are (generally) tempted to make invidious comparisons. Obvious comparisons would be between spear and rifle (or nuclear missile), grass hut and skyscraper, or bark canoe and airplane.

Implicit in such comparisons is usually the belief that material progress confers a superior degree of "progress" or a higher stage of "civilization." Our study will chronicle major stages in the development of such a cultural attitude toward technology (and science). It is crucial to recognize, at the outset, that such a cultural perspective is unique, rather than universal in human society. There have existed throughout history (both unrecorded and recorded)—as well as at the present time— societies which have fashioned ways of life that simply do not place great value on technological change. The Polynesian islanders, studied by anthropologist Raymond Firth in the late 1920s, are one such group. Firth found that they were not particularly interested in making new things or in improving traditional techniques for making old ones. Although they acknowledged the superiority of the "white man's" artifacts, they were not envious of foreign technological success nor did they seek to emulate it. By Western standards, the Polynesian islanders were (in the 1920s) technologically stagnant or backward. By their own standards, however, a quite modest level of technology was appropriate to their culture. Such contrasting perspectives will present themselves throughout our study (Worster, 1985). The increasing prominence given to advances in science and technology constitutes a defining characteristic of industrial civilization. The symbol of this civilization is *homo faber*: man the maker. ■

C. Agricultural Society: Animal Husbandry and Plant Breeding

■ ■ ■

Archaeology affords evidence of manufactured products—materials that were intentionally modified for an increasingly widening and more specialized range of uses—from hundreds of thousands of years ago. The seeds of cultivated plants and the bones of domesticated animals appear, however, much later in history. With their appearance, the human species had embarked upon an agricultural revolution that radically altered the course of human cultural evolution (Rindos, 1984). Agriculture was certainly not "invented," in the narrow sense of the word, but was the result of a process of progressive change from one situation to another (Gille, 1986, vol. 1, p. 153). It arose in widely separated regions of the earth, probably quite independently from place to place. Therefore, it seems highly unlikely that agriculture had but a single origin. It is, in fact, likely that it had several origins in both the Old World and the New (Heiser, 1990, p. 10).

By roughly 5000 B.C., early farming communities had been established over a somewhat limited area of the Near East—from the more favorable valleys of mainland Greece in the West, through southern Anatolia (in eastern Turkey), Syria and south into Palestine, in the Mesopotamian valley and in the upland valleys and on the plateaus of what today are northern Iraq and Persia. Mesopotamia, the land "Between the Rivers," played a central role in the origins of science and technology. It occupies the flat alluvial areas between the Tigris and Euphrates rivers. Together with the areas north and west—which stretch in a curve from the Tigris round to the coasts of Syria, Lebanon, and Israel—it forms what was called the "Fertile Crescent." On some of the larger Mediterranean islands, such as Cyprus and Crete, similar communities had come into being.

These communities were the centers of the agricultural revolution. The basic rule of these novel forms of social and economic organization is, to later eyes, deceptively simple: not to use the entire harvest of nature for food, but to set some of it apart and replant it. Behind this new procedure, however, lay a series of complex thought processes and cultural innovations. First of all, the "gatherer-farmers" had learned that the growing cycle was constant, that it repeated itself at regular intervals. Then they learned which of the edible plants had particularly high yields. Finally, they made the seemingly senseless choice of literally taking the bread from their mouths and burying it, hoping to multiply their agricultural "investment" in a few months. This was achieved. The agricultural revolution provided Neolithic farmers with harvests that had previously been simply inconceivable (M. Cohen, 1977).

Regular, abundant harvests permitted a communal food surplus which greatly exceeded the subsistence levels of earlier hunting communities. This surplus permitted the feeding of a (gradually) increasing population. The constant supply of agricultural products also provoked (or facilitated) a series of related and profound socioeconomic and political innovations. These included (Clutton-Brock, 1981):

1. Domestication of animals, which could become a permanent activity and could be extended to new species such as the horse and various types of cattle (that is, to many more species than had been marginally domesticated by previous groups of humans, such as the dog). These domestic animals took on a dual role as suppliers of physical power and as living food reserves;

2. Maintenance of a constant communal food surplus, which allowed some members of the community to be freed from primary production and used for specialized jobs, such as making tools and implements;

3. This surplus could be traded for materials or merchandise that the community itself did not possess. Trade could also be used to enlarge the sphere of individual needs to include not only

survival, but clothing and household goods. The demand for household goods—as well as the need for adequate containers to store provisions—brought about a spectacular development in ceramics and various basket-weaving techniques. Similarly, wheeled vehicles, such as carts and wagons, were developed both for long-range transport and to shift heavy loads over short distances;

4. Finally, the development of the plough and the yoke integrated domestic animals fully into the human agricultural revolution and led to advanced methods of cattle-raising (Heiser, 1990, pp. 43–45).

The agricultural revolution, then, prepared the human species for a dramatic "take-off." The cultural complex that associated humans, plants, and animals can be regarded as the starting point of that attempted "mastery of nature" which became one of the dominant goals of subsequent human social and technological evolution. It was during this period, from roughly 5000 to 3000 B.C., that two other innovations appeared which were destined to alter *homo sapiens'* future: the emergence of cities and the creation of writing. Both were first developed to aid in the administration of increasingly sophisticated agricultural societies. Cities served as centers of storage and distribution, while writing served to record such items as receipts for payments or where tributes were going. These twin achievements would provide for an accelerated and ever more profound development of scientific thought and technological innovation.

Notable cities began to take form, from around 4000 B.C. onward, in the area stretching from Egypt to Mesopotamia. There, the agricultural system acquired the form that leads directly to "civilization"—literally that type of development of human society which brings the "city" to the fore as the dominant social form. The basic human groups became organized into (more or less) large territorial units, of similar ethnic characteristics. These larger units were linked together by the community, or network, of social, economic and defensive organization. The typical feature of all of these first civilizations was the city. These cities shared the following traits: (1) a complex division of labour; (2) literacy and a literate class (usually the priesthood); (3) monumental public buildings; (4) political and religious hierarchies; (5) a kingship (or some variant) believed to be descended from the gods, and, ultimately, (6) imperial status (or the claim to rule over subject peoples).

It was, therefore, the cities that came to store a major portion of the food supply *as well as* house the military and religious leaders and the most dynamic members of the artisan class. Thus emerged the separation, both social and territorial, between rural and urban areas. The rural majority remained engaged in food production while the urban—but highly significant—minority managed (on both the secular and religious levels) the community's wealth and knowledge. It was in the cities that the evolution of technology and science—practical and intellectual innovation—began to accelerate. The countryside, in contrast, remained—and would long remain—attached to traditional family structures and patterns of agriculture and cattle raising as well as to traditional techniques of basketweaving, weaving of cloth and simple pottery making. Already there was visible the dichotomy between the "civilized" world and the "barbarian" world beyond. There were, in fact, repeated—sometimes successful—attempts by nomadic peoples to conquer the civilized communities. The widespread introduction of firearms, however, in the late Middle Ages tipped the balance of history in favor of urban, industrial societies. ■

D. Origins of Science: The Ancient Civilizations

■ ■ ■

One crucial form of urban management took the form of recording and transmitting information. To administer the new city-communities it was necessary to keep records of such things as the taxes to be paid and the services to be provided by individual citizens or smaller dependent communities. Between 4000–3500 B.C. there appeared—among the Sumerians (in Mesopotamia)—the beginnings of a system of writing in which signs were made on slabs of wet clay. Such signs would most likely have been in some form of picture-symbols or "pictograms." Wheat in storage, for example, was recorded by an ear of wheat, oxen by an ox head, and so forth. These slabs were then dried and were stored as a "written" record (some of which exist to this day). This writing is called *cuneiform*, because of its wedge-shaped characters.

Like their Mesopotamian counterparts, the Egyptian rulers found it necessary to keep records. Instead, however, of using clay tablets, the Egyptians devised a lighter and more convenient way of storing information in the form of papyrus rolls. These rolls were made from the papyrus reed which grows prolifically in the Nile delta. (Our own word "paper" is derived from the word for papyrus. However, paper, in fact, is a quite different material from papyrus, and was invented by the Chinese, not the Egyptians.) Papyrus was an easy material on which to write with "pen and ink" and the Egyptians developed their peculiar, stylized form of writing known as *hieroglyphs*. Very early on, the Egyptians reduced their hieroglyphs to a highly simplified cursive form that could be rapidly written by hand. The invention of writing was of vital importance for most aspects of the development of civilization. It was absolutely essential for the growth of abstract science and its transmission. The evolutionary ideas of Charles Darwin and Alfred Russel Wallace, for example, could never have achieved the momentous impact they had without writing.

These first ancient writings were all sacred. Scribes worked in the temples or in the courts of the deified rulers. In Egypt, the scribes worked in the tombs where the written word perpetuated the spoken word and made it "eternally" effective. (It is interesting to note that the god of the Jews was the first whose will was declared in writing.) In spite of a high degree of codification and a gradual reduction in the number of written symbols, however, early writing remained extremely complicated. It was accessible to only the (few) scribes and priests. Neither hieroglyphics nor cuneiform scripts were "alphabetic." They were "syllabic" in that each symbol represented a syllable, not a sound. The decisive steps that transformed writing from a mysterious art into a readily accessible technique occurred (roughly) in the period 2000–1500 B.C. A novel principle was used to effect a drastic change: the signs were no longer associated with entire words or syllables, but with single sounds (or "phonemes"). These "letters" could then be combined to form syllables, with the complete "words" written from right to left.

These early alphabets culminated with the appearance of the Phoenician alphabet around 1700–1500 B.C. The Phoenicians lived in the coastal regions of present-day Lebanon as well as parts of what are now Syria and Israel. Their writing was truly alphabetic and contained 22 letters. The Phoenician alphabet quickly spread throughout Syria, Arabia and Palestine and even further. For, the Phoenicians were great traders and established colonies and trading posts throughout the Mediterranean. The introduction of alphabetic script was the last step in a (relatively) rapid evolutionary process of written communication (Ronan, 1983, pp. 32–34).

The Phoenician alphabet (the basis of many modern scripts) accomplished more effectively than any previous writing system an extraordinary thing: a whole spoken language, with the full range of its meanings, variants and nuances, could now be recorded unambiguously on a material surface. Relatively easy to learn, it took writing out of the domain of an elite few and became a tool for many to use. This tool became the means by which abstract ideas could become powerful practical forces in social and cultural evolution and in the development of science and philosophy. With the formulation of special systems of signs (notation) to indicate numbers—especially the Babylonian adoption of "positional" notation for writing numbers—the first decisive steps towards developing the quantitative sciences, such as mathematics and astronomy, were taken.

It must be emphasized that there were profound links between science and practical cultural needs from the outset. In Egypt, for example, astronomical observation and the related activity of measuring time (notably in the development of the calendar) took on particular importance because of agriculture's need to forecast when the Nile floods would begin each year. Sophisticated and comprehensive systems of weights and measures, essential for trade and commerce, also were developed by the Sumerians and Egyptians. The remarkable achievements of the first ancient civilizations—particularly the Sumerian/Babylonian and Egyptian advances in mathematics, astronomy, and medicine—set the stage for subsequent developments in science and technology (Clagett, 1989). Indeed, in one sense the formal grandeur of the Egyptian pyramids appears to reflect a perception that mathematics offers one critical key to the relationship between the human species and the universe (Arnold, 1991). Yet, it is equally true that, in another important sense, it is difficult to call the achievements of the Sumerians, Babylonians and the Egyptians "science." Despite areas of striking clarity, in the final analysis natural events were still believed to be controlled by supernatural powers whose wills could not be known. For the precursor of modern science to emerge, the gods had to be relegated to the background and an attempt made to explain the world in natural, rather than supernatural, terms. This was the great achievement of the ancient Greeks. Among all the peoples of Western antiquity, it was the Greeks who not only collected facts but ordered them according to a *comprehensive rational plan*. In this sense, the Greek philosophers of nature were the first thinkers who devised explanations that did not rely on (at least some major aspect of) magic or superstition. The outlook of the Greeks—which itself developed only very gradually and owes much to the earlier civilizations of the eastern Mediterranean—underlays what we may call the modern scientific approach to nature (Ronan, 1983). ■

E. The Classical World: Greece and Rome

■ ■ ■

It is often said that the Greeks "invented" science and philosophy (Nicolacopoulos, 1990). Certainly, such a statement requires important qualifications—we have seen that Mesopotamian and Egyptian societies made notable beginnings in science and technology. It is, however, clear that the Greeks developed a new and—for the development of science and technology—profound approach to understanding the natural world (Lindberg, 1992, p. 13). Like Mesopotamian and Egyptian cultures, the Greek world was populated by gods and divinities. But the Greek gods differed in one important respect from the gods of the earlier civilizations. Their actions in the physical world were "reasonable" and, therefore, capable of comprehension by humans. Furthermore, in the absence of (relatively infrequent) acts of intercession by the gods, the universe *continued* to operate according to natural laws (Lloyd, 1979).

It is this strikingly different role played by the gods in Greek society that paved the way for a new outlook towards nature. In the poems of Homer and Hesiod there is less of the terror felt by the Babylonians for their gods and less of the cozy confidence in divine beneficence experienced by the Egyptians. As Homer makes clear in the beginning of the *Iliad*, the gods could wreak havoc upon mortals, as Apollo does by spreading a plague among the Greeks for having insulted one of his priests. But the gods were not so great that humans could *only* implore their forgiveness and hope that catastrophe could be averted. For though the gods had supernatural powers, they also possessed many human attributes and were not above human defiance and persuasion. Indeed, the relations, both social and sexual, among the gods and people in the Greek world was intense. Such an attitude towards divinity left its impression on Greek culture, especially in science and philosophy.

Although the Greeks revered their gods—and recognized that many human attempts to imitate the gods might result in disaster or punishment for pride—they maintained a far more critical stance than earlier cultures with respect to the divine powers. The Greeks, like almost all primitive peoples, attempted to account for their origins and the origins of the world. These attempts first took the form of myths in which the gods played primary roles. But could the gods of Homer and Hesiod *really* be the creators of the vast and orderly universe which even the most superficial study of natural phenomena revealed? It was the Greeks who first answered "No" to this question. They sought to find the physical principle, or principles, which would explain the cosmos. The word "cosmos" itself is Greek. Its original meaning was "order." The first great Greek contribution to the history of science, therefore, was the recognition that (1) there was an inherent order in the universe and, most significantly, (2) such order could be understood, clearly and logically, by the human mind (Clagett, 1957).

One of the most striking things about the Greeks is that, for the first time in history, we are able to affix specific names to the authors of particular writings. No longer do we have to rely upon the anonymous—and generally composite—texts of earlier civilizations. Henceforth, particular theories and ideas can be attributed to particular individuals (or their "schools"). The invention of writing now takes on a more powerful role in the development of scientific theories and the controversies generated by them. [It should be noted that the passage from oral tradition to written culture was not yet complete. Socrates, in the fifth century B.C., still preferred oral teaching and Plato, in the next (fourth) century, wrote in "dialogue" form]. Historians have called what developed in the seventh century B.C. a "scientific age"—the first in human history. Greek science represented the remarkable achievement of separating the investigation of the laws of Nature from any religious questions of the relationship between humans and the gods.

Why science should have suddenly begun to blossom here, on the eastern side of the Mediterranean, is a question to which there is no categorical answer. There would seem to be no geographical or ethnic reason why this should have been so. All we can say is that here were colonists living in a new political, social and economic environment. It was largely of their own making and not imposed from without by another culture or empire. In an area which was new to them, the islands and coasts of the Aegean Sea, they were bound to ask questions and seek novel answers. This questioning of nature might not have occurred so readily if the Greeks remained settled in a more traditional way of life. The Greek world however was an active commercial and trading area. Merchants and travellers came from the east and southeast, from the Fertile Crescent and further regions, from Iran and from India, and even from China. In this complex and stimulating environment, it seemed "natural" that a new way of looking at things might bring about all kinds of "improvements" in society. The Greeks, in their busy harbors and thriving marketplaces, could see that frequently there was more than one solution to a particular problem. Moreover, it became clear—though we cannot cite any specific point in time—that it might not always be desirable to do things as they had "always been done." We touch here upon that crucial question of why certain societies adopt scientific and technological outlooks and why others do not (Sallares, 1991). Suffice it to say, that the first culture which may be termed scientific (in a modern sense) arose among the Greeks between the eighth and seventh centuries B.C. In cities like Miletus and Ephesus, technical and economic innovations were conducive to (though they did not cause) the rise of a rational outlook in science and philosophy. It must be emphasized, nonetheless, that non- and pre-Greek traditions, and non-Western cultural achievements (especially Indian, Egyptian, and Chinese), all played fundamental roles in the creation of what we now know as modern science (Rochberg, 1992, p. 547).

Development of Greek Science

The origins and development of Greek science is a vast subject (Clagett, 1957). Here we can list only a (very) few of the major figures and accomplishments of that process. Among the earliest Greek thinkers to make a significant contribution to the history of science was Thales of Miletus (c. 624 –c. 546 B.C.). Thales's fame rests primarily on his cosmology, astronomy and mathematics (especially geometry). He is said to have theorized that the earth was a flat disk which floats on water. Thales was also a practical man, making a fortune in Miletus by leasing all the olive presses in that city in a bumper year. Thales appears to have been the first to display clearly that quality which was to characterize Greek science: to give a natural, not supernatural, explanation of the world. He sought to derive underlying theories from the facts of observation and experience. Other prominent early thinkers who excluded the gods as explanatory devices include Anaximander (fl. 550 B.C.), Parmenides (fl. 480 B.C.), Heraclitus of Ephesus (fl. 500 B.C.) and Zeno (fl. 450 B.C.), famous for his paradoxes of infinity. Although their theories may not now seem particularly sophisticated, the critical point is that they were entirely naturalistic (Bowen, 1991).

Another extremely important figure in the development of scientific thinking was Pythagoras (c. 560–c. 480 B.C.). He discovered that the note produced by a lyre string was determined by its length. He found, moreover, that the simple musical harmonies bore simple mathematical relations to one another. For example, the length of a string which produced a note an octave higher than another note was exactly half as long as the string for the lower note. This discovery is of basic importance in the history of science for it marks the first clear introduction of mathematics into physics. It is not self-evident that nature ought to contain mathematical relationships. Pythagoras' discovery created a whole new, and potentially extremely powerful, instrument for the analysis of the world. For, if a physical property could be expressed in mathematical terms, then it ought to be possible to operate theoretically on this property with the full power of mathematical logic. Science could now correlate physical phenomena to exact mathematical relationships in theory, and not merely in practical tabulations and measurements (as the Mesopotamians and Egyptians had done previously). The mathematical approach to science initiated by Pythagoras and his followers was to prove decisive in the formation of the modern scientific outlook. Galileo, many centuries later, would deploy the Pythagoreans' numerical vision to great effect (see sections 2a, 2c).

There were many brilliant thinkers who flourished in the Mediterranean world from the fifth century onwards, and continued the development of Greek science (Lloyd, 1979). Mention may be made of Empedocles (c. 492–c. 432 B.C.; famous for his theory of the "four elements" [see section 2a]), Democritus of Abdera (fl. 410 B.C.; famous for his atomic theory), Euclid (fl. c. 295 B.C.; famous for mathematics, especially geometry), Archimedes (c. 287–212 B.C.; famous for both theoretical and applied mathematics), Hipparchus of Nicaea (d. after 127 B.C.; the greatest astronomical observer of antiquity who discovered the precession of the equinoxes), and Apollonius of Perga (fl. c. 210 B.C.; famous for his work on conic sections). These are but a few of the many participants in what has been called the "Greek miracle," that is, the development of a scientific outlook (Lloyd, 1987).

Two of the greatest philosophers of classical Greek civilization—Plato and Aristotle—also made significant contributions to scientific thought. Plato was born in 427 B.C., probably in Athens, and died there in 348 or 347 B.C. He was an aristocrat but decided not to take an active part in political life. Instead, like his master Socrates (c. 470–399 B.C.) before him, Plato devoted his career to teaching, learning and philosophical investigation. About 387 B.C., Plato bought a plot of land outside the western gates of Athens, where he founded the "Academy." The Academy was, in essence, the first great institute of higher education. Among other religious and political functions it also served as one of the first centers for scientific research. Plato's greatest contribution to science—both through his own teachings and writings and those of his pupils—was his insistence on the role of mathematics and logic. Platonism exerted a profound impact on the course of medieval science (especially astronomy [see section 2a]) and philosophy. It must be noted, however, that Plato's distrust of experimental observation and empirical results was to exert a negative influence on the development of western science.

Plato's greatest pupil was Aristotle. Aristotle was born in 384 B.C. in Stagira (in Macedonia), the son of the physician to Philip II, King of Macedonia. When he was seventeen, Aristotle enrolled in Plato's Academy where he studied under Plato and others. In 343 B.C., Philip II invited Aristotle to act as tutor to his son Alexander (later famous as "Alexander the Great"). Aristotle remained in Macedonia until 335 B.C. Then, once Alexander succeeded to the throne, he returned to Athens to set up his own school and research center. Aristotle's "Lyceum" became famous for its library and museum, as well as for his teaching. The museum contained collections of natural objects of various kinds and was funded by Alexander. Unlike Plato, Aristotle believed that empirical observation and collection of facts was as necessary to science as theory and mathematical logic. He was keenly interested in biology (Lloyd, 1987). Again, unlike his master Plato, Aristotle felt it was in keeping with the intellectual dignity of the scientist to observe phenomena—including the habits of living creatures—under natural conditions. Aristotle's entire system of thought was strongly influence by his biological investigations. For him, the most appropriate scientific metaphor as a representation of the universe was organic, not mechanical. Aristotle's cosmos was alive and its elements were to be understood, whenever possible, in biological terms. (This Aristotelian emphasis on an organic model for science was to be relegated to a subordinate position in the "mechanical philosophy" of the seventeenth-century Scientific Revolution [see section 2c]). Aristotle also made significant contributions to physics and astronomy. His doctrines of (a) four "causes," (b) "natural place" and "natural" vs. "violent" motions, and (c) the sharp distinction between the behavior of matter in celestial and terrestrial regions, were all to be extremely influential in the development of medieval science (Judson, 1991) (see section 2a). There was, in fact, hardly a field of science in which he did not make valuable contributions or provide an insight for others to pursue (Lindberg, 1992, Chap. 3).

With Aristotle's death in 322 B.C., an era in Greek science and philosophy came to a close (Lindberg, 1992, p. 69). The conquests of Alexander the Great opened the Greek world to a flood of knowledge and ideas from the newly conquered lands. In turn, however, Greek science and philosophy were among the most important "exports" to the Near East and Egypt. Indeed, it was the new seaport in Egypt—Alexandria—which replaced Athens as the focus of science and philosophy. The Museum at Alexandria—which contained the greatest library of antiquity—was an institution for scholarship and advanced study in all fields, including science. Alexandria became the focus of "Hellenistic," meaning "Greekish," culture and exemplified the great flourishing of Hellenistic science in the third century B.C. (Hellenistic culture dates from Alexander's death in 323 B.C.; it is differentiated by historians from the previous, unadulterated Greek, "Hellenic" culture.) Euclid, to cite but one example, worked at the Museum at Alexandria between about 320 and 260 B.C. There he wrote the *Elements*, which dominated western geometry until the twentieth century. In fact, Euclid's *Elements*—with its axioms, postulates, theorems, and proofs—has been said to have affected the Western mind more than any other book except the Bible. Copernicus, Kepler, Galileo, Newton and Einstein, to mention only a few of the greatest scientists, were "brought up" on Euclid. Another towering figure at Alexandria was Claudius Ptolemy (c. 100–170 A.D.). Ptolemy's *Almagest* did for astronomy what Euclid's *Elements* did for geometry. The *Almagest* dominated western astronomical science until the Copernican Revolution (see section 2a).

Roman Science and Technology

The process by which Greek science ultimately was transmitted to Renaissance Europe to form the basis of the Scientific Revolution of the seventeenth century is complex (see section 1g). The first stage in this remarkable historical process was the meeting of the Hellenistic world with the world of the Romans. As early as the third century B.C., Rome was already ruler of Italy. Two hundred years later the Romans controlled almost the entire Mediterranean, including the Greek world. They set up an empire that was to provide an unprecedented degree of cohesion and law to a region from Egypt to Britain. The Hellenistic states, born out of the break-up of Alexander's vast empire, did not seem able to resist Roman penetration effectively. What took place in the emerging Roman empire was an extremely complicated interaction between two very diverse cultures. The unity imposed by the empire—enshrined in the Roman towns and roads built everywhere—was responsible for the transmission of Hellenistic culture and learning, including science, to previously "backward" areas of Northern Europe. But Greek science was to undergo important, and not entirely beneficial, transformation in the Roman world (Lindberg, 1992, pp. 133–137).

From the beginning of Greco-Roman contact on a large scale, the conquering Romans found themselves in a somewhat ambiguous position. There could be no doubt of the superiority of Greek thought in almost every intellectual area. In most of the sciences, Greek theory and practice went far beyond anything the Romans had devised. In medicine, the Greek recognition of the complexities of clinical symptoms and their advanced anatomical and physiological knowledge and speculation far surpassed the medical learning of the Romans. Yet the Romans were conquerors and the Greeks their vassals and slaves. The Romans might well ask themselves of what use scientific learning and speculation was in a world dominated by military power. (Our own age sees a far more direct link between science and military power [see sections 6a, 6b]. For all their respect for Greek thought, the Romans tended to push aside Greek scientific accomplishments in favor of the more characteristic Roman intellectual achievements of law, administration, war and politics (Taton, 1963, pp. 268–269).

Thus, the great Greek advances in science underwent a certain period of neglect in the Roman Empire. The Romans were, essentially, a more "practically oriented" people than the Greeks. Roman genius tended to manifest itself in the foundations of law and in great technological accomplishments. Indeed, technological applications were a priority in the Roman world (Bruun, 1991). The Romans soon learned everything they could from the Greek scholars about navigation and building harbors, roads, aqueducts, and "war machines." Indeed, one of Rome's greatest historical achievements was its system of roads (Gille, 1986, vol. 1, pp. 366–367). In Greece, the roads had been mere paths or tracks. Only for the religious processions to the great temples were short paved roads laid down. The Romans, on the other hand, wanted to move their imperial armies quickly and efficiently. They built their roads, as far as possible, in a straight line. Small hills were cut through, tunnels were made through mountains, and paths were cut through forests. The surfaces of Roman roads were paved with stones, and drainage ditches dug along them. Rivers were crossed by bridges, some of which still exist and carry modern traffic. These roads made possible swift communication and transportation throughout a vast empire, enabling Rome to maintain its military domination and to administer a vast territory. Their roads were the Romans' greatest contribution to developing technological civilization.

It is known that the Romans were already using steelyards in the third century B.C. During the second century B.C., they developed devices which used the operating principles of pulleys to lift heavy building materials. Suction and force pumps were also well known. New drainage methods introduced by the Romans improved mining techniques, making it possible to dig deeper mines (beyond the limits of water tables). The great aqueducts built in (Roman) Spain furnished enough water to carry ores, making wide-scale production of tin possible (Hill, 1984). The art of glass-making also flourished in the Roman Empire. First opaque, then transparent glass was widely used for windows in houses. Around 200 A.D., the first mirrors also appeared.

A dominant feature of Roman scientific culture, then, was the emphasis placed on the wholly practical aspects of scientific enquiry (Stahl, 1962). Given this technological orientation, the most important Roman scientific writings tended to be works of synthesis (from previous authors) and arrangement, rather than original investigations. Great encyclopedias and compendia were the characteristic productions of Latin scholars. In biology and medicine, the major figure was Galen (A.D. 129 –c. 200). He wrote numerous treatises, including ones on anatomy and physiology, which remained the standard medical texts for more than a millenium. His medical and biological philosophy owed much to Aristotle, whose teachings Galen was to promulgate effectively. (Galen's work in anatomy and physiology, however, was hampered by the ancient prohibition on human dissection. Like many of his contemporaries and later medieval scholars, Galen was forced, when he wanted to carry out dissections, to use the bodies of animals. This often led to inaccurate speculations regarding human anatomy and physiology.) It is a measure of Galen's persuasiveness, that it was the Aristotelian viewpoint which permeated Western medicine down to the seventeenth century. Perhaps the most typical Roman technological work is Vitruvius' *De Architectura*, published in the second half of the first century B.C. Vitruvius (d. c. 25 B.C.) had a wide variety of cultural and scientific interests, and most of the problems he confronted required a considerable knowledge of physics. His knowledge, however, was always conditioned by utility and his work is a technological rather than a scientific treatise. *De Architectura* includes sections not only on the principles of architecture, but also on the following: (1) town planning, (2) civil engineering, (3) water supply (and the various machines used for raising, storing and transmitting it to the user), (4) civic defense and the design of the necessary siege-engines and catapults, and (5) valuable discussions of the various building materials available to Roman architects.

One of the most famous Roman encyclopedias is the magnificent multi-volume *Natural History* of Pliny the Elder (A.D. 23–79). Pliny's work is an immense compilation which has preserved for posterity much of the knowledge and many of the opinions of natural science during his own and preceding periods (Lindberg, 1992, pp. 141–144). What fascinated Pliny (and presumably his readers) was the curious, the bizarre, the entertaining. He had little interest in discovering the principles or "scientific laws"—some unifying thread—which might tie his numerous observations together. Moreover, Pliny was not always reliable in his quotation of sources and was also somewhat uncritical. Fabulous or imaginary accounts appear side by side with prosaic descriptions of natural history. Yet Pliny's *Natural History* remained for many centuries the authoritative work on natural science for the Roman world. The worship of authorities, the often uncritical copying of earlier works, and the sheer joy in the contemplation of the odd and the bizarre—as well as the ordinary—facts of natural history would also characterize the scientific writings of the medieval scholastics of the twelfth and thirteenth centuries. Pliny's work may be taken to epitomize the best and the worst of Roman science. It served to preserve and transmit some accurate observations and provide a few guidelines for further research. It also perpetuated the fancies and folklore of antiquity. Pliny's work may not be modern science, or even have achieved the standards of earlier Greek science; but it did popularize previous discoveries and thereby stimulate wide interest in the natural world for centuries to come (Beagon, 1992). Pliny died, characteristically, while attempting to follow the course of the great volcanic eruption of Vesuvius (near Naples) in A.D. 79 at (too) close range. ■

F. Science and Technology in China, India and the Arab World

■ ■ ■

The history of modern western science and technology dates largely from the revival of original Greek learning in the Latin West from the twelfth century onwards [see next section]. Mention must be made, however briefly, of the contributions of Chinese, Indian and—above all—Arabic civilization to the development of science and technology.

China

Chinese science and technology for much of its history developed in comparative isolation. Although there were sporadic contacts between China and India, Islam and the West, the Chinese outlook on the world remained insular and was quite different from that of the West (Bodde, 1991). In particular, the Chinese holistic attitude to the universe differed from the more interventionist character of science and technology which came to characterize the Scientific Revolution and what we term modern science. Significantly, there is renewed interest today in this holistic approach, which is now recognized to be less destructive environmentally than certain aspects of the Western approach to Nature.

The Chinese made notable advances in several sciences, including astronomy, chemistry and mathematics (Ronan, 1983). The Chinese also showed a pronounced ability to apply knowledge to practical ends. They have been called the "applied scientists *par excellence*" of early modern history. Chinese technology included impressive engineering developments in the design of efficient bellows and pumps, in iron and steel manufacture, in drilling deep boreholes, in shipbuilding, and in porcelain manufacture. In these and many other technical accomplishments, Chinese mechanical ingenuity and inventiveness often preempted the West, in some cases by more than a millenium. Three Chinese inventions in particular profoundly affected the history of civilization: the mechanical clock, the magnetic compass, and gunpowder (Needham, 1978). The "escapement"—the device that allows the rotation of a shaft to occur only in regular steps, by permitting a train of gears to "escape" by only one tooth at a time—is the essence of all mechanical clocks. It was first devised in China about A.D. 723. In this, the Chinese preempted the West; mechanical clocks did not arrive in Europe until early in the fourteenth century, 700 years after the invention of the escapement in China. An early version of the magnetic compass was a familiar sight in China by the second century A.D. In time, it was adopted by sailors and was common on Chinese ships perhaps as early as the tenth century, and certainly by the eleventh. Chinese navigational usage of the magnetic compass thus preceded its adoption in the West by at least 100 years. The Chinese also discovered that magnetic north and south do not coincide with geographical north and south, several centuries before that discovery was made in the West.

It is not known precisely how or when gunpowder was first discovered. Most probably, it was Chinese familiarity with nitric acid in industrial processes which brought them into contact with potassium nitrate ("saltpeter"). Saltpeter was probably first used in alchemical experiments (perhaps to obtain an "elixir" to help in achieving immortality), in combination with charcoal and sulfur. Such experiments would have led the Chinese to the discovery of gunpowder. A form of gunpowder had been known in China since before 900, and in 1040 some recipes for gunpowder mixtures appeared in a printed book. First used for fireworks, gunpowder was quickly appropriated for military purposes, being adopted in battle in the tenth century. During the next two hundred years, gunpowder played a regular part in military operations in China. It appears not to have become known to the outside world until the thirteenth century, when it was used in Islam. In 1249, for example, gunpowder was used against the Crusaders in Palestine with particularly terrifying effect (Pacey, 1990, p. 45). Gunpowder reached Europe in the late thirteenth century. Whether this was the result of transmission of technology or an independent invention is not clear. In any event, the introduction of gunpowder—and the powerful new weapons it made possible—was to profoundly affect the subsequent course of European, and international, warfare and history (McNeill, 1982).

In the field of astronomy, one of the most interesting observations was made by Chinese (and Japanese) scholars toward the middle of the eleventh century. This was the report of the sudden appearance of a star of extraordinary brightness in 1054. Recent studies have made it possible to identify this event with the explosion of a supernova, that is, a star that explodes, creating vast envelopes of hot, brightly glowing gas. Thus, it may appear where no star has been observed before because it was previously too dim to be visible—hence the name of "nova" (new). It was, therefore, in China that the first recorded description of the explosion of a supernova was made, more than 500 years before the novae of Tycho Brahe (in 1572) and Johannes Kepler (in 1604).

Finally, mention must be made of Chinese advances in biology and medicine. One particularly significant Chinese insight into medical treatment is the use of "acupuncture." The earliest documented use of acupuncture dates from about 600 B.C. The principal idea behind acupuncture is to be found in the Chinese belief in the close link between humans and earthly things (the "microcosm") and the entire universe (the "macrocosm"). The original acupuncture points bore a specific relationship to the compass points and to the arrangement of the heavens. Acupuncture also reflected the Chinese biological view of a kind of "vital spirit" or "air," which moved within living things. The motion of this vital spirit, which played an important role in the development of Chinese medicine, was believed to be facilitated by the implantation of needles. Acupuncture has continued to be used in China since its appearance. It is often used now in conjunction with modern Western medicine, for instance as an anaesthetic during surgery. Acupuncture is now also accepted by the non-Chinese medical profession, and is occasionally used as a means of treatment in other countries. The technique is currently being investigated in the light of modern scientific medical knowledge. It appears that acupuncture is an effective practical method of stimulating the natural responses of the body to the onslaught of disease. Like many other branches of science, Chinese medicine advanced to a high level (Sivin, 1990).

India

In the period before the Scientific Revolution, Indian science made a number of original contributions that were later developed in China, in Islam, or in Europe (Ronan, 1983). This was particularly true in mathematics. Hindu mathematicians developed a convenient form of writing numbers, which comes close to our modern system. In fact, these Hindu numerals were adopted, with some modifications, by Arab mathematicians in the ninth century A.D. Three hundred years later, Hindu numerals entered Europe when Adelard of Bath (fl. 1116–1142) and other scholars began translating Arabic works into Latin during the twelfth century. It was for this reason that they became known as Arabic numerals, though their origin was really Hindu. In astronomy, Hindu scholars digested and modified the astronomical knowledge received from other civilizations outside India. In the course of time, this knowledge was handed on to Islam where it was put to great use.

It must be said, however, that because of the specific religious tone of Indian civilization, modern science failed to develop there. The basis of Hinduism is an animistic religion with a large number of different gods, not unlike those of the ancient Egyptians. The Hindu religion tended to encourage spiritual enquiry rather than detailed investigation of the natural world. The ideas of Hinduism combine a reverence for all forms of life with a certain disdain for the material aspects of civilization. These tendencies were developed in an extreme form by the teachings of Siddhartha Gautama (c. 564–c. 483 B.C.), who is known as the Buddha, or the "Enlightened One." He taught that the sole aim of life was the achievement of *nirvana*, or the release from the cycle of rebirth and of the suffering that characterizes life. Buddhism taught that nothing in the material world has any reality equal to the achievement of nirvana. A renunciation of the material world and of individuality are both essential to the followers of Buddha. Consequently, Buddhism was not conducive to detailed researches in the natural sciences. The case of Indian science testifies to the fact that mere possession of scientific and technological skills was not sufficient for the emergence of the modern scientific outlook (Kulkarni, 1987). Modern science is the product of a specific constellation of religious, political, economic, philosophical as well as technical forces. The rise of modern science would take place in a society—Renaissance Europe—with a far more individualistic and materialist/mechanist outlook than in India.

Islamic Contributions

The critical contributions of the Arab world to the history of science and technology are two-fold. First, the Arabs—particularly during the so-called "golden age of Islam" (from the eighth century A.D. to the eleventh), when Islamic cultures flourished in Spain, north Africa, Syria and

Iran—made important original scientific advances. Second, by their translation of Greek texts into Arabic, Arab scholars preserved and transmitted those original masterpieces to the Latin West. The development of modern (western) science is deeply indebted to the sudden influx of Greek learning which came to the west with the great influx of Latin translations of Islamic texts from the late eleventh and twelfth centuries onward (Lindberg, 1992, p. 215).

The dominant fact in Arab history is the emergence of Islamic culture. The culture of Islam is, in turn, dominated by the life and work of Mohammed. Mohammed was born in Mecca about the year 570 A.D. One night, he saw a vision of the angel Gabriel who spoke to him. Mohammed assembled his revelations in the *Koran*, the holiest of Islamic books. The Koran is of great significance in the history of science because it first acted as a stimulus to the progress of Islamic science and, finally, as an ultimate barrier. By his death in 632 A.D., Mohammed had made many devoted converts. His followers then undertook (and quickly achieved) the enormous task of uniting the different tribes of the Arab peninsula. With this conversion accomplished, the Muslims burst upon a surprised world. Within less than a century, by 750 A.D., the religious warriors of Islam controlled a continuous empire that stretched from Spain to the Indus Valley in India. Despite their missionary zeal and often fiercely puritanical teachings, the Islamic invaders were prepared to accept much of the cultures of the peoples whom they conquered. This included (among others) the heritage of Greek science and philosophy that survived in many Hellenistic cities of the Middle East. Islamic scholars enthusiastically translated Greek texts into Arabic. This assured a spread of Greek scientific and philosophical ideas with the use of the Arabic language and script throughout the Islamic world. In fact, the Arabic language was to prove a highly flexible and appropriate medium for the expression of scientific concepts.

The absorption of Greek science and philosophy into Islamic culture facilitated the development of an indigenous system of science. An important element in the growth of science has been the way in which different societies have carried on a dialogue with one another in their investigations of Nature. Such was the case in Islam (Butt, 1991). Arab geographers, for example, respected the skill of their Greek predecessors. But they felt free to correct them, when later observations proved the earlier ones false, and to construct original scientific treatises themselves. The same spirit of innovation characterized Islamic studies in mathematics, astronomy, medicine, and other fields. Islamic scholars also came in contact with non-Greek sources of science. Particularly important was the influence of India whose medical, astronomical, and mathematical heritage was absorbed into Islam. Non-Greek sources also served to stimulate valuable criticism of certain Greek ideas. The so-called Arabic numerals are of Indian origin and their eager acceptance by Arab mathematicians gave a significant push to the development of Arab mathematics (Dijksterhuis, 1961, pp. 109–115).

Arabs made fundamental contributions to many branches of mathematics, particularly in the development of the two powerful techniques of algebra and trigonometry. The Arabic word "al-jabr" is the source of the English "algebra." In physics, Alhazen (965–c. 1040) made significant contributions to the science of optics. His finding that the refraction of light is caused by light rays travelling at different speeds through different materials (media) was used in the seventeenth century by Kepler and Descartes. His major book, *Optics*, marks the high point of Arabic physics. It is strikingly modern in character. Much like the physicists of the Scientific Revolution, Alhazen took a mathematical and experimental approach to his subject. Medicine also was advanced by Arab scholars. Two Arabic physicians stand out. Rhazes (c. 854–c. 925) was the director of the Hospital at Baghdad which attracted medical students from all over. His masterpiece was the

Treatise on Smallpox and Measles which provided such good clinical descriptions of these diseases that it was used in the West until the nineteenth century. The second great medical figure is Avicenna, or Ibn Sina (980–1037), one of the major figures of Islamic science and famous as a source of Aristotelian philosophy and science to the West. Avicenna's *Canon of Medicine* was the most widely read and best known Arabic work of medicine and profoundly influenced the development of medicine in both East and West. In fact, along with the works of Rhazes, the anatomical and physiological writings of Galen, and the *Aphorisms* of Hippocrates, Avicenna's *Canon* remained the basis of most medical education until the eighteenth century (Siraisi, 1990).

Finally, mention must be made of alchemy and chemistry. Arab alchemy—whose greatest practitioner was Jabir ibn Hayyan (whose work spanned the late eighth and early ninth centuries)—was a complex mixture of science, magic, mysticism, theology and chemical technology. The transmission of the rich, if confused, corpus of Arabic alchemy to the West became an important source for the emergence of modern chemistry during the Scientific Revolution (see section 2b). The Arabs also made notable improvements in agriculture and industry. The paper and bookbinding industries, for example, improved so much that by the ninth century in Baghdad, factories were established for making standard sizes of paper and special qualities were being produced for carrier pigeon service. This development of the paper-making industry in the Near East and Western Mediterranean was one of the main technological triumphs of Islamic civilization. It was, also, a milestone in human history. Science, literature, philosophy and all fields of knowledge became available to all literate persons in every Muslim country (al-Hassan, 1986, pp. 190–192).

Yet, for all the remarkable scientific and technological achievements of Islam, that culture never gave rise to a modern scientific outlook or world-view. Islamic religion extols the value of revelation and submission to God above all else. This is not to say that reason or the investigation of Nature were entirely discredited. Islamic scholars during the golden age of Islam studied science, often with brilliant results. By the twelfth century, however, for a complicated set of religious and political reasons, science and (independent) philosophy came to be regarded as dangers to the faith of Islam. Although it is no longer possible to view (as did some earlier scholars) the history of the rise of modern science as one of inevitable conflict with religion, the "battle" metaphor holds with respect to Islam. Science had begun to be perceived as heretical. Islam made a conscious choice of faith over science. The legacy of Islamic science was, however, to have a profound—and very different—effect on the culture of the Latin West during the Middle Ages. ■

G. Medieval Science and Technology

■ ■ ■

The term "Middle Ages" itself is somewhat confusing. It is actually a collective name covering a few very distinct periods, roughly from the fifth century to the mid-fifteenth century. The first medieval period extends from the break-up of the Roman Empire in the West during the fifth century until the beginning of the eleventh century. This is generally called the "Dark Ages" in Europe. It was a time of invasion, economic recession and political disorder. Scientific pursuits, which had reached such a high state during the Hellenistic and, to a lesser degree, Roman eras, declined notably. Much of Greek scientific thought was lost in the almost universal disruption of learning which followed the final collapse of the Roman Empire. (It should be noted, however, that the eastern half of the Roman Empire, centered at Byzantium—the "New Rome" established and renamed Constantinople in 330 by the Emperor Constantine—enjoyed an amazing prosperity and vigor for over a thousand years.) In the Christian cathedral, monastic, and court schools of early medieval Europe, most scholars concentrated their energies on theological and mystical questions. Certain scholars—most notably Boethius (c. 480–c. 524), Isidore of Seville (c. 560–636), and the Venerable Bede (c. 672–735)—did serve to transmit, however imperfectly, some ideas of Greek and Roman authors on science and technology.

Science, however, was only a small part of their scholarly interests, which focused rather on Christian faith. It was Bede who first used as his anchor date the birth of Christ, thus initiating the use by historians and others of the concept of the Christian era. We still denote the period since Christ by the letters A.D., Anno Domini, meaning "in the year of the Lord." More attention was paid to practical matters of technology. By the ninth and tenth centuries, the West (particularly in Northern Europe) had improved systems of crop rotation and ploughing. This was followed by advances in the use of nonhuman power, at first in agriculture but later in certain early industries. The invention of a new method of harnessing and the introduction of the nailed horseshoe in the ninth and tenth centuries made it possible to use draft-animals to pull heavy weights (Marcorini, 1988).

A second period of the Middle Ages denotes the eleventh and twelfth centuries. This period witnessed a general intellectual reawakening and economic recovery in Western Europe (Price, 1992). It was during this period that the Latin West became acquainted again with the brilliant scientific achievements of the Greeks, largely through Arabic translations. Technology continued its advance. By the twelfth century, the introduction and widespread use of the watermill (known in antiquity) and the windmill (reported from Persia in the seventh century) allowed the effective use of waterpower and windpower in agriculture and industry. With the emergence of universities during the thirteenth and early fourteenth centuries—such as Paris (founded c. 1200) and Oxford (founded c. 1220)—a golden age of "scholastic science" characterized the later Middle Ages (Lindberg, 1978). This late medieval scientific advance was to undergo a dramatic, indeed revolutionary, development during the Renaissance. Beginning in Italy in the mid-fourteenth century, the Renaissance covers the period in European cultural history to the beginning of the seventeenth century. The Renaissance approach to science and technology would lead to the Scientific Revolution (see Chapter Two).

Transmission of Greek Science

It is the recovery and revival of Greek learning, particularly science, by the Latin West about the middle of the twelfth century which directly concerns us here (Lindberg, 1992, chap. 10). There were two main channels through which Greek science entered the Latin West. The more significant, in terms of immediate impact, was through translations from the Arabic. These came mainly from Spain, where large territories were reconquered by the Christians from the Moslems during the Crusades. The more accurate channel, however, was through translations directly from the Greek, coming largely through Italy.

As we have noted, with the expansion of Islam—particularly with the conquest of Alexandria and Syria—the Arab world had come into contact with Greek science, which included the scientific views of Aristotle and Plato. This science was translated into Arabic by Moslem scholars from Greek and Syriac texts. After the city of Toledo in Spain was reconquered by the Christians in 1085, a wealth of Arabic scientific literature became available to those who could read it. Under the patronage of its archbishop, Toledo became a center for the translation of this literature into Latin (through the medium of the Spanish vernacular). Because of the intricacy of the subject matter and the complicated technical terminology, words whose meanings were imperfectly understood were often simply transliterated from their Arabic form. Many of these words have survived thus down to the present day as, for example, "alkali," "alembic" (the upper part of a distilling vessel), "elixir," "zenith," "algebra," "algorithm" and "lute."

These translations stimulated scholars from all over Europe to hasten to Spain in search of scientific knowledge. An Englishman, Adelard of Bath (fl. 1116–1142), made the first complete translation of the *Elements* of Euclid. A number of scholars wrote popular works incorporating the new scientific ideas. The most important, and most prolific, of the twelfth-century translators was an Italian, Gerard of Cremona (c. 1114–1187). He is credited with translating over 70 works from the Arabic into Latin. These included important scientific and philosophical works of Aristotle (and his commentators), Ptolemy's *Almagest*, many works of Galen and Hippocrates, as well as Avicenna's *Canons of Medicine*. Translations of original Arab works brought new ideas in mathematics, medicine, alchemy, magic and astrology to the West. These latter were to be an important, if controversial, ingredient in the development of modern science up to the seventeenth century (see section 2c). The translations in Spain also serve to spread the Arabic system of numbers (itself borrowed from the Hindus). The great merit of this system was that it contained a symbol for zero. Any number could be represented simply by arranging digits in order, the value of a digit being shown by its distance from zero (or from the first digit on the left). The Arabic/ Hindu numerical system had great advantages over the cumbersome Roman system and was to prove important in the rapid development of modern science.

The second great avenue of transmission of Greek science was Sicily and Northern Italy. Here, however, in addition to translations from the Arabic there appeared some of the earliest translations to be made *directly* from the original Greek. Sicily was a particularly significant source of "new" Greek scientific ideas. By 1090, this island—which had been dominated by Byzantium and, then, Islam—had become a Norman kingdom. Latin, Greek and Moslem subjects lived together in conditions even more favorable than those in Spain for the work of translation. During the late twelfth and early thirteenth centuries, the proportion of translations made directly from Greek to those made at second hand through Arabic gradually increased. The translations made from Greek provided more accurate renditions of Greek scientific and philosophical ideas for Western scholars. The combined impact of the translations from Greek and Arabic texts was to provide a profound and powerful impetus to the study of science in the West during the later Middle Ages (Murdoch, 1984).

The brilliant achievements of medieval scientists and scholars, which paved the way for the Scientific Revolution, can be mentioned only briefly (Grant, 1971). They include: (1) The recovery of the Greek idea of theoretical explanation in science. Medieval natural scientists and philosophers developed the basis for a sophisticated (and essentially modern) concept of scientific explanation, including how to construct and to verify or falsify theories. They also analyzed the relation between theory and experiment; (2) The extension of mathematics to the whole of physical science, at least in principle. The medieval scientist began to ask the kind of question that could be answered by a mathematical theory within reach of experimental verification. Especially in optics, astronomy and mechanics, the thirteenth and fourteenth centuries witnessed a turn from a predominantly *qualitative* to a more *quantitative* approach to natural phenomena (Weisheipl, 1971); (3) A new approach to the central problems of physics, namely, the questions of space and motion (Clagett, 1959); (4) In the biological sciences and medicine, some advances were made including the beginnings of a more accurate description and classification of the flora and fauna of different regions. In geology, new observations were made and the true nature of fossils appeared to have been understood by some writers; and, perhaps most significant, (5) The idea, first explicitly expressed in the thirteenth century, that the aim of science was to gain *power over nature* to be used for human purposes.

Medieval Technology

In technology, the later Middle Ages also saw significant advances (Pacey, 1990). These included major developments in mining, metallurgy (especially with respect to iron), glassworking, shipbuilding, architecture and cartography. Advances in cartography were of crucial importance for the subsequent diffusion of culture, including science and technology. When the magnetic compass first appeared in Europe about the year 1200, its potential navigational usages had been known to the Chinese for at least two centuries. However, the compass would have been of little use if reasonably accurate maps—with specific accompanying details for navigators—were not also available. It was in the thirteenth century that the first "portolani" (portolans) appeared. These contained written accounts of coasts and ports, navigational advice, tables of distances, and lists of obstructions and of navigable channels—in addition to accurate maps.

It was Portugal, under the direction of King Henry the Navigator, which took the lead in oceanic exploration in the fifteenth century. Precise though these portolans were in regard to distance and direction, they were not intended to represent large areas of the earth's surface. They are the marine equivalent of the medieval road map, a kind of schematic representation of a route. With the first Latin translation of Ptolemy's *Geography* in the early fifteenth century, the situation improved dramatically. A knowledge of mathematical cartography was rediscovered and quickly adopted and developed by Western Europe (Pryor, 1988). Reasonably accurate world (two-dimensional) projection maps and terrestrial globes soon followed. The links between technology and the nascent economic/political power of industry were beginning to emerge (DeVries, 1992). One of the most striking examples of this is provided by the Fugger family. From small beginnings in the fourteenth century, the Fuggers had by the sixteenth century built up tremendous capital from their very effectively worked silver-lead mines of Styria (in present-day Austria), the Tyrol and Spain. They were thus in a position to finance the big guns and mercenary troops on the scale required by a new European ruler like the Emperor Charles V. One of the most significant industries—for the history of civilization as well as the history of science—to become rapidly mechanized at the end of the Middle Ages was the production of books.

There were many different technical innovations which led, finally, to the development of printing. The manufacture of linen paper seems to have begun in China in the first century A.D.; it then spread westwards through the countries dominated by Islam, to enter Christian Europe (through Spain and southern France) by the twelfth century. This was a more suitable material for printing than the older parchment and brittle papyrus. Presses were already known in the manufacture of wine and the printing of cloth. The most essential element, type, was made possible by skills acquired by wood engravers and by goldsmiths who had developed a technique for casting metal. Type developed in three main stages, first in China and then in Europe. Since the techniques used in these two regions were very different, it is difficult to say to what extent the one influenced the other. In China, printing from wooden blocks—a separate block being cut for each page—appeared in the sixth century. Printing from movable wooden characters was introduced around 1050, so that it was no longer necessary to carve a whole page of writing, as it could be set up from a stock of reusable type. Printing from movable metal type appeared in Korea in the fourteenth century. In Europe, the use of wood cuts for the elaborate initial letters of manuscripts first appeared in the twelfth century. Block printing first appeared at the start of the fourteenth century, and was common throughout Europe by the fifteenth century. Movable metal type came in around the end of the fourteenth century. The advantage of cast metal type was that hundreds of copies of each letter could be cast from a single mould instead of having to be carved separately as with wooden type. Between 1447 and 1455, the goldsmith Johannes Gutenberg (c. 1400–c. 1468) and his associates (in Mainz, near Frankfurt) brought the use of accurately set movable metal type to perfection. With this crucial development, the printing—which means rapid multiplication—of books on a large scale became possible. Artists, too, recognized the significance of making exact replicas of their work. The German painter Albrecht Durer (1471–1528), regarded as the inventor of etching, combined engraving with the printing of his own books. A technological revolution of profound import for civilization had occurred. Books of every kind could be set up from a stock of separate alphabetical letters. This invention would thereafter determine the course of daily life to a remarkable extent (Wightman, 1972, pp. 57–63).

The process of printing spread quickly from Germany throughout Europe. By 1500, at least 30,000 individual editions had been published in the countries of Western Europe. Of these titles, the majority were, naturally, religious—from the Bible to various works on theology. However, other types of books, equally reflecting the demand, followed. For, no more then than now did publishers wish to publish what they thought the public would not buy. Significantly, a number of these early printed books dealt with scientific subjects (Clair, 1976). There was a mixture of popular science (for example, books on astrology and alchemy as well as elementary treatises on medicine, arithmetic, and geometry), manuals on chemical and other industrial practices, scientific encyclopedias, Greek and Latin classics, and medieval and early Renaissance textbooks. These latter included major works on scientific method and philosophy of science by the Oxford scholar Robert Grosseteste (c. 1168–1253) and Roger Bacon (c. 1220–c. 1292), who argued for the harmony between the natural sciences and religion. Central to this medieval synthesis of faith and reason were the books of Albert the Great (c. 1200–c.1280) and his pupil, the Italian theologian (and later Saint), Thomas Aquinas (c. 1224–1274).

The invention of printing had a number of crucial consequences for the development of science and technology. It hastened the creation of a modern international community of scientists by making scientific ideas available to all who could gain access to books. By making texts readily available, it diffused knowledge, providing a wider audience than could have ever been the case without printing. Printing thus may be seen as a powerful extension of that earlier invention, writing. It served to emphasize the authority of the written word, in science as in other fields. The influence of writing, printing, and paper on Western civilization has been immense. The spread of printing and the popularization of education (and, thus, literacy) were to render writing a main agent in the formation of industrial society. Moreover, our modern societies—dependent as they are on written records for administration and information flow—would have been unthinkable without access to vast quantities of cheap paper. Economically, politically, and culturally, twentieth-century technological societies are literally based on paper as the medium of information storage and transmission. At the start of the twenty-first century, we are witnessing another profound revolution as computers become the new information tools of civilization (see sections 5b, 5c).

Printing had a particularly critical influence on the biological sciences. It made possible the dissemination of identical, accurate illustrations for natural history. Much fifteenth and sixteenth century work in anatomy, zoology and botany depended for its effect primarily on illustrations. These illustrations enormously aided identification of specimens as well as standardization of technical terms. Accurate illustrations (free from the inevitable errors of human copyists of earlier manuscripts) could only be produced in quantity through printing (Lindberg, 1992, p. 345). With the cooperation of contemporary artists, books of astonishing beauty—as well as technical exactitude—poured from the presses, and increased further the popularity of science. Finally, the printing press also made the advance of science itself easier. It became increasingly the norm (by the time of the Renaissance) to publish one's discoveries. This ensured that new ideas were not lost, but were available to provide a basis for the work of others. Not all scientific advances, however, were completely dependent on the printed word. Some scientists, most notably Nicholas Copernicus (1473–1543), witheld their work from the press for many years. But this attitude became increasingly rare. Publication greatly facilitated that process of dissemination and critical discussion of ideas which was to provide a critical ingredient for the Scientific Revolution. It became generally true that—as is the case today—scientific work not printed (or otherwise recorded) had very little chance of influencing others. Perhaps the most conspicuous example was the work of the Florentine artist, engineer and proto-scientist Leonardo da Vinci (1452–1519). Da Vinci, who worked in comparative secrecy and published nothing, failed to have the immediate, widespread impact on his contemporaries that he deserved (Hart, 1985, pp. 94–113).

The Medieval Synthesis

What, then, was this medieval legacy to the rise of modern science and technology? (Lindberg, 1992, chap. 14) One of the great achievements of medieval thought, certainly, was the rediscovery of the classical heritage of Greek philosophy and science. But the writings of the Greeks (and to a lesser degree of the Arabs) did not remain in "pure" form. The Greek tradition, as epitomized by Aristotle, presented a threat to medieval Christian faith. Many of the doctrines of Greek philosophy clearly contradicted fundamental articles of Christian theology. A glaring case was the conflict between Aristotle's clearly reasoned conclusion that the world was eternal and *Genesis'* account of the creation (that is, that the world had a definite beginning in time). More importantly, Aristotle tended to bring theology under the dominance of reason and logic. Yet medieval Christianity was, to a large degree, a "mystery religion" based upon such concepts as the Trinity and the ultimate free will of every individual Christian. These concepts could not be explained rationally—they had to be "accepted on faith." The contradiction between Greek and Christian thought was no trivial matter. For, to many, what was at stake was whether the newly recovered Greek learning was worth the price of possible damnation. If Aristotle (and the Greek corpus) was to be made acceptable, he had to be "sanitized" for orthodox Christians. This task was accomplished by St. Thomas Aquinas (Dijksterhuis, 1961, pp. 128–135).

Aquinas achieved the most brilliant synthesis of Aristotelian and Christian thought for the Middle Ages. These attempts by Aquinas and others to reconcile Aristotelian science and logic with Christian doctrine were given the general name of "scholasticism" by later generations of philosophers (Dales, 1992). Aquinas succeeded in making Aristotle (and Greek thought in general) acceptable to orthodox Christians. Among other things, he emphasized that Aristotle's hierarchical cosmos—from formless matter through the "great chain of [living] being" to the "intelligences" that moved the planets and, finally, to the "Unmoved Mover" (upon which ultimately all form and motion in the universe depended)—was analogous to the medieval Christian cosmos. This latter was predicated on a hierarchy stretching upward from serf, bourgeois, noble, king, angel and, finally, to Christ. The important point is that Aquinas constructed a world-view for medieval Christianity that could include science. But the "price" paid was the ultimate subordination of science to religion. Aquinas had "purified" ancient and medieval science (and technology) by ridding it of pagan elements and adding an explicit spiritual and theological dimension to science. This meant, however, that to criticize any single aspect of the medieval legacy of science meant criticizing the whole, carefully balanced, Christian framework. Aquinas had won a central place for science by rooting it firmly in Christian dogma. By 1500, the assimilation of Aristotle, Galen, and Ptolemy was essentially complete. The views of the Greeks had been incorporated along with Christian doctrine in a vast synthesis, backed by the powerful authority of Church and State. Successful as this synthesis was for medieval thought, however, it posed potentially grave problems for the advance of science and technology.

Criticisms of certain aspects of classical science became common in the thirteenth and fourteenth centuries. With new observations and advances in scientific method, flaws in traditional explanations of, for example, the fall of a stone to earth or the appearance of the rainbow were exposed. Such isolated corrections at first posed no serious threat to Christian orthodoxy. By the time of the early Renaissance of the fifteenth century, however, a more intensely critical tradition had developed which threatened to disrupt not only accepted scientific doctrines but religious dogma as well (Iorio, 1991). Scientific innovation—the very basis of modern science—appeared to be more and more equated to religious heterodoxy. Attacks on tradition came not only from scientists. The Protestant Reformation was itself a powerful attack on the medieval/Catholic world-view. In the vigorous and challenging climate of the fifteenth century, people began to look at the nature and function of science and technology in ways far different from their medieval predecessors (Crombie, 1959, vol. II, pp. 109–110). The combined impact of religious revolt, growth of capitalist expansion, elements of political independence, and discovery of new sea routes and new areas of the world (especially the totally unexpected "New World" to the west of Europe) was such as to encourage a new spirit of scientific enquiry and technological endeavor during the Renaissance (Boas, 1962).

Science, Technology, and Society: The Critical Links

It is clear that the development of a modern scientific and technological culture is not simply a function of novel scientific ideas or technical innovations. Although these surely are the necessary conditions, by themselves they do not ensure that such a culture will develop. Ancient Greece and medieval China, for example, possessed prodigious scientific and technical talents. Yet a pervasive techno-scientific culture did not arise in either civilization. What seems to be required for science and technology to flourish and become characteristic, indeed defining, features of a given society is a complex network of specific cultural, sociopolitical and economic forces. There are at least seven such essential factors (Seitz, 1992, pp. 18–19):

1. The society must be sufficiently advanced in the evolution of agriculture and animal husbandry that it permits what might be called leisure and professional classes. That is, it must be civilized and have significant centers of culture. Such a society must also contain a certain number of individuals having the ability to ponder, from curiosity, the nature of the world about them.

2. A reasonable fraction of those individuals must have the material support necessary for their pursuits. In the early phases of the development of science, such as in ancient Greece, their requirements will be quite modest (beyond the essentials of life).

3. There must be readily accessible institutional frameworks which permit the contributors in the search for knowledge to function in an environment that is reasonably compatible with their needs. In our own day, we have universities, research institutes (both private and public), and distinguished industrial laboratories.

4. There must be systems of communication and information storage which permit the investigators to interact as broadly as possible. This will assure an essential exchange of ideas over a period of time, both to provide criticism and to permit systematic development.

5. There must be great pressure within the evolving system to promote, and indeed insist upon, the critical analysis of conclusions which are drawn by individuals. These individuals, therefore, form part of a community of investigators who strive to reach common agreement on principles that are valid as common working tools—at least for a period of time until a valid reason for change, arising primarily out of science itself, may appear as part of the process of development of science. Observed deviations from commonly accepted conclusions must form the basis for careful reexamination of such conclusions.

6. There must be a strong interest in experimentation, that permits ever deeper and more thorough understanding of the world. Greek science failed to develop its full potential in part because this basic requirement was not adequately met.

7. Finally, those involved in the pursuit of science and technology must be substantially free from dogmatic pressures which impede their freedom of speculation and experimentation. Such pressures can arise from forces within the social structure, external to the group of investigators, and deflect them forcibly from their activities. Or such pressures may be embedded within individuals as part of their indigenous cultural heritage in a form that is essentially impossible to overcome. This latter factor may have impeded the development of science in medieval China (Bodde, 1991).

Historically, the appropriate mix of the above factors did not begin to coalesce until roughly around the late fifteenth century. It was during the period between 1500 and 1700 that an emerging techno-scientific culture first became apparent. ■

Science and Technology in the Renaissance and the Enlightenment 2

The movement generally known as the Renaissance was one of the most significant in European history. It effected a fundamental change in human attitudes toward the major questions of human existence. Beginning in the Italian city-states of the mid-fourteenth century, the Renaissance saw not only a rediscovery of the ideas and texts of classical antiquity—giving rise to the dominant movement known as humanism—but also a new discovery of the world itself (Goodman and McKay, 1990). It was an age of geographical exploration and a period of great economic, political, and religious upheaval (Grafton, 1992). Although there is much debate as to the precise definition and dating of the Renaissance, there is little doubt that the period from the late fourteenth to the late sixteenth centuries marked a break in many important respects from medieval culture. However deeply the Renaissance may have been rooted in medieval soil, it was everywhere uprooting accepted ideas (Kaufmann, 1992). The spirit of the Renaissance permeated many areas, including science. In this chapter, we shall focus on one of the most significant episodes in Renaissance history, namely, the Copernican Revolution. Copernicus' lifetime, 1473–1543, occupied the central decades of the Renaissance and the revolution which bears his name exemplifies the spirit of innovation.

By the seventeenth century, certain aspects of European thought and society began to take on those forms that historians call early modern culture. Central to these developments was the Scientific Revolution, the period roughly between 1550 to 1700. During this time the conceptual and institutional foundations of modern science were erected upon the discredited medieval, largely Aristotelian, world-view. A new mechanistic philosophy of nature, championed by René Descartes, Pierre Gassendi, Thomas Hobbes and Robert Boyle (among others), provoked major transformations in physics, astronomy, biology and other technical disciplines. This being said, it must be noted that magical and mystical traditions continued to influence the development of modern science in some important areas. Nowhere is this interplay of various traditions more obvious than in the origins of modern chemistry, which owes much to alchemical thought and practice. This chapter examines the revolution in chemistry which culminated in the late eighteenth century in the work of Antoine Lavoisier.

The Scientific Revolution had broad repercussions in general culture: scientific ideas and methodology permeated the thought of the age. The clearest indication of the impact of scientific thought and practice occurs in the cultural context of the European Enlightenment. The twin symbols of "reason" and "nature" dominated Enlightenment efforts to establish objective "sciences of humanity" and the "science of society." This chapter concludes with an assessment of the Enlightenment program and its significance for nineteenth- and twentieth-century attitudes toward the cultural context of science and technology. ■

A. Astronomy and the Changing Nature of Facts: The Copernican Revolution

■ ■ ■

The revolution in astronomy which is associated with the name of Nicholas Copernicus (1473–1543) is one of the watersheds in the rise of modern science. The development and validation of the heliocentric, or sun-centered, theory constituted a decisive alteration in humanity's conception of the physical structure of the universe. It also signalled a dramatic shift in humanity's conception of its place in that universe. More than most events in the history of science, the Copernican Revolution exemplifies the rise of the modern Western world-view. In natural philosophy, it replaced a finite, earth-centered cosmos, which had been reconciled with Christian teaching, by an infinite, uniform, nearly empty universe. The Copernican Revolution also ratified a conception of knowledge based on experiential facts rather than on ecclesiastical authority (Ravetz, 1990, pp. 201–202). To fully understand the nature and significance of the Copernican Revolution, it is necessary first to examine briefly the system which Copernicus' theory ultimately replaced: the Ptolemaic, or earth-centered, universe.

At the beginning of the sixteenth century an educated European would have known the way in which the universe worked. He or she would have "known" that the earth was stationary at its center. It would also have been clear that a giant sphere marked the physical outer boundary of the universe. Furthermore, this sphere rotated once each day, carrying with it the fixed stars. Between the central, spherical earth and the sphere of the fixed stars—the "two-sphere" universe—would have been located the moon, the sun and five planets. Finally, each of these seven bodies would have followed a complex yet predictable path in the heavens, compounded out of simple circular motions. Such a view of the universe—called the Ptolemaic system after the great Egyptian astronomer Claudius Ptolemy (c.100–170 A.D.)—was fully consistent with our hypothetical European's astronomical observations, his/her physical theory, and his/her philosophical and religious framework.

By the end of the seventeenth century an educated person would also have known the way in which the universe worked. He or she would have "known" that the earth, like the other planets, revolved around the central sun. The earth's path, like that of the other planets, would be known to be elliptical, prescribed by the force of gravity. The earth, moreover, would be understood to rotate once each day on its axis. The moon, of course, would still be understood to revolve around the earth. Such a view of the universe—called the Copernican or heliocentric system—would be fully consistent with our (second) hypothetical European's astronomical observations, his/her physical theory, and (to a greater or lesser degree) his/her philosophical and religious framework.

In the period which had elapsed a revolution had occurred: the Copernican Revolution. It may be considered to have been bounded in time by the publication in 1543 of Copernicus' great treatise *On the Revolutions of the Celestial Spheres* (generally known after its abbreviated Latin title *De Revolutionibus*) and the publication in 1687 of Isaac Newton's *Principia* (*Mathematical Principles of Natural Philosophy*). In the century and a half between these two dates, the educated person referred to above would have had a choice between the old and new astronomies. During that period of intellectual ferment there would have been two theories competing, in effect, for the status of scientific truth.

The notion that science affords a set of objective criteria upon which such choices can be made is rendered suspect by an examination of this period of revolution. The older Ptolemaic astronomy carried with it a set of assumptions about the universe which were consistent with human experience, both religious and physical. Copernican astronomy carried with it a different set of assumptions about the universe. The clash between the two astronomical systems—as exemplified in the famous conflict between Galileo and the Catholic Church during the seventeenth century (see section 2c)—was not, as it is often depicted, a clash between scientific reason and religious obscurantism or fanaticism. It was, rather, the contest between two theoretical systems, both of which were honestly and competently defended by their respective adherents. And the choice between the two systems could not be made on clear, objective scientific grounds alone. For each system could count on extensive empirical support and mathematical rigor. During the period of transition which saw the Copernican *paradigm* replace the Ptolemaic *paradigm* as the dominant model for astronomy, a scientific consensus among astronomers simply did not exist. And when a consensus did finally emerge among astronomers by the close of the seventeenth century, adherence to the Copernican theory rested on a complex set of empirical, mathematical and philosophical as well as cultural arguments (Kuhn, 1957, pp. 226–228).

The Copernican Revolution plays so important a role in the history of science not only because it provided the basis for the development of modern astronomy. It also provides an excellent case study from which we can learn something of the nature of theory change in general in science. Furthermore, the defense and refinement of Copernicus' heliocentric theory, particularly by such figures as Galileo, Kepler and Newton, present a rich picture of the genesis of the modern scientific outlook. The emergence of Copernican astronomy reveals science as inextricably linked to its historical and social context. Copernican astronomy was inseparable from the philosophical, religious and sociopolitical controversies of the sixteenth and seventeenth centuries. An understanding of the Copernican Revolution, then, assists us in also understanding the culturally complex nature of the scientific controversies which dominate our own age.

Ptolemaic Astronomy

Perhaps the most remarkable fact about the Ptolemaic system was that it continued to be the most widely held picture of the universe, by scientists and laymen, for nearly 1500 years (Crombie, 1959, vol. I, p. 82). What is known as Ptolemaic astronomy is not merely Ptolemy's own astronomical system. His major work, the *Almagest*, appeared in the second century A.D. Although Ptolemy made many original contributions, his system depended upon ideas of earlier Greek astronomers. Like Euclid's *Elements*, however, the *Almagest* was so brilliant an exposition of the earth-centered universe that it came during the Middle Ages to symbolize that system.

Ptolemaic astronomy is, moreover, much more than an astronomical theory. Though largely mathematical, the *Almagest* is based on Aristotelian physics and rests on certain philosophical notions. These include Aristotelian arguments which show the earth to be stationary, in the center of the universe. Ptolemy's system is also predicated upon Plato's doctrine of perfect circular motion. Plato maintained, largely on the basis of *a priori* reasoning, that only uniform circular motion was appropriate to the realm of perfection, the realm of God's pure, untouched creation.

Aristotle elaborated on the Platonic insistence of circularity, and made explicit its relevance to astronomy.

Aristotle's cosmology did not offer a *mathematical* solution to the problem of the motion of the planets. But in his cosmology, the planets (including the sun) were recognized as having each its own distinct *qualitative* motion. The heavenly regions beyond the sphere of the moon—the *superlunary* region, which included the planets, the sun, and the fixed stars—were assumed to manifest perfection. Thus, according to Platonic philosophy, the orbits of the heavenly bodies about the central earth had to be circular. Below the sphere of the moon—the *sublunary* and terrestrial regions—the motion of bodies was not circular, but naturally radial, that is, to or from the center of the earth.

The universe of Aristotle was also a system of *concentric* spheres, nesting one within the other. Aristotle based his cosmology on the ancient concept of the two-sphere universe. But

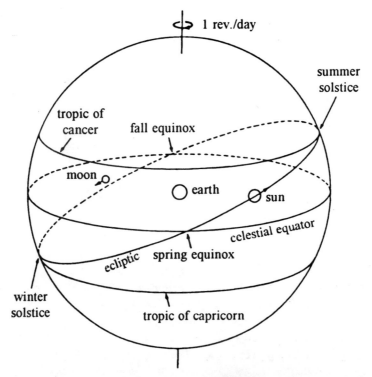

Figure 2.1. Two-sphere model of the cosmos.
From David C. Lindberg, *The Beginnings of Western Science,*
Copyright © 1992 by The University of Chicago. Reprinted with permission

he incorporated between the stellar sphere and the earth a crystalline sphere for each of the seven known planets (including the sun and the moon). This spherical construction was reflected in the earth also. The four terrestrial elements—earth, water, air and fire—were located, according to the doctrine of "natural place," in concentric spheres. The element earth was "naturally" located at the center. Around it, in order, were the spheres of water, then air, and, finally (and closest to the moon), the sphere of fire. Unlike the perfect motion of the heavenly bodies, which were made up of a fifth element, the "aether," the bodies comprised of the four elements underwent noncircular motions. Thus the physical motion of bodies located in the realm of mankind, below the moon, were disturbed and dislocated by the processes of change and decay. Above the sphere of the moon was the perfect motion of the fixed stars (so called because they presented an unchanging aspect to earthly observers). The Gods themselves were located in a bounding shell, the *primum mobile* or "prime-mover," whose motion was transmitted down through the planetary spheres, causing the perfect but complex motion of the planets (Olby, 1990, pp. 559-560).

Ptolemy's great achievement was to provide a detailed, *quantitative* solution to the observed motions of the planets, the sun, and the moon. By means of a brilliant conceptual scheme based on a system of *epicycles* and *deferents*, Ptolemy was able to show mathematically that each planetary orbit about the central earth was the result of a *combination* of perfect circular motions. Now, the result of these compounded motions would "appear" to an observer situated on the earth to be slightly irregular. That is, each of the planets would occasionally appear to move backwards in its orbit—or exhibit *retrograde motion*—for brief periods of time. In "reality," however, the planets too obeyed the doctrine of uniform circular motion. It must be emphasized that Ptolemy's

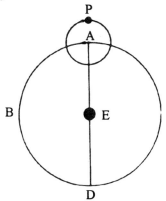

Ptolemy's epicycle on deferent model.

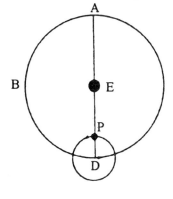

Ptolemy's epicycle on deferent model, with the planet on the inside of the epicycle.

Retrograde motion of a planet explained on the epicycle and deferent model. As the epicycle moves counterclockwise on the deferent, the planet moves counterclockwise on the epicycle. The actual path of the planet is represented by the heavy line.

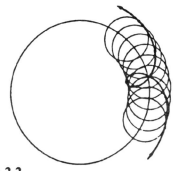

Figure 2.2.
From David C. Lindberg, *The Beginnings of Western Science,*
Copyright © 1992 by The University of Chicago. Reprinted with permission

mathematical theory allowed astronomers to compute the orbital motions of the planets not just approximately, but to within the degree of accuracy permitted by the observational data of the time. Moreover, and this is crucial, there is no limit to the potential accuracy of such a system. By adjusting geometrically the relative size of epicycles and deferents, an astronomer could achieve as close an approximation to any path as required by observational data (Lindberg, 1992, pp. 98–105).

Ptolemy's computational astronomy, when incorporated into the metaphysical systems of Plato and Aristotle, provided a cosmological system that satisfied technical as well as philosophical demands. The cosmos was finite and spherical. It was divided into two qualitatively distinct regions, the sublunary and superlunary, each with its own physical laws. The order of the heavenly spheres, working inwards from the fixed stars, was: Saturn, Jupiter, Mars, Sun, Venus, Mercury, and Moon. Finally, the spherical earth rests stationary at the center of the universe. It is interesting to note that Ptolemy was familiar with earlier Greek notions of a sun-centered universe, but rejected them. Ptolemaic astronomy was logically consistent and quantitatively accurate (to the demands of the empirical data of the time). It provided a rigorous conceptual scheme, or model, for the structure of the universe that served a number of significant functions (Kuhn, 1957, pp. 64–77).

First of all, it both accorded with existing observational data and *explained* them. An observer of the heavens with the Ptolemaic system in mind, will find that the conceptual scheme imposes and *discloses* a pattern among otherwise unrelated observations. Moreover, Ptolemy's system was predictive. A Ptolemaic astronomer would expect nature to show properties that exist, even if he or she had never observed them. For example, the behavior of the sun, the stars and the planets are determined, since they are fastened to the celestial spheres. Their behavior and motions even in parts of the world that had not yet been visited by Greek astronomers, such as in the southern hemisphere or at the poles, were knowable in principle if not yet by observation. Ptolemy's conceptual scheme also suggested areas for further research and, ultimately, discovery of new information. It thus became the scientifically accepted model of the universe for nearly a millenium and a half. Moreover, during the Middle Ages the Aristotelian/Ptolemaic universe became incorporated into Christian theology by St. Thomas Aquinas and other scholars by the close of the thirteenth century (Weisheipl, 1971, pp. 60–62). Toward the end of the Middle Ages, then, Ptolemaic astronomy was deemed scientifically valid, cosmologically satisfying, and theologically endorsed. Ptolemaic astronomy was, therefore, technical astronomy linked to broader philosophical, cosmological and religious issues. To disturb that cosmology would require not only a scientific revolution, but a cultural one as well.

Copernicus' Doubts

When Copernicus was born in Torun (in what is now Poland) in 1473, the Ptolemaic system represented astronomical orthodoxy. The founder of modern astronomy lost his father in 1483, when he was only a little more than ten years old. Thanks to the assistance of his maternal uncle, Copernicus was able to enter the University of Cracow in 1491. Through the influence of this same uncle, who had become a Polish bishop, Copernicus was elected a canon of the cathedral chapter of Frauenburg, whose members enjoyed an ample income throughout their lives. He attended the Italian Universities of Bologna and Padua, where he studied medicine and canon law, and the University of Ferrara where he took his doctorate in canon law. Settling in Frauenberg in 1512, Copernicus thereafter led an extremely busy life. He was an active church administrator, a practising physician, and a writer on economics and, of course, astronomy (Rosen, 1971, pp. 401–402).

By the time Copernicus had finished his preliminary studies at the University of Cracow, he would have learned from his professors of astronomy that the Ptolemaic system was in need of some reforms. But there was nothing in his education to prepare him for overthrowing the Ptolemaic system. He saw his contribution to astronomy, rather, as a mathematician or geometer. For the task that Copernicus set himself was to do a better job than Ptolemy in setting up a geometric account of the motions of the heavens (Mendelsohn, 1984, p. 68). In particular, Copernicus disliked the device known as the equant which Ptolemy used. In Ptolemy's system, a planet moved with uniform motion not around the geometric center of its orbit, but around a mathematical point—the equant—slightly displaced from that center. Copernicus felt that the equant violated, or diluted, the Platonic doctrine of uniform circular motion. When Ptolemy failed to give complete mathematical satisfaction on this and other technical matters, Copernicus turned to a reexamination of alternative, earlier Greek views on the problems of astronomy—rival ideas which the Ptolemaic system had rendered obsolete by its overwhelming success. Again, there was nothing drastic or uncommon about scholars of Renaissance Europe reexamining the ancient Greek texts on many subjects. Copernicus' attitude was not revolutionary; indeed, he never intended it to be. He was not a pioneer, and attempted nothing that others had not tried before. Many other sixteenth-century astronomers were using the ancient texts to refute or modify Ptolemy on certain, minor details. Copernicus alone chose a system—the heliocentric one—which was to have profound implications for astronomy. Even this, however, would not become apparent for another generation or more. Copernicus was a conservative thinker (Dijksterhuis, 1961, p. 288). Yet seldom has such a conservative thinker been so bold, even inadvertently, in accepting what was considered scientifically improbable at the time.

The hypothesis Copernicus turned to was a heliocentric one. Up to the third century B.C., a heliocentric tradition of cosmology had existed alongside the geocentric one. Heraclides in the fourth century B.C. had offered a system in which the earth rotated and the planets Mercury and Venus circled not the earth but the sun. Aristarchus in the third century B.C. offered an account which was in outline identical with the Copernican system. However, Greek thought had selected the two-sphere universe and its elaboration by Aristotle as the model on which to build a detailed quantitative account of the motions of the heavenly bodies. Ptolemy's brilliant achievement settled the matter in favor of a geocentric astronomy and the heliocentric alternative was discarded. Until, that is, Copernicus retrieved it. He believed that by removing the earth from the central place it occupied in the Ptolemaic system and putting it, theoretically, in orbit around the sun (and with a rotation on its own axis), he could produce a geometrical account which he felt was superior to Ptolemy's.

Copernicus' Innovation

At the heart of Copernicus' innovation lies the point which required, for him, the most carefully reasoned argument: the attribution of motion to the Earth (Kuhn, 1957, chap. 5). It was this attribution that caused Copernicus to fear that astronomers would refuse to take him seriously. For, to assume that the Earth moved, in the sixteenth century, required such a straining of well-assured fact as to be equivalent to an argument put forward today that the Earth is stationary. It is difficult in the twentieth century to understand this. We are convinced that the Earth moves because we have been told so since childhood, though relatively few people can readily offer proof of this motion. In the sixteenth century, everyone knew, for similar reasons, that the Earth stood still. And no one needed arguments to prove what the evidence of the senses confirmed.

To be sure, scientists and philosophers conventionally offered various kind of proof, logical and scientific (nearly all derived from Aristotle and Ptolemy), to demonstrate the Earth's immobility. Thus, for example, it was habitually pointed out that the Earth belonged at the center of the universe because, according to Aristotelian physics, that was the natural place for the heavy element "earth" of which it is chiefly composed. It was argued, further, that it was inherently improbable that any such naturally heavy and sluggish object should move. And the natural motion of the earth, in any event, was rectilinear—unlike the natural motion of the celestial bodies which was circular. Finally, if the earth did move about the sun, or rotate on its axis, either the atmosphere or else missiles or birds moving through it, would be left behind. Similarly, a stone dropped from a tower would not hit the ground at the foot of the tower. These arguments—which seemed entirely compelling at the time—were the ones Copernicus had to refute before his system could even gain a hearing.

Copernicus first countered the argument that the Earth could not be assumed to move, because to move was contrary to its own nature. Copernicus responded that it was easier to imagine that the relatively small Earth moved, than that the great heavens hurled themselves around every twenty-four hours, a feat that must require truly enormous speed. Even to call the earth "relatively small" required a bold imagination that others could not encompass as readily as Copernicus did. Surely, so he argued, it was easier to imagine that the apparent motion of the heavens was really the result of the motion of the earth, turning on its axis once every twenty-four hours. As for Ptolemy's fears that in that case the atmosphere would be left behind, surely these fears were groundless. For the atmosphere was a part of the whole terrestrial region, and as such would share, like things suspended in it, the motion of its central body, the Earth. By positing the earth's motion, Copernicus was forced to modify the rigid distinction between celestial and terrestrial physics which had for so long been an essential tenet of the Aristotelian cosmos. He denied that there was any fundamental difference between the physics of the terrestrial and celestial regions. For example, he argued that the spherical nature of the Earth fitted it to move in circles as much as did the spherical shape of the heavenly bodies.

Copernicus was the first modern astronomer to begin to break down the old barriers between the Earth and the celestial regions. One by one these traditional barriers would be demolished by his successors until in the Newtonian universe modern physics presented a unified cosmos. However, Copernicus himself never carried his own arguments that far. His method was thoroughly Aristotelian in spirit if not in content. He insisted that "We conceive immobility to be nobler and more divine than change and inconstancy." So, if the heavens were nobler, as Aristotle taught, they should be at rest, while the baser Earth moved. Since it was *possible* in principle that the heavens were at rest and the Earth in motion, Copernicus felt that it was also *probable* if the "facts" so warranted (Kuhn, 1957, p. 153).

This was to be the crux of the revolution that Copernicus' innovation began. Would the *possibility* of his system being true be converted by empirical and mathematical reasoning into the *probability* of its being true? Simply put, would the Copernican hypothesis come to be accepted as the "true" picture of the universe in place of the Ptolemaic cosmology? (Lindberg & Westman, 1990, pp. 105–108). Indeed, it is not clear from Copernicus' own works whether he intended the motion of the earth to be a device confined to paper which usefully served as a computation tool, or whether he really believed the earth to be a planet in motion through space. In any event,

Copernicus died in 1543, the year in which his *De Revolutionibus* was published. The debate about the two competing astronomical systems would be conducted without him. The debate of the following hundred years, culminating with Galileo and Newton, was a vigorous one. The debate was intense in the broader cultural context because so much seemed at stake. Philosophy, religion and cosmology were in an agitated state for a century. But the debate was also intense from a more narrowly technical perspective. To the astronomers of the late sixteenth and seventeenth centuries, the Copernican system appeared at first to create as many new scientific difficulties as it could rightly claim to have resolved.

In the Copernican system, the (now familiar) order of the universe was: at the center, the Sun; then the spheres of Mercury, Venus, the Earth with its Moon, Mars, Jupiter, and Saturn; finally, the (now stationary) fixed stars (still) forming a boundary and limit to the universe as a whole. It must be emphasized that Copernicus' innovation was more than just replacing the earth with the sun as the center of planetary motions. Copernicus' heliocentric astronomy consisted of a number of additional, and equally crucial, assumptions. First, he had to assume that there was no single center of motion for all the heavenly bodies. For, although he postulated that the planets all revolved around the Sun, the Moon still clearly revolved around the Earth. This Copernican dichotomy was considered, at the time, a disadvantage. For one of the niceties of the Ptolemaic geocentric scheme was that all the heavenly bodies revolved around the same point.

By removing the Earth from the center of the universe, Copernicus exposed his system to another criticism. Physics and cosmology no longer seemed to support one another. According to Aristotelian physics, heavy bodies fell to a central Earth precisely because it was the *natural* place for the terrestrial element to come to rest. When Copernicus made this explanation no longer possible, he left gravity as a completely mysterious and inexplicable phenomenon. Gravity, or the tendency of heavy bodies to fall, needed an explanation in a way that it had not before. Copernicus could only postulate that, in fact, gravity was common to all planets, without any explanation. The result was to raise a new and fertile problem to be tackled by later cosmologists. At the time, however, it seemed another insuperable objection to Copernicus' system (Cohen, 1985a, pp. 47–50).

Copernicus next made an assumption concerning the size of the universe. It must, he declared, be so vast that the distance of the Earth to the Sun (roughly the dimension of the solar system) must be negligibly small compared with the distance from the Sun to the sphere of the fixed stars. This was an extremely necessary postulate for Copernicus. For it alone could account for the fact that the motion of the earth around the Sun is not reflected in an apparent motion of the fixed stars, as it otherwise would be. The fixed stars in the Copernican system ought to exhibit the phenomenon of "parallax." That is, any one star should appear—to an observer on the moving earth—to move slightly to and fro against its background of more distant stars during the year. This is due to the fact that the Earth travels from one side to the other side of its orbit around the Sun every six months. This phenomenon of parallax is similar to the way in which a photographer's view of a group posed before him varies as he walks to and fro in front of it. But the fixed stars did not appear to exhibit any parallax. This fact is hardly surprising, since stellar parallax continued to evade telescopic detection until 1838–9. The absence of any observed parallax was another grave weakness for sixteenth and early seventeenth century astronomers debating the relative merits of the Copernican vs. the Ptolemaic systems. The best that Copernicus could do was to insist (correctly as it later turned out) that the parallax was there, but that it was too small to be detectable owing to the immense distance of the stars from the earth.

The remaining assumptions concerned the position of the Sun and the motions of the Earth. Copernicus stated explicitly that the center of the planetary system—the solar system—was, in fact, the Sun. This assumption seemed a decided *advantage* to Copernicus and his supporters. It explained much that had hitherto been somewhat mysterious. For, it was curious that the Sun, if only a planet like Venus or Mars, should be so visibly distinguished from the other planets. Why, moreover, was it the Sun alone which shed light and warmth that fostered life itself. Now at last the unique properties of the Sun were recognized as corresponding somehow to its unique position.

Concerning the earth's motions, Copernicus' ideas seemed to confer further clear advantages over the Ptolemaic system. Copernicus assumed that the earth's diurnal (daily) rotation on its axis produced the *apparent* rising and setting of the sun, planets, and fixed stars every 24 hours. He postulated that it was the Earth's annual motion (revolution) around the Sun that produced the apparent annual motion of the Sun along the *ecliptic*. But this second, annual motion of the Earth did much more than replace the Sun's yearly motion in Ptolemaic astronomy. It served as well to regularize the various (apparent) peculiar motions of the planets. For example, the observed retrograde motions of the planets were explained quite simply—and shown to be only apparent, not actual motions—when the earth became a moving "observation platform." In the Ptolemaic system, major and cumbersome epicycles were required to "explain" what was believed to be real physical retrogression. In addition, observations since antiquity had shown that Mercury and Venus, unlike the other planets, were always near to the Sun in the sky. Venus, for instance, sometimes sets just after the sun—hence its designation then as the evening star—and sometimes rises just before the sun, as the morning star. This phenomenon is referred to as limited elongation. In the Ptolemaic system, it had to be explained by judicious, and artificial, relation of the devices governing the orbits of the sun and these planets. In the Copernican system, it followed naturally, indeed automatically, from the fact that Mercury and Venus moved around the Sun in orbits far smaller than the Earth's orbit. Thus, neither planet could ever appear to be far away from the Sun to an observer stationed on the Earth (Rosen, 1971, p. 408).

Debate in Astronomy

Given the relative strengths and weaknesses of both the Copernican and Ptolemaic systems, on what grounds could a sixteenth- or seventeenth-century astronomer choose between them? More to the point, which hypothesis was scientifically correct? To an open-minded contemporary of Copernicus, it was clear that he had provided a powerful alternative to Ptolemy's astronomy. By removing the Earth from the center of the universe and placing the Sun at the center of the planetary system, Copernicus achieved a number of things. By making the fixed stars truly fixed and by using the several motions of the earth to explain a wide array of observed phenomena, he rendered the heliocentric hypothesis a compelling one. He argued that by these means he had introduced a greater measure of simplicity, order, harmony and uniformity into astronomy. He believed that his system corresponded, far better than Ptolemy's, to Plato's original conception of a universe mathematically expressible in terms of circular motion. It is true that Copernicus still had to use epicycles and deferents. But their use had long been interpreted as legitimate devices conforming to the philosophical requirement of a *combination* of circular motions. Moreover, every astronomer knew how to manipulate these and would have regarded a universe without them as strange indeed. His heliocentric system, however, did not require the "equant." This was a dubiously satisfactory mathematical contrivance, and one without physical meaning. Copernicus had also explained away the awkward retrograde motions of the planets as mere appearances owing to the earth's own orbital motion. These were two of the strongest arguments in Copernicus' own eyes for the superiority of his system. They afforded a mathematical elegance that Copernicus was convinced would appeal to theoretical astronomers. Finally, the mathematics of the Copernican system were a little easier to manage than the mathematics of the Ptolemaic system.

But were these advantages enough to convert one to a belief in the *truth* of the Copernican system? Would one readily accept a system so reasonable, but so *unprovable* at the time? There were advantages surely in Copernicus' model. But the crucial issue was whether these advantages warranted destroying the scientific work of centuries. With what justification could one substitute Copernicus for Aristotle and Ptolemy? Even granting the cogency of his arguments, the fact remained that Copernicus could offer no proof of the truth of his ideas.

There simply was no sign in everyday experience that the inhabitants of earth needed to readjust their most basic and time-honored notions. On the contrary, everything in common sense showed the Sun moving and the Earth standing still. Copernicus' argument for the plausibility of a moving earth from the well-known facts of the peculiarities of relative motion was suggestive, but hardly definitive. It was true that the passengers on a moving ship, for instance, *could* imagine that they were stationary while the land moved or the shore line receded. However, the passengers recognized almost immediately that their senses were playing tricks with them. There was nothing comparable to suggest that the Earth's motion was really around the Sun, with the Sun itself stationary. Moreover, if the Earth were moving and not the center of the universe, what about gravity? Copernicus' explanation for the reason why heavy bodies fall was rather a plea for understanding than a scientific demonstration. Worse than this: if the Earth were not the center of the universe, what happened to the dignity of man? Had God not created the universe for man's enjoyment, and put the Earth at its center to prove it? Certainly—and in accordance with religious teaching—the Earth was the *unique* abode of humans. The uniqueness of its astronomical position seemed to follow. Finally, Copernicanism appeared to contradict the firmly rooted medieval belief in astrology. Why did the motions of the planets influence the Earth and its inhabitants if the planets actually circled the Sun, and not the Earth? To us, knowing that Copernicus was right makes the arguments opposing him seem trivial. However, in simplifying the debates on Copernican astronomy in such a manner, we do an injustice both to the historical realities of his time and to the actual cultural climate in which *any* scientific controversy necessarily occurs. We demean—and misconstrue—both the achievement of Copernicus *and* the difficulties which stood in the way of accepting his theory if we fail to recognize the historical complexity of the Copernican—or *any* scientific—Revolution. Copernicus had good reason to fear rejection, even scorn, for his theory (Hall, 1983, pp. 71, 117). His scientific position seemed at the time so untenable as to approach the absurd.

Copernicus himself clearly perceived the difficulties of his situation. He thought that his assumptions about the motions of the universe were valid, and that his hypotheses were reasonable enough to be probably true. He did not, however, expect observations to confirm this, because his own experiences suggested that a sufficiently high degree of accuracy could not be expected. The famous Danish scientist Tycho Brahe (1546–1601), a pioneering observational astronomer, was forced to reject Copernicus' hypothesis on just these grounds. Tycho's own instruments, which set a new standard in the accuracy of naked-eye observation, failed to detect stellar parallax. Torn between the competing systems, neither of which could be proven to be true, Tycho generated his own system. His famous astronomical compromise maintained the attractive technical features of the Copernican system while leaving the Earth stationary, as custom and common sense demanded. In Tycho's model, the Sun orbited the Earth but the orbits of the planets were sun-centered. It was as if in a working model of the Copernican planetary system, the Sun were to be detached from the base and the Earth pinned down. The *relative* motions of the planets and the Sun are conserved, but the Earth is no longer in motion. This model is geometrically equivalent to the Copernican system and shares the same simple account of retrogression and limited elongation. Yet owing to the immobility of the Earth in Tycho's compromise system, the absence of observed stellar parallax is no longer a problem and common sense and traditional cosmology are no longer violated (Kuhn, 1957, pp. 200–209).

Copernicus' Supporters

The debates about the Copernican hypothesis from the time of the publication of *De Revolutionibus* to the start of the seventeenth century, inconclusive as they were from an empirical point of view, served one crucial scientific function. They kept a plausible, if as yet unproved, hypothesis alive. In the sixty years or so since 1543, Copernicanism had been so thoroughly debated and so widely discussed that even laymen knew the arguments for and against it. These years of critical discussion and public controversy rendered the system familiar, and reduced its shocking novelty. They gradually weakened the force of some anti-Copernican arguments which had become trivialized by repetition. Most importantly, these debates helped to make Copernicus' system more readily acceptable when new and more definitive arguments in its favor were forthcoming.

As history records, those arguments emerged during the course of the seventeenth century. Whatever its other disadvantages, the Copernican theory proved extremely useful in stimulating astronomers to pursue new lines of research and encouraged further critical attitudes toward the Ptolemaic theory. One of the characteristics of science, ideally, is the constant testing of received ideas and the expectation that new experimental findings will either substantiate or contradict aspects of an existing paradigm. During the seventeenth century, arguments in favor of the Copernican system gradually but decisively gained ascendancy over those favoring the traditional astronomy. These arguments can be seen as comprising four principal steps in the acceptance of the new cosmology (Hall, 1983, p. 121):

1. Copernicus' supporters had to discredit further the philosophical—as well as theological—arguments against the possibility of the Earth's motion. This involved a careful criticism of existing ideas, particularly the authority of Aristotelian/Ptolemaic prejudices against a moving Earth. Such effective criticism was essential in order to establish a new framework in which such motion would no longer be considered impossible, or even implausible;

2. The second step, which was a necessary complement to the first, was to revise theories of physics. This revision of physics showed that the objections to Copernicus which were based on traditional ideas—such as the Aristotelian conception of natural place to explain gravity—were no longer valid;

3. The new astronomy was greatly enriched by sophisticated qualitative observations—made with the newly invented telescope. These observations suggested forcefully that many previous Ptolemaic explanations were inadequate, if not false or misleading;

4. Finally, exact quantitative measurements of a degree of accuracy and precision unknown to astronomers before provided new data for recalculating planetary orbits. This led ultimately to the abandoning on precise empirical grounds of the traditional preconception in favor of circular motion (to which Copernicus himself remained bound). New mathematical laws were formulated which established the true planetary orbits as elliptical, not circular.

The completion of the revolution in astronomy begun by Copernicus rested on the contributions of many individuals. Three names, however, stand out as preeminent: Galileo Galilei (1564–1642), Johannes Kepler (1571–1630), and Isaac Newton (1642–1727).

Galileo Galilei

Galileo's contributions are associated with the first three of the above steps. He was not an astronomer in the technical sense of being concerned with the mathematical details of positional astronomy (such as preoccupied both Ptolemy and Copernicus). Rather, as a philosophical scientist he was intrigued by the cosmological implications of Copernicus' theory. Although Galileo did not invent the telescope, as is often thought, he was the first to appreciate the potential role of the new tool for astronomy. When he made his first telescopic observations of the Moon in December 1609, Galileo embarked upon a program—ultimately a campaign—which was to transform astronomy. He realized that the telescope both revealed new observational facts *and* raised the level of empirical debate beyond the scope of previous naked-eye observational techniques. Although Galileo's telescopic discoveries did not prove the Copernican hypothesis, they effectively removed the major physical objections to it (Hall, 1983, pp. 122–124).

Galileo issued his first report on his astonishing observations, which followed quickly from the first ones concerning the Moon, in March 1610. The *Sidereus nuncius* ("Starry Messenger") contained startling and unexpected scientific news for the lay reader as well as the technical astronomer. It was one of the first books to show naturalistic representations of heavenly phenomena. Galileo drew a number of pictures of the moon as seen through the telescope. Although these representations are somewhat distorted, so that modern astronomers have had difficulties in dating the observations, on the whole they are completely recognizable pictures, or portraits (Winkler and Van Helden, 1992, pp. 196–197). Galileo showed that the Moon's surface was rugged, like the Earth's. It contained features such as mountains and valleys and perhaps seas. Galileo even estimated the height of the Moon's mountains from their shadow lengths. His telescope resolved part of the Milky Way into a dense cluster of individual stars and showed the heavens to be full of minute stars invisible to the naked eye.

Galileo described in detail how Jupiter was surrounded by four hitherto unsuspected satellites. He named them the "Medicean stars" in honor of his patrons, the Medici of the royal House of Tuscany (Segre, 1991, pp. 19–22). Galileo first spotted them in early January 1610, but it took him several days to understand that they were circling the planet in permanent orbits. He remarked that Jupiter's satellites might comfort those Copernicans who were troubled by the singularity of the Earth alone possessing a Moon. In Saturn, Galileo detected a peculiar variation of shape. This was interpreted, half a century later, as an enclosing plane ring. When Galileo turned his telescope to Venus he was able to discern that the planet's appearance varied between a long thin crescent and a small, full disc. These "phases," which resembled the phases of the Moon, could not possibly be accounted for in the Ptolemaic system. Ptolemy's limited elongation for Venus tied the center of that planet's epicycle on or near the line from the Sun to the Earth.

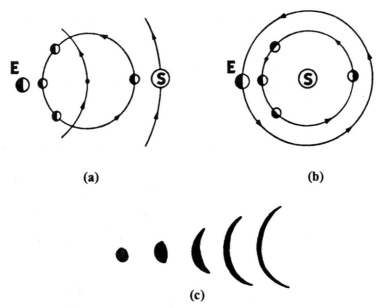

(a)   **(b)**

(c)

Figure 2.3. The phases of Venus in (a) the Ptolemaic system, (b) the Copernican system, and (c) as observed with a low-power telescope. In (a) an observer on the earth should never see more than a thin crescent of the lighted face. In (b) he should see almost the whole face of Venus illuminated just before or after Venus crosses behind the sun. This almost circular silhouette of Venus when it first becomes visible as an evening star is drawn from observations with a low-power telescope on the left of diagram (c). The successive observations drawn on the right show how Venus wanes and simultaneously increases in size as its orbital motion brings it closer to the earth. From Thomas S. Kuhn, *The Copernican Revolution,* Copyright © 1957 by the President and Fellows of Harvard College. Reprinted with permission.

Venus could never appear in full illumination and would always appear in "new" or crescent form. In Copernicus's system, on the contrary, Venus was in orbit around the Sun and not always between the Sun and the Earth. Thus Venus should, and did, display phases.

Finally, Galileo was one of the first to observe sunspots. To be sure, sunspots are sometimes visible to the naked eye. But Galileo's telescopic observations led him to realize their astronomical significance: sunspots indicate changes on the surface of the Sun and also its rotation upon an axis.

In Galileo's hands the telescope proved almost at a stroke how inadequate all philosophical (and popular) accounts of the universe had been (Cohen, 1985a, pp. 56–58). Even Copernicus had left ideas on the *physical* nature of the heavens practically unaltered. He still believed, for instance, that the planets were carried on the surface of crystalline spheres. Now, to anyone who was prepared to think openly, the discoveries that followed upon the invention of the telescope would suggest a train of thought both non-Aristotelian/Ptolemaic and pro-Copernican. Physical astronomy, in essence a creation of the telescope, altered decisively the nature of the Copernican debates. Previously, both Copernican and Ptolemaic adherents were restricted in their arguments to their differing analysis of the position and motion of the heavenly bodies. They could not consider the physical characteristics of stars and planets in any empirically meaningful way. Speculations concerning the nature of the Sun, the Moon, the planets and the stars lay in the province of cosmology and astrology. Galileo challenged the cosmological basis of Ptolemaic astronomy. His discoveries demonstrated that changes occurred in the heavens as well as on Earth. The hallowed dichotomy between terrestrial and celestial phenomena was shattered. The heavens were no longer immutable. More important, the universe was a physical structure governed by laws similar to those that governed the motion of bodies on/near the Earth.

The celestial regions could no longer be considered to be a realm completely distinct from terrestrial phenomena. Galileo's telescopic findings indicated that the heavens were not composed of some immutable, aetherial substance. Instead, they indicated that the heavens were composed of two types of physical bodies. The first, the stars—including our Sun—were incandescent sources of light. They were plainly physical, since they were not invariant. Moreover, they were not equally remote but distributed, somehow, throughout space in incredible numbers. The second type of celestial body, the planets, were physical objects practically indistinguishable from the Earth itself (if it could be seen from afar). The Earth could now be placed, without hesitation, in the class of solar satellites on physical grounds as well as by virtue of its orbital motion.

Galileo's deployment of physical astronomy was a crucial, and dramatically controversial, element in the Copernican Revolution (see section 2c). By demolishing the cosmological basis— Aristotelian physics—of Ptolemaic astronomy, he underscored the need for a new science of physics—incorporating *both* terrestrial and celestial phenomena. The creation of this mathematically exact and dynamically correct astronomy was achieved most clearly in the work of Kepler and Newton (Westfall, 1971, pp. 23–24).

Johannes Kepler

Kepler was a small, frail man, near-sighted, plagued by fevers and stomach ailments, yet nonetheless resilient. Not a great observational astronomer—poor eyesight would have hindered him had he tried to be one—he yet insisted upon closer agreement between theory and experiment than any astronomer before his time. A passionately devoted mathematical computer, he cared only for those mathematical representations of the heavens which offered the possibility of interpretation in physical terms. Yet, for Kepler the mathematical harmonies and order of the physical universe were a direct reflection of God the Creator. Mystical and rational at the same time, Kepler transformed metaphysical speculations into astronomical relationships of the utmost importance. Totally dependent for his best work on the observations of Tycho Brahe, he was a firm and unwavering Copernican. He found an astronomy whose clumsy planetary mechanisms typically erred by several degrees. He left an astronomy with a unified and physically meaningful heliocentric system, and one far more accurate. He was a prodigious worker, author of a couple of dozen books on astronomy, optics, mathematics, and religion. At the same time he conducted a voluminous correspondence with the leading scientists of his day.

Kepler played a different role from Galileo in completing the Copernican Revolution. Although Kepler wrote prolifically on astronomical subjects, his intensely personal cosmology was not very appealing to some of his rationalist contemporaries. A much greater audience awaited Galileo. A gifted polemicist, Galileo became the most persuasive propagandist for the new cosmology. Kepler, on the other hand, was an "astronomer's astronomer." It was the technical astronomers who recognized the immense superiority of his work. For them, Kepler's improvement in predicting exactly the planetary positions was forceful testimony to the power of the

Copernican system. In another sense, however, Kepler's life was unfortunately similar to Galileo's. After succeeding Tycho Brahe as Rudolph II's Imperial Mathematician (of the Holy Roman Empire), the latter part of Kepler's life was nonetheless made wretched. Being a Protestant, he was torn between his need for religious toleration and his financial support from a Catholic Emperor. He personally suffered during the Thirty Years' War (1618–1648). He died, after many wanderings, in an inn at Regensburg, in Bavaria (Gingerich, 1973, pp. 306–308).

While Kepler's discoveries would have been impossible without the refinement of observation attained by Tycho Brahe, more than mathematical precision was involved in them. Before the telescope, the only materials available for the construction of a planetary theory were angular measurements—principally determinations of the positions of the planets in the zodiac when Sun, Earth and planet were in the same straight line. Consequently, the most that a planetary theory could achieve was to predict the times at which a planet would return to the same relative situation, and its position at those times. The mathematical analysis of the solar system as a number of physical bodies moving in three-dimensional space had never been attempted, as such, by the older astronomers. They had been contented to leave such problems to philosophers. They had never concerned themselves with the *real* path of a planet in space. So long as their model predicted with tolerable accuracy the few recurrent situations in which naked-eye observations could be made, they were satisfied. The whole tendency of the Scientific Revolution, however, was to rebel against this view of the astronomer as a theoretical mathematician only. More was required. The new astronomer could not merely devise models to "save the phenomena." One now had to see astronomy as comprehending the totality of knowledge concerning the heavens and the relations of the Earth to the celestial regions (Westfall, 1971, pp. 4–5).

Kepler had a modern conception of the universe as a system of bodies whose arrangement and motions should reveal common, physically verifiable, principles. He believed that the general laws of astronomy were to be demonstrated from observations, not from metaphysical axioms alone. For Kepler, the astronomer's task was not to study the universe piecemeal—to construct models for each separate planet. Rather, by studying and interpreting it as a whole, Kepler believed that the astronomer could prove that the phenomena of each part of the universe were consistent with a single, overall scientific order. His aim was to provide a fitting theoretical pattern, empirically confirmed, of the new mathematical astronomy. This Kepler accomplished with his famous Three Laws. These are: (1) the orbit of each planet is in the shape of an *ellipse*, with the Sun located at one focus; (2) the line joining a planet to the Sun sweeps out equal areas in equal time intervals; and (3) the squares of the periodic (orbital) times [T] of each planet are proportional to the cubes of the mean distance [D] of each planet from the Sun [$T^2/D^3 = k$]. Kepler's Laws, when applied to the Copernican hypothesis, transformed the science of astronomy. With the recognition that planetary orbits are elliptical, Ptolemy's (and Copernicus') commitment to the doctrine of circular motions was shown to be erroneous. When the Law of Equal Areas is substituted for the doctrine of uniform velocities about some central point, the true regularities which governed planetary motions were revealed. Finally, the Third Law, which established an exact relation between the speeds of planets in different orbits, pointed to a crucial regularity in the solar system never before perceived. Kepler banished all need for epicycles, eccentrics, equants and other *ad hoc* devices in astronomy. His beautifully simple laws fully described the (accurately) observed movements of the planets (Cohen, 1985a, pp. 137–147).

Thus Kepler set scientists, when they began to understand the significance of his three laws, directly on the road to modern celestial mechanics. The new physics—a necessary basis for

Copernican astronomy—was to involve a deep revision and clarification of the concept of *force*, and new ideas about the nature and physical activity of universal matter. Kepler had proved that mathematics, measurement, and physical principles could be united in a true scientific synthesis—even if he had left the business incomplete. Cosmologists, and natural philosophers, could not indefinitely ignore the challenge to be (a) mathematically demonstrative and (b) observationally exact in the Keplerian manner. Kepler had gone far beyond the bounds of the astronomical problem of the two previous generations—does the Earth move or not?—to assert fundamental principles of celestial motion. The answers which cosmic physicists could now provide would thoroughly challenge traditional notions of what either philosophy or astronomy should be. The formulation of this new outlook is most successfully exemplified in the work of Newton. Kepler's Laws, for all their genius, were empirical. It was Newton who provided the theoretical proof for Kepler's Laws and thereby demonstrated the scientific truth of the Copernican system (Hall, 1983, p. 145).

Isaac Newton

Born on Christmas day, 1642, Newton was an only child. He was, apparently, sent to Cambridge University because his mother (a widow) could find no practical or "useful" abilities in him. At Cambridge, his undergraduate years seem fairly unremarkable. Yet in 1669, at the age of 27, he became the second Lucasian professor of mathematics in the University. Surely something in this step is testimony to Newton's remarkable gifts and genius. For almost 30 years he remained as an industrious, though virtually non teaching, academic fulfilling his professional duties conscientiously enough by the standards of his day (Hall, 1983, pp. 306–307).

Newton's achievements are legendary. With his work the Copernican Revolution—and the Scientific Revolution—reached its climax. A model for the physical sciences had been created in his *Principia* (1687). Galileo's and Kepler's confidence in the mathematical structure of nature was fully justified in Newton's grand synthesis of terrestrial and celestial motions. The unity of nature was revealed in his system which showed the applicability of the same laws, the same forces, the same principles of explanation in the heavens and on the Earth. The planetary movements of Copernicus, Kepler's Laws, the discoveries made by Galileo and the Dutch physicist Christiaan Huygens (1629 –1695) relating to the phenomena of gravity and motion, were all shown to follow from Newton's Theory of Universal Gravitation. The force that keeps the planets in orbit around the Sun, that keeps the Moon in orbit around the Earth, that governs the movements of the stars, and that causes an apple to fall toward the Earth is the same force: universal gravitation. Newton's cosmology finally erased the long-standing Aristotelian dichotomy between celestial and terrestrial physics (Westfall, 1993).

By showing that one and the same force operates throughout the universe, Newton completed the unification of the physics of the heavens and the Earth begun by Galileo and Kepler. The "problem of the planets" was solved at last (Kuhn, 1957, chaps. 6, 7). Gravity is *the* motive force governing phenomena near the Earth's surface, in our Solar System, and throughout the universe. With Newton, physics and astronomy were put on an immensely successful path of prediction, exact mathematical explanation, and empirical verification. Mankind's ancient efforts to account for the observed regularities in celestial and terrestrial movements culminated in his work. The crisis in astronomy which initiated Copernicus' innovation was resolved by a new conceptual scheme. Newton's paradigm itself would remain supreme for more than 200 years. It provided a scientifically fertile and culturally provocative metaphor for the eighteenth and nineteenth centuries (Cohen, 1985a, pp. 164–184). In the twentieth century, Newton's system would confront its own crisis in the work of Einstein. That, however, is the subject of a later chapter (see section 4a). ■

B. Alchemy and the Origins of Modern Chemistry

■ ■ ■

Chemistry as an integrated, modern science is a product of the Scientific Revolution (see next section). The ancients and their medieval successors had no such distinct science. They had, to be sure, much scattered empirical knowledge of a chemical nature. They also had theoretical principles that pertained to what we call chemistry. It is often stated that alchemy was the root of modern chemistry—a sort of primitive or "pre-scientific" chemistry. But alchemy was both more and less than chemistry (Olby, 1990, p. 226). It was broader with respect to its mystical and philosophical pretensions and associations. But it was less in its restricted range of experimental techniques. Modern chemistry certainly owes a great deal to the alchemical tradition. However, it derived also from a number of other traditions. (We will see a similar pattern in the development of evolutionary biology from the diverse fields of natural history, geology, ecology, and—even—political concepts [see section 3b]). These included mining (which by the sixteenth century had become a crucial economic activity in Europe), medicine and pharmacology, physics, and some of the craft processes of early technology including the making of glass, pottery, gunpowder, salts and acids. During the sixteenth and seventeenth centuries, the changing attitude toward nature in general which characterized the Scientific Revolution manifested itself also among those who studied chemical phenomena.

The accumulated theories, concepts, and technical procedures of previous centuries would be critically reexamined in a new light—that of the modern scientific method. Some of these would be rejected and new concepts and techniques devised in their place. Other traditional aspects of chemistry would be refined and incorporated into the new science of matter. The modern scientific method—which combined theory and experiment in an innovative manner and which was proving so decisive in transforming physics and astronomy—made itself felt in the chemical study of nature. The rejection of the ancient cosmology of the *four elements* in the astronomical field led to their rejection in the chemical field as well. Ultimately, the path to modern chemistry, slow and complex, culminated in the work of the great French chemist Antoine Laurent de Lavoisier (1743–1794). It begins, however, partly with the four element theory.

The Four-Element Theory

Expanding upon the views of early Greek philosophers (including Plato) on the nature of matter, Aristotle developed the four-element theory. For him, all matter was composed of earth, water, air, and fire. [Aristotle added a fifth element, the "quintessence" or "ether." The ether was, however, not material and was confined to the celestial regions. It did not, therefore, enter into the composition of terrestrial (sublunary) substances.] These four elements were, however, not original bodies but different aspects of one primary matter, each displaying different qualities. Onto this primary matter, different forms could be impressed, much as a sculptor can make different statues from one block of marble. All the different forms in which matter can reveal itself are "potentially" contained in it. This view is the crux of Aristotelian physics and its original contribution. The potential forms contained in this primary matter are expressed in the effects of four fundamental qualities: cold, heat, dryness, and moistness (or humidity). These qualities are never found by themselves, but always exist in pairs. Since contradictory (opposite) qualities [cold/heat, dryness/moistness] can not combine in nature, there are only four actual pairs of qualities. Each pair of qualities defined one of the elements. The four pairs are, thus, (a) cold/dry, (b) cold/moist, (c) hot/dry, and (d) hot/moist.

When primary matter is affected by the pair cold/dry, it becomes the element earth. Similarly, water is formed by the pair cold/moist, fire by the pair hot/dry, and air by the pair hot/moist. These four elements, according to Aristotle, then combine in different proportions to constitute all the many natural substances. Moreover, each of the different forms or qualities can be removed from the primary matter and be replaced by one of the other qualities. The transformation of one element into another thus becomes possible in Aristotle's philosophy. For example, water could be transformed into air by boiling, etc. Actual substances, since they were composed of varying amounts of the different elements, could—theoretically—be transformed under suitable conditions into one another by altering the proportion of their qualities. This idea of transmutation was to play a crucial role in medieval alchemy (Lindberg, 1992, pp. 54–56).

The Alchemical Heritage

Alchemy produced many ideas and techniques that would be incorporated into modern chemistry. The tradition of alchemy is of great antiquity. It was practiced centuries before the birth of Christ. Its heyday was from about the ninth to the close of the sixteenth century (Stillman, 1960, pp. 182–183). The practitioners of alchemy ranged from kings, popes and emperors to minor clergy, parish clerks, smiths, dyers and tinkers. Such important figures as St. Thomas Aquinas, Roger Bacon and, later, Isaac Newton were deeply interested in the meaning of alchemy (Dobbs, 1991). Alchemy was of a two-fold character. Its *exoteric*, or outward, aspect was concerned with attempts to prepare specific substances and bring about actual chemical transformations. Its *esoteric*, or mystical and psychological, aspect was manifested in a complex, almost devotional, system. In this, the alchemist's laboratory and the visible transformation of metals and other substances became the symbolic transformation of sinful man into a purified being through prayer and submission to God's will. The esoteric aspect of alchemy appears to have developed from the belief that the preparation of such important substances as the "philosopher's stone" could only be achieved with divine favor and grace (Martels, 1990).

The two aspects of alchemy are inextricably linked. The Arabic word "al-Kimya" itself was used to denote technological and philosophical aspects of both alchemy and chemistry (al-Hassan, 1986, p. 133). When reading certain alchemical texts now, for instance, it is often unclear whether the author is talking of actual chemical reactions. The possibility that the language of exoteric alchemy is being employed to express mystical or philosophical beliefs and aspirations is always present. What, for example, are we to understand by expressions such as "mercury is the womb in which embryonic metals can be gestated" or that "a fertilized 'seed' of gold could develop into a nugget?" Alchemists attributed sex to metals and minerals, and described their reactions in reproductive and organic metaphors. The modern reader must, therefore, be cautious in interpreting alchemical recipes as early or primitive expressions of actual chemical processes.

Even the central alchemical concern of transmutation is problematic. Alchemy represents an amalgamation of certain chemical technologies and philosophical speculations. The origins of alchemy are obscure. Besides the more clearly documented Egyptian beginnings, there are claims for Chinese, Hindu, Mesopotamian, and Hebrew early activities. As a formal discipline, however, alchemy may be considered to have developed toward the end of the first century of the Christian era. It probably arose among the Greek scholars of Alexandria in Egypt. Alchemy then spread through the lands of the eastern Mediterranean, particularly Syria, before being taken over by the Arabs following the rise of Islam. Later, interest in the subject was transmitted to the Latin West with the transfer of Arabic scholarship to Spain and Italy in the twelfth century. In Egypt, in the first century A.D., Greek philosophers could observe the activities of metalworkers. These artisans would enhance the appearance of ornaments fashioned from less precious metals and stones. These workmen doubtless realized that they were fabricating imitation jewelry when they alloyed and gilded materials. The Greek philosophers, however, conceived the technical processes in a broader framework. They were versed in Platonic ideas with the stress on perfection. Aristotelian notions regarding alterations of elemental materials by adjustment of forms and qualities were also influential concepts. The transmutation of base metals into gold would not appear to them to be an unreasonable undertaking (Ihde, 1964, p. 11). It was easy, perhaps, to be convinced that what the Egyptian artisans produced was genuine gold and silver. Was this technology or philosophy?

The possession of alchemical lore or secrets seems always to have been something of a mixed blessing. The history of alchemy is filled with accounts of alchemists whose lives were endangered because they were believed to possess the philosopher's stone. Since this was presumed to confer the ability to create gold from the transmutation of base metals, alchemists sometimes excited the avarice of contemporaries or incurred political and legal penalties. Similarly, suspected possession of the "elixir of life" could be risky. This particular kind of philosopher's stone was believed to prolong human life indefinitely. If the alchemist agreed to demands for curing a disease but failed, the consequences might indeed be unfortunate for both alchemist and patron.

For reasons of safety and/or cupidity—that is, the desire *not* to share potentially valuable secrets—the alchemists frequently employed enigmatical language to describe their theories, materials (ingredients) and experiments. This secrecy is in marked contrast to the modern science of chemistry. One of the most notable aspects of the revolution in chemistry, associated primarily with the achievements of Lavoisier, was precisely the reform and clarification of chemical terminology. Whereas alchemical symbols are often mystical, ambiguous and qualitative, modern chemical symbols are quantitative and refer uniquely to specific atoms and compounds. John Dalton's (1766–1844) *atomic theory* enabled chemists—if not everyone else—to understand just what was meant by their symbols and formulae. Alchemists, in contrast, would often interpret the same symbols differently in different contexts.

Astrology and Alchemy

A further characteristic of alchemy was its link to astrology. By the sixth and fifth centuries B.C., a very complex system of astrology had been elaborated by (among others) the Greeks and Babylonians. Many human activities, including craft practices, were carried out to the accompaniment of religious and magical procedures. Supposed connections were seen between metals, minerals, plants, animals *and* the planets, the Sun, the Moon, and the Gods. Many of the operations which the alchemists employed, such as metallurgy and coloring of materials, were related to the above activities. Alchemists, therefore, also accepted much of the astrologers' speculations (Partington, 1960, pp. 22–23).

The major tenet of astrology was the harmony between the *macrocosm*—the universe—and the *microcosm*—humanity. All that went on in the universe had its influence on, and parallel with, human activity. For example, the soul of man was believed to enter the body by way of a particular star and leave by the same path at death. The signs of the *zodiac* thereby assumed a profound significance. The zodiac refers to the band of the celestial sphere, extending about eight degrees to either side of the ecliptic, which represents the path of the principal planets, the moon and the sun. The zodiac is divided into twelve equal parts, called signs, each 30 degrees wide, bearing the name of a constellation. Of obvious importance was the configuration of the planets and stars at the moment of a person's birth. (This belief continues today. A person may be asked: What is your sign? Gemini or Capricorn or which?) Casting horoscopes—which are diagrams of the signs of the zodiac based on a particular aspect of the heavens, such as at a person's birth—to predict a person's future became common. Horoscopes to discover the most favorable conditions for activities ranging from embarking on travel to the preparation of specific drugs and alloys were also frequently cast. The calculations used in making these horoscopes often required the use of mystical numbers such as magic squares. An esoteric numerology and symbolism arose which became part of many alchemical treatises.

Because astrology was regarded as demonstrating the influence of the stars on *all* the happenings of nature, alchemists paid particular attention to its relevance to the operations of their craft. They developed a symbolic language which linked the stars to specific metals and reactions. The metal gold, for obvious reasons, was linked to the Sun. In similar fashion, silver was linked to the Moon, iron to Mars, mercury to Mercury, tin to Jupiter (because of that planet's brightness) and so on. The symbols of the planets became the symbols for the various metals. Such symbols would sometimes be coupled. Electrum, a gold/silver alloy, was thus represented by a coupling of the symbols for sun and moon. This extensive alchemical symbolism is in part a precursor of modern chemical notation for elements, compounds and reactions. But it must be emphasized that whereas chemical symbolism and nomenclature aims at clarity, alchemical terminology by its very nature was often obscure and mystical.

In tracing the development of chemistry during the Scientific Revolution, we see, therefore, that it was not simply the result of the gradual refinement of alchemy. Nor was it the development of any other single preexisting conceptual tradition. In contrast, Copernican astronomy (at least before Galileo and Newton) was in many respects a development from the combined theoretical and empirical approaches of more traditional astronomy. Certainly, the concept of a moving earth, itself borrowed by Copernicus from some of the speculations of antiquity, necessitated a revolution in astronomy. But Copernicus' system would have been readily understood—even if disputed as the true explanation of the facts—by Ptolemaic astronomers. Chemistry shows no such clear evolution from a previous tradition. It drew upon alchemy, technology, medicine, and other diverse sources (Olby, 1990, p. 872).

Prelude to Modern Chemistry

Before modern chemistry could develop, a period of critical examination of these sources was necessary. First of all, up until the sixteenth and seventeenth centuries there were really two quite distinct strands in the early history of chemistry. What we would call chemical *theory* was really a branch of general "natural philosophy." Chemical changes were conceived within the pattern of traditional ideas on the nature of matter. The most important influence here was the four element theory, derived primarily from Aristotelian physics. Essentially independent of the above, was the accumulated *empirical* tradition of practical chemical knowledge. By the Middle Ages, there was a vast body of facts and technical processes which owed little to philosophical speculation. This empirical tradition included glassworking, refining of metals, distillation of alcohol, manufacture of medicaments, glazing of pottery and preparation of pigments, and discovery of the mineral acids (such as hydrochloric, sulfuric and nitric acids). Certain medieval alchemists, however, stressed the conclusion that humanity could significantly change the order of the natural world by altering natural substances by these chemical methods. This technological dream, however premature, was to be reflected in the direction taken by Western culture during the seventeenth century and after (Newman, 1989, p. 443). Operations such as oxidation and reduction of materials were gradually mastered—through improvements of furnaces and other apparatus—even though their theoretical explanation remained unknown.

By the sixteenth and seventeenth centuries, these two strands came together. Figures such as the Swiss physician Paracelsus (c. 1493–1541), the Flemish chemist and doctor Johann Baptista van Helmont (1579–1644), the German chemist Johann Rudolph Glauber (1604–1670), and the British natural philosopher Robert Boyle (1627–1691) sought both to add to empirical knowledge and to fit these facts into current (and changing) scientific theory. For, as Galileo was to show, although experiments are crucial to the development and verification of science, experimental results mean little without a theoretical structure. In the development of modern chemistry, two major questions had always to be kept in mind. First, how could the changes in the properties of bodies brought about by various manipulations (primarily with the aid of heat) be accounted for in the light of existing scientific theory. And second, how were the existing and newly invented techniques of craft practices, as well as of the laboratory, related to those theories. Stage by stage, the science of chemistry developed a coherent framework and independent character from the rest of general natural philosophy.

Paracelsus' place in the history of science is controversial. There is no doubt that much of his work and teachings are confused, obscure, mystical and—quite simply—mistaken. Yet there is no doubt that in other respects he did have a positive impact. He is considered one of the main founders of the school of iatrochemists, or "medical chemists." Paracelsus and his followers attempted to apply chemistry to the preparation of medicines and to the explanation of processes in the living body (Debus, 1965, pp. 32–34). His fame was due to his being a good surgeon, to his understanding the use of metallic remedies, to his striking cures with opium, and especially to his use of preparations of mercury to cure certain diseases which had resisted all the old remedies. Paracelsus was also, apparently, the first to use the name "alcohol" for strong spirit of wine, and the first scientist in Europe to mention the metal zinc.

In theory, Paracelsus believed that matter was comprised of the three chemical principles of salt, sulfur, and mercury—the so-called *tria prima*. This view contrasted sharply with the four-element theory of the Aristotelians. The tria prima was connected with the behavior of matter toward fire and heat. Salt was the principle of "fixity" and "incombustibility," mercury of "fusibility" and "volatility," and sulfur the principle of "inflammability." The last two had long been recognized by alchemists, but Paracelsus seems to have been the first to add salt. These three principles had only a superficial connection with the substances whose names they bore. But their philosophical and experimental connotations in Paracelsus' interpretation influenced his contemporaries. Especially as developed by his immediate followers, who made his theories more precise and less mystical, Paracelsian ideas became one ingredient in the matrix from which modern chemistry emerged. The very idea that there was a specifically *chemical* way of looking at matter and its properties was effectively absent prior to the sixteenth century, and gained ground only slowly thereafter. Medieval alchemy and Aristotelian "chemistry" were really branches of philosophy and cosmology. When, however, certain experimenters in the sixteenth and early seventeenth centuries began speaking of metals (for example) as being compounded of "sulfur" and "mercury"—although these terms did not refer to the same things as our common modern elements of these names—it became possible to speak of a chemical approach toward substances. Matter was not defined simply by its physical properties. It was also coming to be defined by its different proportions of *experimentally verifiable* substances or elements. These elements were, moreover, now defined by specific chemical properties.

One major problem which had to be faced was *chemical identity.* Different substances had been confused with one another since antiquity. Identical substances were frequently known under a variety of names and considered to be different things by different "authorities." There was no clear recognition of the fact that some substances were actual—as opposed to "philosophical"—building blocks of which other substances were composed. Without such recognition, the nature of chemical reactions and the replacements which take place therein remained obscure. It was one of Paracelsus' followers, van Helmont, who in rejecting the tria prima made some initial—though still murky—progress toward a truer understanding of chemical entities.

Van Helmont's most significant work was done with chemically produced gases, which he distinguished from ordinary "air" (Partington, 1969, vol. 2, pp. 227–232). He recognized that the gas produced during the burning of combustible substances like charcoal or alcohol—which he called "gas sylvestre"—was identical to such gases as are given off (1) during the fermentation of grape juice or grain mash, (2) by the action of vinegar on sea shells, and (3) by the reactions which take place in certain caves. Van Helmont's "gas sylvestre"—our carbon dioxide—also included other gases such as that given off during the reaction of silver with nitric acid. He also distinguished a flammable gas produced by the heating of organic matter, or by putrefaction. This gas, named "gas pingue," was actually a mixture, primarily of hydrocarbons. Despite some confusions, however, van Helmont shrewdly recognized differences between gases. Most significantly, he realized that a unique gas—a single chemical entity—might be produced in several alternative ways from different sources.

Glauber, a younger medical contemporary of van Helmont, acquired extensive knowledge about acids and salts and their interrelationships. He improved the current methods of preparing several mineral acids. The German medical chemist Otto Tachenius (fl. 1650) recognized that salts are the product of the reaction of an acid and a base (Partington, 1969, vol. 2, p. 293). His use of "spot tests"—such as nutgall extract for detecting iron compounds—helped lay the foundations of *qualitative analysis.* Perhaps the most important work along this line was that of Robert Boyle. He was a wealthy Englishman whose Baconian enthusiasm for the value of science helped stimulate the formation of the Royal Society of London [chartered by King Charles II in 1662]. By 1662, with the aid of the physicist Robert Hooke (1635–1702), Boyle had carried out the famous experiments with the air pump which led to the discovery of the pressure-volume relationship in gases which still bears his name ("Boyle's law").

Robert Boyle

In 1661 Boyle published *The Sceptical Chymist*. The purpose of this famous work, as its title implies, was negative rather than positive. Boyle set out to demolish the two reigning—and in his mind false and misleading—theories of matter: Aristotle's four elements and Paracelsus' three principles. He showed, with an extensive array of experimental evidence, that there was no sound basis for regarding these postulated entities as "elemental" in any real sense, since they could not be extracted from any substance. Boyle pointed out that the "clearest-speaking" chemists looked upon elements in a more practical manner. In his oft-quoted definition (found in the appendix of the second edition of *The Sceptical Chymist*), elements are "certain Primitive and Simple, or perfectly unmingled Bodies; which not being made of any other bodies, or of one another, are the Ingredients of which all those call'd perfectly mixt bodies are immediately compounded, and into which they are ultimately resolved" (quoted in Leicester and Klickstein, 1965, p. 42).

It is doubtful whether Boyle himself considered any known chemical substance as an element. Despite the modern ring to his definition, he nowhere gives an example of an element. As a follower of the *corpuscular philosophy,* Boyle believed in a primary matter out of which all substances were formed. He sought therefore, to explain the properties of substances—including what we would now consider elements—on the basis of increasing aggregations of those primary particles. Yet his criticism of existing concepts concerning elements was extremely influential. Like van Helmont—whose work he studied with great care and to whom he frequently refers as an authority—Boyle attacked the three principles of the then orthodox chemists on the grounds that substances could not be resolved into them. As part of the rigorously experimental approach which characterized all of his work, Boyle's views on elements were an important part of the new outlook on chemistry (Olby, 1990, p. 995).

Boyle was one of the outstanding theorists of the corpuscular (or "mechanical") philosophy and a consummate experimentalist in both physics and chemistry. His works are among the first to consist largely of clear descriptions of experimental research. He contributed powerfully to the development of precise chemical technique, the principles of chemical analysis, and the study of chemical composition. He fully controlled the extensive work done in his own research laboratory, particularly when assisted by others. He noted the precise details of each experiment. Boyle was probably the first chemist to appreciate the importance of using pure substances and of viewing operations critically. He was well aware too of the importance of repeating experiments. Boyle realized that although identical experiments should yield the same results, the possibility existed that slightly different results might occur when different individuals performed the same experiment. He did not take the results of a single trial to justify sweeping conclusions, in the manner of most of his predecessors.

Boyle undertook to prove to philosophers that chemistry could be more than simply a collection of recipes. He sought to demonstrate to more traditional chemists that in revealing nature's secrets they had a more noble aim than transmutation of base metals or the preparation of medicines (however crucial the latter task might be). Endowed with an innovative philosophical outlook, Boyle sought to build a bridge between the new chemistry and the new physics—the two sciences most concerned with the properties of matter. He was almost unique among contemporary physicists in wishing to master all the details of chemical technique and nomenclature. He was, in the same way, almost unique among chemists in substituting for their vague qualitative notions the precise, and potentially quantitative, mechanical concepts of the physicists of the seventeenth century (Boas Hall, 1970, p. 380).

Boyle's studies on the nature of combustion—one of the most important problems facing chemists at that period—were significant. Fire had always been the principal energy source utilized by chemical philosophers to study combustion reactions. But their explanations of the action of fire were inclined to be highly speculative. Boyle, and Robert Hooke, examined the behavior of combustible substances under various but precise experimental conditions, including the use of evacuated vessels. They observed that combustion stops when air is withdrawn. They noted further that sulfur "fumes" when heated in a vacuum but does not ignite. But gunpowder burned under water! They realized that "air" was involved in some way in the combustion of most substances, but that saltpeter might serve as a substitute for air in gunpowder.

Boyle also observed that metals gained in weight when heated in air. He reasoned (erroneously) that the gain was due to the absorption of "igneous particles" which passed even through glass. Boyle believed that air consisted of three kinds of particles. Only one kind was really "air" particles. The other two, he thought, were "exhalations" from the earth and celestial bodies. He concluded that the role of the air in combustion, calcination, and respiration was due to these extraneous particles which were present in only minor amounts.

Other London chemists were also moving toward recognition of the part played by air in combustion. Hooke suggested independently of Boyle that the air acted as a solvent for "sulphureous bodies," their union producing heat. John Mayow (1641–1679) published a book in 1674 which emphasized the role in combustion of "nitro-aerial" particles both in the air and in saltpeter. He also believed that a "sulphureous" substance must be present in combustible matter. It must not be thought, however, that Boyle and his London contemporaries anticipated the discovery of oxygen. Their ideas, although clear, were still highly speculative. Their experiments were necessarily limited in character since there was as yet no convenient way of preparing and manipulating gases in the laboratory. Consequently, their ideas could not resist the rise of the *phlogiston theory* introduced by two German chemists, Johann Joachim Becher (1635–1682) and his disciple Georg Ernst Stahl (1660–1734).

Phlogiston Theory

In his *Physicae subterraneae* (1669) Becher proposed that bodies were composed of air, water, and three "earths": "terra lapidea" (fusible or vitreous), "terra mercurialis" (mercurial) and "terra pinguis" (inflammable or fatty). He considered combustible substances—such as charcoal or oil—to be rich in terra pinguis, which was then lost during burning. Here, Becher was in accord with the prevailing scientific outlook of his time. Since heat and light palpably accompanied such reactions—and because, until the late eighteenth century, the gaseous state of matter was generally ignored by chemists—the usual theoretical interpretation was that a fiery constituent or principle was being removed. In particular, metals which burned readily contained some of the inflammable earth. Stahl later developed these ideas into an elaborate chemical system in which the term "phlogiston" replaced "terra pinguis."

The potential scope of the phlogiston theory proved remarkably broad. Not only did the theory explain combustion and calcination [the heating of metals] as being caused by the *loss* of phlogiston. It also explained the smelting (reduction) of metallic ores to their metals, by exposure to heat, by the *addition* of phlogiston. Since the ore ("calx") of a metal is converted into the metal by heating with charcoal—a substance rich in phlogiston—Stahl argued that phlogiston was transferred from the charcoal to the calx. The calx was thereby converted into the metal: calx + phlogiston = metal. Respiration and many other chemical changes were readily explained in terms of phlogistic concepts. In an era in which qualitative measurements were still rudimentary, the loss and gain of phlogiston did not appear paradoxical. The fact that *loss* of phlogiston appeared to *increase* the weight of a substance, while *gain* of phlogiston seemed to *reduce* it, was not perceived as a problem for the theory. Various explanations, such as attributing "negative weight" to phlogiston, were advanced at times by Stahl and his followers. During this period, such discrepancies in the phlogiston theory seemed minor when compared to its achievements. The phlogiston theory was a decisive turn away from alchemy. It (1) linked together a large number of experimental facts into a coherent body of chemical doctrine, (2) suggested new experiments, and (3) led to many important discoveries during the eighteenth century.

The phlogiston theory, despite its weaknesses, was a marked improvement over most preceding attempts at developing a scientific framework for modern chemistry (King, 1975, p. 605). Stahl's influence on early eighteenth century chemistry was crucial for several reasons. First, the phlogiston theory provided a useful provisional conceptual scheme for the interpretation of many experiments. It thus reinforced the "Galilean" tradition—which was championed also by Boyle—in chemistry; theory and experiment were constantly played against one another. Second, Stahl's system enabled him to give a consistent explanation to experimental data concerning combustion reactions—the most important reactions for eighteenth-century chemists. Stahl achieved a major scientific clarification (and simplification of theory) when he showed combustion and calcination [the heating of metals] to be identical processes. Third, under Stahl's framework, chemists gained a valuable insight into a vast number of chemical processes in actual laboratory terms. They learned to treat natural substances, such as sulfur, carbon, salts, metals, alkalis and acids, as the truly active ingredients in chemical reactions. Their emphasis thus shifted away from unverifiable abstractions (idealized concepts), such as the four Aristotelian "elements" or the three principles of seventeenth-century chemists. Finally, chemists thinking in the phlogistic manner were induced to make rigorous and fertile experiments.

Joseph Priestley's (1733–1804) famous discovery of the elemental gas oxygen—which he termed "dephlogisticated air"—was made entirely within the framework of the phlogiston theory. Priestley, a nonconformist minister of Leeds—and a member of the Lunar Society of Birmingham, which included Erasmus Darwin and James Watt (see section 3c)—assumed, from the teachings of Stahl, that a candle on burning gives out phlogiston. It is extinguished in a closed vessel after a time because the air becomes saturated with phlogiston. Ordinary air, therefore, supports combustion because it is only partially "saturated" with phlogiston, and can absorb more of it. Substances burn in air with only a moderate flame, whereas in the new air [that is, the oxygen he obtained from his experiment] the flame is vivid. Priestley, therefore, concluded that the new gas must contain little or no phlogiston. Hence, he called it "dephlogisticated air" (Partington, 1960, p. 118). It is worth noting that Lavoisier could often simply invert the phlogistic doctrine to yield his oxygen theory. Where Stahl, for example, had seen a loss of phlogiston, Lavoisier saw a gain (combination) of oxygen. Although, as we shall see, Lavoisier's achievement was far more profound than this, the conceptual symmetry between the two theories is evidence of the service that the phlogistic hypothesis had performed for eighteenth-century chemistry.

Lavoisier's Attack on Phlogiston

Antoine Laurent Lavoisier was born in Paris in 1743. His father was a lawyer who held the important position of solicitor to the Parisian Parlement, the chief Court of France. His wealthy mother, who also came from a lawyer's family, died when he was only five. Not surprisingly,

Lavoisier's education was geared to his expected entry into the legal profession. This meant that he attended the best school in Paris, the Collège des Quatre Nations (known popularly as the Collège Mazarin). The building still survives and now houses the Institut de France, of which the French Academy of Sciences is part. Lavoisier spent nine years at the College, graduating with a baccalaureate in law in 1763; but his spare time was always to be devoted entirely to scientific pursuits (Guerlac, 1975, pp. 49–50). In 1766, two years before he reached his legal majority of 25, Lavoisier's father made a large inheritance over to him. To further his complete financial independence, in 1768 Lavoisier bought a share in the Ferme Generale. This was a private finance company which the government employed to collect taxes on tobacco, salt, and imported goods. In exchange for this privilege, shareholders payed the state a fixed sum of money each year. Such a tax system was clearly open to abuse and consequently the "fermiers" were universally disliked. They were to reap the dire consequences of their membership of the company during the French Revolution. Indeed, Lavoisier was to be guillotined on 8 May 1794. Much of Lavoisier's personal fortune was spent on the best scientific apparatus that money could buy. Some of it was so complex and unique that his followers had to simplify his experimental demonstrations in order to verify them. Elected to the Academy of Sciences in 1768, Lavoisier helped to prepare its official reports on a whole range of subjects—ranging from the water supply of Paris, hypnotism and food adulteration to the manufacture of gunpowder and the respiration of insects.

It was the mid-eighteenth-century developments concerning gases which provided Lavoisier with the stimulus for his scientific studies on combustion. His work on this matter proved to be the downfall of the phlogiston theory. These investigations on gases occurred, as we have seen, within the framework of Stahl's system. Hydrogen, discovered in 1766 by the British natural philosopher Henry Cavendish (1731–1810), was identified with pure phlogiston. Oxygen was called dephlogisticated air. Nitrogen was named phlogisticated air. It was only when these gases were subjected to careful and quantitative experimental analysis that the phlogiston theory became an impediment to scientific advance. Lavoisier, from his own experiments and those of certain of his contemporaries, recognized three fundamental facts which contradicted—or at least rendered highly questionable—the phlogiston hypothesis.

First, Lavoisier confirmed that metals *gained* in weight upon calcination [combustion]. This had been first convincingly demonstrated in 1772 by L. B. Guyton de Morveau (1737–1816). Second, he showed that when a metallic calx [what we now call the oxide of the metal] was "reduced" [that is, heated] in the presence of carbon, the metal itself was formed. In addition, a "fixed air" [what we now call carbon dioxide] was formed. And third, he proved that when a metallic calx was reduced by itself—that is, decomposed by heat in the absence of air—the metal was formed *plus* a "new air." This new air was now called oxygen. Oxygen was decidedly different in its properties from fixed air. The combination of these three experimental facts led Lavoisier to conclude that phlogiston was probably nonexistent.

Stahl's system taught that phlogiston was a substance emitted during all combustions and absorbed during all reductions. According to this theory, when a metallic calx was heated in the presence of carbon ["pure" phlogiston] phlogiston would be absorbed. As a result, the metal would be produced. Stahl, thus, considered the metal to be a compound (calx + phlogiston). Conversely, when a metal was heated by itself, the phlogiston would be driven off, leaving a calx behind. Stahl maintained, in effect, that metals were compounds, whereas calxes [our "oxides"] were simple elements. The reverse, of course, we now know to be true.

Lavoisier's experiments showed, in contrast, that there were specific airs or "gases" which were involved in the various phenomena of combustion and reduction. Moreover—and this was the crucial fact—these gases could be observed in the laboratory and their presence or absence measured precisely in *quantitative* terms. For all its modernity and usefulness, the phlogiston theory still shared aspects of the qualitative philosophy of the ancient and medieval alchemists regarding the concept of elemental substances. Lavoisier's interpretation challenged certain of these qualitative hypotheses. We should remember, however, that Lavoisier's "new chemistry" was itself not entirely free from some traditional qualitative perspectives. He considered heat and light, for example, to be "weightless elements." They could, to be sure, be measured by instruments such as the calorimeter. But they could not be measured by that increasingly important instrument, the "chemical balance."

Lavoisier's attack on phlogiston and the announcement of his new theory of combustion appeared in a series of papers and books during the 1770s and 1780s. He declared that he had embarked on an immense series of experiments intended to reveal the properties of the different airs, or gases, which were coming to be understood as key agents involved in chemical reactions. Experiments with the newly invented airpumps in the 1660s, for example, had allowed Boyle and John Mayow to deduce that combustion and respiration were related phenomena. In 1727, the English physiologist Stephen Hales (1677–1761) had hit upon a way to isolate and collect for study and precise measurement the air produced from a heated solid. Building upon these and related techniques, Lavoisier was able to pursue his famous investigations leading to the oxygen theory of combustion. Although he did not discover oxygen [it had been previously isolated by Joseph Priestley and Carl Scheele], Lavoisier was certainly the first to understand the consequences of its discovery.

He realized the true nature of oxygen as a chemical element. This perception (in one sense) reversed the assumptions of the phlogiston theory. Lavoisier and his contemporaries (especially Guyton de Morveau) were able to conceive and execute an ingenious series of quantitative experiments which established the true chemical nature of combustion and calcination. Lavoisier's brilliant achievements symbolize the revolution in chemistry at the close of the eighteenth century. In making modern chemistry begin with Lavoisier, however, undue emphasis has perhaps been placed on his theory of combustion. There are other doctrines—notably Joseph Louis Proust's (1754–1826) law of constant proportions [i.e., constant composition of elements as the test of a true chemical compound as opposed to a mere mixture] and John Dalton's (1766–1844) atomic theory—which were also fundamental to the development of the science of chemistry. Yet Lavoisier's contributions are preeminent.

His theory proved that combustion was due to the fixation or combination of a specific part of the air—oxygen—with the burning substance. Furthermore, the weight gained by the burning substance was equal to the weight of oxygen consumed in forming the new compound. The heat (which Lavoisier called "caloric") and light that was emitted during every combustion came from the action of the gaseous oxygen, and not (as Stahl had maintained) from the inflammable substance. In this way, Lavoisier completely revised ideas of chemical composition in terms of elements and compounds. And although the analogy between respiration and combustion had been noted before by others (e.g., Boyle), it was Lavoisier who developed the concept that respiration is the oxidation of the carbon in food (Holmes, 1985).

The Chemical Revolution

Lavoisier's decisive refutation of the phlogiston theory resembles Galileo's attack on Ptolemaic astronomy in several important respects. Like Galileo's demonstration of the validity of Copernicus' ideas, Lavoisier's combustion theory built upon, and further verified, the work of certain of his predecessors and contemporaries. Like Galileo in his critique of the Ptolemaic system [in *Dialogue on the Two Chief World Systems* (1632)], Lavoisier eloquently exposed the inconsistencies of the phlogiston theory. He showed that phlogiston was both redundant and contradictory. It had come to mean widely different things to different chemists. Thus, there was no single, coherent "phlogiston theory." And like Copernicus' theory when compared to its Ptolemaic rival, Lavoisier's theory of oxidation could explain *all* the experimental data of Stahlist chemistry, more accurately and more simply. Most importantly, Lavoisier's theory was able to incorporate all the quantitative data gathered in the eighteenth century on the newly recognized role of gases, as Stahlist chemists could not. Moreover, once the pattern of substituting the oxygen theory for the phlogiston system became established among scientists, Lavoisier's combustion theory could be extended by analogy to many other chemical reactions—e.g., burning substances in an atmosphere of sulfur, chlorine, and so forth (Perrin, 1990, pp. 264–277).

Lavoisier codified—and propagandized for—the new system of chemistry in his textbook (published in 1789) called *An Elementary Treatise of Chemistry*. Together with Antoine Fourcroy's (1755–1809) larger textbook published in 1801, this became a model for chemical instruction for the first decades of the nineteenth century. A book on chemistry written before this time would probably be unintelligible today to anyone but a historian of science. Lavoisier's text, in contrast, reads as if it were an older edition of a relatively modern chemistry textbook. In it, Lavoisier defined a *chemical element* as any substance which could not be analyzed [broken down] further by chemical means. Such a definition enabled him to identify some 33 basic substances as elements, including some which were later shown to be really compounds (Lavoisier, 1965, pp. 175–176). By the mid-1790s, Lavoisier's new system of chemistry had effectively triumphed. Only a few prominent chemists—notably Joseph Priestley—continued to defend the phlogistic system. Lavoisier's revolution in chemistry, based on his brilliant synthesis of theory and experiment, was quickly established as the new paradigm for that discipline (Donovan, 1990, p.272). Another, political, revolution was shortly to put an end to any further contributions by him to the new science in whose creation he played so crucial a role (see section 2d).

By the close of the eighteenth century, then, chemistry was established on a modern foundation. The achievements of Lavoisier and his associates set the stage for the dramatic advances in both science and technology based on modern chemical knowledge and procedures which have characterized the nineteenth and (especially) twentieth centuries. Building upon the early efforts at chemical reform of van Helmont, Boyle and others during the seventeenth and early eighteenth centuries, Lavoisier completed the reform of alchemy and medieval chemistry (Melhado, 1985). The advances in pneumatic chemistry during the mid-eighteenth century called attention to the key element oxygen in many chemical reactions. Lavoisier's and his colleagues' brilliant experiments on combustion, respiration, and the compound nature of water established the nonexistence of phlogiston—and gave the death blow to the ancient concept of air and water as irreducible elements. Enhanced by his reform of chemical nomenclature in collaboration with Fourcroy, Guyton de Morveau, and Claude Louis Berthollet (1748–1822), Lavoisier's new system set chemistry on its modern course.

Lavoisier and his colleagues believed that the language of chemistry should reflect a clear description of a substance's actual composition. Recall that much of alchemical nomenclature was ambiguous or allegorical. Greek, Hebrew, Arabic and Latin words were used, sometimes interchangeably. There was widespread use of analogy in naming substances, such as "father" and "mother" for sulfur and mercury. Moreover, the same substance might receive a different name according to the place from which it had been obtained, such as "Spanish green" and other designations for copper acetate. In contrast, the new system of nomenclature was to be based on fixed names for substances which directly reflected their chemical composition. It was also to be based on the oxygen theory of combustion. Lavoisier's suggestions for linguistic reforms were initially resisted by those who adhered to the phlogiston theory. Fairly quickly, however, the triumph of the new chemistry facilitated the adoption of the new nomenclature.

Perhaps the most significant assumption in the new nomenclature was that substances which could not be decomposed were simple elements. Lavoisier and his colleagues believed that the names of these elements should form the basis of the entire nomenclature. Thus, the elements oxygen and sulfur, for example, would combine to form either "sulfurous" or "sulfuric" acids, depending on the quantity of oxygen combined. These acids when combined with metallic oxides would form the two groups of salts known as "sulfites" and "sulfates." In 1813, the Swedish chemist J. J. Berzelius (1779–1848) introduced the modern notation whereby an atom of an element is symbolized by the initial letter of its name (Melhado, 1992). Two letters are used where elements with the same initial letter (such as Carbon=C but Copper=Cu [from the latin "cuprum"]) might be otherwise confused. Berzelius' symbols, which could be easily arranged algebraically to represent compounds, became generally adopted from the mid–1830s onward. At about this time, chemists also began to represent reactions by means of equations. The establishment of modern chemistry—a complex process involving philosophical, linguistic, and sociocultural as well as scientific and technological factors—constitutes a revolution in science. ∎

C. The Scientific Revolution

■ ■ ■

The term "Scientific Revolution" describes the transformation of thought about nature which took place in Europe during the period roughly between 1500 and 1700 (Schuster, 1990, p. 217). It refers primarily to that process by which the tradition of Greek, Islamic, and Medieval ideas concerning the physical universe was replaced by "modern science." The phrase has been current since the late seventeenth century, when people first became conscious of the profound extent and importance of the intellectual changes that had recently occurred. During this period, revolutionary advances were made first in a small group of sciences, particularly astronomy and physics. The procedures by which these changes were effected has come to be known as the "scientific method." Although the Scientific Revolution was the product of the work of many individuals in several countries, we shall focus on the contributions of four major figures: the British essayist, philosopher, and statesman Francis Bacon (1561–1626), the French natural philosopher René Descartes (1596–1650), Galileo Galilei (1564–1642), and Isaac Newton (1642–1727).

The social context of the Scientific Revolution is as important as the fundamental intellectual transformations which constitute its core. The latter are inseparable from the former. The Scientific Revolution was contemporaneous with the advent of European global dominance and the rise of capitalism. Economic and political factors and new cultural attitudes toward society and nature were crucial to the formation of the modern scientific spirit and outlook (Moran, 1991).

The rise to power of the bourgeoisie and merchant classes created a climate in Europe which was particularly hospitable to the production and application of scientific and technological knowledge. The rise of efficient nation-states, such as England, France and the Low Countries, facilitated the spread of technocratic ideas in government and trade. The growth of cities and the spread of urbanization when coupled with a decline in agrarian traditions proved most receptive to industrial innovations. Voyages of discovery broadened Europe's cultural outlook and material horizons. All of these factors served to weaken traditional authority in religion, politics, education and ideology in general. This new secular outlook was responsive to the claims and promises of emerging modern science. Certain aspects of Protestantism (utilitarianism and empiricism), too, appeared favorable to scientific innovation and discovery, especially during the later seventeenth century (Gieryn, 1988, p. 591).

Meaning of Science

The very word science itself underwent a profound change in meaning. Prior to the seventeenth century, the word "science," in English, in Latin, and in the Romance languages, meant no more than "knowledge" or "understanding"—as opposed to mere belief or practical skill—in its general sense. What is now called science was then known as "natural philosophy." But the more advanced thinkers, especially in England and France, began to separate science from the larger and vaguer body of metaphysics and learning. They began to give the word its modern significance (Ross, 1990, pp. 800–802), for the word science acquired its modern connotation when it came to be felt that humanity's truest—indeed, perhaps its only certain—knowledge is derived by the scientific method. Descartes and others proclaimed the power and superiority of that new method which uncovered a body of systematically collected and accurately observed and measured (quantified) natural phenomena, tied together by general theoretical laws.

One of the first important authors to use the word science in this modern sense was the French philosopher and mathematician René Descartes. Toward the end of the seventeenth century, the *Dictionary* of the French Academy—reflecting this linguistic shift—defined science as "the certain and evident knowledge of things by their causes." Although Bacon's use of the word implied something similar, this change in the connotation of the English word did not become generally accepted until the eighteenth century. And not until a still later period, the nineteenth century, did the German "Wissenschaft" take the place of the older "Kunst." The word "technology" first appeared in English in the early seventeenth century.

These changes in language are highly significant because they record a profound change in thought. Not only were science and technology deemed more important than ever before in history, the method of science was also elevated to a radically new level of influence. It came to be regarded as a major (and useful) instrument for discovering truth. It was also regarded by some as the *only* instrument for discovering truths about the world. Of course, there were many who refused to accept the arguments of the new scientists. Some of these critics rejected science as a method for discovering anything truly meaningful or significant about the world. Others maintained that scientific knowledge was inferior, and therefore subservient, to other sources of knowledge—such as religion. There is no doubt, however, that the scientific method was about to triumph in certain societies and cultures. The rise of modern science, with its capacity for benevolent *as well as* detrimental cultural changes, is a dominant theme of nineteenth- and twentieth-century history. The remaining chapters of this book are devoted to examining the fundamental yet ambivalent roles and impacts of modern science and technology.

There was, to be sure, no univerally agreed upon "method of science" in the seventeenth century. The specific contributions to the development of the scientific method by Bacon, Descartes, Galileo, Newton and their peers are all crucial, albeit different (Hall, 1983, chap. 7). The controversies as to the most appropriate or proper method were vigorous in the seventeenth and eighteenth centuries, and continue to our own day. But historians agree that after the Scientific Revolution, scientists viewed their tasks and fields quite differently from previous thinkers. Ancient and medieval philosophers most often emphasized notions of "qualities" [as opposed to quantification], "purpose" [teleology], and certain religious and mystical precepts in their study of the natural world. Modern scientists, in contrast, emphasize verification of hypotheses and theories, empiricism, and quantitative laws.

The Scientific Revolution, like all historical short-hands, contains many anomalies. Like the French Revolution, for example, it was neither entirely consistent nor final. Contemporary science differs in some crucial ways from the Newtonian and Cartesian models. These differences include both the conceptual and technical tools modern science employs and its content and conclusions. Nevertheless, most contemporary scientists would argue that the evolution of science since the late sixteenth century displays a certain fundamental consistency in method and structure (McMullin, 1990, p. 29). Most significantly, modern science—particularly in the advanced industrial societies—studies and affects the world in ways markedly different from the manner in which Nature was explored by previous civilizations. One of the most eloquent and influential proponents of this new outlook was Francis Bacon.

Francis Bacon

Bacon was the son of Sir Nicholas Bacon, lord keeper of the great seal. He was educated at Trinity College, Cambridge, from 1573 to 1575. He entered Gray's Inn in 1575, and became a barrister in 1582. Bacon's life was spent in court circles, in politics, and in the law. He was knighted on the accession of James I in 1603, became lord chancellor in 1618, and was made viscount St. Albans in 1621. Forced to resign the chancellorship in 1621, Bacon lived in retirement near St. Albans. He devoted the remaining years of his life to natural philosophy (Wormald, 1992). Bacon was the greatest propagandist for the new science. He was central to the success of the Scientific Revolution. For it was he who—despite certain defects in his view of scientific method—enunciated the vision of scientific and technological *progress* which has been a cornerstone of many societies since the eighteenth century. Bacon believed that mankind had been prevented from achieving intellectual and material progress in the past by a misuse of its reasoning faculties. He pointed out four major obstacles to truth—that he termed Idols—which had hitherto enslaved the human mind and spirit in antiquity and the Middle Ages (Bacon, 1960, pp. 47–49). The first group of obstacles Bacon named "Idols of the Tribe." These were the inherent limitations that humanity suffers because of its biological nature. Because of these limitations—including its relative physical weakness and deficient senses of sight, touch and smell as compared to other animals—humanity has been handicapped in its attempt to control or alter nature. Bacon's emphasis that humanity should try to overcome these limitations in order to *control* nature is a radical departure from most traditional cultural viewpoints. These, as we have noted, generally adopted a relatively passive, or partnership, role of humanity with respect to physical nature.

The second group of obstacles Bacon called the "Idols of the Cave." These comprise the limitations which people suffer because of the restrictive education they had traditionally received or their particular individual interests. Bacon criticized what he felt were the sociopolitical limitations posed by previous cultures. The third set of obstacles were called the "Idols of the Theater." These referred to the great authoritarian philosophical systems of the past which controlled and circumscribed human thought and action. Bacon was particularly—if somewhat unjustly—critical of Aristotelianism. He believed that all dogmatic systems of tradition had militated against real human progress. Finally, Bacon referred to the "Idols of the Marketplace." These were the deceptions of words, those limitations imposed by the ambiguous languages used to discuss the natural world. Bacon believed that previous languages did not represent reality accurately. He was especially critical of the language of medieval scholasticism. This, he claimed, mistook words for actual things and often elevated mystical entities to real status. In this respect, Bacon was a major figure in the seventeenth-century movement (in Europe) to reform and modernize language.

These four Idols symbolized to Bacon the major hindrances to the advancement of knowledge. In effect, he had analyzed the cultural reasons for the failure of past civilizations to develop fully their scientific and technological potentials. His opinion of the ancient Greeks, for instance, although controversial is most revealing of his new vision of progress. Bacon dismissed their knowledge as verbal and barren. The ancient Greeks had no history to speak of, only fables and legends of antiquity. They knew only a small part of the world. Africa south of Ethiopia, Asia east of the Ganges and the entire "New World" were unknown to them. Not surprisingly, Bacon held that excessive respect for antiquity would necessarily obstruct the advance of science. He was fully aware of the broader significance of recent voyages and discoveries. Not only were Europeans becoming acquainted with new cultures and new foods and techniques. Voyages of material discovery also symbolized, for Bacon, new prospects and new futures for the societies of Europe. He believed it would be disgraceful if, while new regions of the Earth, the seas, and of the stars had been recently revealed, the intellectual globe should remain shut up within the narrow limits of old discoveries. Bacon declared that the most significant items of this new global commerce would be, not "gold, silver, or jewels; nor silks. . . [or] spices," but the exchange of knowledge (Basalla, 1984, p. 521)

Bacon's Four Idols constitute, in effect, the first sociological analysis of the cultural role of science and technology. He argued that a radically novel attitude towards science and technology was essential if humankind were to overcome what he perceived to be the limitations of the past. Bacon's view of tradition as being oppressive was surely a minority view of the time. Many regarded tradition as the revered source of authority. They regarded continuity with the past, rather than any social change or "progress," as being the desired goal of human thought and action. Bacon's striking descriptions of the *value* of change, therefore, both reflected and inspired the beliefs and actions of those who participated in the Scientific Revolution. He epitomized those individuals who saw in science and technology the tools by which society would be modernized (Martin, 1992). Bacon cited three inventions, unknown to the ancients, which dramatically expressed the potential of science and technology: printing (see section 1g), firearms (see section 1f), and the compass (see section 1g). Like several of his contemporaries, Bacon recognized that these three mechanical inventions (and their successors) had begun to exercise a far-reaching impact on the course of human history.

Technology and Maritime Empires

In fact, by Bacon's time, the compass and other navigational inventions were enabling European explorers to commence that series of voyages which would profoundly alter the status of global power. When, at the end of the fifteenth century, Columbus crossed the Atlantic and Portugese mariners sailed round Africa into the Indian Ocean, they opened the way to new continents. They also inaugurated a new science of navigation. Before this period, ships had either kept to narrow seas, or used regular winds to bring them to known landfalls. Now that they had to establish their whereabouts in unfamiliar waters, seamen needed recourse to the instruments of the astronomers, to find their location from the positions of Sun and stars. Instruments such as the astronomical astrolabe and the (simpler) quadrant were modified for use at sea (Gille, 1986, vol. 1, p. 571). Though less complex than the original devices, some mathematical training was needed to handle them. The Spaniards developed a system of teaching and certifying pilots to navigate their ships. Books on the new art of the compass and celestial navigation appeared, then were translated, copied and improved.

The links between astronomy, navigation and exploration in the two centuries preceding Bacon represent a clear example of science and technology in their social context. The impulse to use astronomical knowledge to improve navigational methods came at first, like the impulse to Atlantic exploration, from the Portugese prince, Henry the Navigator. He himself went on only one expedition, and that in his early youth: across the straits of Gibraltar to assist in the capture of the Moorish fortress of Ceuta in 1415. But until his death in 1460, he was the chief European exponent of the value of Atlantic explorations along the coast of Africa and of the value of astronomical aids to such navigation (Pacey, 1990, p. 57). To this joint end, he set up an early naval and colonial research institute at Sagres, on the southwest tip of Portugal. Although the institute lapsed with his death, the impetus given by Prince Henry to improve navigation, and to explore, was powerful. Portugal became so famous for its navigational interests that, by the late fifteenth century, Lisbon had emerged as a major European center for practical astronomy.

The cultural impact of these navigational advances was profound. Before 1500, civilizations had been essentially land-centered, and contacts by sea were relatively unimportant. Although there were some notable water-centered cultures previously in history—such as those of the Mediterranean and the Indian Ocean—direct sea contact between different continents was relatively unimportant. This changed after 1500. With the conquest first of the Atlantic and then of the Pacific Oceans, the beginnings of a "global village" appeared. This resulted in an extension of the stage of international history to regions which had hitherto gone their way in comparative or complete isolation. It was the European voyages of discovery in the sixteenth, seventeenth, and eighteenth centuries which opened all the seas to the ships of those nations.

First Spain and Portugal, then Britain, France and Holland sent their ships of exploration worldwide. With the economic benefits came political power. Spain and Portugal conquered the "New World" of the Americas (Greengrass, 1991, pp. 53, 65–66). France also made significant inroads there. In the East, the most formidable European group throughout the seventeenth century was the Dutch East India Company. First formally incorporated in 1602, it quickly became Europe's biggest trading corporation and established a monopoly on many of the most valuable world trade routes. The English East India Company, incorporated in 1600—although somewhat smaller than its Dutch rival—opened up trade routes during the seventeenth century with India (cotton goods and pepper) and China (tea and porcelain). Coupled with inroads made across the Atlantic and into the Caribbean, the stage was set for the rise of Britain to global superpower status and "ruler of the seas" during the nineteenth century. All this, of course, takes us far beyond Bacon's time. But in some important respects his vision included the rise of these maritime empires.

New Atlantis

Bacon's crucial insight was to realize that if science and technology were to have their fullest impact, society would have to adopt a *systematic* approach to their development and applications. In his most famous work, the posthumous *New Atlantis* (1627), Bacon describes (in this utopia set on a mythical, remote island—Bensalem—in the South Seas) a unique institution called "Salomon's House." This is, in effect, an organization for the production and dissemination of scientific and technical knowledge. He describes in detail the role of the salaried [a momentous innovation] employees of Salomon's House. Their duties included carrying out experimental investigations, assessing results, and using the scientific knowledge thus gained to make further practical inventions. There was also to be a hierarchical system which included novices and apprentices. In many respects, Salomon's House seems quite modern in spirit, resembling a large research organization. Bacon included what today we would call overseas sales and technical representatives, research and development departments, policy-making executives, and even agents for scientific and technical espionage. Bacon's ideas concerning the organization of research were prophetic. This particular element of his broader vision was incorporated into the new scientific societies, such as the Royal Society of London (1662), which first appeared in Europe in the late seventeenth and eighteenth centuries (Ravetz, 1990, p. 120). We may also see a Baconian spirit in the professional scientific and technical organizations, such as in England and Germany, which proliferated during the nineteenth century (see section 3a). The "think-tanks" and research institutes that characterize the science of the major advanced industrial nations of today may also be regarded as distant heirs to Salomon's House (see sections 7a, 7c).

Bacon's views on the social organization of science and technology were remarkably innovative (Rossi, 1968, pp. 22–23). It is hard for us to realize, after more than three centuries of continuous and extraordinary technical development, just how peripheral science and technology were considered to be in Bacon's own time. He sought to liberate science and technology from the constraints of traditional cultural attitudes. We are today more aware of the negative environmental, ethical, and sociopolitical impacts of certain scientific and technological advances than Bacon could have been. Yet his vision of their potential benefits was an exciting and influential one during the Scientific Revolution. Bacon believed that, if judiciously used, science could further "the relief of man's estate."

Bacon's vision of technical progress and intellectual transformation has become an integral aspect of many societies since the seventeenth century. Bacon could have had little or no inkling of science-based industry or the ramifications of modern industrial society. But his belief that the betterment of the human condition is possible by the concerted development and practical application of scientific and technological knowledge is now a commonplace. Science and technology *have* overcome certain of humanity's physical limitations. The telescope, the microscope, Newcomen and Watt's steam-engines, and a myriad of other inventions have greatly augmented human abilities. But alongside Bacon's comments on science as dominion over nature, there must also be set his more insistent view that knowledge should be applied in works of compassion and "for the benefit and use of life." If Bacon is the patron saint of those heroic engineers who have built cathedrals, railroads, and space vehicles, he is also the spiritual parent of those who see their scientfic and technological vocations as social and humanitarian ones (Pacey, 1983, pp. 172–173).

Education in the sciences and the raising of the social status of craftsmen and engineers have created the preconditions for modern industrial civilization. The language of science has been reformed and has become international in many respects. The use of the computer is an excellent example of this process. And, most significantly, science—in many domains—has replaced traditional political and religious authorities as the new measure of truth and power. This idea of a scientific "priesthood" had its roots in the seventeenth century. The experimentalists of the Royal Society prided themselves on being the "priests of nature" (Shapin & Schaffer, 1985, p. 319). The social quest for scientific and technological progress has become a dominant feature of modern history. Although the socially related functions of science and technology have turned out to be more complex and controversial than even Bacon anticipated, his historical significance is indisputable. He was one of the first to envision and propagandize for a pervasive cultural role for science and technology. However, the full realization of Bacon's program for the application of scientific research to the solution of major technical problems would be achieved only in the nineteenth and twentieth centuries (Dorn, 1991, pp. 145–146) (see sections 3a, 3c).

Baconian Empiricism

The basis for Bacon's optimism concerning the benefits of science, turned, of course, on a method for achieving those results. Bacon is also important to the Scientific Revolution for his attempt to formulate an explicit method of scientific enquiry. He aimed at a predominately experiential and inductive approach to the question of scientific knowledge (Hesse, 1970, p. 374). Bacon believed that the natural philosophers of the past had not paid sufficient attention to the methods by which the range of knowledge could be enlarged. He also condemned them for not testing their theories against the facts.

Bacon argued that scientific knowledge could best be built up by posing questions about nature that experiment and observation could answer. Since Bacon's science was to deal with real things, its results must be real and perceptible. Measured by these standards, he regarded Aristotelian and medieval science as hollow structures. He believed they dealt with barren abstractions, rather than objective phenomena. Although Bacon's view of medieval science was polemical, he was justified in maintaining that the storehouse of factual knowledge about the physical universe was meager. His remedy was to return to a consideration of the facts of material phenomena. The facts might be collected from experience, from reliable reports, from the lore of craftsmen, and, above all, from designed experiments. Bacon clearly conceived of experiment not merely as a trial to "see what happens," but as a way of answering specific questions. One task of the scientist, then, was to pose questions capable of an experimental answer.

Bacon's emphasis upon fact-collection and experimentation became important ingredients in the formation of the modern scientific method. Even the routine verification of measurements, or the establishment of precise constants [such as the force of gravity], have been productive of original discoveries. But Bacon's suggestion that scientists would achieve significant results and valid generalizations simply by collecting facts could not by itself ensure scientific advances. In certain fields—such as chemistry, biology and geology—Baconian guidelines were relevant for the early stages in creating those sciences in a modern form. In these sciences, where theories were less advanced and the natural processes under study quite complex, the straightforward acquisition of accurate information was an important task. After that, scientists could—as they did during the eighteenth and nineteenth centuries—more plausibly and profitably propose theories to account for the observed phenomena. In contrast, in physics and astronomy—where accurate experimental observations had long existed [in some instances, since antiquity]—seventeenth-century thinkers like Galileo and Newton had already transcended mere data collection. Baconian empiricism and induction provided only a partial clue for researchers. More explicit guidelines for theory construction were needed. Opposing Bacon in the effort to formulate a viable scientific method was René Descartes.

René Descartes

Descartes was born into the minor nobility, whose members contributed notably to intellectual life in seventeenth-century France. At Jesuit schools, he received a modern education in mathematics and physics—including Galileo's telescopic discoveries—as well as in philosophy and the classics. He became financially independent owing to inherited family property (Crombie, 1971, p. 51). Unlike Bacon, Descartes sought to create a *metaphysical* foundation for modern science. He attempted to establish a complete system of nature embracing the explanation of all phenomena, mental as well as physical. Descartes promised not merely a guide to scientific knowledge, but an unfailing method of discovery. He is one of the founders—along with B. Spinoza (1632–1677) and G. W. Leibniz (1646–1716)—of modern *rationalism*. This is the philosophical system which maintains that the general nature of the world, though not necessarily its details, can be established by nonempirical *deductive* reasoning. For Descartes, the structure of natural science was theoretical and logical. He believed that the truths of science could be discovered through the use of clear and distinct ideas, whose content was independent of sense-experience (Sorell, 1987, pp. 66–67). Once reason uncovered these fundamental ideas, the scientist could then deduce general theoretical "laws of nature." Though Descartes did not ignore empiricism, experimentation played no more than a minor role in his system.

As outlined in the famous *Discourse on Method* (1637) and other writings, Descartes began his search for the proper method for the natural sciences by embracing the certainty of the existence of mind and God. Rejecting empiricism as a starting point, he declared that all knowledge of truth is implanted by God. It is this intellectual faculty of clear perception—the only source of metaphysical certainty and permanent knowledge—which enables us to engage in an inquiry into truth and to successfully construct science (Markie, 1986, p. 72). In this, Descartes did not differ from the mainstream of medieval philosophy. Rather, his innovation was to stress that the task of the scientist is to frame all propositions as clearly and distinctly as those of geometry. According to Descartes, the "enigmas of nature" will reveal themselves to the proper use of logic. The universal truths of science, or the laws of nature, therefore, will be detected by reason (Hatfield, 1990, pp. 111–112).

Thus, the system of Descartes, unlike the "new philosophy" of Bacon or Galileo, did not aim only to establish correct scientific statements. It aimed to provide a fundamental, rational structure of the universe, whose relevance to particular empirical facts becomes the secondary task of the scientist. Descartes' laws of nature are deductive, not inductive or empirically based. He was so confident of his method that, he asserted, the main features of his philosophy were necessarily true—as with a theorem in mathematics. Descartes claimed that the formal, axiomatic truths of mathematics, such as those of geometry, were the true model for all scientific explanation. His deductive ideal exerted a powerful influence on many of his contemporaries and continued as an intellectual force during the Enlightenment (see next section). In particular, his exposition of the new "mechanical philosophy" and his views on the corpuscular structure of matter dominated much of physical science for the next century (Cottingham, 1992, pp. 282–283).

Despite the brilliance of his system, however, Descartes offered an ultimately unsatisfactory method for the natural sciences. Too often rigidly "a prioristic," Descartes moved further and further from the world of empirical reality. His magnificent conception of nature—logically impeccable as it was—could not withstand the onslaught of experimental data. His system was called by even so staunch a disciple of his as Christiaan Huygens (1629–1695) "un beau roman de physique." Although aware of the significance of experimentation for science, Descartes' deductive method afforded an inadequate place for it. The important eighteenth-century Swiss physiologist Albrecht von Haller (1708–1777), who championed the cause of Baconian empiricism, condemned Descartes for being "too hasty for the experiment, the street was too long for him" (Roe, 1984, p. 275).

Reduced to bare essentials, the methods of Bacon and Descartes were not concerned with the same things nor with the same functions. Thus, neither could stand as a wholly adequate or valid model for scientific investigation. The inductive method alone was a poor tool for expounding the universe. Similarly, deductive logic needed a sound, empirical picture of the real world to work upon, for scientific concepts and laws do not crystallize spontaneously from natural histories and data gathering. Neither can they be created as pure abstractions from the human intellect. What was needed to guarantee scientific advance in the seventeenth century (and beyond) was a method which combined the crucial insights represented by Bacon and by Descartes. This synthesis between *theory* and *experiment*—the modern scientific method—was first clearly achieved in the work of Galileo Galilei.

Galileo Galilei

Galileo, the eldest of seven children, was born in Pisa, Italy, on 15 February 1564. His father was Vincenzio Galilei, a musician and musical theorist and a descendant of a Florentine patrician family distinguished in medicine and public affairs. Galileo's name is now synonymous with that decisive change in the balance between speculative philosophy, mathematics and experimental evidence which characterized the Scientific Revolution. The period covered by his scientific publications began with the announcement of the first telescopic astronomical discoveries in 1610 in his *Sidereus nuncius* (or *Starry Messenger*). Galileo's use of the telescope revealed the moon to be mountainous, the Milky Way to be a congregation of separate stars, and Jupiter to be surrounded by four (hitherto unsuspected) satellites. By naming them for the Medici dynasty, Galileo acquired royal patronage and legitimation of a sociocultural status higher than most other scientists in early seventeenth-century Italy (Biagioli, 1990, p. 236). All this was contrary to traditional Ptolemaic/Aristotelian teaching (see section 2a). Galileo's scientific writings ended with the first systematic attempt to extend the mathematical treatment of physics from "statics" to "kinematics" [the study of the motions of bodies] and with the strength of materials in 1638, in the *Two New Sciences*. The same period witnessed Kepler's mathematical transformation of planetary theory and William Harvey's (1578–1657) experimental discovery of the circulation of the blood. Galileo's life and works are of central importance to an understanding of the Scientific Revolution. His personal (and famous) conflict with religious authority dramatizes vividly the extent and profundity of the changing approach to nature associated with the Scientific Revolution (Drake, 1972, pp. 237–238).

With respect to method, Galileo's work affords a compromise between the ideas of Bacon and Descartes. He did not, as they did, construct an explicit methodology of science. But the elements of the modern scientific method can be extracted readily from his writings. Like Bacon, Descartes, and the other major critics of traditional approaches to science, Galileo was faced with two fundamental problems. First, on what foundation was the new intellectual structure of science to be built? Second, what criteria for satisfactory and valid explanation were to replace those of the past, such as Aristotle's emphasis on teleology [purpose in nature]? For Galileo, the method of science was not only the collection of data, as Baconian induction taught. Nor was it the exclusive concern with deductive logic as Descartes had emphasized. Rather, Galileo believed that science aimed to establish a logically consistent description of phenomena which is at the same time rooted in empirical reality. He recognized that while the scientist must employ theoretical concepts which are constructed from mathematical reasoning and intellectual imagination, these concepts must ultimately be tested against reality (Cohen, 1985a, p. 197).

Galileo's Scientific Method

Galileo's method for arriving at scientific laws and generalizations includes four major components. The first is *abstraction*. This means that the essential generalization for any scientific phenomenon is not to be taken as the end-product of the logical examination of an idea, as the Aristotelians maintained. Instead, the Galilean scientist begins the study of a particular problem by separating the fundamental characteristic of the phenomenon from the surrounding properties. For example, in studying the acceleration of falling bodies, Galileo temporarily ignored friction and air resistance in formulating the question. Abstraction involves the second of Galileo's methodological principles, the *distinction between primary and secondary qualities*. Galileo claimed that by abstraction it is learned that the primary, or basic, properties of bodies are purely physical. These would include size, shape, and motions of particles. In contrast, secondary properties such as color, taste, and smell of objects, while real, are not inherent in the bodies themselves. Instead, they are the names given to sensations stimulated in the observer by the physical constitution of the objects he/she perceives (Hatfield, 1990, p. 133).

This aspect of Galileo's philosophy of science is related to his adherence to the "corpuscular," or mechanical, philosophy. During the seventeenth and eighteenth centuries, the mechanical philosophy—and its related ideal of *reductionism*—was responsible for some of the most notable achievements in science. Aristotelian and medieval physics had focussed upon explanation of change and movement in terms of the "qualities" of bodies [such as "natural place" and "affinity"]. In contrast, Galileo, Descartes, Robert Boyle, Newton and their colleagues sought to frame a corpuscular physics of a qualitatively neutral matter composed of geometrical and mechanical properties alone. Matter, in this view, could be moved only by external force, having no inherent force or tendency to motion (Tamny, 1990, p. 597–598).

Much of the corpuscularianism of Galileo, Descartes and Boyle was given a rigorous mathematical framework by Newton in his *Principia* (1687). This book's analysis of gravitational attraction became a model for certain eighteenth-century attempts to incorporate Nature's other forces—such as magnetism—into a mathematical physics. But Newton himself remained publicly noncommittal about the mechanism of attraction. This led certain Newtonians, and many of his important critics, to feel that Newton had actually reintroduced occult qualities into physics (Schaffer, 1990, p. 617). More important, after certain initial successes, the corpuscular philosophy proved inadequate to a complete scientific explanation of a number of significant chemical, biological and psychological processes. The debates over the comprehensiveness of the corpuscular philosophy continued throughout the eighteenth and nineteenth centuries. There is no doubt, however, that in the hands of Galileo and others, the corpuscular philosophy was a critical ingredient in the Scientific Revolution.

The next aspect of Galileo's method was *mathematics*, which was a crucial aid in the process of abstraction. By transposing the conditions of a problem into mathematical language (when possible), Galileo believed that certain of the defects of traditional physics could be avoided. Further, mathematical manipulation might expose connections between phenomena that would otherwise remain unknown or undetected. Thus, the core of science for Galileo was to transfer a problem, properly defined, to this abstracted physical universe. As greater complexities are then added back to this initial statement, the scientist approximates more and more closely the actual universe of our observation. The architecture of the real world for Galileo is mathematical. To him, the book of nature was "written in mathematical language . . . the letters being triangles, circles and other figures without which it is humanly impossible to comprehend a single word" (Hall, 1983, pp. 179–180).

Galileo recognized, however, that while mathematical logic is infallible, a logically consistent scientific hypothesis might rest on false assumptions. This was the case with Ptolemaic astronomy and (even) Cartesian "vortex" physics. It appeared all too easy to mistake one of nature's circles for a triangle. For Galileo, therefore, the final step in scientific investigation had to be *experimentation*. Only then could the scientist determine whether his (abstracted) image of the universe represented faithfully things as they "actually are." Galileo's linkage of experimental validation to theoretical structure is one of the triumphs of the Scientific Revolution and remains a hallmark of the modern scientific method (Drake, 1990, pp. 233–234).

Galileo and Experiment

Galileo's attitude toward experiment differs in an important respect from that of Bacon (Cohen, 1985b, p. 141). The latter emphasized mainly the role of experiment as a means of obtaining new information. Galileo, in contrast, recognized the additional role of experiment in testing a theory. In his view, the questions which the scientist asks of nature are most useful when they are not random. They should be designed so that a single, unambiguous response can be elicited from a given experiment. To be sure, this approach to experiment had occurred to certain earlier thinkers. But with Galileo it became a main pillar of scientific research. Experiment is now a test of knowledge, confirming a necessary deduction in the development of a sound theory.

Galileo's name is also linked to the concept of "thought-experiments." A scientist should be able to claim, in principle, that if one performed a possible experiment, one should get a particular result—even if one never actually performs the experiment. Suppose, for example, that theoretical examination suggests that under specified conditions event "B" will follow event "A." Such reasoning can be tested, Galileo suggested, by creating those conditions and performing the experiment. In this sense, Galileo viewed experiments as demonstrative and corroborative of true theories, rather than only as genuine tests of them. The precise relation between theory and experiment in the work of Galileo—and in science in general—continues to be a matter of philosophical dispute. However, the modern scientific method—with its twin base in theory *and* experiment—appeared most clearly first in the writings of Galileo (Hall, 1983, pp. 182–184).

Not all his contemporaries greeted Galileo's scientific achievements with enthusiasm. In particular, his astronomical discoveries threatened an accepted way of looking at the world.

During the Middle Ages, Aristotelian natural philosophy, Ptolemaic astronomy and Christian theology had been merged into a union of belief and knowledge with an explicit and satisfying cosmology. This medieval cosmology was, to its adherents, an adequate—even necessary—explanation of both the phenomena of nature and the human condition. Presenting an Aristotelian with evidence against his beliefs in science compares with confronting a modern physicist with evidence against, say, the theory of relativity (see section 4a). Galileo's new science of physics and astronomy was just this controversial. More to the point, however, was the fact that Galileo's defense of Copernicanism appeared to threaten the very basis of Catholic orthodoxy (see section 2a).

Theological Controversy

From the early stages of his career, Galileo's Copernican views became the topic of conversation and controversy among theologians as well as astronomers, philosophers, and educated laymen. In the *Letter to the Grand Duchess Christina* (composed in 1615 and eventually published in 1636), Galileo sought to clarify what he thought was a necessary distinction between science and theology. He argued that neither the Bible nor Nature could speak falsely. Morality, the service of God, and the salvation of souls were the legitimate concern of the theologian. However, Galileo claimed that the investigation of nature was the special province of the scientist. But such a neat separation is not always possible. In fact, the Bible often speaks on physical matters.

One such famous passage is known as the "Miracle of Joshua." Joshua, seeking a lengthening of the day in order to prolong a battle, calls out "Sun, stand thou still." As a consequence of divine intervention, the Bible tells us that the "sun stood still in the midst of the heavens" and the day was miraculously prolonged. A literal interpretation of this passage would contradict the Copernican hypothesis that the sun is immobile at the center of the universe [and hence could not have been moving]. In the *Letter to Christina*, Galileo argued that the Bible is not to be taken literally in all instances. He maintained that the text of the Bible is often written in common language so that it might be understood by simple persons. Particularly in matters of physics—which, according to Galileo, are not the Bible's major concern in any event—confusion has often been avoided by casting casual references to astronomical phenomena in simple language, such as "the sun stood still."

If this language contradicts demonstrated scientific evidence—as Galileo held Copernicanism to possess—then the Bible must not be interpreted literally in such passages. Galileo was arguing that in physical matters, we should use our (God-given) senses as the prime source of knowledge. Moreover, in those parts of the Bible which are not concerned with religious matters, he said we can employ scientific knowledge to clarify our biblical interpretation. Galileo was actually saying much more. In attempting to establish what he regarded as the appropriate demarcation between scientific and theological language, he embarked upon a course that could lead to a divorce between science and religion and faith from reason. And this is how certain of the leaders of the Catholic Church interpreted Galileo's argument.

For, in claiming for scientists a sphere of their own—where they would be immune to criticism by nonscientists—he was also claiming an absolute authority for science. Galileo was, in fact, doing more than defending his right to discuss freely the Copernican system. He took the Copernican theory to be a proven account of reality and believed its conclusions to warrant the status of scientific truth. And if those conclusions, particularly the motion of the earth around the sun, contradicted certain teachings of the Catholic Church, then the Church should yield on those points. Theologians saw—quite correctly, as it turned out—that Galileo's argument that the Bible should be interpreted to correspond to soundly demonstrated physical truths could have far broader implications for faith and institutionalized religion. For, where is the definition of science to end? Could it not be possible that sense experience and scientific method might yield answers to moral and ethical problems.?

The *Letter to Christina* represents an epitome of what has been called the "crime" of Galileo. For the next two decades, Galileo's new cultural program for science brought him into direct and indirect conflict with the Catholic Church. Finally, the publication of his *Dialogue Concerning the Two Chief World Systems* in 1632—a major polemical treatise in favor of Copernican-ism—brought matters to a head. In 1633, Galileo was brought to trial by the Inquisition (de Santillana, 1959, chap. 12). Although the specific details of the charges, and of the evidence brought to bear against Galileo, are still the subject of some historical dispute, the outcome of the trial was never in doubt. The Galileo affair was an affair of state, a very serious affair of state. The room for the Church to maneuver was extremely restricted, and a trial for Galileo—his official condemnation—was the only way out (Redondi, 1987, p. 258).

Contrary to popular accounts, Galileo was never tortured. He was, however, "persuaded" to acknowledge that he had gone too far in his arguments for Copernicus in the *Dialogue*. On the basis of that admission, or recantation, Galileo's book was put on the Papal Index and prohibited. [The Roman Catholic Church officially conceded that it had erred in condemning Galileo only in 1992.] He was also sentenced to "formal prison," but that amounted to a series of comfortable suites in approved palaces and villas. During the next few years, Galileo, by now nearly blind, returned to the study of physical dynamics. In 1638, he published *Two New Sciences*, on which his fame as a natural scientist primarily rests. Galileo died in 1642, the year in which Newton was born. The controversies concerning science and religion engendered by his trial, as well as the influence exerted by his powerful approach to scientific method, endure to this day. In Italy, the Church's decision led to a decline in Italian science following Galileo's death (Segre, 1991, pp. 141–142) His significant successors would be found henceforth in northern Europe.

The early applications of that scientific method were often brilliant. Particularly in the hands of Isaac Newton and his peers, did this combination of theory, mathematical analysis, quantitative precision, and experimental verification achieve revolutionary breakthroughs. So dazzling was Newton's success in physics (see section 2a), in fact, that his name came to symbolize the triumphal march of science in general for the eighteenth century (Stewart, 1992). As a model of scientific investigation and synthesis, Newtonian science seemed—to many—unrivalled.

In many respects, Newton's *Mathematical Principles of Natural Philosophy* (1687) was the culmination of the seventeenth-century Scientific Revolution. His public career and his scientific accomplishments justified the hopes which certain important figures had placed on the new approach to Nature. Newton's universal law of gravitation was recognized as vindicating the scientific endeavor of the seventeenth century: the efforts to experiment and mathematize, the reaction against tradition, and the search for new and firmer conceptual foundations. Although Newton himself remained tied to certain traditional philosophical and religious concepts, he was generally regarded as the herald of a new age (Dobbs, 1991).

During the eighteenth century, the scientific ideal—precisely because of its undoubted first successes in physics, astronomy, and mathematics—appeared to provide the clue for removing falsehood and obscurity from other disciplines. Biology, chemistry, and medicine were the next targets for modernization. Some thinkers went even further. The architects of the Enlightenment believed that the scientific method held the key to enlargement of knowledge in *all* fields. Psychology, economics, history, the study of society, even morality and religion themselves, were proclaimed as ready for—in fact, desperately needful of—scientific reform. If applied properly, the inevitable result of the scientific approach would be a steady improvement in the human condition. Science would become the engine of social progress. ■ *Question* ʼ

D. Science and the Enlightenment

■ ■ ■ *The scientific method held the key to enlargement of knowledge in all fields.*

The new approach toward natural science in the seventeenth century, which culminated in the work of figures such as Galileo, Boyle, Descartes, Kepler, and Newton, was to be applied with continued success during the eighteenth century. To the French mathematician Jean Lerond D'Alembert (1717–1783), the Scientific Revolution was a dynamic intellectual and cultural force. He regarded his own time as one displaying a "new method of philosophizing, the kind of enthusiasm which accompanies discoveries, a certain exaltation of ideas which the spectacle of the universe produces in us—all these causes have brought about a lively fermentation of minds, spreading through nature in all directions like a river which has burst its dams."

D'Alembert was one of that brilliant group of mid-eighteenth century French intellectuals—who included Voltaire, Denis Diderot, Julien Offray de La Mettrie (1709–1751), and Georges-Louis Leclerc, Comte de Buffon (1707–1788) among many others—called the *philosophes*. The philosophes were united in a belief that natural science could become one major ingredient in a progressive reform of culture and society. Other Europeans—David Hume (1711–1776) in Great Britain and Immanuel Kant (1724–1804) in Germany are notable examples—and North Americans—Thomas Jefferson (1743–1826), third President of the United States (1801–1809), is a famous example—shared the views and ideals of the philosophes. All these thinkers are part of the general movement of thought and activity during the eighteenth century known as the *Enlightenment*.

The term was coined by the philosopher Kant. When asked in 1785 to characterize the times in which he lived, Kant replied that "we are living in an age of enlightenment." For Kant, enlightenment—or, as it was called in France, the "siècle des lumières" ["century of light"], because of its emphasis on reason, rather than revelation, as the surest guide to knowledge and understanding—meant humanity's exit from a self-imposed and restrictive state of infancy. He believed that humankind had not yet been bold enough to transcend the limitations of ignorance. Kant felt that science was one element in a new self-confidence for the human race. Like D'Alembert, he thought that the Scientific Revolution was still in progress. But the Scientific Revolution for the Enlightment signified a far broader concept than the intellectual revolution of the seventeenth century (Hankins, 1985, pp.1–2, 159–161).

The distinguishing characteristic of the Enlightenment was its prevalent confidence in "reason." The philosophes and their followers had been duly impressed with the striking success of applying the scientific method to various disciplines during the preceding century. It is significant to remember, however, that these initial successes were achieved first in physics, mathematics, and astronomy. The philosophes, emboldened by the progress in science, believed that the same method—or some approximation to it—could achieve similar reforms in other areas of thought and culture.

The world-view of the Enlightenment was partly inherited from previous cultures. The ideals of ancient Greece, for example, were widely praised, if not always put into practice (Gay, 1966, pp. 31–203). But it is also, in major respects, primarily a product of the new outlook of the Scientfic Revolution. The philosophes inherited from their ancient and medieval predecessors the belief in absolute truth and in a "reasonable" and comprehensible universe. But the Enlightenment found in modern science a new standard of truth. In particular, seventeenth-century astronomy provided a novel and verifiable scheme of the universe. Newton appeared to many to be the preeminent exemplar of the scientific spirit. His discovery of the law of universal gravitation was regarded as a clear expression of science at its most powerful. Newton's physics also seemed to offer a model, or at least a guide, for uncovering truths about other aspects of culture. In the work of the Abbé de Condillac (1714–1780), Newton's methodology was authoritatively linked with the broader commitment of progressive social change (Gillispie, 1971, p. 382).

Bacon and the Enlightenment

The "Age of Reason," as the Enlightenment is also called, was not merely an intellectual movement. It aimed to be eminently *practical* as well. Echoing Baconian optimism, Enlightenment spokespersons maintained that it was society's duty to use the knowledge gained from scientific investigation to improve the conditions of human existence. Bacon had been explicit on this point. The head of Salomon's House—the scientific academy in Bacon's utopian *New Atlantis*—declares their goal to be the use of scientific and technical knowledge to enlarge the boundaries of human empire, to "the effecting of all things possible." For Bacon, the social endeavor to "establish and extend the power and dominion of the human race itself over the Universe" was a far nobler ambition than any mere pursuit of personal economic or political gain (Rossi, 1968, p. 27).

This Baconian vision owes much to the spirit of the Renaissance. It reflects the confidence in human abilities generated by recent technological achievements, inventions, and bold undertakings in navigation and exploration. But Bacon went further. He urged humanity to exercise its intellectual powers to achieve power *over nature*. Here Bacon even had the Bible on his side. He quoted enthusiastically from the Book of *Genesis* to support his conviction that God had indeed created man in his image and had granted him dominion over nature. Though mindful of the dangers inherent in a too reckless exercise of that power, Bacon believed that humanity—if guided by wise, moral principles—could reassert its rule over the rest of creation.

Bacon's program had a number of crucial, and controversial, consequences for the Enlightenment and for the Nineteenth Century (Elkana, 1984, pp. 494–499). First, it was argued that more of society's energies should be directed toward subduing and "conquering" nature than had been the case in the past. To be sure, the ancient and medieval worlds had their notable technological achievements. But science had been regarded principally as a key to *understanding* rather than *changing* nature. The nonhuman environment had been seen largely as a fixed background against which the drama of human life unfolded. Hopes for an improvement in material conditions were limited. Much of the energy devoted to improving humanity's lot was focussed on spiritual rewards and the (possibly) benign environment of the hereafter. Bacon and certain of his contemporaries manifested a radically new and optimistic attitude toward nature.

A major impetus for this newly expressed optimism of the sixteenth and seventeenth centuries was, as we have seen, the remarkable progress in science and technology. For Bacon and his followers, science and technology would provide both the intellectual and practical tools to exercise fully the human "right" to dominion over nature. They become, in effect, society's principal instruments for achieving ethical and social, as well as technical, progress (Ravetz, 1990, p. 121). Most of the philosophes shared this Baconian vision of science and technology as humanity's noblest aids. The deification of science and technology—which is so notable a feature of many of our modern attitudes toward nature—soon followed. This new social reverence for science was to find bold, if ambivalent, expression during the French Revolution at the end of the eighteenth century (Emerson, 1990, pp. 974–975).

Voltaire and the Philosophes

Francois Marie Arouet de Voltaire (1694–1778) was one of the first and most prolific and persuasive of the philosophes. In addition to his celebrated literary achievements—of which *Candide* is perhaps the most well-known—Voltaire also published (in 1738) a popular tract on *Elements of the Philosophy of Newton*. Like Bacon, Voltaire propagandized for the new scientific world-view. Significantly, Voltaire had a long and intimate—intellectual as well as personal—relationship with Gabrielle-Emilie de Breutil, the Marquise du Châtelet (1706–1749), probably the best-known woman scientist of the Eighteenth Century. Her translation of Newton's *Principia*, with a commentary, remains today the standard French translation of that work (Schiebinger, 1989, pp.59–65). During the Enlightenment, Voltaire and his associates fought a powerful campaign on behalf of science and reason. In books and pamphlets, in vast encyclopedias and in newspapers and journals, in poetry and prose, by serious argument and by witty mockery, the disciples of Enlightenment created a brilliant—and controversial—polemic for social and cultural change.

It was a fundamental conviction of theirs that humanity's foremost task consisted in the establishment of greater and greater control over the environment—both material and social. This was indeed the dream of Anne-Robert-Jacques Turgot (1727–1781), the most enlightened of mid-eighteenth century French royal administrators. As controller general of finance, his brief reforming ministry (1774–1776) epitomizes the relationship between science and politics in pre-revolutionary France (Baker, 1990, p. 159). In that capacity he attempted bold reforms on a national scale, thus earning an enduring reputation as the most courageous official of the old regime.

Turgot's interests and talents were far-ranging, touching upon languages and literature as well as many fields of science. He contributed a major chemical article in the Diderot *Encyclopédie*, which apparently had some influence on Lavoisier (see section 2b). More significant than Turgot's own scientific activities was his role as a patron and public official who regularly sought the advice of scientific experts. He was motivated by the conviction that the results of scientific research, applied to technology and taught to peasants, craftsmen, manufacturers, and others, could provide a firm foundation for social progress. Turgot's views were not necessarily original, being shared by the philosophes and other contemporaries. What makes his so notable, however—and what separates him from the other philosophes—was his political power to implement those views. Translated into policy, his attitude led Turgot to devise some projects of his own (such as the collection of accurate statistical data about France), solicit suggestions from scientists, sponsor translations of scientific treatises, and encourage the work of inventors (Rappaport, 1976. pp. 494–495).

For Voltaire, Turgot and their peers, the scientific method pointed the way. From physics, mathematics, and astronomy, the new approach was adopted in the other natural sciences. Biology, chemistry, and medicine would soon—or so it appeared to some—be revolutionized in the same way as the physical sciences had during the previous century. It was in the Enlightenment that many of the categories of modern scientific thought with which we are today familiar first began to take shape. Physics, mathematics, and optics were assuming a more clearly modern form. The so-called "social sciences" were making their preliminary appearance. These changing categories of science were a reflection of changing views of nature and its study that the Enlightenment inherited from the seventeenth century and further refined (Charlton, 1984, pp. 66–67).

Franklin and Electricity

The investigation of electricity provides one of the clearest examples of this changed outlook. Of all the natural phenomena investigated during the Enlightenment, electricity was the one that caused the most excitement and attracted the most researchers. The study of electricity became the model for experimental physics, both in the kinds of experiments performed and in the construction of apparatus. Electricity had several advantages over the other fields of experimental physics. Once research began in earnest, experimenters rapidly discovered new electrical phenomena. This experimental work proved rewarding in a financial as well as scientific context. Many of these electrical experimenters found places in the universities and the scientific academies of Europe. A small but significant proportion supported themselves by giving public demonstration lectures. Because of their often dramatic effects, electrical experiments were popular and suitable for recreational purposes. The Abbé (and physicist) Jean-Antoine Nollet's (1700–1770) electrical experiments were particularly impressive. They provide a significant example of the impact that science was beginning to have on even those outside the scientific community. Though many in the audience were probably unaware of the theoretical principles involved, Nollet's dramatic demonstrations foreshadow the use of science-as-entertainment which is commonplace today. This was especially the case after 1746, when the discovery of the Leyden jar made it possible to accumulate very large electric charges (Hankins, 1985, pp. 53–57, 67–71).

Benjamin Franklin (1706–1790), born in Boston, was the first North American to win an international reputation in pure science and the first scientist to gain fame for work done wholly in electricity (Cohen, 1990). His principal achievement was the formulation of a (then) widely used theory of general electrical action. He advanced the concept of a single "fluid" of electricity and was responsible for the introduction into scientific discourse of such terms as "plus" and "minus," "positive" and "negative," "charge," and "battery."

Franklin is best remembered for his experiments showing that the lightning discharge is an electrical phenomenon. Upon this demonstration, together with his experimental findings concerning the action of grounded and pointed conductors, he based his invention of the lightning rod. In a paper published in 1750, Franklin discussed the possible electrification of clouds and the nature of lightning discharge. Later, when the experiments were made, Franklin found that another function of the lightning rod, apart from "disarming" a passing cloud, would be to conduct a lightning stroke safely into the ground. His experiments to test the electrification of clouds, including the famous kite experiment of 1752—which was, however, not entirely original with him since certain French researchers were then performing similar experiments to draw electricity from clouds—achieved an immediate and widespread international renown.

The lightning experiments and the erection of "lightning rods" on public buildings in Philadelphia and elsewhere, caused Franklin's name to become known throughout North America and Europe. He became well-known to the public at large, as well as to the scientific community. One reason for the popular fascination with his discovery was that it subjected one of the most mysterious and frightening natural phenomena to rational explanation. It also proved that Bacon had been correct in asserting that a knowledge of how nature really works might lead to a better control of nature itself. Franklin demonstrated that valuable practical innovations might indeed result from pure, disinterested scientific research. In addition to his scientific accomplishments, Franklin became famous as a stateman. He was one of the authors of the "Declaration of Independence" and played a crucial role in the political and diplomatic activities leading to the creation of the United States (Cohen, 1972, pp. 129, 132–135, 138). Franklin, moreover, is one of the first public figures whose *initial* international reputation was gained in science. Thus he prefigures the politically active scientist-statesmen who play so conspicuous, if controversial, a role in our own day (see sections 6a, 6c, 7a, 7b).

The association of electricity with lightning and the discovery that all substances could be electrified moved electricity from the fringes to the center of scientific attention. Recall that Newton had constructed a complete world system from the single idea of universal gravitation. He also concluded that other attractions and repulsions between atoms would likely account for most of the phenomena of chemistry and physics. Electricity seemed to be the phenomenon that was most likely to exhibit these interatomic forces. The pioneering efforts of Franklin, Nollet and others would be brilliantly developed by Michael Faraday, James Clerk Maxwell, and other physicists who established the foundations of the science of electromagnetism during the nineteenth century.

Medicine, physiology, and chemistry also witnessed fundamental changes in concepts and techniques during the eighteenth century. Chemistry, in particular, assumed a modern aspect by the close of the century. Historians speak of the Chemical Revolution associated with the work of Lavoisier and others (see section 2b). The study of zoology, botany, geology, and meteorology began to emerge as distinct disciplines. What we call science today was, however, still called (by many) "natural philosophy" during the Enlightenment. Biology and sociology were names and disciplines that would not assume a recognizably modern tone until the nineteenth century. Yet there was a marked change in outlook which governed the study of all natural science during the Enlightenment. It makes the eighteenth century a period of transition from the Scientific Revolution of the seventeenth century to the emergence of the more fully developed modern sciences of the nineteenth and twentieth centuries. But the advocates of the Enlightenment were not content to rest there. They aimed at little less than the transformation of all sociopolitical institutions in obedience to the dictates of reason.

The Science of Society

This extension of the scientific method to include the study and reform of a broad array of human activities is one of the most characteristic features of the Enlightenment. From the natural sciences, the new pattern of the scientific method was adopted in—or adapted to—other fields of thought and action. The philosophes believed that history, when properly understood, could furnish a new knowledge of human nature. And this human nature was, according to the thinkers of the Enlightenment, assumed to be as much subject to scientific law as was inanimate nature. Gradually, politics, psychology, education, economics, aesthetics, and even religion were considered to be amenable to the methods of science. All these fields—dominated still by what was considered the yoke of tradition—were investigated, criticized, explained and reformed accordingly. Science also provided a new opportunity for cultural achievement by women. Although still restricted by custom and lack of access to formal education and training, eighteenth-century female scientists began to challenge successfully certain traditional stereotypes. Chemistry, in particular, became increasingly popular among women. Elizabeth Fulhame, an early convert to Lavoisier's theory, became well-known for her research and publications on the new chemistry (Alic, 1986, p. 99). By the beginning of the eighteenth century, a surprisingly large number of women had achieved a degree of prominence in astronomy in Germany (Schiebinger, 1989, p. 79).

Far from regarding the new and powerful scientific method with suspicion, hostility, dread or incomprehension—as had many in the seventeenth century—advocates of the Enlightenment encouraged its widespread application. In the search for truth, the methods of experiment and mathematical analysis had already been justified by their successes in most of the natural sciences. The sciences describing and predicting human behavior, both individually and in society—what would soon be termed the "social sciences"—would, it was believed, be marked by similar success. No longer, it was argued, could cultural traditions, the sanctity of biblical revelation, nor even the authority of the state be used to prohibit the acceptance of scientifically established truths.

Certain individuals of the seventeenth century, as we have seen, had also maintained that science and its methods could shed new light on fields other than strictly scientific ones. In the preface to his *Histoire* of the Paris Academy of Sciences, its "perpetual secretary" Bernard de Fontenelle (1657–1757) wrote (in 1699) that the new "geometric spirit" could also improve studies on politics, morals, literary criticism and even public speaking. But it had still been considered prudent, and in some cases such as that of Galileo obligatory, to conceal or downplay such thoughts. Even the Royal Society of London's stated purpose, in the words of one of its founders, "precluded matters of theology and state affairs" to focus exclusively on the natural sciences.

Such a restricted scope for the scientific method was foreign to the outlook of the advocates of Enlightenment. Their view of science was radical in the sense that they saw it as a tool to criticize and reform social and political structures. In England, Joseph Priestley's (1733–1804) important work on the chemistry of gases was firmly rooted in the social conditions of the English Enlightenment (Golinski, 1992, p. 63). The philosophes believed that the human environment—in both the physical and cultural senses—could be changed for the better with the proper use of critical reason as a guide. Scrutinizing tradition in all fields, and casting it off when reason demanded it in the name of progress, the philosophes firmly believed that they were uncovering the laws that governed the social world. Just as in physics and astronomy, so would ideas about politics, religion, psychology, economics and education be made scientific by an appropriate application of experiment and theory. The term "scientific" had been largely irrelevant to, or deemed harmful for, social and political issues in previous ages. Among the followers of the Enlightenment, in sharp contrast, the term "scientific" became not merely relevant to social and political questions, but the only certain guide to truth in those domains. The Enlightenment's belief in the certainty of progress—and even the ultimate perfectibility of humanity and the human condition—was based on the new faith in science and technology (Meek, 1976, pp. 75, 177, 230).

The Encyclopédie

One of the most impressive manifestos of this creed was the massive cooperative venture of the philosophes, the *Encyclopédie*. Its twenty-eight volumes, under the editorial leadership of Denis Diderot (1713–1784) and d'Alembert, appeared from 1751 to 1772. Its contributors included Voltaire and most of the prominent philosophes. The *Encyclopédie* epitomized the ideas, outlook and aspirations of the Enlightenment. Its subtitle was "An Analytical Dictionary of the Sciences, Arts, and Trades." Eleven of the 28 volumes were devoted to beautiful plates illustrating the apparatus and practices of the various arts, crafts, and sciences. No other general encyclopedia had come close to including such a large number of plates—twenty-five hundred. Most of these describe technology, as do such ample articles as the 44-page piece on glassmaking. Many of its articles provided the most up-to-date resumes of technical developments in various fields. These served, in many cases, to take such knowledge out of a situation of relative secrecy or obscurity, and bring it before a wider audience. In composing articles and plates, Diderot and his collaborators frequently relied on direct, personal observation of trades and industries rather than on book learning or copies of earlier plates. The article on printing, for example, was written by the foreman of the printing shop that produced the *Encyclopédie* (Donato and Maniquis, 1992, pp. 21–22).

In this respect, the *Encylopédie* is a forerunner to the science encyclopedias and "how-to" manuals of our day. However, most of the material in the remaining volumes was pure propaganda from a consistent Enlightenment viewpoint. It was a powerful vehicle for spreading and popularizing the new faith in scientific reason. These ideas, clearly and emphatically presented in all 28 volumes, included: (1) the desire for progress and the optimism that accompanied it; (2) the belief that people are everywhere the same and subject to universal laws of human nature; (3) the conviction that only irrational customs and unjustifiable, restrictive laws accounted for discrepancies among the different nations and societies; and finally (4) the commitment to scientific and technological "useful" knowledge as the remedy for irrational customs and beliefs.

Part of the aim of the *Encyclopédie*, as it was the aim of the Enlightenment in general, was precisely to convince people—including, hopefully, those in positions of power—to abandon traditions which were restrictive, reactionary, or completely false. The *Encyclopédie* penetrated the country in its various editions, sold well in provincial capitals, and was well known to large segments of the reading public (Doyle, 1988, p. 85) The philosophes and their disciples saw themselves as completing the Scientific Revolution by establishing, or attempting to establish, a science of moral and social phenomena. They were convinced that jurisprudence, religion, and morality were no less subject to scientific formulae than were astronomy or physics. Certainly, the idea of a natural law, a natural ethics, and even a natural religion—all based on the method of science—could be found in the ideas of various thinkers of previous centuries. But this search for a science of society now became a dominant, albeit controversial, goal of the Enlightenment (G. Rousseau, 1991).

One part of the new scientific approach was to identify and remove those barriers to human progress which seemed to be associated with irrational traditions and laws. When they came to study existing institutions and customs, the philosophes advocated active reforms in most cases. They demanded freedom of thought and expression, without which what they regarded as truth would be handicapped in its struggle with power and authority. Although few of the philosophes actually preached political revolution in the name of science, their ideas tended in the direction of "rational" reform of existing institutions.

One area where such reformist arguments were needed and beneficial was the law. The followers of the Enlightenment argued for, and partly achieved, reform of many of the more glaring inequities, injustices, and cruelties of traditional legal practices. One of the most significant writers here was the Italian Cesare Beccaria (1738–1794). He was a professor of law at Milan, an avid philosopher, and an original thinker. Beccaria sought to substitute reasonable penalties for crime in replacing the often cruel and barbarous practices which then counted for law in much of Europe. His famous essay on *Crimes and Punishments* (1764) was one of the most influential works of the Enlightenment (Venturi, 1972, pp. 154–164). Penology, the theory and practice of prison management and criminal rehabilitation, essentially began with this treatise. Beccaria's ideas on prison reform caught hold particularly in England, though it required a couple of generations for them to work effective changes in the English criminal law. Their first international fame came, however, in the influence they had on Catherine II's instructions for the reform of Russian law. Beccaria's ideas also exerted considerable influence on Napoleon's reform of the criminal code in France (and its colonies).

A second, equally ambitious, goal of the Enlightenment's program for achieving social progress, after the errors of the past were identified and eliminated, was to construct a new society. The blueprints for the new society were as varied as the individuals presenting them. Yet all these visions of a more perfect social order were rooted in the conviction that science would provide the fundamental laws—if not the specific details—governing humanity's proper actions. It was at this level that the Enlightenment's faith in science would be put to the critical test. Would the same methods that proved so successful in creating the modern physical sciences also prove successful in creating the social sciences? It was philosophes like Turgot, his brilliant protégé the Marquis de Condorcet (1743–1794), and their circle who first used the term social sciences. The term itself is highly significant. For these individuals believed that it would be a *science* of society—based on the scientific method's combination of reason and experiment, and using statistical thinking and quantitative methods whenever possible—which should and would replace the various systems of tradition and authority that had previously governed human history. Recent political and economic developments, including the early impacts of industrialization, were compatible with a mechanistic view of society that favored quantitative social analysis. As society was broken down into its material components of population, resources, industry, and so on, the reduction of human beings to anonymous social atoms became a more common theoretical device. (Johannisson, 1990, p. 361).

Science, Technology and the French Revolution

One of the first sociopolitical situations in which science and technology were applied directly by government was the French Revolution. The causes, events, and consequences of that tremendous upheaval at the close of the eighteenth century are exceedingly complex. They have been the subject of intense historical debate and conflicting interpretation. This period saw immense pressure for change in both science and political ideology. Science was used to sanction not only progressive and Utopian beliefs, but also certain conservative ideologies. Attitudes toward the relation between nature and politics, which had seemed somewhat consistent during the Enlightenment, became more complex and ambivalent. In all cases, however, science was invoked to validate political beliefs and outlooks, whether new or old (Outram, 1990, p. 1019). The head of the Revolutionary tribunal which tried and executed Lavoisier in 1794 is reputed to have declared publicly "The Republic has no need for experts." In point of fact, however, scientists and engineers played a crucial role in several aspects of the Revolution. The mathematician and engineer Lazare Carnot (1753–1823), for example, served as Minister of War. He was spoken of as the "organizer of victory." Although most of the major figures of the Enlightenment were dead by 1789, when the Revolution broke out, their ideas concerning a science of society were utilized in certain Revolutionary programs and reforms. Condorcet, one of the most optimistic and visionary of the philosophes, did attempt to put certain of the Enlightenment's ideals into practical operation.

Particularly in the area of public education and constitutional reform, Condorcet actively promoted the scientific analysis of human nature and social institutions during the early years of the Revolution. He believed that the social sciences had developed to the point where they could begin to be applied effectively to the solution of economic problems and to the art of government. Such applications were possible because recent developments in the mathematics of probability now enabled scientists to construct theoretical laws which described, and ultimately would predict, the behavior of aggregrate groups of people in society. It was a brilliant idea, the essential foundation of modern empirical social science (Gordon, 1991, p. 167). The brutal political events of the period known as the Reign of Terror, however, brought about his untimely death in 1794. Condorcet's Enlightenment vision of a social science which could bring about social and political reform would, nonetheless, inspire the ideologists of Progress during the nineteenth century.

Science also played a crucial practical role in the Revolutionary struggles (Meadows, 1987, pp. 102–103). During the blockading of French ports by other countries, scientists and engineers were co-opted for military and economic activities. For example, since metals for munitions could no longer be imported, techniques were devised for extracting strategic metals—such as copper—from scrapped church bells. A process to manufacture saltpeter [sodium nitrate]—an essential ingredient of gunpowder—instead of importing it from India was developed. Perhaps the most significant effect of revolution was the realization that France needed experts in large numbers. This led in 1794 to the establishment of the *École Polytechnique*, whose students were given advanced courses in mathematics, engineering and chemistry. Most of the next generation of France's best research scientists were graduates of this school, which continues to play a dominant role in French intellectual life in the present day.

The quantifying spirit united with the purposes of the Enlightenment and the Revolution to produce the metric system of weights and measures (Heilbron, 1990, p. 207). It can be argued that one of the most enduring results of the French Revolution was the establishment of the metric system. European scientists had for many years discussed the desirability of a new, rational, and uniform system to replace the many national, and even regional, variants that made scientific communication difficult. During the Revolution, and before its brief suppression in 1793, the French Academy of Sciences standardized weights and measures. It introduced the system based on "meters" [defined in 1790 as one ten-millionth of the distance between the North Pole and the Equator on the meridian passing through Paris] and "grams" [the mass of one cubic centimeter of pure water at 4 degrees centigrade (the temperature of its maximum density)]. The metric system became legally binding in France in 1840. It soon became adopted internationally by the scientific community, though its official adoption by many other nations was delayed until the twentieth century.

When Napoleon became Emperor in 1804, he continued the Revolutionary practice of employing science and scientists. On the Egyptian expeditions in 1798, the chemist C. L. Berthollet (1748–1822) and the mathematicians Jean Baptiste Joseph Fourier (1768–1830) and

Gaspard Monge (1746–1818) accompanied him. Monge had earlier served as Revolutionary Minister of the Navy. The chemist Antoine Francois de Fourcroy (1755–1809), also active during the Revolution, later became Napoleon's Minister of Public Instruction. During the French Revolution and immediately following, science and scientists were deployed on a larger scale than ever before for political, economic and military functions. Many of the complex and controversial aspects of the cultural role of science and scientists of our own day can be traced to their novel and active roles in the late eighteenth century.

The various uses and interpretations of science during the French Revolution warn us against assuming that there was a single, unified approach to the Enlightenment. The science of mankind for Jean-Jacques Rousseau (1712–1778)—author of influential works on political philosophy, education, and morality—for instance, was a very different thing from that of Voltaire or Condorcet (Charlton, 1984, pp. 219–220). Yet all the philosophes were united in their conviction that the benefits resulting from the application of the scientific method would include social reform and progress. They believed that with science as a guide, humanity would at last be able to control desires "rationally" and pursue mutual concerns more justly and humanely. The Enlightenment was predicated on the idea that social progress would automatically issue from an increased satisfaction of material needs (including medical advances) *coupled with* a general liberation of the intellect from superstition and irrationality. The twin fruits of the scientific method would consist in rational mastery over both the physical and social environments. We shall see how ambiguous progress in the name of science and technology has been in actual historical contexts. There is no doubt that the human species has been able to use science and technology to transform both physical and social environments radically since the beginning of the nineteenth century. Whether that transformation has been on the whole a beneficial one or not is a matter of increasing debate in our own day. That we are engaged in such a momentous debate is testimony to the power, if not the complete correctness, of the Enlightenment's vision (Hulme and Jordanova, 1990).

Comte and Positivism

One of the nineteenth century figures most influenced by the Enlightenment's praise of science was the French philosopher Auguste Comte (1798–1857). Comte is famous for his theory of *positivism* (Laudan, 1971, pp. 375–380). This term was first used systematically by the social philosopher Claude Henri Saint-Simon (1760–1825), the founder of French socialism. Comte adopted Saint-Simon's ideas and developed the comprehensive system of positivism. Positivism is a theory of nature which holds science to be the key to all knowledge and action. According to Comte, action depends on science, and science is fundamentally concerned with "prevision" or prediction.

Comte believed that all human thought passes successively through three phases, or stages, in its historical development. The first stage he termed the "theological." People here explain the world around them in anthropomorphic terms. Natural phenomena are conceived of as the products, sometimes whims, of theological agencies or human-like gods. The second stage Comte termed the "metaphysical." Here, deities and supernatural causes are replaced by abstract concepts and imperceptible, but nondivine, forces. The final stage Comte call the "positive" one. Here, humanity repudiates both gods and abstract causal forces. Instead, knowledge restricts itself to expressing precise, *verifiable* correlations between *observable* phenomena.

Comte held that although the theological and metaphysical stages of human culture are based on a "misconception" of natural processes, they were essential historical preparations for the emergence of positive knowledge. Those stages were "natural" for civilizations which lack the appropriate philosophical, mathematical and experimental techniques for investigating nature. Moreover, Comte maintained that it is not only knowledge in general, but every *branch* of knowledge which evolves through the three stages. However, different branches of knowledge evolve at different rates. In his six-volume *Cours de philosophie positive* (1830–1842), Comte arranged—or ranked—the sciences in a hierarchy according to which they have attained (progressed to) the positive state. He maintained that mathematics had—by the start of the nineteenth century—most fully reached the positive stage, followed (in order) by astronomy, physics, chemistry, biology, and, finally, the least positive field, sociology or "social physics."

The system of positivism is patterned (partly) on what Comte perceived the Scientific Revolution to represent in human history (Chant, 1989, pp. 42–43). He believed that the scientific method—the "tool" of positivism—first received significant expression in the physics and astronomy of the seventeenth century. Like Galileo and Newton, Comte considered the proper method to be a sort of middle ground between the overly empirical approach of the Baconians and the excessively deductive approach of the Cartesians. He recognized the creative role of the intellect in formulating theories, but at the same time put rigid empirical checks on the conjectures about nature which the mind produces (McMullin, 1990, p. 832). It is by subjecting theories to the test of experimental verification that they are established as scientific, or positivistic.

Comte's most original and probably most influential idea was the last element in the hierarchy of sciences, social physics—or, as he called it after 1840, sociology. Comte is often regarded as the founder of sociology. In his opinion, previous thought about the nature of society had been speculative and deductive, rather than cautious and empirical. Certain moral, religious, and philosophical perspectives and prejudices had stood in the way of an objective study of society. Comte held that an empirical study of human social institutions would yield the valid laws of social progress. Such a study included the historical development of societal forces and structures, such as customs and family composition and roles; also relevant were the biological and psychological characteristics of the individuals and groups which comprise a society. Using the scientific method, which unites theory with experiment, the Comtean positive sociologist would know the past, understand the present, and—most significant—predict the future course of social development. Both Comte and Saint-Simon promoted the idea of a *technocracy* of neutral experts as the new ruling class of industrial society. Their views have contributed to certain movements for social engineering in the twentieth century, such as scientific management and industrial psychology (Waites, 1989, p. 316) Comte became so obsessed with the concept of a ruling scientific elite, that he devoted the latter part of his career to the scientific "religion of humanity." Replete with positivistic saints, such as Newton, and festivals, it was aptly (if somewhat sarcastically) described by Charles Darwin's friend Thomas Henry Huxley as Catholicism minus Christianity (Porter, 1990, p. 1033)

Comte represents, in many ways, the nineteenth-century culmination of the Enlightenment. His influence can be discerned in the work of such important figures as the French physiologist Claude Bernard (1813–1878), the English political theorist John Stuart Mill (1806–1873), the French philosopher of science Pierre Duhem (1861–1916), and the American mathematician and logician C. S. Peirce (1839–1914). Positivist concepts became part of the "cult of science" which was so notable an aspect of nineteenth-century culture, particularly in Europe and North America

(Marx, 1992, pp. 459–460). This refers not only to the growth of science and technology, however crucial these developments were (see chapter 3). It means also the attempt to answer most, if not all, questions scientifically. In addition to Comte's science of society—sociology—the nineteenth century witnessed a new "religion of science" (Ernest Renan), a "scientific socialism" (Karl Marx and Friedrich Engels), a "science of human nature" (J. S. Mill), an "experimental novel" governed by "scientific principles" (Émile Zola), and so on. Comte was one of the most powerful voices in the nineteenth century calling for the spread of science and the scientific method—as the only truly reliable knowledge—to all fields of human activity. He is a major figure in the modern attempt to construct a valid social science. The controversies which surrounded the cultural role of science and technology in the nineteenth century continue to envelop our attitudes toward science and technology today.   ■

Science and Technology in the Nineteenth Century

3

A. The Professionalization of Science

■ ■ ■

Among the most important developments of the late eighteenth and nineteenth centuries was the gradual transformation of scientific activity. Especially in Europe and the United States, science changed during this period, slowly but decisively, from a (generally) part-time pursuit of individual private researchers to a regular vocational pursuit of full-time research and development by professional scientists (Morrell, 1990, p. 982). Of course, the professional scientist had existed previously in history. We have only to recall the names of Copernicus, Galileo, and Newton to recognize individuals whose lives were devoted to the pursuit of scientific knowledge. But after the Industrial Revolution, the number of individuals who practiced science as a full-time career increased dramatically. This development—professionalization—had profound implications for the magnitude and direction of scientific activity (Frängsmyr, 1990). Significantly, the rate of scientific discovery and technical innovation quickened—a prelude to the rapid growth of science in the twentieth century.

Professionalization also changed the character of the social institutions of science. The British Association for the Advancement of Science (BAAS), for example, was founded in 1831 to provide a forum for bringing together both amateur and professional scientists. Meetings were held annually and in different cities throughout Britain. The BAAS served to disseminate the latest results of the different scientific disciplines. Although not the first scientific society (see sections 2c, 2d), the BAAS is typical of the newer nineteenth-century organizations devoted to spreading scientific knowledge. It also provided a forum for the discussion of issues relating to the interaction of science and society. Such discussions frequently dealt with the ways in which scientific education and research should be organized and funded. By the middle of the nineteenth century, similar bodies existed in France, Hungary, Germany, Italy, Scandinavia and North America. Governments became increasingly involved in science by supporting research and influencing what research was undertaken. In the United States, the Smithsonian Institution was founded in 1846 as a government center for research and publication in science. It had as its first director (or as the position was called then and since, its first secretary) the distinguished physicist Joseph Henry (1797–1878). The establishment and development of the Smithsonian has been crucial to the evolution of federally supported science in America (Seitz, 1992, pp. 45–46). There was also a growing interaction between scientific research and technological/industrial advances (see section 3c).

This transformation of the nature of scientific activity is significant historically for two major reasons (Ben-David, 1991). First, the professionalization of science and the increased links between science and technology radically transformed the international balance of geopolitical power. At the start of the nineteenth century, Great Britain was the undisputed world leader in technology and industry and a giant of scientific achievements. The Crystal Palace Exhibition of 1851 attested to this fact. By the close of that century, however, several European nations (notably, Germany, France and Belgium), the United States and, to a more modest degree, Japan were rivalling Great Britain in scientific accomplishments and equalling or surpassing her technologically. Thus, an understanding of how particular cultural and sociopolitical factors influenced the advance (or retardation) of science and technology can help us understand much of the course of modern history.

The second (and related) reason for studying the professionalization of science during the eighteenth and nineteenth centuries is that this period witnessed a marked growth of governmental involvement in the funding and organization of scientific research and education. With increased government funding came political, social, economic, or military pressures which influenced whether or not national—and often local—governments would, or could, support specific scientific and technological projects. Today, governments are increasingly involved in the funding and utilization of scientific and technological research and education. The more we learn about the reasons for which eighteenth- and nineteenth-century governments became thus involved, the more we may understand our contemporary controversies surrounding science and technology. We come to understand how systematic arguments emerged (and have evolved over time) to justify such public expenditures; we also gain useful insights into the public pressures, or apathy, toward those arguments. The cultural debates about science and technology which first emerged clearly during the nineteenth century foreshadow the intense debates of today (see chapters 6, 7).

The organization, and reorganization, of science during the Industrial Revolution is, therefore, an important area of study. Some of the specific aspects that scholars have analyzed are:

1. Changes in the cost patterns of scientific research and administration;
2. Changes in the social backgrounds and occupational status and expectations of scientists (e.g., the rise of a new technoscientific elite);
3. Trends in the development of scientific education and advanced degree granting;
4. The growth of scientific journals and communications networks (crucial for the development of modern science);
5. Differential rates of growth in different fields (e.g., was biology developing more rapidly than physics?) and in different countries;
6. Patterns in governmental support of science and technology under competing international economic and military pressures;
7. A comparison of changing national attitudes towards science and technology within the broader context of cultural, sociopolitical, and economic developments.

Emergence of the Scientific Research Laboratory

One of the most characteristic features of modern science is the research laboratory. Today, one can find research laboratories in universities, private firms, and in government agencies. Yet, it is difficult to identify an established laboratory before the nineteenth century. There were, certainly, anatomical theaters dating to the early years of the Renaissance, where the lecturer and his assistant demonstrated the gross anatomy of the body to the aspiring physician. But these were not medical laboratories in the modern sense and the student himself rarely put his hand to the cadaver. Similarly, although some scientists had humble "labs" in the kitchens or basements of their homes, none of these was readily available to other scientists or students.

The first major step toward laboratory instruction is generally taken to be the establishment of Justus von Liebig's (1803–1873) chemical laboratory at the University of Giessen (Germany) in the late 1820s. There, students were given formal instruction in their chosen science. Prior to Liebig's innovation, direct laboratory instruction had been available to only the lucky few privileged to work in the small private "labs" of wealthy individuals such as the great Swedish chemist J.J. Berzelius (1779–1848). Liebig's laboratory, in contrast, was open to a wide range of aspiring chemistry students who could work together with advanced researchers each day. There, they learned the techniques and analytical operations which were the basis of the developing science. Liebig's seemingly modest innovation revolutionized the progress of science when it spread throughout Europe and North America during the nineteenth century (Holmes, 1973, p. 330). It ranks as one of the great inventions in the *organization* of science (see section 2c).

Liebig's and similar laboratories enabled the labors of many people to be brought together to a critical point in a way usually impossible before. Consequently, a mass of interlocking problems could be tackled which would have daunted the lone researcher. The workers in such a laboratory need not even be of first–rate ability, so long as they are competent. A "second-rater" will simply make a smaller contribution than a first-rater. As the number of laboratories increased, the numbers of students studying science increased dramatically—with obvious implications for the scientific strength of each nation. Moreover, the emergence of the teaching/research laboratory served to foster intensive research at that early stage in a scientist's career when, as recent data indicate, he/she is at his/her most creative and productive. When, in the 1870s and 1880s, the first industrial research laboratories were organized by synthetic dye manufacturers in Germany, Liebig's innovation was pushed in a new direction—with dramatic possibilities for the future role of science and technology (Basalla, 1988, p. 124).

Reform of Scientific and Technical Education

The brilliant advances of modern science during the seventeenth and eighteenth centuries were accomplished, in most cases, by either individual wealthy scientists or scientists lucky enough to be supported by patrons (Galileo springs naturally to mind). Such research and, more significantly, its encouragement was largely ignored—with few exceptions—by the great universities of Europe. Indeed, well into the nineteenth century the older universities such as Oxford, Cambridge and the Sorbonne were largely resistant to the needs of science. These traditional universities eventually did incorporate more science into their curricula, albeit gradually. However, two other developments provided the new educational institutions necessary for the further development of modern science.

First, new universities independent of the medieval giants were founded which could welcome and encourage science. Notable here are the German universities of Bonn and Berlin and North American universities such as Johns Hopkins (1876) in Maryland and McGill in Canada (1821). Hopkins was a great success. In the years 1878–1889, for instance, while Yale produced 101 doctorates and Harvard 55, Johns Hopkins granted 151 Ph.D.'s (Reingold, 1991, p. 180). Coupled with the research laboratories, these new universities were to revolutionize the progress of science. The second development was the adoption of the revolutionary model of the École Polytechnique, founded in France in 1794.

The École Polytechnique established the pattern of professional training for engineers and marked a major step forward in the growing interaction between technology and the state. It was a public institution under the direct control (at different times) of the Ministry of the Interior and the Ministry of War. Two of its related schools of applied engineering, the École des Mines and the École des Ponts et Chaussées, both came under the control from the 1830s onwards of the Ministry of Commerce and Public Works. On a somewhat different level—because it fed private industry rather than the state services—was the private École Centrale des Arts et Manufactures. It was, however, later taken over by the Ministry of Commerce in 1856, nearly thirty years after its foundation as a private institution. Two other important schools with no ministerial attachments were the École Municipale de Physique et de Chimie Industrielles (founded in 1882) and the École Supérieure d'Électricité (1894). This rich and expanding provision for technical education in France was completed by the *écoles d'arts et métiers* and numerous other lower-level trade schools, most of them under the control of the Ministry of Commerce (Fox and Weisz, 1980, p. 8).

The French pattern of technical education was followed in Europe and, to a lesser degree, in North America during the course of the nineteenth century. In these polytechnical institutes the emphasis was completely scientific and mathematical—the forerunners of our modern engineering schools and technical colleges. One crucial consequence of this sophisticated and organized attempt to tie science and technology directly to the industrial and commercial interests of society was to broaden the supply of technically competent individuals (Buchanan, 1992, pp. 223–225). In addition to the preparation of engineers, the new technical colleges also prepared teachers of mathematics, physics, and chemistry for the civil and military institutions of the state; this multiplied dramatically the sheer number of practicing scientists and engineers. It must be noted, however, that as these technical schools developed in the nineteenth century, their policies tended to exclude women and thereby prevented them from pursuing such careers (Carter and Kirkup, 1990, p.9).

The ultimate result of this reform of scientific/technical education was to ensure the production of great numbers of "second–rate" professionals. The term "second–rate" is not used in any perjorative sense here, but simply to indicate a lower level of training and professional standing. These scientists and engineers actually fuelled the explosive development of nineteenth-century industrial research laboratories and scientifically oriented businesses. One needed no longer to be a Newton or a Galileo to contribute to society's scientific advancement.

In one notable case—Germany—the commitment both to scientific research and professional technical training was to have profound geopolitical consequences. Germany's rise to international power status and industrial preeminence by the close of the nineteenth century owed much to her generous support of science and technology. From the 1840s onwards, Germany attracted increasing numbers of young scientific foreigners. People came from Great Britain, Holland, Scandinavia, Italy, Russia, the United States, Canada and Mexico. They came either because they could not get an equivalent education at home or because it was relatively cheap—or both. In Germany, fees for scientific education were kept deliberately low. By 1900, as one example, there was hardly a British chemist of any standing who did not possess a German Ph.D.—a degree still not obtainable in the home country (Crosland, 1976, p. 189).

Specialization of Science

Although the separate sciences had been pursuing different paths at least since the seventeenth century, the links between different branches of science was still strong throughout the eighteenth century. The demarcation lines between chemistry and medicine, chemistry and geology, mathematics and astronomy, chemistry and experimental physics, for example, were often blurred. Many important scientists made significant contributions in several fields. During the nineteenth century, however, the professionalization of science demanded a more rigorous specialization to ensure advances (Rudwick, 1985). As the methods and theories of each field developed, it became necessary to define the particular nature of each discipline and to train its practitioners differently. Chemists came to occupy a different professional niche from that of biologists, for instance, but each science divided even further. The science of chemistry itself differentiated into organic chemistry, inorganic chemistry, and electrochemistry. Biology witnessed the emergence of specialized fields such as physiology, ecology, paleontology, and evolutionary biology.

As scientists came gradually to occupy more clearly demarcated niches as professionals, they concentrated more intensively on more restricted fields of research (Secord, 1986). Different branches developed more specialized methodologies and procedures. In the process, each branch of science came to establish a greater independence from other intellectual disciplines. This is not to say that the links between science and philosophy, or science and religion, did not remain strong. The debates over evolutionary biology, geology and religion, for example, amply demonstrate such interplay (see section 3b). But the intricate interdependence of science and philosophy which characterized the Medieval period, the Renaissance, and the period of the Scientific Revolution itself, was loosened (Kohn, 1985, pp. 943–946).

The prestige—indeed respectability—of science increased notably during the nineteenth century. Certain disciplines such as history, psychology, sociology, and economics sought to divest themselves of aspects of their philosophical past and acquire the aura of science. An influential school of "scientific historians," especially in Germany, sought to place modern historiography on a scientific basis by establishing canons of objectivity for the study of documents and sources. Although the debate on the precise relationship between the social sciences and the natural sciences continues to our own day, the Enlightenment ideal of a scientific model for all explanation exercised a profound allure for thinkers as diverse as Jeremy Bentham and Karl Marx (Gordon, 1991).

Another aspect of the professionalization of science was the increasingly quantitative approach to theoretical and practical problems. In chemistry, John Dalton (1766–1844) established the basis of the atomic theory and the Italian A. Avogadro (1776–1856) developed the molecular hypotheses which laid the quantitative foundations for modern chemistry. Sadi Carnot (1796–1832) and the Scottish physicist William Thomson (Lord Kelvin) (1824–1907), among others, laid the foundations for the mathematical handling of heat transformations essential for thermodynamics—a science which also was fundamental for steam engineering. Electricity and magnetism, which had attracted great interest primarily as scientific curiosities in the eighteenth century, became established as exact sciences in the next century. The research of the Dane H.C. Oersted (1777–1851), who discovered the magnetic effect of an electric current, and of the English scientists Humphry Davy (1778–1829)—who developed applications of electricity to chemistry and who identified six new metallic elements—and Michael Faraday (1791–1867) led to the establishment of electromagnetic theory. This was to have momentous implications for physics and chemistry. Davy was also an excellent lecturer, who quickly attracted large audiences to the Royal Institution (founded in 1799) in central London. By the time Faraday attended his lectures in 1812, Davy had made the Royal Institution one of the preeminent scientific centers in Great Britain. Faraday's public lectures, starting in the 1820s, set the pattern for the brilliant popularizaton of science which continues to be one of the noteworthy contributions of the Royal Institution to this day (Thomas, 1991, p. 192)

Ironically, as Europe and North America fostered the professionalization of science—and witnessed the social transformation of the scientist's role—their general populace became more divorced from any actual comprehension of science's methods and achievements. Because of specialization, the increasing social impact of science was accompanied by a *decreased* ability on the part of the general public to comprehend the scientific or technical basis of that impact. Although science and technology still impressed, indeed awed, the layman—even highly educated ones—fewer were able to participate directly in its developments. Voltaire and Diderot (see section 2d) had few successors in this respect in the nineteenth century. A failure to achieve one of the Enlightenment's greatest goals, namely, a scientifically literate public, seemed to many an inevitable cost of the professionalization of science during the nineteenth century. The effective popularization of science was a challenging problem which attracted some attention but insufficient action. To some degree, this attitude persists in the twentieth century. In our own times, the problem of educating the general public about science/technology and their societal and environmental consequences is emerging as a crucial area of research and action (see sections 7a, 7b, 7g and 7h).

The full scope of the professionalization of science during the nineteenth century can be encapsulated in a brief look at the BAAS. Recall that the preeminent symbol of British scientific achievement, the Royal Society of London, had been officially chartered in 1662. It was a wholly private creation; royalty gave patronage, but nothing more. The Fellows of the Royal Society enjoyed neither privilege nor pension. They were granted no buildings or funds. Therefore, the Society remained, down to the nineteenth century, impoverished and inadequately housed. It had never possessed laboratories, or other than honorary means of promoting research. Furthermore, for over a century and a half the qualifications for a Fellowship included wealth and influence as well as scientific merit; without such support from the politically powerful, the Society would have collapsed. During the eighteenth century, the Royal Society came to be seen more as a place for the privileged in search of notoriety than as a forum for scientists. By 1830, not a single one of the 63 nobles who held fellowships contributed a significant scientific paper. Criticism of the Royal Society increased and when the BAAS was organized in 1831, it quickly moved to redress the defects for which the Royal Society had been attacked. From its inception, membership in the BAAS was restricted to practicing scientists.

Most significantly, the BAAS did not cater to the geniuses of science. Although these continued to play an active role, the BAAS sought to further the recognition of those individuals referred to as "the cultivators of science"—those of the second and third rank who in their more modest, but equally crucial, way advanced scientific research and application. It became clearer (as it had earlier to Francis Bacon and his associates) that science in an industrial society could no longer depend for its progress solely upon the achievements of an isolated Newton or Descartes. Related to the growth of specialization was the realization that investigators of more limited range and talents were now essential to the advance of scientific knowledge and its applications. In the

United States, it became increasingly possible for people of more modest abilities (and modest financial means) to find employment and a lifetime occupation as scientists. The growth of the scientific enterprise encouraged this development of a large body of trained, competent, mid-level scientists—many of whom, of course, were talented and had quite creditable research records. They were not, however, geniuses or charismatic leaders of science (Reingold, 1991, p. 41).

This is not to imply that the newer professional institutions, like the BAAS, radically transformed the social basis of science. There is much evidence which shows that the BAAS was still controlled by a gentlemanly group of professionals who were now paid to do what they wanted to do anyway as amateurs. The BAAS and other leading British organizations, such as the Geological Society, were still very much collections of powerful, influential and well-connected scientists (Morrell, 1990, pp. 987–988). The crucial point remains, however, that they were now all professional scientists.

In one important respect, the BAAS was socially innovative. From its foundation, the BAAS had to confront the "woman question." At first, females were permitted to attend the social functions but not the scientific meetings of the Association. Finally, after much agitation and demonstration, in 1839 women were admitted to all the sessions (though confined to separate galleries or railed-off areas). Although the first official woman member was not admitted until 1853, from 1840 onward women were active participants in the BAAS. The Zoological Society of London (1827) and the Royal Entomological Society (1833) both admitted women on the same terms as men from the outset. This gender egalitarianism was not characteristic. The Linnean Society of London, the Royal Microscopical Society, the Geological Society, and the Royal Society itself did not admit women until the twentieth century. Moreover, women were barred, except in a few special cases, from the most important centers of nineteenth-century science, the universities. Similarly, the eminent École Polytechnique, founded in Paris in 1794, did not admit women until 1972 (Alic, 1986, pp. 178–181).

With the growth of professionalization and specialization came a shift—gradual at first, but more perceptible by the close of the nineteenth century—in the social origins of scientists and engineers (Desmond, 1989). Science in the seventeenth and eighteenth centuries had depended primarily upon individuals who either possessed independent means or who were fortunate enough to secure some type of patronage. By contrast, the late nineteenth-century scientist was increasingly of middle-class origin. These persons needed to be paid a living wage for doing scientific work. Thus, an expectation of a certain level of remuneration and a recognizable career structure became part of the defining characteristics of a professional scientist. Interestingly, in this restricted sense, neither Charles Darwin nor Alfred Russel Wallace, the codiscoverers of the theory of evolution by natural selection, were professional (though they were brilliant) scientists. Darwin was independently wealthy while Wallace had to struggle throughout his long career to earn a living variously as an author, lecturer, and editor (see next section).

The success of scientists in achieving professional status—with the concomitant sense of corporate identity, level of minimum certified competence, and acceptance of certain social obligations—was a remarkable development in nineteenth-century history. The professionalization of science has implications which society is still assessing. Moreover, this initial professionalization was limited mainly to Europe and North America. Those countries—such as Islamic lands subjected to colonial rule by Western powers during the nineteenth and early twentieth centuries—which did not share in this science-based industrialization were deterred from making similar advances (al-Hassan and Hill, 1986, p. 283). The great global question posed by the accelerating integration of science, technology, and industry was stark: which nation or nations would most effectively support and exploit the new profession and to what ends? That question first became highly significant in the nineteenth century. It is, perhaps, an even more crucial question today (see sections 5b, 5c, 5d, 6a, 6b, 6c, 7a, 7c, 7e). ■   *Question 2*

Question 3

B. Darwin, Wallace and the Origin of Species: Evolutionary Biology and the Science of Humanity

■ ■ ■

Few scientific theories have had an impact equal to that of the theory of evolution by natural selection, discovered simultaneously by Charles Darwin (1809–1882) and Alfred Russel Wallace (1823–1913). Although the contributions of both men were equally crucial to the enunciation and development of that theory, historians and the public generally tend to equate "evolution" with Darwin's book *Origin of Species*, first published in 1859. For this reason, it is convenient to use the *Origin* as a shorthand symbol of the scientific and cultural revolution effected by both Wallace and Darwin (Ruse, 1989). The impact of evolutionary theory during the nineteenth century was far-reaching (Oldroyd and Langham, 1983). The continued development of evolutionary biology, and the contemporary debates spawned by that development, constitute a fundamental part of the history of twentieth-century science.

Background

The publication of the *Origin* engendered tremendous controversies. Darwin's and Wallace's work clarified and presented in a rigorous fashion a view of evolution that already was present in a number of eighteenth and nineteenth century scientific, as well as cultural, hypotheses. Their conception of evolution by natural selection thus represented not merely an isolated scientific hypothesis, but the popular expression of the ideas of a broad intellectual and cultural movement. At its appearance in 1859, all of the *Origin's* religious, philosophical, sociopolitical, as well as scientific implications were understood at once. It was praised or damned for reasons far beyond the narrow scientific arena to which Darwin and Wallace first restricted themselves publicly (Hodge and Kohn, 1985, p. 205).

Preevolutionary theories in biology were dominated by some version of the concept of "special creation." Naturalists of the late seventeenth and eighteenth centuries maintained, or hoped, that their scientific findings would confirm the pervasive belief that nature exhibited a rationally ordained system of divine means and ends. This theory of special creation held that all living organisms—animals and plants—which existed at the present day had been created in precisely their present forms by God. Furthermore, they had been perfectly preadapted to suit their particular environments and geographical locales. It followed, therefore, that there had been *no* change (or only insignificant variations) in any species since the beginning of time. Thus, it was argued, there can have been no evolution, nor any evolutionary connection, between different species. *Homo sapiens*, it was further maintained, was a unique species with no animal (or prehuman) ancestors.

The "argument from design" was the basis of the creationist position, which flourished well into the early nineteenth century. Creationism maintained that the adaptive features of each characteristic structure of animals and plants had been *purposely* created by an Intelligent Designer. It was argued that the order and complexity of the natural world, particularly as exhibited in the (nearly) perfect structure and functioning of organic beings, could not be the product of natural forces alone. Only God, it was asserted, could impose such a system of design on nature. A frequent analogy drawn upon by naturalists was that of the relationship between a watch and a watchmaker. No one, surely, could believe that the pieces of metal that form the works of a watch had assumed their complex shapes "naturally." We know, of course, that there existed a watchmaker who designed and manufactured them. Since nature contained in itself no such innate tendency to build up the complex structures of an animal or plant, it was argued that there must be a Designer for organic beings. Moreover, creationists held that the structure of living beings illustrated the Creator's power, wisdom, and benevolence. The form given to every organ is adapted to the function it performs in the animal or plant's living activities. This demonstrates, for the creationists, that God cares for the welfare of His creatures. Such arguments were called utilitarian, because they assumed that every characteristic of an organism had a useful purpose. Humans, of course, were the supreme example of God's design. The perfect structure of the human hand and eye seemed the most obvious illustration of how our bodies had been created to serve us (Bowler, 1989).

The scientific and popular adherence to the doctrine of special creation during the eighteenth century was symbolized in the person of the great Swedish botanist and taxonomist Carl Linnaeus (1707–1778). His *System of Nature* (1735) assigned to every plant and animal its particular place in one great, hierarchical "chain of being." Linnaeus' taxonomic system—which introduced our modern binary system of biological nomenclature (each species is known by its *generic* plus *specific* name)—assumed that all the characteristics of every species are knowable to humans. This implied that the classification of animals and plants was rationally comprehensible, because the biologist's classifications mirrored the natural system which had been created in all its details by God. Linnaeus and other serious naturalists realized that it was impossible to conceive of the whole of nature as being created explicitly for humanity's use and enjoyment. However, they believed that every species revealed itself, in some way, as the product of God's wisdom and plan.

Linnaeus, himself, gradually developed certain doubts that nature was a divinely ordained scale of unchangeable forms. In later works he suggested that new species might be formed by the interbreeding of different species (hybrid generation) or by the influence of climate and geography. In exceptional circumstances he even believed that some species could become extinct. Still, the prestige of his name was clearly on the side of a static view of nature. Like Newton, Linnaeus was regarded as providing definitive scientific support for a theological viewpoint. He developed a sophisticated version of Aristotle's concept of fixed species, which formed "natural" groups of related forms. Moreover, his theory seemed the ideal guide to the practical problems of eighteenth-century naturalists. They had to fit the vast number of new types of animals and plants being discovered during the commercial and scientific voyages of European travellers and explorers into some meaningful framework. Linnaeus' system seemed to provide the best model for biological classification. It attained worldwide influence not only through his writings, but also through his students. A great many foreign students came to Linnaeus in Uppsala to learn the foundations of systematic natural science. All of them later helped to spread the Linnean doctrine in their own countries (Lindroth, 1973, p. 379)

Forerunners to Wallace and Darwin

During the Enlightenment and early nineteenth century, a number of critics of the creationist view challenged the concept of fixity of species. They maintained that taxonomies predicated upon biological immutability were unscientific. One of the most influential critics was the French naturalist and philosopher Georges-Louis Leclerc, Comte de Buffon (1707–1788). Buffon's work is of exceptional importance because of its diversity, richness, originality, and impact. He was among the first to create an autonomous science, essentially free of any theological influence (Roger, 1970, p. 581). A man of independent fortune, Buffon typified the challenging spirit of the Enlightenment (see section 2d). He held that although creation and extinction of species belonged, ultimately, to God alone, many varieties could be produced by natural causes. His massive and widely read 36 volume *Histoire Naturelle* (1749–88) attributed the wide diversity of nature to the operation of a system of natural laws and forces rather than to the Divine Mind. Buffon argued that the natural world could not be understood by trying to discover some "blueprint" of creation. Rather, one ought to look for uniformities in the way natural objects presented themselves to one's senses.

A second obstacle to the successful study of natural history, according to Buffon, was the belief in *teleology* or final causes. Teleological biologists emphasized that it was the function, or purpose, of things which explained their origin and structure. The complex structure of the human eye, for instance, was explained as the product of divine plan to enable humans to see efficiently. Rejecting this idea categorically, Buffon asserted that the scientist should assume that the various structures of living forms could be explained by natural causes only. Instead of attributing the habits and mechanisms by which birds build their nests, for example, to God's design, the scientist should search for naturalistic explanations. Buffon's theory involved important departures from the prevailing fixist view of nature in the mid-eighteenth century. His concept that the present array of species was the *outcome* of natural forces operating over long periods of time, rather than a static expression of some ideal pattern, was to become a critical part of evolutionary thought. Buffon, himself, never pushed the variability of nature as far as considering it a possible explanation for the *appearance* of new species (Kohn, 1985, pp. 267, 905). He did stress, nonetheless, that the stability of species was owing to humanity's limited time perspective. His ideas suggested that given enough time, species might alter. He also emphasized—unlike many of his contemporaries—that no moral lesson could, or should, be drawn from nature. Nature should not be viewed as a divinely orchestrated stage for God's handiwork. Buffon's concept of nature as the outcome of scientifically explicable forces acting over long periods of time would be incorporated into the early evolutionary ideas of Wallace and Darwin. However, the tendency to draw moral guidelines from Nature continued to be a powerful one among many evolutionary thinkers, including Wallace.

Another and more direct, if controversial, influence on nineteenth century evolutionary thought were the ideas of another French naturalist, Jean Baptiste de Lamarck (1744–1829). He espoused a materialist philosophy similar to that of Enlightenment philosophes such as Diderot and Paul d'Holbach (1723–1789). Lamarck rejected the concept that living matter required any divine intervention for its various manifestations. Even highly complex organisms, capable of sophisticated actions and behaviors, were the product of matter in motion. Mental phenomena, including intelligence, were no exception. For Lamarck, these were the attributes of fundamental "atoms" of matter and needed no divine causation. Rejecting the Cartesian dualism of mind and matter, he adopted a radical materialism which implied that even psychology should be considered a branch of biology (L. J. Jordanova, 1984).

Lamarck believed that particular forms of living beings were the outcome of matter interacting with its (various) environments. He drew the significant conclusion that the stability of any species was directly proportional to the stability of its surrounding conditions. Lamarck's geological studies (he was influenced by Buffon, among others, in this area) had taught him that the earth's surface had undergone constant, albeit gradual, change through time. This geological *uniformitarianism*—which some historians have compared to Lyell's later, and more famous, doctrine—encouraged Lamarck to consider it unlikely that living organisms had remained unaltered during the earth's long history. Since they depended for their very existence on close adaptation to environments which changed, they could hardly retain fixed structures and behaviors. As had Buffon, Lamarck stressed that the *apparent* immutability of species—their stability—arose from a limited human time perspective. He argued that the odd thing was not that species (even genera and orders) had been transformed during the earth's history, but that some forms had changed so little over time.

Thus, the mutability of species, hinted at by Buffon and others, became Lamarck's starting point. Change, not fixity, was the postulate which determined his approach to natural history. He argued persuasively that the adaptation of organism to environment was a dynamic relationship. The environment was not a divinely created arena arranged so as to minister to life. On the contrary, it established the constantly changing conditions to which all living things must adapt if they were to survive. Lamarck's specific evolutionary hypothesis—the famous theory of "use and disuse of parts," or, the inheritance of acquired characteristics—(although it intrigued Darwin) was not so significant a contribution to the development of nineteenth century biology. Far more crucial was his insistence that some form of evolution *had* occurred (Corsi, 1989, pp. 40–46).

From the time of his earliest scientific studies, Lamarck was always more interested in the broad picture of nature and in general interrelations than in details. While he did give scattered examples to support his theories, Lamarck appeared to feel that they were sufficiently obvious not to require extensive proof (Burlingame, 1973, p. 592). His emphasis on the process of organisms to survive amidst changes in the environment offered an alternative strategy to those biologists dissatisfied with creationist explanations. When coupled with Buffon's concept of random variations to produce organisms which might become unfit for their environment—and thus possibly become extinct—Lamarck's transformist ideas encouraged evolutionary speculations. In addition, theories of geological uniformitarianism, such as in the work of Lyell, provided a vastly expanded time-scale for the earth's history. Although Lyell himself initially opposed Lamarck's transformism, he and other geologists emphasized the role of natural, as opposed to divine, causes as the *direct* agents of terrestrial phenomena. Such were the ingredients which lay at hand for the young Wallace and Darwin as they worked towards the scientific revolution with which their names are associated (Desmond and Moore, 1991, pp. 220–225).

Wallace, Darwin and Natural Selection

The joint discovery of the principle of natural selection by Wallace and Darwin is among the most celebrated episodes in the history of science. And although their paths to discovery were similar, there is no doubt that the two naturalists arrived independently at similar conclusions concerning the origin of species (Kottler, 1985, pp. 369–371). It is significant that, for both men, it was the impact of extensive first-hand observations of the flora and fauna of exotic lands coupled with certain speculations of the English political economist Thomas Robert Malthus (1766–1834)—in his *Essay on the Principle of Population* (1798)—which provided the direct clues to the mechanism of evolution (Winch, 1987). In particular, Malthus' ideas on the tendency of rapid human population growth to outstrip increases in available food supply were critical in both Darwin and Wallace's formulation of natural selection (McKinney, 1972, pp. 80–96). Malthus' book unleashed a storm of controversy that is still active in contemporary debates on global population growth (Simpkins, 1974, pp. 67–70).

For Darwin, it was the famous voyage aboard the *Beagle* to South America—in particular, to the Galapagos Islands—during 1831 to 1836, which began the transformation of the youthful natural theologian into a convinced evolutionist. Wallace's travels to South America (1848–1852) and to the Malay Archipelago (1854–1862), while less well-known, were equally decisive. When he left England on 26 April 1848, at age 25, embarking for Para (now Belem, Brazil), Wallace was an amateur naturalist. He wanted to pursue his "favorite subject—the variations, arrangements, distributions, etc., of species." When he returned to England from the Malay Archipelago 14 years later, he was a biologist of established reputation. He had successfully developed his early evolutionary speculations (first suggested in a letter to the entomologist Henry Walter Bates in 1845) into the rigorous theory announced by him and Darwin in 1858 (Fichman, 1981, p. 29).

It is crucial to distinguish at the outset between the general theory of evolution and the specific theory of natural selection. Both Darwin (preeminently, of course, in the *Origin of Species*) and Wallace convincingly demonstrated the *fact* of evolution. Their various writings provide a vast and well-chosen body of evidence showing that animals and plants cannot have been separately created in their present forms, but must have evolved from earlier forms by slow transformation. Their unique innovation, however, was to provide a *mechanism* by which such transformations could, and would, be brought about: natural selection. Natural selection rendered the idea of evolution scientifically intelligible. It therefore exerted a decisive impact on subsequent intellectual and cultural history. Yet while many endorsed the first part of Darwin and Wallace's theory—evolution—the principle of natural selection elicited considerable criticism from the start. Wallace himself later came to question its complete sufficiency, especially in the case of human evolution (Kottler, 1974). In the crucial period of the late 1850s and early 1860s, however, both Darwin and Wallace insisted that both parts of their theory were inseparable.

Biogeography

Many factors stimulated the first evolutionary ideas of the young Darwin and the young Wallace. Biogeographical questions were central to the growing dissatisfaction each felt with regard to creationist explanations of the still puzzling facts of animal and plant distribution. Biogeography is the science which studies the geographical occurrence—or range—of each animal and plant species over the globe (Browne, 1983). Wallace was to devote much of his long scientific career toward establishing biogeography on a secure evolutionary foundation. For Darwin, the Galapagos islands represented isolated ecosystems which served as different natural "laboratories" to compare and contrast species and varieties. The islands of the Malay Archipelago served a similar purpose for Wallace. Thus, travel to exotic lands was absolutely central to the discovery of the principle of natural selection. Three types of observations in South America especially struck Darwin. Although these observations did not provoke his *first* theorization on speciation, they did provide him later with excellent examples of speciation, once natural selection had been identified as the probable cause. Darwin's conversion to the theory of evolution—once thought to have been a typical "eureka" experience stemming from his famous visit to the Galapagos Archipelago—is now generally seen as a slow and largely post-voyage development in his scientific thinking. The *Beagle* voyage, therefore, served primarily as a catalyst in shaking Darwin's adherence to special creationism (Kohn, 1985, p. 146). Once that bond was shattered, he was able to turn to evolutionary hypotheses as alternative explanatory tools (Sulloway, 1982).

First of all, Darwin found that species of Galapagos finches differed slightly from island to island. But the species showed general resemblance to one another and also to other finches on the South American mainland to which the islands were nearest. If, he queried, each species had been specially created, why should there have been such an inordinate amount of "creative activity" here? Should not the identity of conditions and location of the several volcanic islands of the Galapagos have caused these creatures to be identical? For, the theory of special creation held that each species of animal and plant had been created perfectly adapted to its particular environmental niche. Moreover, why—Darwin pondered—did the Galapagos species so closely resemble the finches of the nearest coast of lush, tropical South America, where environmental conditions were so dissimilar. Shouldn't they resemble, instead, those species of birds on the Cape Verdes Islands (off the northwestern coast of Africa) whose harsh volcanic character and mid-oceanic position afforded a climate and ecology so similar to that of the Galapagos?

As Darwin travelled up and down the mainland of South America, he saw that species occupying a particular ecological niche in one region were replaced in neighboring regions—even those with dissimilar environments—by other species that, while different, appeared closely related in structure. Why, for example, do the rabbit-like animals on the savanna of La Plata resemble the peculiar South American rodent which lives near the savannas? Should they not resemble, rather, the savanna-dwelling rabbits of North America or the Old World? Darwin generalized these findings, which were inconsistent with special creation, to conclude that the fauna of the different climate zones of South America are *historically* related to each other. They showed little or no relationship to the fauna of equivalent climate and ecological zones on other continents, precisely because they were not related to them (in any direct evolutionary sense).

Darwin's Fossils

Finally, Darwin found in the pampas of central Argentina fossil remains of large mammals (*Glyptodon*) covered with bony armor like that of the armadillos now living in the same region. (When Darwin returned to London, these spectacular fossils would be the young naturalist's entrée into the world of professional science [Desmond and Moore, 1991, p. 205]). Why were these extinct animals built on the same plan as those now living? According to special creation, fossils represent extinct species from earlier epochs separated in time by universal catastrophes (like the biblical Deluge). Since new, post-catastrophe species were, supposedly, created by God to fit entirely new environmental conditions, there should be no relation between fossil and living forms. Moreover, fossils should display similarities, if any existed, to contemporary fossils found elsewhere on the globe, since all would have been created for the same (earlier) geological epoch. On the hypothesis that species were immutable and had not changed since they were originally created, there was no scientifically consistent creationist answer to any of Darwin's questions (Barrett, 1987).

On the other hand, such observations were wholly consistent with an evolutionary explanation. If species *were* subject to modification through time and to divergence into different lines (new species), then all of Darwin's queries could be resolved simply. The finches of the Galapagos resemble each other and those of South America *because* they are descended from a common ancestor. They differ slightly because each has *adapted* to its own particular mode of life and, in some instances, is restricted to one island only. Further, although the volcanic nature and ecological conditions of the Galapagos and Cape Verdes Islands are so similar, their species are *historically* unrelated to each other. Instead, they are related to those of their (respective) adjacent continents. The Galapagos species share a common ancestor with South American species. The Cape Verdes species share a common African ancestor. They do not, despite their similar environments, share a common ancestor with each other. In like manner, the hares of South American grasslands are related to neighboring rodent species because all share some common (South American) ancestor. Finally, the fossil Glyptodon resembles the armadillo now living because both share a common ancestor (DeBeer, 1963).

The example of the armadillo/Glyptodon relationship is particularly important. If living animals and plants display affinities with extinct species, then there is no reason to believe—as catastrophist biologists asserted—that extinct organisms have no living descendents. They may, in fact, have representatives alive today. This meant that the entire fossil record was available to Darwin and Wallace as paleontological evidence for evolution (Desmond and Moore, 1991, p. 210). To be sure, nineteenth-century paleontology was an undeveloped science. Darwin admitted (in Chapter 10 of the *Origin*) the difficulty posed by the incompleteness of the geological record for the acceptance of evolutionary theory. There was an absence of any graded sequence of fossils illustrating the probable course of evolution of even a single species. It is to Darwin and Wallace's great credit that they were able to formulate the principle of natural selection despite such obstacles.

Descent with Modification

The vast accumulation of data by Darwin and Wallace during their respective travels armed them with a powerful working hypothesis: species have undergone change and have originated one after the other by "descent with modification" from common ancestors. Groups of such descendent species share the same common ancestor. The general theory of evolution, when supplemented with natural selection as the mechanism of species change, was soon recognized as bringing together a broad and diverse range of biological phenomena under the explanatory potential of a single, unified scientific framework (Young, 1993). A relationship was disclosed between the data of hitherto separate fields of study. Such data could be drawn from embryology, comparative behavior, comparative anatomy, mimicry (the fact that certain species so closely resemble another unrelated species as to be mistaken for the latter), animal and plant breeding (domestic variation), and, of course, paleontology. The data from these different fields was boldy—and correctly—reinterpreted by Darwin and Wallace as the consequence of descent with modification, geographical or reproductive isolation, and divergence of species owing to their occupying different ecological niches (Brooks, 1984).

What, then, was the mechanism of natural selection? For Darwin and Wallace, at first almost alone among their contemporaries, evolution was, scientifically, a two-step process: first, the appearance of variations (later called mutations) in nature, and second, the sorting of this variation by natural selection. Darwin and Wallace argued that the existence of *heritable* variations within a species, coupled with the production of more offspring than could possibly survive, constituted the conditions under which "favorable variations" tended to be preserved and "injurious variations" eliminated. Over long periods of time—that is, over many genera-tions—and under the continued selective influence of the environment (the so-called "struggle for existence"), a group of organisms would eventually have accumulated many new favorable variations. They would, then, differ sufficiently from their ancestors to constitute a new taxonomic status: thus, the "origin of species." Both Darwin and Wallace realized that evolution must be a universal phenomenon. If different species of finches could evolve from a common ancestor, then, given enough time, entire genera, families, even classes and orders of plants and animals, could also be formed in a similar process. Ultimately, all living organisms must be related through their common descent from some simple, original form (or forms). Furthermore, since all organisms vary and all reproduce themselves in greater numbers than can survive, there must always be competition (whether direct or indirect) between variants for scarce resources. Thus, the principle of natural selection, too, is universally valid (DeBeer, 1963).

The joint Darwin-Wallace announcement of the theory of evolution by natural selection at the meeting of the Linnean Society of London on 1 July 1858 marks a turning-point in the history of biology. Surprisingly, it seems that the announcement generated little immediate notice or response. It was the publication of the *Origin* the next year (1859) which brought Darwin and Wallace's theory to the attention of the wider scientific community and to the general public. During the 1860s, and continuing to the present day, evolutionary theory and the principle of natural selection generated vigorous controversy. Certainly, there were inadequacies and discrep-ancies in the initial formulation of the theory. Some of Darwin and Wallace's scientific peers were quick to point these out (Hull, 1973).

Criticism of the Darwin-Wallace theory was inevitable, since much of mid-nineteenth century biological knowledge relating to evolution was poor or confusing (Bowler, 1990). Little was known, for instance, of the precise nature of heredity or variation. Although the revolutionary ideas of Gregor Mendel (1822–1884) on genetics were available from 1865, they had little impact until the start of the twentieth century. Thus, the cause and mode of transmission of heritable variations—the fundamental "raw material" for natural selection—remained obscure for several decades after the appearance of the *Origin*. The science of ecology was still in its infancy and a fuller understanding of the nature of environmental adaptation was therefore impossible. The fossil record was still incomplete. It took time for convinced evolutionists, such as the English biologist Thomas Henry Huxley (1825–1895) and the American paleontologist Othniel C. Marsh (1831–1899), to trace plausible evolutionary trees of the ancestry of creatures such as the horse, so as to strengthen the case for evolution. Marsh's classification and description of extinct vertebrates (he described eighty new forms of dinosaurs, both giant and tiny) were major empirical contributions to knowledge of evolution (Shor, 1974, p. 134). Claims for the discovery of fossilized human remains were always fiercely contested. Many scientists, including Darwin's close friend and colleague, the brilliant geologist Sir Charles Lyell (1797–1875), were perturbed on religious grounds about possible human historical coexistence with lower and now extinct creatures. Lyell felt that this would indicate a religiously unacceptable evolutionary prehistory for the human species. However, Lyell's important *Antiquity of Man* (1863) presented to the reader a broad array of evidence which indicated that man had probably evolved from lower animals over long periods of time. Lyell's evidence was drawn from sources such as skeletal remains (e.g., the skull of the Neanderthal Man which had been discovered in Germany in 1857) and the gradual divergence of the European languages from a common ancestral root language. Despite his own ambivalence on the question of human evolution, Lyell's geological and biological writings were ultimately of immense support to Darwin, Wallace and their advocates (Wilson, 1973, p. 574). Finally, the time-scale of earth's history as estimated by many geologists and physicists seemed grossly inadequate for the lengthy time needed for *gradual* evolution to have occurred (Burchfield, 1975). These and other objections, however, have been rendered substantially ineffectual by subsequent scientific investigation. The theory of evolution by natural selection stands as a basis of modern biology (Mayr, 1991).

Human Evolution: Science and Culture

As momentous as the theory of natural selection has been for the history of science, its impact on general culture has been equally profound—if often controversial or misguided. That the *human* implications of evolution are paramount for most people should come as no surprise. Indeed, both Darwin and Wallace were from the outset of their respective careers deeply concerned with the question of human evolution and its bearing on philosophical, religious, and sociopolitical matters (R. Smith, 1972). Surely, Darwin's closing statement in the *Origin*—a lengthy treatise conspicuous by its omission of any significant mention of the species *homo sapiens*—ranks as one of the greater understatements in history. "Light," Darwin suggested, "will be thrown on the origin of man and his history" (Durant, 1985, p. 284).

To understand the full impact of Darwin and Wallace's ideas it is necessary to grasp the temper of the age in which they lived. The world of the mid-nineteenth century witnessed dramatic advances in science. But "science" meant only partly the empirical approach to nature. More immediately, more tangibly, science meant to most people the secondary results of that empirical method: the products of technology. During the long reign of Queen Victoria, science and technology transformed many of the conditions of people's lives. The first railroad was built in England in 1825, when Victoria was a little girl. Before that, the maximum speed of land travel was, for up-to-date Englishmen as it had been for Caesars and Pharaohs, the speed of the horse. But before the Queen and Empress died, at the century's close, almost all of Great Britain's now existing railroads had been built. Science had begun that liberation of humans from animal muscle, that acceleration toward (then) inconceivable velocities, which is characteristic of the twentieth century.

Science was also impressive. It was *doing* things, making things *work*. The practical, empirical British (and European and North American) mind was fascinated. While Victoria occupied the throne, transatlantic steamship service was begun, power-driven machines revolutionized industry, the telegraph and telephone were developed, and the electric lamp and the automobile were invented. Eight years before the *Origin*, in 1851, the Victorians celebrated Progress at the first world's fair in the dazzling Crystal Palace Exhibition held in London's Hyde Park. When Darwin and his family, wealthy even by comfortable Victorian standards, visited the Crystal Palace, they were representative of those who had benefited handsomely from Britain's global industrial supremacy (Desmond and Moore, 1991, pp. 391–397). Science seemed to many (but not all!) to banish doubt. In this cultural milieu, evolutionary theory was new, revolutionary, even heretical—yet it was persuasive.

It was persuasive because science was persuasive. Evolution became a watchword to the late Victorians. By the end of the nineteenth century, hardly a field of thought remained untouched by the "new" concept. Historians had begun looking at the past as a living organism. Legal theorists studied the law as a *developing* social institution. Psychologists and philosophers explored the implications of evolutionary theory for their fields (Richards, 1987). Critics examined the evolution of literary "types" or genres. Anthropologists and sociologists invoked natural selection in their analyses of social forms. Apologists for wealth showed how the poor are (so it seemed to them) the "unfit" and how Progress, under the leadership of the "fit," was inevitable. And novelists "observed" their fictional creatures as they evolved in an "empirical" way (Beer, 1983). Half a century after the publication of the *Origin*, evolution—which in 1800 had been a word used in mostly narrow and technical scientific senses—seemed capable of explaining just about anything. The titles of major books of that period are symptomatic: *The Evolution of Morality* (1878), *The Evolution of Religion* (1894), *The Evolution of Modern Money* (1901), and, finally, *The Evolution of the Soul* (1904).

The application of Darwin and Wallace's ideas to nonbiological realms—whether legitimate or not—was encouraged by the very language of natural selection theory (Young, 1985). Although the controversies surrounding evolution and religion are perhaps the most well-known (Durant, 1985), there was scarcely any subject which remained immune to evolutionary incursion. Darwin and Wallace themselves often probed the cultural implications of evolution. Wallace wrote frequently on subjects as diverse as spiritualism and land nationalization and other sociopolitical issues (C. H. Smith, 1991, pp. 66–201). The vocabulary they employed in first presenting their theories drew heavily on the terminology of the social sciences and political philosophy. Recall that it was Malthus' *Essay*, with its vivid depiction of the most morbid aspects of struggle and conflict in human as well as animal societies—war, cannibalism, infanticide, epidemics, famine—which contributed one spark to both Wallace's and Darwin's earliest thoughts on natural selection. And Malthus was only one of the numerous authors who appeared obsessed with the idea of struggle. Victorian Britain, with its unchecked industrial expansion, seemed to demand the metaphor of struggle in politics, religion, economics as well as science. It was, moreover, Herbert Spencer's phrase "survival of the fittest" that Wallace preferred to his and Darwin's own expression "natural selection." He thought that "survival of the fittest" was less subject to (erroneous) personification than "natural selection" and considered it to be a more direct, rather than metaphorical, expression of the process of evolution.

The impact of evolutionary thought upon late-nineteenth century culture was pervasive, if controversial (Moore, ed., 1989). The scientific contributions of Wallace and Darwin were used, transformed, and sometimes distorted in a bewildering variety of contexts. The interaction between biology and social thought was complex because scientific terminology and concepts were incorporated into existing sociopolitical debates which themselves were complex (Jones, 1980). Many of the political thinkers who dealt with evolution held deeply opposing views, for example, on the question of whether "nature" or "nurture" is the most important factor determining a person's character. The role of "nature" in determining behavior was central to the controversies concerning biology and gender (Russett, 1989).

Those who believe that nature—that is, heredity—is the most basic influence will most likely reject any strong claim that improved conditions and education can have a lasting, beneficial effect on character. If a person inherits "bad" traits, then nothing can help him/her and it is a waste of money even to try. This attitude led to conservative political arguments based on the need to limit the numbers and influence of the lower classes. These latter, presumably, represented the chief reservoir of bad traits. Elimination of the unfit could take place by either natural or artificial selection. Darwinism and Mendelism both could seem—to some—to offer a scientific basis for eugenics because both theories stressed the power of heredity to determine the biological character of an individual (Kevles, 1985).

At the other biological extreme, the Lamarckian emphasis on the inheritance of acquired traits provided a basis for believing that "nurture" could triumph over the limitations imposed by "nature." Followers of Lamarckian ideas maintained that human beings can be improved by exposure to better environmental (including economic and educational) conditions. They further believed that such acquired improvements could be inherited, and thus become fixed in succeeding generations. In fact, under Stalin, Lamarckism enjoyed a major—if somewhat unfortunate—vogue during the 1930s and 1940s in the Soviet Union (Graham, 1992). T.D. Lysenko even succeeded in having (his version of) Larmarckian biology incorporated for that period into official Communist ideology. Lysenko argued that Western or "capitalist" genetics, with its emphasis on the immunity of genes to most external influences, locked biology into patterns of heredity which could change only very slowly over time. Lamarckism, in contrast, provided communism—according to Lysenko—with a science capable of quickly changing genetic characteristics by appropriate environmental manipulation (Lecourt, 1977). The debate as to whether nature or nurture—or, most likely, some interaction between the two—is the dominant force influencing human development continues to the present (Gould, 1981).

Another attitude which seemed to be reinforced by some versions of evolution was the tendency to think of human differences in hierarchical terms. In principle, Darwinian evolution should have undermined the concept of a strictly linear ranking of species. Darwin and Wallace had emphasized the branching nature of evolution, using the metaphor of a broad tree of life. The new species which arose from ancestral species were not higher but rather "later" in the evolutionary framework. It was very easy, however, for many thinkers to equate more recent species (or varieties) with a more highly evolved status.

This hierarchical ranking was most often applied to the human species itself. The question of the scientific status of the races of mankind became a hotly debated subject in the nineteenth century. It seemed only too obvious to some writers that those groups of people which had more primitive levels of technology and industry than other groups were therefore lower in the evolutionary scale. Europeans almost invariably assumed that other races were inferior to themselves. Moreover, the degree of inferiority was best measured by the (lower) level of technological and social development. It was all too simple for some biologists and anthropologists to assume that these so-called lower races corresponded to earlier stages in the evolutionary process by which the highest form of humanity had gradually emerged from prehuman ancestors. Some of the major founders of nineteenth-century anthropology argued, explicitly or implicitly, that the races of mankind could be ranked scientifically along a linear scale from least to most highly evolved (Stocking, 1987). The legacy of such views, which tend to see human racial differences in hierarchical terms, has been an unfortunate one. Most biologists and anthropologists of the late twentieth century would regard any attempt to buttress racism with pseudoscientific arguments as invalid and unscientific. This tendency to rank different races hierarchically had an analogue in certain political theories. Eugenics and (some types of) Social Darwinism were based on a similar ranking of individuals within a single society or nation. Thus some groups within a given society were assumed to be "naturally" more able than others. This was deemed to be a fact, reflected in the natural division of society into higher and lower classes (Adams, 1990). Gender issues also bore the imprint of hierarchical arguments.

For all these reasons, there is perhaps no clearer example of the complex interaction between scientific theory and sociopolitical thought than with evolution. The debates over the scientific status and cultural implications of evolutionary theory were often bitter during the nineteenth century—nowhere more so than in religious matters. Despite Darwin's own reluctance to engage in theological controversy, many of his defenders engaged the established church head-on (Kohn, 1985, pp. 475–476). These debates continue, in some quarters, to be equally bitter in our own time (Strahler, 1987). ■ *Question 3* ↑

C. The Steam Engine: The Interplay of Science and Technology

Question 2 ↓

■ ■ ■

From the perspective of the history of science, technology and society, the year 1769 is of particular significance. In that year, two patents were issued which, in part, symbolize the Industrial Revolution. In January 1769 the Scottish engineer James Watt lodged his patent for the condensing steam engine. In May of the same year, Richard Arkwright patented his water-frame for the mechanical spinning of cotton and wool. These two inventions—along with the inventions of John Kay (flying shuttle, patented 1733, permitting the weaving of fabric much faster than before possible), James Hargreaves (hand-operated spinning jenny, 1764), and Samuel Crompton ("Crompton's mule," 1779, a machine which made it possible to produce any kind of yarn)—revolutionized the textile industries. They thus set a precedent for the modernization of many more enterprises during the nineteenth century (Donnelly, 1991). Arkwright's innovation was largely independent of the scientific knowledge of his time. In contrast, Watt's invention was the product of a sophisticated interplay of scientific and technological knowledge, particularly of the then known laws of heat and of the properties of steam.

James Watt

James Watt (1736–1819) was the grandson of a teacher of mathematics and the son of a merchant in Greenock, Scotland. In 1757, through the influence of friends on the faculty of the University of Glasgow, he gained an appointment as "mathematical instrument maker to the university." Watt thus found the setting that would foster much of his technical and scientific work. He soon was on friendly terms with a select circle of scientists and philosophers at the university. These included the chemist and physicist Joseph Black (1728–1799) and the political economist Adam Smith (1723–1790). Indeed, it is Smith's famous description of the manufacture of pins that stands as one of the earliest depictions of the division of labor and mass production which characterized the Industrial Revolution. Watt's approach to the problems of earlier versions of the steam engine (notably the Newcomen engine) was academic and scientific rather than simply practical. This theoretical approach to a technical question was relatively novel and foreshadowed the growing interplay of science, technology, and industry which marked the nineteenth century and is a central aspect of our own time.

The gradual development of the steam engine constitutes a classic example of the interaction of science and technology. The crucial work of the French physicist Denis Papin (1647–1712), the military engineer Thomas Savery (c. 1650–1713), and Thomas Newcomen (1663–1729) owed much to the earlier scientific investigations of such men as Robert Boyle and Christiaan Huygens. Watt's relationship with Black—discoverer of the principle of latent heat—in his own development of the steam engine has often been referred to. But Watt's own scientific abilities frequently have been inadequately appreciated. He was, early in his career, on friendly terms, not only with Black and Smith, but with other professors at Glasgow and Edinburgh universities (notably John

Robison). Later, he communicated with Joseph Priestley, (Charles Darwin's grandfather) Erasmus Darwin (1731–1802), and most other eminent philosophers in England, and also with many French, German, and other continental scientists. He was not merely a brilliant mechanic, but an engineer and chemist, well-versed in contemporary scientific knowledge and constantly engaged in scientific experiments.

Educated at Greenock Academy and trained as an instrument-maker, Watt early exhibited strong interests in mathematics, mechanics, and chemistry. Before he was fifteen he had read the Dutch physicist W. J. 'sGravesande's (1688–1742) famous *Mathematical Elements of Natural Philosophy*. Later, when appointed instrument-maker to Glasgow University, he started learning German and Italian so that he might read relevant technical treatises in those languages. Before his famous improvements on the steam engine, Watt had read J. T. Desaguliers' (1683–1744) *Course of Experimental Philosophy* and other scientific writings related to this subject. His improvements were the outcome of careful experiments on steam and on models of Savery and Newcomen engines, in which he consulted with Black. Watt was able to produce tables on the thermal efficiency of steam engines, based on mathematical theory as well as practical experiment. He also appears to have rediscovered the principle of latent heat, independently of Black. Watt, like Matthew Boulton, Josiah Wedgwood (1730–1795), James Keir, and other prominent industrialists, was made a Fellow of the Royal Society.

As Watt's career indicates, applied science was helping to bring about the Industrial Revolution. On the other hand, we should not fall into the error of supposing that the latter was simply a product of the Scientific Revolution. There were a host of sociopolitical and economic factors which were necessary if science and industry were to be successfully integrated (Musson and Robinson, 1989). France, for example, was ahead of every other country in scientific achievements during the eighteenth century. Yet the Industrial Revolution did not first manifest itself there. Instead, it was in Great Britain that the earliest clear signs of industrialization appeared. A number of circumstances in Great Britain facilitated the development and spread of modern industry. These included: (1) availability of rich resources of coal and iron; (2) foreign trade was greatly expanding; (3) capital could more easily be mobilized; (4) enterprise was relatively freer from state and local restrictions, and (5) a social and political climate favorable to economic development. In this appropriate set of circumstances, there were greater opportunities initially for applying scientific knowledge to industrial concerns than elsewhere in Europe.

A Closer Union of Science and Technology

Of course, science and technology had interacted at certain times previously in history (see sections 1d, 1e, 1f, 1g). Yet Watt's accomplishment is indicative of the new, closer relationship between science and technology which developed during the Industrial Revolution and which became characteristic during the nineteenth century. For, technology is more than just another name for applied science, or the application of scientific theory to the solution of practical problems, although at times it can be that.

Rather, as we have seen, technology is as old as human society (Kranzberg and Pursell, 1967). It existed long before scientists began gathering the knowledge that could be used in shaping and controlling nature. Stone-tool manufacture, one of the earliest known technologies, flourished for over two million years before the advent of mineralogy or geology. The makers of stone knives and axes were successful because experience had taught them that certain materials and techniques yielded acceptable results, whereas others did not. When a transition was made from stone to metal (the earliest evidence for metal working has been dated c. 6000 B.C.), the early metal workers, in a similar fashion, followed empirically derived recipes that gave them the copper or bronze they sought. Not until the late eighteenth century, however, was it possible to explain simple metallurgical processes in chemical terms. Even now there remain procedures in modern metal production whose exact chemical basis is unknown.

Technology, unaided by science, is capable of creating elaborate structures and devices (Marcorini, 1988). How else can we account for the monumental architecture of antiquity or the cathedrals and mechanical technology (windmills, water-wheels, clocks) of the Middle Ages? How else can we explain the many brilliant achievements of ancient Chinese technology? Furthermore, the arrival of modern science did not put an end to endeavors that were primarily technological. People continued to produce technological triumphs that did not draw upon theoretical knowledge. Many of the machines invented during Great Britain's Industrial Revolution had little to do with the science of the day. The textile industry, at the heart of eighteenth-century economic growth, was not the result of the application of scientific theory. The inventions of Kay, Arkwright, Hargreaves, and Crompton, referred to above, which were crucial to increased textile production, owed more to past craft practices than they did to science (Staudenmaier, 1989).

Yet by the end of the eighteenth century, the degree of interaction between science and technology had altered significantly. Science began to have a more direct and substantial influence on technology. Watt's achievement pointed toward the rapid expansion of science-based technologies. He prefigured the scientist-engineers of the nineteenth century who created the synthetic dye production and electric light and power industries. These science-based industries revolutionized communications, transport, clothing manufacture and many other aspects of general culture. Despite the contrast between Watt's modest achievements as a scientist and his extraordinary originality and inventive power as an engineer, his career displays one of the key developments in the history of science—the entrance by engineers into the world of research. During the eighteenth century the traditional affiliation between engineering and craftsmanship was being revised in favor of a merger of engineering with theoretical and experimental science. In Watt's work in chemistry (he is credited with being one of the first to state that water is not an element), in his close association with chemists and other scientists, in his employment at the University of Glasgow, and in his membership in the foremost British scientific societies, there exists one of the clearest and earliest examples of that new union between science and technology (Dorn, 1976, pp. 197–198).

Watt and the Newcomen Engine

According to many popular accounts, the young Watt is said to have been inspired to invent the steam engine as he watched steam rising from the spout of a tea kettle. As George Basalla points out, however, this fanciful but simplistic legend—one of many which embellish the history of science and technology—is undermined by the fact that working Newcomen engines existed in England at the very moment Watt was contemplating vapors from the boiling tea water: the larger versions were an established power source in half the world. Watt's successful version of a full-sized steam engine (1775), in fact, grew out of his dissatisfaction with a small-scale model of a Newcomen engine he was asked to repair (Robinson and Musson, 1969).

The basic principle of the Newcomen engine is simple. The pressure of steam forces a piston upwards. When the steam condenses, the vacuum created enables atmospheric pressure to drive the piston back down again. Because the engine was devised to pump water from mines, it took the form of a long pivoting beam with a pump rod attached to one end and the piston rod to the other. A large piston (five to six feet in diameter) was fitted into a cylinder that had inlets for steam and the cold water used to condense the steam, and with an outlet for the waste water. After the pressure of the atmosphere had pushed the piston down to its lowest position, and lifted the pump rod to its maximum height, the weight of the pump mechanism caused the pump end of the beam to descend, raising the piston and making it possible to fill the cylinder with steam again so that the cycle could be repeated. Two aspects of this engine deserve special attention: first, the weight of the atmosphere, not the expansive power of steam, did the work; and second, the cylinder was alternately heated and cooled as steam and cold water were injected into it (Basalla, 1988, p. 35).

Watt's Separate Condenser

In the winter of 1763/4, when Watt began his repair and study of a model Newcomen engine, he was troubled by some of its features. In attempting to remedy them, Watt drew upon some recent advances in the science of physics concerning the theory of heat transfer and heat loss. Apart from the limitations resulting from the use of atmospheric pressure, Watt perceived the existence of another problem: that of the considerable heat loss, without any corresponding mechanical effect. Heat was lost during the forming of condensation. And there was a loss of steam when it was introduced into a cooled cylinder. Watt's solutions to these problems were the following: the process should take place in a closed, not an open, cylinder; and condensation should take place outside the cylinder, not within. Between 1765 and 1769, Watt perfected several vital elements:

1. A separate condenser was incorporated. This meant that the cylinder would be kept at a constant heat, instead of heating and cooling it during each cycle;
2. The condenser was kept constantly cool just for the purpose of condensing the steam;
3. The cylinder was insulated to prevent heat loss;
4. Water was ejected by means of a condenser pump;
5. Atmospheric pressure was no longer used. It was replaced by the action of steam, applied first to one side and then the other side of the piston.

(Gille, ed., 1986, vol. 1, pp. 608–609)

Thus, expanding steam pushing against the piston did the work in Watt's engine. The first double-acting steam engine with a separate condenser was built in 1783, but the most fully developed example was installed in 1784 at the Albion mills in London. It dominated steam engine design for the next half-century.

Watt's steam engine was much more expensive and more complex than the simple Newcomen engine. It was, however, as Watt's experiments showed, much more economical in fuel. This last factor made it a salable proposition in those places where power was urgently needed and where economy of fuel was crucial. It is instructive to recall that the first working Newcomen engine had been constructed (in 1712) for a very specific purpose—pumping water from mine pits. Mining was one industry that could not readily accomodate itself to the geographical restrictions of waterpower. Textile factories, for example, could be sited next to good waterpower sources. Coal or tin mines, fixed in location, obviously could not. At best, canals might be dug to carry water to the mine's waterwheel. Alternatively, power generated by a close-by stream could be transmitted by a system of linked rods to operate pumps at the mine. However, neither method was completely satisfactory. Consequently, the Newcomen engine, often burning the fuel mined on the spot, first

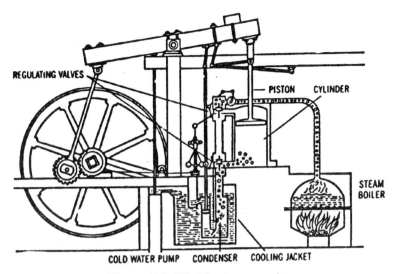

Figure 3.1. Watt's steam engine.

Figure 9.2 from ASIMOV'S NEW GUIDE TO SCIENCE by Isaac Asimov.
Copyright © 1960, 1965, 1972, 1984 by BasicBooks, Inc. Reprinted by permission of
BasicBooks, a division of HarperCollins Publishers Inc.

found a place in mining regions. But the motion generated by a Newcomen engine was a
reciprocating, or back and forth, one. This was well-suited to operating pumps but not factory
machinery. The problem, then, was to obtain *rotary* motion from a steam engine. Watt's inventive
work between 1780–1800 resulted in a direct rotative engine and completed his achievement:
smooth rotary motion could now be obtained from a dependable and efficient steam engine. Steam
could now replace the vertical waterwheel as the dominant supplier of industrial power.

Watt's steam engine was a seminal invention which spawned a wide variety of other
mechanical devices. The hot air and internal combustion engines are two of the most important
power sources that have evolved from the steam engine. As early as 1759, hot air was proposed as
a substitute for steam in an engine. The first working model of such a device was, however, not
built until 1807. Later in the nineteenth century Robert Stirling, in England, and John Ericsson,
in America, designed hot air engines that were sold to the public. By 1900, the hot air engine was
supplanted by yet another variant of the steam engine, the internal combustion engine. This
replaced the *external* combustion of the steam or hot air engine with an *internal* combustion
within the cylinder. The world's first production model of an internal combustion engine was
designed by the Belgian inventor Jean Joseph Etienne Lenoir (1822–1900) in 1860. The Lenoir
engine, fueled by illuminating gas, was closely patterned after Watt's double-acting horizontal
steam engine. Watt's double-acting engine admitted steam on both sides of the piston and hence
did work in both directions. In analogous fashion, Lenoir's engine exploded a gas and air mixture
at both ends of the cylinder, thereby driving the piston forward and backward. Later improvements
of the gas engine included the German manufacturer Nikolaus Otto's (1832–1891) single-acting
four-stroke model of 1876. The Otto engine served as the prototype of the modern automobile
engine (see section 5a). Although the gaseous medium had been changed from steam to hot air to
exploding mixtures of fuel and air, the basic configuration of Watt's original cylinder-and-piston
remained a constant element of design (Basalla, 1988, p. 40).

Boulton and Watt

Watt entered into a partnership with the Birmingham manufacturer Matthew Boulton to create an economically viable version of his costly engine. Their successful collaboration to launch the steam engine on its impressive career symbolizes that unique merging of scientific, techno-logical, social and economic factors which characterized the Industrial Revolution. In twenty-seven years of collaboration (1773–1800), their firm built approximately 500 engines. After 1800, when all of Watt's patents simultaneously entered the public domain, the construction of steam engines expanded greatly. The steam engine, to be sure, was not the sole reason for the accelerated growth of modern industry in Britain and elsewhere during the nineteenth century, but it contributed to a considerable degree (Daumas and Gille, 1979, pp. 56–58.) It must be appreciated, however, that for some European economies, especially those which possessed minimal coal reserves, the cost of steam production may well have outweighed its potential advantages. For these countries, particularly Switzerland and Italy, the exploitation of water power represented a more viable energy source. Just as there existed different national paths to industrialization in the nineteenth century, so also was there a choice between alternative types of motive power. Steam was critical, but not omnipotent (Musson, 1976).

Boulton—whose renowned Soho works at Birmingham specialized (among other things) in precision work in metals—was typical of those late eighteenth-century businessmen, such as Josiah Wedgwood, who combined commercial expertise with scientific interests. It was in the rapidly expanding industrial urban centers that the alliance between science and technology developed most strongly. The Manchester Literary and Philosophical Society and the Lunar Society in Birmingham were the most famous of the several local philosophical societies (including also those such as in Derby and Liverpool) in which there was much coming and going between the laboratory and the workshop. Men like Watt and Wedgwood were equally at home in both settings. They doubtless benefited a good deal from their regular intercourse with such scientists as Erasmus Darwin and Priestley. The interaction between science and industry which characterized these local societies foreshadowed the increasingly closer links between science and technological innovation in the nineteenth and twentieth centuries (Musson and Robinson, 1989).

Of this new breed of scientific businessmen, Boulton was among the most prescient. He was possibly the only man of his time who foresaw clearly the coming age of steam power. Boulton envisioned a world in which steam engines would be used not only for pumping out mines but for a whole range of other purposes as well. Only such a remarkable vision could really have justified the risk that he, a successful manufacturer, took when he entered into partnership with the poor, inexperienced but immensely gifted young laboratory assistant from Glasgow (Cardwell, 1972, pp. 89–90). Boulton's remark to Watt in 1769 was to prove prophetic: "it is not worth my while to manufacture your engine for only three countries; it is well worth my while to make it for the whole world."

The firm of Boulton and Watt, then, was a crucial forerunner of the science-based industrial enterprises which emerged during the nineteenth century. Their conspicuous feature is the *planned* convergence of science and technology to create new industries. These science-based industries, by the successful marketing and sales of a new innovation or product, can have a profound—at times revolutionary—impact on the societies in which they are disseminated. Boulton and Watt, in some important senses, completed the program first enunciated by Francis Bacon in the seventeenth century (see sections 2c, 2d). They established one model for transform-ing science, via technology and industry, into a sociocultural force. In the words of the famous twentieth-century philosopher-scientist Albert North Whitehead (1861–1947), Boulton and Watt contributed to the "greatest invention of the nineteenth century [which] was the invention of the method of inventions." This phrase "the method of inventions" does not refer to any set of "rules" for inventing—which is a complex creative act in any event. Rather, Whitehead's phrase refers to the devising of *institutions* to ensure technological progress: the research laboratory (staffed, in part, by professional scientists), the design/development departments of corporations, and technical sales and services units.

Global Industrial Competition

Historically, the actual establishment of industrial research laboratories in the modern sense occurred not in Great Britain but in Germany. Germany quickly proceeded to surpass Britain as the leading industrial nation by the close of the nineteenth century. And the main agents of this change were the increasingly numerous groups of highly trained professional engineers and scientists who appeared in significant fashion first in Germany and France and, then, the United States. By the mid-1870s, for example, Alexander Graham Bell, Thomas Alva Edison, and other scientist-inventors perfected the electric telegraph and telephone, making U.S. companies (like Western Union) world leaders in new forms of rapid communication (Gorman and Carlson, 1990, pp. 137, 147). What had once, therefore, been the highly distinctive feature of a firm like that of Boulton and Watt became commonplace in all countries with advanced technologies (Hoddesdon, 1981). The critical role played by government and private support of science and technology in the late nineteenth century has become a central feature of the so-called "high-tech race" of the late twentieth century (see sections 7a, 7c).

Indeed, it was owing largely to the activities of the firm of Boulton and Watt and similar enterprises, that British industrial leadership seemed uncontested during the first half of the nineteenth century. The history of the dissemination of the steam engine exemplifies this. Between 1712 and 1850 virtually every improvement in the heat-engine and every name associated with it—with the exception of certain critical figures like Sadi Carnot—was British. A visitor to the 1851 Crystal Palace Exhibition in London could look at any one of the engines on display and know that every principle, every detail, every refinement was due to British "genius." This would not have been chauvinism; it would have been an undeniable, universally conceded fact. But Boulton and Watt steam engines not only conquered Great Britain. They were introduced into other lands by experienced engine-erectors routinely sent out from England to Germany, France, Holland, Spain, Austria, Sweden, Belgium, Switzerland, Hungary, Italy, Denmark, Portugal, Russia, and, significantly, the United States. In some of the more remote and less industrialized countries, these men found the local populace lacking in the mechanical skills that were taken for granted at home. In 1805 a Boulton and Watt employee in Russia warned that the engine he had just completed there was likely to be harmed through Russian incompetence. During the next few decades, however, these inexperienced Europeans came to know a great deal more about machinery. This was, ironically, a direct result of the English mechanics who appeared in their midst to build steam engines during the eighteenth and early nineteenth centuries. But after 1851 the situation changed decisively. Great Britain was no longer the world's undisputed industrial leader.

Great Britain's displacement from the international industrial pinnacle was not limited to steam engines (Mathias and Davis, 1991). One of the best-known examples of loss of leadership by the British was the synthetic dyestuffs industry. Here was a new field, based on the rise of organic chemistry in the early nineteenth century. Some of the finest work in the field had been done by a young Englishman, William Henry Perkin (1838–1907). In 1856, Perkin—then an 18-year old student at the recently founded Royal College of Chemistry in London—synthesized a purple dye from aniline, one of the coal tar chemicals. This was the first dyestuff to be produced commercially from coal tar (Edelstein, 1974, pp. 515–516) Coal tar, which is formed as a by-product during the production of coke and coal gas, had become a serious industrial nuisance by the mid-1800s. Perkin's work thus offered, among other things, a profitable path to "recycling" part of this industrial waste. Perkin quit school and embarked on manufacture of the dye with his father and brother. Since there was no tradition of fine-chemicals manufacture, it was necessary to develop equipment, processes, and know-how. It was also necessary to overcome the dyers' aversion to any dye from a "nonnatural" source. The British public, too, did not accept aniline purple at first. But after the color became popular in Paris as "mauve," or "mauvine," it became very fashionable in England. Perkin's main market was the enormous British textile industry. There was enough capital and willingness to innovate to ensure success in the first two decades of Perkins' new industry. But by 1900 the industry had almost entirely emigrated to Germany.

Even as early as 1875, the synthetic dye industry was becoming concentrated in Germany. During the 1860s, small German firms were still struggling for a part of the dyestuffs market while English firms prospered. The English manufacturers, however, were blinded by their early successes with an essentially empirical approach. They failed to perceive the necessity for theoretical ("basic") scientific research in coal tar chemistry. In Germany, on the other hand, there was a genuine enthusiasm for the chemical industry. German politicians and businessmen realized that England had gained a dominant position in textiles and steel during the early Industrial Revolution. Germany, an ambitious nation under Bismarck, hoped to become preeminent in *new* industries closely allied with science (Kemp, 1985, p. 100).

Although German chemical firms rose from small beginnings, the economic climate was such that they could become veritable giants by the close of the nineteenth century. Adequate financing, vigorous approach to sales, farsighted management, a favorable patent policy, and mutually agreeable competitive arrangements enabled Germany industry to flourish. Scientific education was given sympathetic support by state and industry. Well-trained chemists were available in large numbers (see section 3a). They carried on the research necessary to expand greatly the knowledge of synthetic compounds and foster the synthetic dyes and other chemical industries. By the close of the nineteenth century, the few chemical firms left in Britain were small and unimportant compared with such German giants as the Bayer Company—which introduced "aspirin" onto the rapidly growing pharmaceuticals mass-market. Germany had revolutionized the relationship between science and technology by employing research scientists to advance industrial goals (Meyer-Thurow, 1982, pp. 364, 373). France also, to a lesser degree, recognized the crucial significance of uniting commercial activity with scientific research. It pioneered in certain aspects of the emerging electrochemical industry, notably aluminum production (Shinn, 1980).

A similar development occurred in the new electrical industry. Britain had been an early leader in this field also. By the mid-nineteenth century, however, a great deal of the most significant innovation in the electrical industry was coming from abroad. Electrical technology depended on knowledge of mathematics and physics, subjects in which Germany's new educational institutes excelled. German firms such as Siemens Halske and A.E.G., as well as the General Electric Company of New York, soon became dominant (Von Weiher, 1980). In areas such as cable manufacture, the electrification of railways, street cars and tramways, and electric lighting, Britain was outpaced. After 1890, the demand for electric power literally "took off" for both industrial and domestic purposes in Germany. Electric motors were widely adopted, and greatly enhanced the efficiency of factory production. By 1907, 48 per cent of engineering firms in Berlin, for example, used electric power. First in Germany, but then throughout Europe and North America, electric power was becoming a permanent replacement for steam power as a motive force in industry (Goodman and Honeyman, 1988, p. 197) In the newest industry of all—motor car construction—the lead had clearly been taken by France, Germany and the United States (see section 5a). By the start of the twentieth century, then, Britain had been overtaken in the science-based technologies by Germany with her superb university and technical college system. At the same time, Britain was outpaced in empirical technology by America.

Mass Production and Mass Consumption

The industrial contrast between Great Britain and the United States is as important as the contrast between Britain and Germany, for science-based technologies were only one aspect of the "new" industrial revolution. Equally crucial was the modernization of work and daily life. Particularly in the US, mass production and the rise of modern consumerism constituted a "consumer revolution." Social classes which had previously not had money to spare, or could not afford expensive products, were now able to buy the new cheap goods of mass production. It is hard for those living in advanced industrial societies to imagine a world without the common gadgets and larger domestic appliances of modern life: electric and electronic devices, clocks, watches, photographic equipment, bicycles and cars. Yet all of these essential elements of the modern consumer's arsenal made their first widespread appearance at the close of the nineteenth century and the start of the twentieth century. In common with the other products of industrialization, they are all items of mass production. The American-led system of efficient and large-scale manufacturing, coupled with equally innovative techniques of marketing and advertising, ensured that the consumer revolution would triumph first in North America and Europe, and then globally (Goodman and Honeyman, 1988, pp. 143–154). A major feature of modernization in societies in the nineteenth and twentieth centuries has been just this mass consumption by millions of ordinary people of goods and services not strictly required for subsistence.

At first, it was primarily the middle and upper classes which had the purchasing power and interest to indulge in the newly available domestic appliances, sporting goods, bicycles, sewing machines and, even, mass-produced upright pianos that began to roll off the assembly lines of Europe and North America. After the 1880s, however, even working-class families, benefiting from increasing real incomes could afford the growing diversity of (relatively) cheap consumer goods—bicycles, ready-to-wear clothing, daily newspapers and comics, radios and motorbikes, and standardized entertainment such as that provided by the earliest cinemas (Chant, ed., 1989, pp. 20, 221). All these consumers were the intended targets of the emerging mass-market industries of the late nineteenth- and early twentieth centuries. Consumer goods manufacturers recognized that mass production and mass distribution were "necessary" steps toward survival in a competitive market. With a burgeoning productive capacity, industry now required an equivalent increase in potential consumers of its goods. In the words of one promoter, "Scientific production promised to make the conventional notion of the self-reliant producer/consumer anachronistic." The modern mass producer could not depend upon a traditional elite market to respond to his productive capacity. Class, regional, even national prejudices for particular types of goods had to be obliterated or melded into a mass-market ideology. It became imperative to endow the numerous workers of industrial society with both the financial power and a pyschic desire to consume. In essence, the future of industrial economies lay in their ability to manufacture customers as well as products (Ewen, 1976, pp. 24–25, 53).

Great Britain, to be sure, was hardly exempt from the consumer revolution of the end of the nineteenth century. There, the number and membership of co-operative societies jumped dramatically and their percentage of total retail sales doubled in the late century. "Marks and Spencer's Penny Bazaar" became a well-known slogan in the north of England. The partners set up their headquarters in Manchester in 1897 and were on the threshold of yet greater commercial achievements. Department stores like Marshall and Snelgrove, Barkers, and Harrods were becoming an essential aspect of middle-class life in Great Britain. Specialized multiple grocers like Liptons, shoe shops like Freeman Hardy and Willis, chemists like Boots (with 150 shops by 1900), newspaper and book stores like W.H. Smith, and scores of others transformed the retail scene. Their products ranged from cocoa and chocolates made by Frys, Cadburys and Rowntrees, to Cherry Blossom Boot Polish and Beecham's Pills. The advertiser also came into his own at this time, making good use of the expanding newspaper and magazine industry (Smith, 1979, pp. 145–147). The rapid growth of advertising in the period after 1860, both reflected the growth in domestic consumption of various products *and* acted as a stimulus to further consumption (Curran, 1977, p. 217). Brand names—Bovril, Colman's Mustard or Pears' Soap—were implanted in the public mind by skillful jingles and pictures.

It was, however, the Americans who pioneered the systematic organization of mass production and mass consumption—being pushed in this direction partly by labor shortages. Americans were also at the forefront of what is called "scientific management" or "Taylorism," after the American engineer Frederick W. Taylor's (1856–1915) system of technological efficiency. His experiments on speeding up factory production implied that human labor could be treated in the same way as inputs and material energy (Nelson, 1980, pp. 36–37). Taylor's methods—which derived from the use of the stop-watch for time studies—aimed at extracting optimal performance from workers. Even the home was rendered a more efficient workplace. By around 1870, writers began to describe in great detail an efficient home's organization and operation. In their 1869 effort, *The American Woman's Home* (1869), Catharine Beecher and her sister Harriet Beecher Stowe scrutinized the kitchen, enumerated its constituents, and explained their proper alignment in terms of the requirement of kitchen work. Food preparation, cleanup, and storage—flour bins, sinks, dishes, strainers—all were analyzed in an effort to reduce kitchen form and activity to a series of specific rules, plans, and procedures. The establishment of domestic science or home-economics courses, usually at land-grant colleges, completed the rationalization of the household. The Scientific Revolution had reached the very hearth and oven of domesticity—as manifested proudly in such general-circulation magazines as *Good Housekeeping* (1885), *American Kitchen Magazine* (1894), and *Sanitary Home* (1899) (Marcus and Segal, 1989, pp. 220–221).

In one important sense, it was inevitable that Great Britain would lose the preeminent position in science and technology that she had gained by simply being the first nation to modernize effectively in that field at the start of the nineteenth century. As science and technology penetrated industry and science-based industry gradually spread to other countries, so too would British monopoly diminish. But we may still ask *why* Britain fell so dramatically from her leading place by the start of the twentieth century?

The reasons suggested by historians—which sound uncomfortably similar to the criticisms being made in many economically hard-hit countries today—include a low native inclination to continue to innovate in science and technology. Rather, Britain relied increasingly upon foreign technical skills and accomplishments and was, quite literally, invaded by foreign, in particular German, scientific and technological talent. The Manchester firm of Beyer, Peacock and Company, founded in 1854 and one of the most progressive and important locomotive manufacturers in England, is a telling example. Carl Friedrich Beyer himself was a young German who had been taught at one of that country's excellent *"technische hochschule."* He had then come over to Britain to complete the practical side of his training as an engineer. Beyer stayed on to become a wealthy and respected citizen of Manchester. Equally significant was the fact that of his firm's eight original draughtsmen, no fewer than three were Germans, or had German names. Many other British manufacturing companies were direct subsidiaries of foreign enterprises.

Britain failed to maintain and build up the indigenous scientific and technological "superstructure" that was necessary to ensure industrial prosperity. Although we have mentioned how Britain did achieve some modest success in modernizing her scientific and technological educational system and in the professionalization of her scientific associations (such as the BAAS), she was no match for Germany. Through the course of the nineteenth century, Germany achieved unparalleled success in establishing a powerful university and technical college system. Germany also had more science-oriented universities and they were—again in contrast to Britain—generously supported by the state. The organization and administration of scientific research was there carried to perfection (Fox and Weisz, 1980, pp. 313-323. The German educational system provided a complete range of scientific and technological personnel. They ranged from research scientists with advanced doctorates, to senior engineers and all the way down to the commercial clerks and travelling salesmen of science-based industry.

In short, Germany seemed to grasp more profoundly than Great Britain the crucial importance in the new world order of science and technology. Her brilliant social organization of research and development when coupled to direct economic and military application was to startle the world at the start of the twentieth century. There had been essentially only a single truly industrialized nation—Great Britain—at the opening of the nineteenth century. By its close, Germany, several other European nations, the United States and, to a lesser but significant degree, Japan had joined the ranks. This spread of the culture of science and technology was to have a critical impact on those nations in the twentieth century which embraced it—or failed to do so. Successive international exhibitions after London's 1851 triumph had elaborated and refined Prince Albert's vision of peaceful contests of industry. But the idea that science and engineering promoted international harmony by creating better communication among the peoples of the world was, by the close of the nineteenth century, being transformed into a compelling advertisement for the superiority of European and North American technology and those whose powerful interests it served. Technological change had become linked explicitly to the advance of Western civilization (Sinclair, 1989, p. 81). ■ *Question 2*

D. Technology and Work: Rise of the Industrial Working Classes

Question 3

■ ■ ■

The triumph of steam power was central to the Industrial Revolution. But this revolution was not limited to major innovations in science or technology. The societal consequences of the Industrial Revolution were equally momentous. This familiar term hints, perhaps, at a sharper, more universal break with the past than historical evidence would suggest. Yet it is hallowed and useful for describing the transformation of European society, particularly in Great Britain, obvious by the close of the eighteenth century. There can be no doubt that Western Europe, and to a lesser degree, North America, had embarked upon an industrial expansion that was to continue practically unabated during the nineteenth century. And the cultural consequences of that technical victory of coal, iron, and steam power were wide-ranging and continue, worldwide, in our own day. The concept of the Industrial Revolution is, ultimately, a useful metaphor for an historically complex phenomenon not otherwise easily described (D.C. Coleman, 1992, p. 42).

Scarcely any aspect of economic life remained untouched by industrialization. Steam power, as the main agent in revolutionizing technological and economic forces, symbolized to many the mighty instrument by which nature would be mastered and harnessed, at last, to the service of mankind. But the age of industrial capitalism was marked by many other great technical advances. In the second half of the eighteenth century, as previously noted, the textile inventions of Hargreaves (the "spinning Jenny"), Arkwright (the "water-frame"), and Crompton ("Crompton's mule," a spinning machine which was essentially a synthesis of Hargreave's and Arkwright's machines), stand out. Coupled with improvements in the production of iron and steel (introduced by the Darbys and others), these and other inventions laid the foundations of a historically unprecedented industrial expansion. Metals, particularly iron and steel, replaced wood in the construction of harbors, bridges, machinery, and railway tracks. Coal was substituted for wood for heating houses, offices and factories. By the time of the Great Exhibition of 1851 in London, Great Britain had been turned into the workshop of the world. The windmill and the water wheel gave way to the steam engine. The steam engine was largely responsible for the establishment of factories, since this form of power could not be used in the domestic workshop. When steam power was applied to transport, the new railways and steamships revolutionized commerce. It was now possible to send heavy bulky commodities such as coal, iron, wool, and grain from one end of the world to another.

Standards of Living

Both contemporaries and historians of this first industrial revolution were then, and continue to be, divided as to the social cost—in both human and environmental terms—exacted by such progress. It was clear to most observers that a new social order was being born. Western culture was transformed under the influence of industrial progress. New political pressures, new social institutions, new modes of thought, belief, and action, and, above all, new conditions of life were the inevitable outcomes of the triumph of science and technology (Harrison, 1985, pp. 211–212).

Two social groupings, or classes, came into a new prominence during the nineteenth century. These were the *bourgeoisie* and the *industrial proletariat*. Both groups, despite their different fortunes, shared certain fundamental characteristics. Each was the agent, as well as the product, of the increasing penetration of science and technology into the fabric of modern society. Karl Marx and Friedrich Engels considered the new urban proletariat as much a creation of the industrial revolution as the factory system itself. For these two eminent theorists of industrialization, both the bourgeoisie and the industrial proletariat carried, though in distinct fashion, the imprint of the materialist philosophy and the "counting-house ethics" of the new age. Marx provided one of the most incisive contemporary analyses of the Industrial Revolution, an original and remarkable amalgam of economic theory, history, sociology, and propaganda (Berlin, 1963, p. 236).

Whether in the office or in the factory, the new worker was bound by a code of modern business. All hands were dedicated, willingly or not, to the task of increasing the output of machines to the very limit so as to multiply the wealth generated thereby. The enterprising "captains of industry," as the owners of the new businesses were flatteringly called by their admirers, symbolized the presumed virtues of the new social order. David Colville (1860–1916), the driving force behind what was to become the dominant firm in the Scottish steel industry by the century's end, possessed a magnetic personality, incredible energy, and a "daemonic drive" which built up the company. He was "*the* master: everyone from the board to the office-boy knew it" (Payne, 1979, pp. 117, 131). These captains of industry (1) exacted hard work in the regularized discipline of the factory, (2) allowed neither themselves nor their mill-hands leisure, (3) preached the evils of "extravagance" and (4) praised (if they themselves did not always practice) the virtues of self-denial and self-discipline. In short, many of the most eloquent spokesmen for the Industrial Revolution seemed driven by a desire for material wealth and power (Kemp, 1985, p. 174). The obligation for all members of the new society to do "something useful" became a norm of society.

While many prospered during the heady early years of the Industrial Revolution—including the new professional scientists and engineers—one great question remained: did all share in the undoubted productivity of industrial society? Although beyond the scope of our study, the sociopolitical consequences of industrialization constitute an essential part of nineteenth- and twentieth century history. The interests of the proletariat and the bourgeoisie—wages, capital accumulation, unions, extended suffrage, labor and urban legislation—would replace landed and rural interests as the dominant focus of politics in Western Europe and North America by the close of the century. The so-called "standard of living controversy" arose as to whether general living conditions ameliorated or deteriorated during the early decades of the nineteenth century (Mathias and Davis, 1990, pp. 39–42).

Clearly, certain of the material conditions of life may have improved during the course of the nineteenth century. But those improvements were neither shared equally among the different classes of society nor even among the working class itself. Did factory and domestic workers, country dwellers and town dwellers, regularly employed or seasonal workers, or, even male and female laborers share equally in the greater productivity of industrial society? The debate is still active among historians today. As put simply by George Rude, did the standard of living fall, as claimed by the "pessimists"; or did it rise, as claimed by the "optimists?" (Rude, 1972).

In the first phase of the debate (roughly from the 1830s to 1840s), opposing sides were fairly evenly drawn. On the optimists' side there were Andrew Ure, author of the *Philosophy of Manufactures* (1835) and G.R. Porter, a classical economist whose *The Progress of the Nation* appeared in 1847. Among the pessimists were the English economists Thomas Malthus and David Ricardo (1772–1823), the English essayist and historian Thomas Carlyle (1795–1881), and the German socialist leader—and collaborator of Karl Marx—Frederick Engels (1820–1895). In his influential defense of the factory system, Ure wrote enthusiastically of the factory children as "lively elves" at play. Clearly, Ure's focus on the economic virtues of machinery in bringing about new achievements in production and productivity obscured the full dimension of the human costs of industrialization (Ure, 1835). Similarly, Porter, in comparing the living standards of the 1840s with those at the beginning of the century, thought it "hardly possible to doubt that here, in England at least, the elements of social improvement have been successfully at work, and that they have been and are producing an increasing amount of comfort to the bulk of the people." On the other side, Carlyle denounced the new factory system as "but a dingy prison-house, of rebellious unthrift. . . [indignant] against themselves and against all men." Engels, fresh from his study of the "Blue Books" (reports) of the early factory inspectors, wrote—in *The Condition of the Working Class in England* (1845)—that, before the industrial revolution, "the workers enjoyed a comfortable and peaceful existence . . . their standard of life was much better than that of the factory worker today."

From the outset, then, it is clear that the controversy concerning the social impact of industrialization was colored by political opinions. The main protagonists were as much concerned with the vices or virtues of early capitalist society as they were with the actual living conditions of the working classes. There is consensus, however, among both pessimists and optimists that living conditions generally began to deteriorate from about 1790 to the 1820s or 1830s, and that things probably began to improve slightly after 1840. What is important to recognize is that living conditions can not be translated into simple quantitative terms, such as wages or articles of consumption (as crucial as these may be). Instead, they depend as much on qualitative factors such as dwellings, health and diet, family life, leisure, work-discipline, intensity of labor, and education. When regional and national differences are added, it becomes clearer still that the standard of living controversy can not be resolved in any direct or unambiguous fashion. In our own day, controversy continues as to whether industrialization necessarily brings improved living standards to so-called developing, or underdeveloped, societies or regions (see section 7e). One critical fact, however, is clear: out of the trials of the Industrial Revolution a "working class" came into being. Though they may frequently have been the unfortunate victims of a process of change they could neither escape nor control, the industrial workers of the nineteenth century struggled and resisted and adapted to suit their needs as and when they could. From these experiences they emerged as a politically distinct working class (Harrison, 1985, pp. 241–42).

Urbanization

There were definite transformations in living and working conditions effected by industrialization. One of the most obvious was the growth of industrial towns and cities, a development fundamental to the alteration of the daily life of working people.

Several factors contributed to this growth. In all European countries, certain industrial towns and cities grew larger as more people moved to them looking for work in the new factories. Capital cities also grew in response to the developing needs of the Court or state administration or as part of the general movement into the towns from the countryside. Much of the urban growth of the nineteenth century occurred in well-established industrial cities whose history stretched back to the Middle Ages (de Vries, 1984). In some cities, such as Marseilles, Hamburg, Barcelona, and even London, increased commercial activity drew more people into the industrial hubs.

After the 1830s, a new stimulant to urban growth was provided by the railways. New towns grew up, like Crewe and Swindon in England, whose main purpose was to build and repair the new railways or act as junctions between one railway network and another. In Crewe, the railway company built the principal schools, established a Mechanics' Institute, and built four churches and over 800 houses for the municipality (Bagwell, 1988, pp. 118–119). The general influence of railways—one of the most obvious and striking symbols of industrialization—on urban growth was noted, with striking prescience, by Robert Vaughan. He wrote in *The Age of Great Cities* (1843):

The new and speedy communication, which will soon be completed between all great cities in every nation of Europe, will necessarily tend to swell the larger towns into still greater magnitude and to diminish the weight of many smaller places, as well as the rural population generally, in social affairs. Everywhere we trace this disposition to converge upon great points.

Two of the largest cities, London and Paris, displayed this pattern of rapid growth. London grew from about 860,000 in 1800 to more than 2¼ million in 1850. Paris grew from a little under 550,000 in 1800 to over 1¼ million in 1850. In addition to these giants, there were by 1850 some forty towns with populations of 100,000 or more (of which ten were in Britain and five in France), where there had been only twenty a half century earlier. Of these, the largest were Constantinople (over 750,000) and St. Petersburg (over 500,000), followed by Berlin, Vienna, Naples, Liverpool and Manchester (over 400,000), Moscow and Glasgow (over 300,000), and Amsterdam and Dublin, each with over 200,000 (Chandler, 1987). But once more, within this general pattern for towns to become cities and cities—particularly capital cities—to grow larger and more quickly, the situation of Britain was quite unique. In most other European states, cities and large towns were scattered islands dotted almost haphazardly over the map. In contrast, by the 1830s England alone showed concentrated regional areas of urban development (the forerunners of today's conurbations), as in the industrial triangle formed by Birmingham, Liverpool and Hull. Engels, writing in 1845, noted that the population of the great woolen region of the West Riding had nearly doubled in thirty years, while the population of Birmingham and Sheffield had almost trebled between 1800 and 1844. He also noted the peculiar quality of London, "where a man may wander for hours together without reaching the beginning of the end, without meeting the slightest hint which could lead to the inference that there is open country within reach." After 1850, a new urban corridor developed which stretched from the Ruhr region in Germany to Northern Italy, based on rapid industrial growth (Hohenberg and Lees, 1985).

Contemporary Impressions

This increasing urbanization—like the growth of industry itself—made a deep impression on contemporaries and stimulated conflicting reactions. Some were filled with awe and admiration (as Engels was, in part, by what he saw in London), or at least disposed to view the new developments with quiet detachment or philosophical calm. Robert Vaughan, for example, observed that "it avails nothing to complain of this tendency as novel, inconsiderate, hazardous; the pressure towards such an issue is irresistible, nor do we see the slightest prospect of its ceasing to be so." Francis Place (famous as a radical tailor and trade unionist), looking back in old age from the 1820s and 1830s, thought London infinitely preferable to the city he had known in his youth a half-century before. Other observers, however, took a gloomier view and were often appalled by what they saw. A notable case was the English journalist and social reformer William Cobbett (1763–1835), to whom London was a "Great Wen," or human ant-heap, draining old England of its wealth and vitality. Engels remarked that "the very turmoil of the streets has something repulsive, something against which human nature rebels." One of the obvious features of his *Condition of the Working Class* is the vigorous, highly charged, and often denunciatory prose with which he describes the environment of urban workers in London and Manchester (D.C. Coleman, 1992, pp. 4–7). The growth of Paris, which took place within a far more restricted area than London's and was accompanied by far more misery and turbulence, provoked even louder protests.

French writers described Paris as a den of iniquity, of crime, prostitution, poverty, wretchedness and despair. Joseph Proudhon wrote of it as a "vast sewer, a place of masters and lackeys, thieves and prostitutes." Where Charles Dickens (1812–1870) wrote almost light-heartedly of many of the antics of urban dwellers of the streets and alleys of London, the picture of Paris painted by the novelists Eugène Sue (1804–1857) in *Les Mystères de Paris* and Victor Hugo (1802–1885) in *Les Misérables* strikes a far more sinister and despairing note. Echoes of this critical view of the modern city continue up to our own day. Its most notable exponent over the past decades has been Lewis Mumford. He writes of the modern industrial city as an "urban hive," "Necropolis" or (sarcastically) a "paleotechnic paradise." Of the nineteenth-century city Mumford declares:

> Between 1820 and 1900 the destruction and disorder within great cities is like that of a battlefield, proportionate to the very extent of their equipment and the strength of the forces employed. . . . Industrialism, the main creative force of the nineteenth century, produced the most degraded urban environment the world had yet seen; for even the quarters of the ruling classes were befouled and overcrowded (Mumford, 1961, p. 447).

To be sure, not all industrialization took place in, or gave rise to, towns. Sometimes—as in parts of Russia—it was cheaper for entrepreneurs to establish businesses in the countryside because labor and transport costs were lower. But urbanization did become the normal concomitant of industrialization. Recent estimates suggest that 7.6 percent of Europe's population lived in cities with more than 10,000 inhabitants in 1600. The figure increased slowly to 1800, when the urban percentage had reached 10 percent. Nineteenth-century urban growth was dramatic by comparison. By 1890, 29 percent of Europe's population lived in cities (Goodman and Honeyman, 1988, p. 30). This increasing trend toward larger cities and towns seemed an inevitable consequence of the increased division of labor between town and country. Additionally, throughout the nineteenth century, the population of Europe was able to grow—and to become even more urbanized, with ever diminishing numbers engaged in agricultural production—because of those technical innovations which augmented farming productivity. Increasing imports of American and British colonial foodstuffs enhanced this process of decline in the proportion of the total population engaged in agriculture (Mathias & Davis, 1990, p. 152). The sharper contrast between urban and rural life, in turn, permitted the economies of scale, transport, marketing, and the maximum exploitation of human capital which industrialization required.

Work, Skill, and Gender Division of Labor

Movement from the countryside to the industrial town meant, for the male rural laborer, a loss of the seasonality of the agricultural year and an adjustment to "industrial time." Hours of work in factories, mines, building trades or transport were not necessarily longer. They were, however, more sharply demarcated from "nonwork," and more regular throughout the year. Many rural migrants brought skills which were easily adapted to mining, urban transport (still largely horse-drawn at the start of the twentieth century), and the construction industry. In factory industries, however, they were confined to unskilled tasks and machine-minding. Several barriers confronted the rural migrant in his search for skilled, highly-paid work. The growing strength of labor unionism in Britain (and, to a lesser extent, in America) and the general force of trade practices limited the number of new apprentices. The already-skilled workers enjoyed an authority over the labor process and reserved certain work and jobs for themselves. For the Slavic immigrant in

Pittsburgh's steel mills, for example, or the Pole in Germany's Ruhr districts, ethnicity made the barrier even more formidable. The workshop-based, artisanal trades—such as coopering [making casks or barrels], working precious metals, cabinet making—still accounted for a huge volume of industrial production. The exclusion of rural migrants from these trades was forceful: skills were guarded and passed from father to son. Migrants were to be found, however, in the "sweatshops" of the tailoring and other trades, and in the "putting out"—or "cottage"—trades (such as paper-flower making). In New York's Lower East Side, for example, whole families of Italian tenement dwellers were engaged in domestic work of this kind.

The girl, or single woman, rural migrant, could also take up factory work as part of her move to the town. Evidence from Britain suggests that females often preferred this kind of work. It provided companionship as well as relatively high wages compared with other female employment and a sense of independence. But a more likely source of women's employment was domestic service. Throughout early twentieth-century Europe, women in manufacturing were concentrated in only three industries: clothing, textiles, and, to a lesser extent, food processing. Of these, only textiles involved working in large factories. Britain, with the world's largest textile industry, provides a perspective on the relatively smaller number of females working in factories. The British textile industry employed some 650,000 women textile workers in 1911. But 1.4 million females worked as indoor domestic servants (Chant, 1989, pp. 11–12).

Yet although women—and children—did enter the industrial workforce in significant numbers during the nineteenth century, a strong gender division of work in both the public and private spheres was established. At first, it seemed that the factory system, with its specialized and often monotonous tasks, might argue against any rationale for sexual division of labor (at least among the industrialized workforce). Yet there is clear evidence that both men and women had firm ideas as to what constituted men's and women's work, and male and female wages for a job. Central to this notion of appropriate female work, was the concept of the "family wage" which emerged in the nineteenth century. Acceptance of this concept—which held that the husband was the significant breadwinner—was fundamental in determining the mix of activities undertaken by women. It ensured that women took primary domestic responsibility for husband and family. Their paid work, therefore, was regarded both by society and by themselves as of secondary importance:

> The family wage became an ideal, held sacred by both working- and middle-class men and women for a variety of reasons. . . . In the late nineteenth century social investigators promoted the idea of the family wage because they felt that a firm division of labor between husband and wife was the best way of securing social stability and the moral integrity of the nation. . . . [It was believed] that the services of a workingman's wife were more valuable economically when they were employed at home than in the labor market [because] men were stimulated to labor only in the hope of maintaining themselves and their families. . . By the 1890s, the wives of skilled men did not usually work, for the ability to keep a wife had become a measure of working class male respectability. . . Where women worked for wages in factories . . . some accommodation had to be reached between the family's need for extra income and male and female ideas about women's proper place. . . [Among] Leicester hosiery workers, men supported women's work so long as they confined themselves to the traditional female task of seaming. Thus sexual divisions in the workplace were underpinned by more general ideas of women's place (Kleinberg, 1992, pp. 154–160).

Gender Stereotypes

Working-class attitudes reflecting male dominance in the family unit had their counterpart in the political reality of the workplace. Protective legislation aimed at women (as well as children) effectively prevented the widespread employment of married women in what were deemed degrading or dangerous occupations (Boxer, 1986). Out of a combination of a perceived risk to women's health and morals and their fears that female workers would undercut male wages, men workers sought to exclude women from skilled occupations. For example, male mule spinners in Lancashire successfully resisted attempts to introduce women (who were quite able to handle the smaller spinning mules), largely because the men provided their employers with an efficient system of labor organization and control in the workplace. Similarly, in the printing trade, male workers were able to turn their political skills against women workers and exclude them from the typographical associations. Because men dominated the guilds and other apprenticeship bodies up to the end of the century, the majority of those in a position to acquire a skill, and become skilled labor, were men. Women might help their husbands in their skilled trade, but only in unusual cases were they permitted to become skilled in their own right (Goodman and Honeyman, 1988, pp. 107–108). Moreover, employers were often loath to employ male and female labor in the same process. As late as the 1930s, a large-scale employer of women refused to consider "the indiscriminate mixing of men and women together" (Kleinberg, 1992, pp. 162–163).

The middle class shared certain of these gender stereotypes. Middle-class married women were also, at least according to the Victorian ideal, effectively excluded from the labor force and confined to the domestic arena. The new professional men of the industrial world—the manufacturers, the wholesalers, the retailers, the bankers, the scientists and engineers—were keenly sensitive of their position as sole family breadwinners. They and their wives and children were entirely dependent on an income from fees or salaries. Life and sickness insurance were devised, in part, to meet their special needs. For professionals, the family was a consuming, not a productive, unit; wives were accountable for expenditure, not income. The culture of this milieu idealized marriage as a partnership of companions. Many books were written to advise the wife on the management of the home, servants and children. With the emergence of the modern urban working-class family, this ideal was propagated outward among the poor by voluntary "social workers": settlement workers, district nurses, and others. These upper- and middle-class women and men were concerned that the working-class wife should learn to manage the home with frugality and foresight.

From the late nineteenth century to about 1950, the dominant social ideal of the modern housewife as a woman entirely dependent on a husband's income—as a consumer exclusively concerned with running a home and raising children—exerted a powerful influence on politics. Social security legislation, employment practices, and the retailing industry itself were all created or modified in response to the altered life experience of millions of women in the emerging industrial societies. Ironically, it was the prolonged economic growth of advanced industrial societies in the Western developed world in the 1950s and 1960s which created new opportunities for married women on the labor market. In these mature industrial societies, legislative and moral changes are evolving which make divorce easier and more frequent. A new feminist consciousness is emerging which challenges the notions of femininity elaborated in the nineteenth and early twentieth centuries (Chant, 1989, p. 14).

Finally, different segments of the urban population were affected differently by industrialization. Moreover, certain regions of the industrializing countries—and, indeed, entire areas of Europe and North America, not to mention the rest of the globe—remained relatively untouched. The great mass of European peasantry continued throughout the nineteenth century to lead lives little different from those of their ancestors. But this persistence of traditional agricultural modes, particularly east of the Elbe River in Germany, only sharpened the contrast between industrial Western Europe (especially England, France, Belgium, Holland, and parts of Germany) and Eastern Europe (especially Poland, Hungary, Russia and the Balkans). The relative cultural homogeneity of the eighteenth century was fast being destroyed in the nineteenth century. The contrasts—political, social, economic—between West and East grew rapidly more pronounced. Industrial Western Europe, with its large-scale technological enterprises, rise of the modern proletariat, political advance of the middle classes, and intellectual and cultural modernism, was drawing far ahead of the largely agrarian East. There, small-scale industries, poor transportation and communications, and dominant clergy and nobility, all slowed social change. The divergent developmental patterns between industrializing and nonindustrializing regions of Europe and North America shaped the course of their nineteenth-century histories (Kemp, 1985). This pattern of divergent response to scientific and technological advances would, when played out on a global stage, have enormous repercussions for the twentieth century. ■

Question 3

Scientific Revolutions of the Twentieth Century

4

A. Einstein and the Theory of Relativity

■ ■ ■

Perhaps no name in science, other than that of Isaac Newton, inspires such awe among scientists as well as in the general public as that of Albert Einstein (1879–1955). Although Einstein is the author of a number of brilliantly original ideas, it is his discovery of the *theory of relativity* which stands as one of the most dramatic episodes in the history of ideas. Einstein's own life was as dramatic as his scientific statements. His involvement in the steps leading to the creation of the Manhattan Project and the development of the first atomic bombs [see section 6a] *and* his later crusades for world peace and disarmament put him squarely at the center of the complex and controversial world of nuclear politics during the late 1940s and 1950s. The theory of relativity itself was an historic turning-point in twentieth-century physics and philosophy. For many of us, what Einstein actually discovered seems almost incomprehensible. Actually, the basic ideas of relativity *can* be easily understood. Einstein himself popularized his ideas in a series of nontechnical books intended for the layperson (Einstein, 1983; Einstein and Infeld, 1971). And insofar as Einstein is said to have revolutionized physical science—indeed, our very notions of space and time—it is essential that we get at least a feeling for the central features of relativity theory (Pais, 1982).

Special Relativity

This section will concentrate on the basic elements of Einstein's Special Theory of Relativity. It is called special because it restricts itself to a consideration of "uniform motion" only. Uniform motion is motion at a constant velocity in a straight line. Einstein developed this restricted version first, before he developed the fuller or General Theory of Relativity. The "general theory," which includes the special theory as one part, covers *all* motion—accelerated and curved, as well as straight line. The Theory of Special Relativity became so well-known partly because some of its predicted effects seemed to contradict common sense. A few examples of such seemingly contradictory predictions include: (1) The slowing down of moving clocks; (2) The contraction of moving lengths; (3) The increase of an object's mass with motion; and (4) The speed of light as being the fastest speed possible for any object in motion *or* for any transfer of information. It is because these predictions have been repeatedly verified experimentally by physicists and astronomers that we have had to readjust—sometimes with great difficulty—our basic notions of space and time. In this sense, Einstein forced a reexamination of many of the concepts of science which were held to be sacred since the time of Newton and the Scientific Revolution [see section 2c] (Hoffmann, 1983, p. 127).

Einstein's theory of relativity is more than just a branch of modern physics. Like quantum mechanics [see next section], it constitutes a radically new way of looking at the physical sciences. It thus implies a new way of looking at our universe, and our place within it. The difficulty most people feel in understanding relativity is not primarily because it is abstract, highly mathematical, or complex. Many scientific theories of the past and of the present century are much more so. Rather, relativity theory forces us to reexamine—and sometimes abandon—some of our most deeply rooted notions of space, time, matter, and motion. Since these basic concepts are those by which we tend to organize both our day-to-day affairs, as well as our fundamental ideas about the universe, it is readily understandable why any challenge to such basic concepts was bound to excite disbelief, opposition, rejection, even ridicule, when first proposed. When a friend asked him why the Chinese had not invented or discovered what we term modern science, in spite of their obviously great creative talents, Einstein's response, probably in part jocular, was to the effect that it is a miracle that modern science evolved anywhere (Seitz, 1992, p. 17) [see sections 1f, 1g].

We have seen how the reexamination of a traditional point of view, in science as in other domains, is often difficult—sometimes painfully so. From a historical perspective, it has taken considerable time and effort (both individual and social) to adjust to the new universe of Copernicus, Galileo, Darwin, Wallace and other now-celebrated names in the history of science and technology. It is a major task of the late twentieth century to adjust to Einstein's universe. Einstein himself commented that it had required a severe intellectual and cultural struggle to arrive at Newton's concepts of space and time. It will require no less strenuous efforts to overcome, or modify, those concepts—a process which is by no means entirely completed. To understand what Einstein's scientific revolution entails, it is necessary to indicate briefly what the central features of Newtonian physics are. We can then appreciate why certain of those ideas were beginning to break down—or become paradoxical—for certain physicists and experimental philosophers at the close of the nineteenth century—the period in which Einstein was growing up.

The Young Einstein

Einstein was born in the small town of Ulm in south Germany on 14 March 1879. His family soon moved to the Bavarian capital, Munich, where he grew up. His father and his uncle ran a small electrochemical plant; so Einstein, from his early days, became acquainted with the young—and exciting—electrical industry (see section 5a). Einstein seemed a slow child and as a schoolboy was thought by his teachers to have little academic ability. When Einstein's father asked what career his son should follow, the headmaster replied: "It doesn't matter; he will never make a success of anything." His family was Jewish in an overwhelmingly Catholic city. The young Einstein may not have shined at school. But he did early become fascinated by science. These interests were first awakened at home—by the mysterious compass his father gave him when he was about four; by the algebra he learned from his uncle; and by the popular scientific books of his day. A geometry text which he devoured at the age of twelve made a particularly strong impression. He especially liked its clarity and certainty. Einstein was able to cultivate his growing interest in mathematics at school. This was one of the few good results he later saw in his schooling, for he had quickly come to dislike the regimentation which characterized European education at that time (Holton, 1988, p. 390).

In 1894, his father's business failed, and the whole family moved to Italy, settling in Milan. The 15-year-old Albert was left behind to continue his studies in Germany. Within six months he quit the school system he so disliked and joined his family in Italy. He finished his formal studies at the Swiss Federal Polytechnic School in Zurich, where he studied physics and mathematics. Einstein's student years were marked again by his independent approach. He spent as much time reading the original works of the great nineteenth-century physicists as in attending lectures. Nonetheless, he graduated satisfactorily in 1900. He was unable to obtain a regular teaching position immediately, and did occasional tutoring and substitute teaching for two years. In 1902, he was appointed an examiner in the Swiss Patent Office at Berne. The seven years Einstein spent at this job, with only evenings and Sundays free for his own scientific work, were years in which he laid the foundations for many areas of twentieth-century physics. They were, in some respects, the happiest years of his life. Interestingly enough, Einstein liked the fact that his job was quite separate from his passionate pursuit of theoretical physics. He felt he could work on his remarkable theories freely and independently, and he often recommended such an arrangement to others later on in his career (Klein, 1971, p. 312).

Einstein started his scientific work at the very beginning of the twentieth century (Gearhart, 1990). It was a time of startling experimental discoveries. The problems and issues which first attracted his attention involved the very foundations of physical science. His approach to those problems led him, ultimately, to produce boldly original ideas which were to revolutionize physics. The closing decades of the nineteenth century were the period when long-held basic theories and principles in physics came under close scrutiny and were directly challenged by a number of investigators. The mechanical philosophy (see sections 2a, 2c), particularly as it was presented in Newtonian (or "classical") physics, had enjoyed great success since the close of the seventeenth century, that is, for nearly 200 years. The goal of explaining all natural phenomena by means of the basic concepts of matter and motion had been achieved in many of the fields of science (notably, physics, astronomy and optics). The impact of the model of Newtonian science had also been felt—although not always with the clearest or best of results—in the new domain of the social sciences (see section 2d).

Certain areas of science, however, seemed to resist a successful interpretation in terms of the mechanical philosophy. The mechanical theory of heat, despite its power, had serious failures and unresolved paradoxes. Most significant, physicists had not been able to provide a really satisfactory Newtonian mechanical foundation for one of the most exciting developments in nineteenth-century science: electromagnetism. To a young man who looked to science for nothing less than an insight into (in Einstein's own words) the "great eternal riddle" of the universe, these basic questions were the most challenging and also the most fascinating. Einstein was impressed with both the successes and the failures of classical (mechanical) physics. But he was already obsessed with the goal that would occupy him the rest of his life. He sought to find a unified foundation for all of physical science (Balazs, 1971, pp. 330–331). Einstein was at the center of the (then) radically new developments in quantum theory and statistical mechanics (see next section). He published three papers in 1905, any one of which would alone have assured his place as a genius in the history of science.

One dealt with so-called "Brownian motion." Here, Einstein explained the curious observations of the Scottish botanist Robert Brown, which had defied scientific explanation since early in the nineteenth century. Brown had noted the fact that pollen grains suspended in water appeared to be in constant but irregular motion when viewed through a microscope. Einstein convincingly showed that it was actually the molecules of water—which were always in motion because of the heat of the solution—which were continually striking the pollen grains from all sides. He concluded that sometimes more water molecules would strike one side of a pollen grain than the other, so causing it to move (Einstein and Infeld, 1971, pp. 58–62). Einstein's explanation of molecular effects was generally accepted as clear evidence that matter is formed from tiny particles too small to be seen by the human eye. His second paper dealt with the "photoelectric effect" and the "quanta" of light (see next section). Einstein's paper was a vital contribution to the development of twentieth-century quantum mechanics. This paper was specifically cited in the Nobel Prize for Physics awarded to Einstein in 1921. It was the third paper of 1905, however, which was to bring, first controversy, and then the greatest fame to Einstein—his first paper on relativity.

Newtonian Space and Time

By the nineteenth century, Newtonian physics had been developed into a seemingly infallible framework for both theoretical and experimental science. Two of the fundamental concepts of Newtonian physics were that of "absolute space" and "absolute time." Newton himself had recognized that most measurements made in science and in daily life are in some sense relative. We measure the motion of a ship, for example, relative to the "stationary" earth (i.e., the shoreline). But we know that the earth is not actually stationary. It is itself in motion—both spinning on its axis, and moving round the sun. We could allow for these motions, by assuming the sun to be a stationary reference point for the earth's motion. But we know that the sun itself is also moving through space, and would have to choose another "stationary" reference point and so on. Newton was troubled by this apparent inability of science to find some absolute frame of reference for the motion of objects. He wondered if there might not be, in theory at least, some way to establish such an absolute frame of reference (Spielberg and Anderson, 1985, pp. 170–171).

Newton postulated that, indeed, there did exist such a stationary frame of reference, which he called *absolute space*. He defined absolute space as the "container" in which the material universe resides. This implies that: (1) When we are at rest relative to space, we are in a state of *absolute* rest. Our state of rest, therefore, is an objective fact, true for all observers, anywhere in the universe; and (2) When we are in motion *relative* to space, we are in a state of *absolute* motion. This motion is, therefore, an objective fact, true for all observers, anywhere in the universe. These implications lead to the idea that a state of rest and a state of motion are *fundamentally* different. Newton believed, therefore, that this difference between absolute rest and motion could always be somehow detected by experiment. As we will see, this belief was to cause serious problems for nineteenth-century physicists.

Newton also needed to measure changes of position of a moving object in *standard* units of time. To do this, he conceived of time as an absolute, unchanging sequence against which the duration of all events—including the motion of an object from one point in space to another—could be measured. Newton accordingly defined *absolute time* as the universal sequence by which we mark the passage of events. This implies that: (1) A moment of "now" exists for the entire universe. Because time is an absolute standard of measurement, there is one, universal sequence of events for everyone, everywhere; and (2) When any given event "A" occurs, everyone, everywhere in the universe, can know about it immediately, "now." These implications lead to the idea that there must be an infinitely fast signal speed bringing the information of the event everywhere in the universe now. This notion was also to cause severe problems for nineteenth-century physicists.

Criticisms of Newtonian Physics

The concepts of absolute space and absolute time were already under critical discussion by physicists when Einstein came upon the scene. It contradicted a basic fact of everyday experience, a fact quite well understood by Newton himself. This fact was referred to as the "principle of relativity." Thus, when Einstein began his examination of the basic assumptions of Newtonian science, he already knew certain well-established, experimental facts. These were: (1) Being at rest and being in uniform motion *feel* the same; (2) Sometimes, it is practically impossible to tell by any experiments if you are, in fact, at rest or in uniform motion. Imagine yourself seated in a slowly moving train at some constant speed. Furthermore, the shades are drawn and the water in your glass is perfectly still. You can not, by any experiment performed *inside* the compartment, distinguish whether you (and the train) are at rest or in uniform motion. Of course, by opening the shades you can tell you are moving if the landscape outside is "passing by". The important point, however, is that no experiment within a closed "laboratory" can readily distinguish between rest and uniform motion; and, finally, (3) It was a fundamental axiom of physical science that the laws of mechanics are the same for all observers moving *relative* to one another at some *uniform* speed.

The problem for scientists was that the concept of absolute space implies that there *is* a fundamental difference between the state of rest and the state of motion (Einstein, 1983, p. 135). Experience and the principle of relativity tell us, on the contrary, that uniform motion is relative, not absolute, with respect to any single, privileged reference point in the universe. This paradox troubled physicists, but they lived with it because Newton's physics and mechanics were so useful in many fields of science, including astronomy. A breakthrough was made in the late nineteenth century when the Scottish physicist James Clerk Maxwell (1831–1879) showed that light is a form of electromagnetic radiation. Light was, according to this theory, an electromagnetic "wave" that propagates through space (Olby, 1990, pp. 342–356). Like all other electromagnetic waves, including infrared and ultraviolet radiation, radio waves, gamma rays, and X-rays, light traveled through space at (approximately) 300,000 km/sec or 186,000 miles/sec.

The Electromagnetic Ether

It seemed evident to nineteenth-century physicists that, to have waves, there must be something present that could transmit them. How, for example, could you have waves at sea if you removed the sea? Maxwell had demonstrated that light consisted of electromagnetic waves. Since we can see the stars, the light from those distant objects must be able to traverse the "apparently" empty space between the stars and the earth. (The same argument would hold for any object we see, no matter how close). Physicists postulated the existence of an "ether" as the medium through which light propagates. The ether seemed to provide the answer to a number of crucial problems.

Physicists thought of the ether as a kind of very rarified—almost weightless and frictionless—jelly through which light and all other objects move through space. Most significant, the ether was stationary in the universe. Light would then have a medium through which it was propagated. But, almost as important to late-nineteenth century physics, the ether could represent absolute space. Instead of measuring the movement of one object relative to another object, scientists could measure the motion of all objects relative to the ether. These would represent absolute measurements. Many physicists believed they had found Newton's absolute space. Moreover, they believed they could experimentally detect the presence of this ether, and thereby conclusively demonstrate the existence of absolute space.

Optical experiments seemed the likeliest candidate for demonstrating the existence of the ether. In a celebrated experiment, two American scientists—Albert Michelson (1852–1931) and Edward Morley (1838–1923)—set out to detect the ether's presence. Their experiment of 1887 used an "interferometer" devised by Michelson, set on a rotating table. Interference patterns occur when two (or more) coherent beams of light interact. Bright bands are seen when the amplitudes of the two waves (of the light beams) reinforce each other. Dark bands are seen where the waves cancel each other out. (Similar principles apply in the new techniques of holography.) In the Michelson-Morley experiment, a light beam was split into two parts moving at right angles to each other and then brought together again. Because of the earth's motion in space, the "drag" of the ether (on the light propagating through it in different directions) was expected to produce a displacement of the interference fringes in the recombined beam. Each light beam, traveling in different directions through the ether, would be slowed down by the ether drag to a different amount. (This would have been similar to the result obtained by measuring the relative speeds of two boats being rowed [at the same speed] in different directions through a moving current.) Their experiment failed in that it did not demonstrate the expected interference patterns. It thus failed to detect any motion relative to the stationary ether. In effect, the so-called "zero result" of the Michelson-Morley experiment failed to detect the presence of an ether (Einstein and Infeld, 1971, pp. 171–176).

No matter how refined their techniques or ingenuity, other physicists, much to their surprise and disappointment, also failed to detect the presence of an ether by any experiment. Einstein was probably not *directly* influenced by the Michelson-Morley experiment, although its results definitely accord with the predictions of special relativity (Holton, 1988, pp. 279–281, 347). At the time, Einstein was pursuing the theoretical question of relative motion in a way far different from that of his contemporaries. His thoughts too were focused on the important and puzzling properties of light and its motion. But unlike most of his contemporaries, Einstein considered what would be the consequences of applying the principle of relativity to the phenomena of light itself.

While he was at the Swiss Patent office, Einstein found the answer to the questions he was asking about the nature of light. This was published in one of the famous papers of 1905. He reasoned that the speed of light, and of electromagnetic waves in general, is unique not simply because it is so fast. The speed of light—symbolized by "c"—is unique because it is the *maximum* permissible speed in this universe. (There are some theoretical exceptions to this. But such faster-than-light particles do not affect the validity of Einstein's reasoning.) No ordinary body can ever reach that speed, so no observer can ever "keep up" with a light wave (Coleman, 1969, pp. 61–62). To arrive at this conclusion Einstein had to assume that however observers moved relative to the source of light, they *always* found the light moving relative to themselves at the same constant speed.

This assumption was at variance not only with Newtonian physics, but also with common sense and experience. If a stone, for instance, is thrown from a passing vehicle, its speed—as seen by an observer standing nearby—will depend *both* on the speed with which it is thrown *and* the speed of the vehicle. Why should this not be true of a ray of light? Einstein's assertion led to even stranger results. Speed is measured in terms of distance covered per unit time, for example kilometers per second or miles per hour. Hence, if the concept of speed has unexpected properties, so also does the concept of distance. One consequence Einstein deduced from this argument was that the apparent dimensions of an object depend on the relative motion of the observer. Equally, time is relative. So the length of time something takes to happen can also depend on the relative motion of the observer.

Special Postulates of Relativity

Needless to say, Einstein's extraordinary ideas—which ran counter to both the established science of his day and to common sense—were hard to accept at first (Miller, 1981). Einstein's **theory of special relativity** begins with two postulates from which everything else is deduced. As a young boy, he had loved studying a geometry book in which basic simple assumptions were made, called postulates. An amazing variety of consequences could be derived from the few postulates of Euclid's geometry, for example. The two postulates which stand as the base of relativity theory are:

Postulate 1: The Principle of Relativity

The laws of physics are invariant in all inertial reference frames. This means that the formulas expressing the various laws of physics must be calculated in the same way for all observers moving uniformly relative to one another.

Postulate 2: The Constancy of the Velocity of Light

The speed of light in empty space is independent of the velocity of its source. This means that no matter how fast a light source is moving, the emitted light always moves at the same speed.

(Spielberg and Anderson, 1985, p. 195)

These two postulates led to an apparent contradiction that, when resolved, forced Einstein to abandon the concepts of absolute space and absolute time. The resolution hinged on how the speed of light is measured. To appreciate the apparent contradiction between the two postulates, imagine the following situation. Suppose you are standing next to a light bulb. As the light spreads from the bulb, you measure its speed. You will find the speed of light is "c," or 300,000 km/s or 186,000 mi/s (in round numbers). Now, suppose the light bulb moves away from you at high speed. The emitted light has no connection (once it is emitted) to the bulb. When you measure its speed, it will still be 300,000 km/s. This "common sense" fact is the same as Einstein's second postulate. But according to the principle of relativity—Einstein's first postulate—the bulb can be considered at rest and *you* are moving away from the bulb at (the same) high speed. If you measure the speed of light in this case, will it still be 300,000km/s?

Now if uniform motion really does *not* affect things, then both situations should be physically the same. In that case, even when you are moving away from the stationary bulb, the speed of the light you measure should still be 300,000 km/s. This conclusion makes complete sense. It is also entirely consistent with Einstein's two postulates. However, think about it again. Our usual way of thinking about velocities does not agree with the above conclusion. A bulb is shining in a street lamp, and the light is propagating out from the lamp at 300,000 km/s. We are in a car speeding down the street away from the street lamp. If we were to measure the speed of light coming from the lamp, our normal way of thinking tells us that we should measure a speed of 300,000 km/s plus the speed of our car. But Einstein's two postulates tell us that we should get 300,000 km/s whether we are standing next to the lamp *or* moving away from it in a speeding car! What he is saying is that the speed of light should be the same for all observers, regardless of their state of motion. By thinking for ten years about why this seems to violate common sense, Einstein finally came up with the idea that our long-held notions about time were wrong (Einstein and Infeld, 1973, p. 178). Put simply, Newton's theory of absolute time (and absolute space) had never been valid.

It is useful to note that the failure of the Michelson-Morley and other experiments to detect the existence of the ether really amounted to the same thing as Einstein's second postulate. These experiments aimed to detect effects of the Earth's motion through the ether. If such effects could be detected, as most late-nineteenth century physicists thought they would, that would be confirmation that uniform motion could be detected optically. Much to most physicists' astonishment, no such effect was detected. They were forced, therefore, to conclude that the speed of light is indeed the same for all observers regardless of their state of motion. This is exactly Einstein's second postulate. He arrived at this result theoretically, by conducting what he called "thought experiments." (This was a process of doing science similar to Galileo's [see section 2c].) Needless to say, many physicists were confused and upset by the failure of their experiments and resisted for some time the full implications of Einstein's theory of relativity (Pais, 1982).

New Concepts of Space and Time

Einstein was, however, deeply convinced that his two postulates were correct and represented a fundamental truth for physical science. Einstein's key insight was that *all* measurements of time involve judgements of "simultaneous events." To take an example from his original 1905 paper, suppose we say "The train arrived at 7 o'clock." What we really mean, Einstein pointed out, is actually a composite of two quite separate things: (1) The train arrived in the station, and (2) Our watch (and the station clock) read 7. Einstein's statement would have seemed simple-minded to many physicists who read it at the time. However, it was the seed that brought forth the relativity revolution that rocked the foundations of twentieth century physics.

To appreciate the idea that simultaneity lies at the root of our very notion of time, it is helpful to look at two more seemingly simple statements. First, "I ate at noon." The simultaneous events are easy to understand. They are "I ate" and "The clock read 12 (at that moment)". Let us now take a second statement which turns out to be not so obvious: "My friend's train arrived, in the station 400 km away from here, at 7 o'clock." What is actually meant is something like the following series of statements: (a) My friend's train arrived in the station 400 km from here; (b) My watch read 7 o'clock; and (c) I knew it was synchronized with the station clock 400 km away, so that must have read 7 o'clock too. The point is that when we talk of events that are actually separated from us, or from each other, in space, we are really talking about at least two separate clocks. To judge the time of events separated in space we need clocks at each event, and these clocks must by synchronized. Two separate clocks can be synchronized in a variety of ways. The crucial point is that only when two clocks are thus synchronized can we actually speak about the time of the events.

Before Einstein, the simultaneity of the above examples of separated events would have been assumed as immediately obvious from experience and left unquestioned by physicists. The conventional understanding of time had been based on such experiences. Einstein maintained that this belief was an illusion. As he later (1936) wrote: "This illusion had its origin in the fact that in our everyday experience we can neglect the time of the propagation of light. We are accustomed on this account to fail to differentiate between 'simultaneously seen' and 'simultaneously happening'; and, as a result, the difference between time and local time is blurred." Einstein realized that the meaning of simultaneity of separated events—and thus the physical meaning of time—was not obvious (Bernstein, 1973, pp. 54–56).

Another crucial insight of Einstein that helped unlock the secret of special relativity, was his further realization that two events which are simultaneous for one person need not be simultaneous for another person. In fact, for another person moving relative to the first at high speeds close to the speed of light (c), the two events will not appear to be simultaneous at all. This can be deduced from Einstein's two postulates. No one had ever suggested that the time interval between two events might be different for two observers who were moving with respect to one another. The problem can be expressed as one of "simultaneity"—the question as to whether two events (which do not occur at the same location) occur at the same time, as seen by two observers who are moving with respect to one another. This question is at the heart of Einstein's theory of relativity.

The following illustration differs only slightly from Einstein's own thought experiment. Suppose a train is traveling along a track at 200,000 km/s (2/3 of the speed of light). Observer A is standing on the ground, just opposite the middle of a given train car. Explosives are set off at each end of the car "at the same time." What does one mean by the phrase "at the same time?" Einstein defines simultaneity as follows: if an observer is midway between the two occurrences and he/she sees those occurrences at the same time, then the two occurrences are simultaneous—they occur "at the same time."

Since light is the carrier of information, the evidence that an explosion occurred at each end of the car comes to the observer at the speed of light. But light has a finite, although great, speed (300,000 km/s). Therefore, it takes time for light to travel from the event to the observer. Because observer A is situated exactly opposite the middle of the car when the two explosions occur, his distance from each explosion is equal. Therefore light requires the same time to travel from each of the two events. Observer A "sees" the two events as occurring simultaneously.

Now suppose observer B is riding on the moving train car, also at its midpoint. Observer B will not see the two explosions as occurring simultaneously. This is due to the fact that observer B is moving toward the explosion that occurred at the front end of the car. The light from the front explosion will reach B *before* the light from the rear explosion "catches up" with the moving observer. Observer B says that the front explosion occurred first. Who is correct, A or B?

Because of your own experience as an earthling who spends most of the time on the surface of the earth (not ever traveling at 2/3 the speed of light), you might prefer observer A's explanation. However, B is no less correct. If you spent your entire life on such fast-moving trains (in thought, at least), then observer B's explanation would seem more reasonable. Einstein would tell you that one observer is no more or less correct than the other. For, there is no absolute time by which one observer is judged to be correct and the other is wrong. Time is relative to the frame of reference from which its passage is being measured. In Einstein's thought experiment, he could have equally set off two explosions in such a way as to make them appear simultaneous to observer B. Then observer A would not have seen them as simultaneous. There are a number of important consequences—some of them still quite strange for us to imagine—which follow from this aspect of the special theory of relativity.

The most fundamental, as we have seen, is that the question of time is really reduced to the problem of clocks, or how we measure time. One statement of the relativity of time is that "moving clocks appear to run slowly to an observer at rest." Another way of expressing this is that time appears (to you) to slow down on a vehicle (or a "laboratory") in motion relative to you. A provocative idea which results from Einstein's special theory concerns the question of "now." If observers in fast relative motion with respect to each other disagree about simultaneity, can there in fact be *one* moment of "now" that exists for the entire universe? A second surprising conclusion derived from Einstein's special theory is that lengths are relative too. This is because, to measure the length of an object, we must measure the position of two ends "at the same time." If moving observers disagree about simultaneity and rates of clocks, they must also disagree about lengths. One way of expressing this is to say that "a moving body appears to contract relative to a stationary observer" (Spielberg and Anderson, 1985, pp. 196–200).

For physicists and chemists, the fundamental properties of a body are typically related to its size and the amount of material it contains, that is, its *mass*. Shortly after publishing his ideas on the relativistic measurement of length, Einstein extended his theory to include relativistic effects on the mass of objects. He showed that the mass of a moving object *increases*, as measured by an observer with respect to whom the object is traveling at some given speed. Like the length contraction of a moving object, the increase in mass was conceived first theoretically by Einstein, in another of his famous thought experiments.

Mass-Energy Equivalence

Einstein was further able to show that there was a fundamental relationship between the mass of a given object and its energy. He expressed this relationship in what is probably the most famous equation in science: $E = mc^2$. The interpretation of this equation is simple but of profound importance. Since "c," the speed of light, is a universal constant, the relationship implies that the energy contained in a substance is directly proportional to its relativistic mass ("m"). Energy addition, therefore, implies a mass increase. If we heat an iron ball, for instance, it should weigh more than it did at a lower temperature. In a chemical reaction which liberates energy, the products would have slightly less mass than the reactants. In both of these cases, however, the mass change would be too small to be easily detectable. Yet, the speed of light is a very large number indeed: 300,000 km/s. It is far larger when squared. Thus, if most of the mass of even a tiny object were converted into its energy equivalent, the result would be a truly enormous release of energy (Calder, 1982, pp. 28–43). This, in fact, is what happens in radioactive decay and atomic and nuclear fission reactions (see section 6a).

At the time Einstein first published his ideas on mass-energy equivalence, the subject was of academic interest only. But developments in theoretical physics and in international politics during the 1920s and 1930s led to an epoch-making "practical" application of Einstein's theoretical prediction. In August 1945, scientists succeeded in liberating the enormous energy locked in matter, according to Einstein's famous equation. The first atomic bombs, dropped on Japan at the close of World War II, constituted one of the most significant applications of science to social affairs in history. We still are learning how to live with its consequences (see section 6b).

The fact that Einstein's theory of relativity implies that an observer sees moving clocks slow down and moving objects contract in length and increase in mass, makes us wonder whether these effects are real. This question launches us into interesting speculations on the meaning of "real," "now" and other related philosophical issues. But if we concentrate just on the physics of the matter, then it is clear that concrete, "physical" things happen in the world that can be explained only in terms of these relativistic effects. One of the best known examples concerns a type of subatomic particle called "mu-mesons." These particles fall to earth as an ordinary constituent of the cosmic showers always coming into the earth's atmosphere. When the number of mu-mesons was measured at the top and the bottom of Mt. Washington in New Hampshire, there were more at the bottom than expected. According to the standard calculations of the half-life of mu-mesons and the length of time it takes for these particles to traverse the atmosphere, there should have been fewer mu-mesons reaching the bottom of Mt. Washington than were actually measured. [The half-life is the length of time required for a given sample of radioactive matter to decline to one-half of its initial value.]

This is a significant experiment because it affords one of the most decisive validations of Einstein's relativity theory. In one version of the experiment, a special detector selected mu-mesons travelling at 99.5% of the speed of light. At the top of the mountain, it detected about 560 of these particles per hour. By contrast, at the bottom of the mountain (some 1900 meters lower) about 410 mu-mesons were detected every hour. The half-life of mu-mesons is about 1.5 microseconds. This means that after 1.5 microseconds, a group of 560 mu-mesons should be reduced to about 280, after 3 microseconds it should be reduced to 140, and so on. Now, it takes about 6 microseconds for the mu-mesons to get from the top to the bottom of Mt. Washington, that is, travelling 1900 meters at a speed of 99.5% of c. Thus, there should have been approximately 35 mu-mesons counted (per hour) at the bottom of the mountain, not the 410 per hour actually measured. For as many as 410 per hour to be arriving at the bottom, the mu-mesons' (radioactive) clocks must have been running much slower. In fact, when the calculation was done, it was found that the clocks were slow by exactly the amount predicted by special relativity for relative velocities of 99.5% the speed of light.

General Theory of Relativity

Einstein later extended the special theory of relativity to include *all* kinds of motion, accelerated and curved as well as constant speed in a straight line. He had been working on this extension of his theory since 1905, but his ideas came to fruition in the middle of World War I. In the first paper he published (in 1915) on his new "general theory of relativity," he showed that gravity—instead of being seen as a pull exerted by an object, as in Newtonian physics—can be viewed as a distortion of the space round the object (Rucker, 1984, p. 79). This distortion produces an acceleration in passing bodies, conventionally labelled "gravitational attraction." Einstein's general theory of relativity, then, includes all types of motion and describes how gravity and acceleration are interrelated. As with the special theory, Einstein's general theory has been validated by successful experimental tests, including those concerning the gravitational red shift of light, pulsars, and black holes (Will, 1986). It provides a comprehensive framework for incorporating the time dimension into the three traditional spatial dimensions of classical physics. One of Einstein's most powerful legacies for twentieth-century physics and philosophy is the concept that we live in a "four-dimensional universe" or "space-time continuum." Einstein noted wryly that, to the nonmathematician, the words "four-dimensional [awaken] thoughts of the occult. Yet [he believed] there is no more common-place statement than that the world in which we live is a four-dimensional space-time continuum" (Einstein, 1983, p. 55)

Up until the close of World War I, Einstein's name had become familiar to the scientific community but was hardly known elsewhere. In 1919, he suddenly became famous to the world at large. In that year, the bending of light passing near the sun—as predicted by his general theory of relativity—was observed during the solar eclipse of 1919. Einstein's name and the term "relativity" became household words. The publicity, even notoriety, that ensued changed the pattern of his life. Einstein was now able to put the weight of his famous name behind causes that he believed in, and he did this. When Hitler came to power in Germany in 1933, Einstein, as a Jew, promptly resigned his position at the Prussian Academy and joined the Institute for Advanced Study at Princeton University (in New Jersey). A few weeks after Einstein's resignation, the famous physicist Max Planck (see next section) expressed his dismay that Einstein had felt it necessary to leave Germany. This and other courageous statements by Planck reputedly so enraged Hitler that he told Planck face to face that only Planck's age saved him from being sent to a concentration camp (Hoffmann, 1983, pp. 168–169). Princeton became Einstein's home for the remaining 22 years of his life. He became a United States citizen in 1940.

During World War II, Einstein lent his prestige and authority to the development of the atomic bomb in the Manhattan Project (see section 6a). After the bomb was used and the war had ended, Einstein, saddened by the role he had played in bringing about the birth of atomic (and later nuclear) weapons, devoted his energies to the attempt to achieve a world government and abolish war once and for all. It is one of the greater ironies of the nuclear age that the initial impetus for the American atomic bomb project came not from U.S. military or political officials, but rather from some foreign-born emigré scientists with distinctly pacifist views. For Einstein, in particular, it was a curious position in which to find himself, after having so long publicly campaigned against the use of technology for military purposes. Yet not to act, for Einstein and the others, opened up the possibility (as it appeared in 1939) of Nazi conquest (Glynn, 1992, p. 90).

He also spoke out against oppression, urging that intellectuals (including scientists) must be prepared to risk everything to preserve freedom of expression. One of Einstein's last acts was his signing of a plea, initiated by the English mathematician and philosopher Bertrand Russell (1872–1970), for the renunciation of nuclear weapons and the abolition of war. He was drafting a speech in April 1955 on the (then) current tensions between Israel and Egypt when he suffered an attack due to an aortic aneurysm. He died a few days later, on 18 April 1955. Einstein left a profound and complex legacy for the twentieth century. His scientific brilliance and social concerns set him apart as one of the greatest figures in the history of science. As Copernicus, Newton, and Darwin and Wallace before him, Einstein initiated a scientific transformation which has required our age to reexamine many of the common sense and scientific prejudices we have inherited. In his work and person, the impact of science upon general culture has truly been revolutionary (Cohen, 1985b, p. 405). ■

B. Quantum Physics

■ ■ ■

The special theory of relativity would have been enough by itself to bring Einstein fame. But the work specifically cited in the 1921 award to Einstein of the Noble Prize for physics was another 1905 paper which explained the long-standing puzzle of the *photoelectric effect*. Einstein's ideas in this field became a fundamental part of the branch of physics called *quantum theory* or *quantum mechanics*. Quantum physics deals with the behavior of particles at the atomic and subatomic levels. Along with the theory of relativity, quantum physics represents one of the major breakthroughs in twentieth-century physical science. Whatever the final verdict on specific details of quantum physics may be, there is no doubt that its scientific and philosophical implications are crucial to our modern understanding of the physical universe. In this sense, its impact will be as significant as the Newtonian synthesis of the eighteenth century (Shimony, 1989, p. 395). To see how it all began, we must go back to an observation that preceded Einsein's ideas on the photoelectric effect.

A major interest for physicists in the latter part of the nineteenth century was the way in which a hot body radiates energy into space. For example, a piece of metal heated to white heat radiates in a different way from one heated to red heat. It proved surprisingly difficult to provide a theoretical explanation of this difference. Finally, in 1900 the German physicist Max Planck (1858–1947) pointed out a possible solution. In order to fit the experimental data he found it necessary to suppose that radiation was emitted in bursts, rather than continuously. This seemed so contrary to both science and common sense, that most physicists considered it just as a device for the purposes of calculation, rather than as being physically meaningful.

Einstein, once again in opposition to mainstream physics at the start of the twentieth century, argued that Planck's idea should be taken seriously. It actually did represent the true nature of radiation. Einstein developed Planck's suggestion that energy may not, in fact, be the continuous phenomenon that was the standard concept in 1900. Planck had proposed that energy can not have every possible value. Rather, energy comes in whole-number multiples of a certain basic value. Planck called this a *quantum* of energy.

Photoelectric Effect

Einstein used Planck's quantum idea to explain the so-called photoelectric effect (Pais, 1982, pp. 378–382). If a metal surface is illuminated, electrons are given off. When the light is strengthened, more electrons are produced, as might be expected. But their energy levels are identical to those of electrons given off in dim light. Thus, the energy of the ejected electrons does not depend on the intensity of the light hitting the surface, as classical physics would imply. Their energy depends, instead, on the wavelength of the light beam. The higher frequencies (such as those from the blue end of the spectrum) give higher energies than lower frequencies (from the red end of the spectrum). Adapting Planck's idea, Einstein explained this by suggesting that radiation (such as light) consists of "packets" or "quanta" of energy, each of which can be absorbed entirely by an electron and dislodge it. He argued, like Planck, that the energy possessed by matter (e.g., kinetic energy) can be changed into radiant energy (radiation) only in integral multiples of quanta. Thus, the energy of each interacting particle is, at all times, a whole-number multiple of its basic quantum unit.

When Planck had evaluated the size of the quantum energy "step," he found it to be 6.6 x 10^{-34} Joule-sec. This is the quantity of which all values of energy appear as whole-number multiples. This number is now referred to as Planck's constant, h. Thus, if a quantum is radiated, its energy would be given by the equation $E = hf$. Here, f is equal to the frequency of the particular radiation. This assertion is known as the quantum hypothesis. For example, the yellow light given off by a sodium vapor lamp is given off in chunks, or quanta, and each such quantum would have precisely the same energy (determined by the frequency of the yellow light). If the light were brighter, this would imply that more quanta were being radiated each second, but each would still have this energy. The value of h is extremely small, and so is the quantum. The units of radiation are so small, in fact, that light looks continuous to us, just as ordinary matter seems continuous. Planck was awarded the Nobel Prize in physics in 1918.

The fact is that Planck's assumption regarding the *quantized* nature of energy actually worked. This led other scientists, including Einstein, to use that same assumption to explain other phenomena associated with the behavior of atoms and their subatomic parts. Significantly, Planck had been one of the first physicists to recognize the importance of the special theory of relativity. "If [it] . . . should prove to be correct, as I expect it will, he will be considered the Copernicus of the twentieth century," Planck had predicted in 1910. Three years later (1913), Planck travelled to Zurich, Switzerland, to meet Einstein and offer him what was probably the best position in Europe for the kind of physicist Einstein was: a directorship at the newly established, and well-funded, Kaiser Wilhelm Institute in Berlin. Although Einstein did not immediately accept Planck's offer—he was reluctant to return to Germany—he did accept the position just before the outbreak of World War I. The joining of the paths of Einstein and Planck was to be critical for the development of modern physics (Cline, 1987, pp. 85–87).

Wave-Particle Dualism

The quantum hypothesis is a wholly revolutionary idea (Cohen, 1985b, p. 405). Coming in chunks or pieces of a certain size is a behavior associated with *particles*. Having a definite frequency, however, is a characteristic of *waves*. In the quantum hypothesis we have both a particle property *and* a wave property, bound in the same simple equation, $E = hf$. This was a particularly upsetting conclusion when dealing with light, since the "wave vs. particle" argument on the nature of light appeared to have been settled decisively a half-century earlier. Classical physics by the second half of the nineteenth century taught that light was a wave phenomenon only. A decisive experiment was needed to overturn the accepted view of light as being wavelike in its nature. This was the significance of Einstein's explanation of the photoelectric effect. For some purposes, Einstein showed that light could be thought of as a wave. But for other purposes, light would have to be thought of as a collection of particles, each produced by a quantum (i.e., discrete) change within an atom.

Einstein perceived that (continuous) waves and (discrete) quanta should behave quite differently in the manner in which they would eject electrons from the metal. First, picture the situation with a continuous light wave washing past an electron in the metal. A certain amount of work, "W," is necessary to break free the electron from the surface. A wave with great energy might be intense enough to do this amount of work on the electron almost immediately and break it free from the metal. A weaker light wave might require a longer time to deliver the necessary energy,

W. Thus, from the classical theory of light as waves, *any* frequency of light should be able to provide electrons with the energy needed, W, to break free and leave the metal surface. A bright light (i.e., light with high energy or frequency) might do it at once. A dim light (i.e., light with low energy or frequency) would have to illuminate the surface for some time until enough energy had been delivered. The point is, wave theory thus predicts free electrons for *any* frequency of light, but with a time delay for a dimmer source.

The prediction from the quantum hypothesis is quite different. If light energy comes in packages, a single package will either contain enough energy to do the job or not. Even with the most intense light source, the probability of a single electron receiving two quanta at once is so small it may be ignored. A single quantum of light, or *photon* (as Einstein named it), will need to have sufficient energy to allow the electron to break free from the surface. But, since the energy of the photon depends upon the frequency of the light, the color of the light (frequency) is of greatest importance. Each metal surface would have a particular color of the spectrum, or "threshold frequency," at which the light photons would have just enough energy to eject electrons. For light whose quanta have less than the required threshold frequency, they could never dislodge electrons. Even if the low frequency light was intense enough to melt the metal plate, it would still produce *no* photoelectrons. On the other hand, any light with a frequency equal to, or greater than, the required threshold level would produce free electrons easily.

Furthermore, the instant that a photon with the required energy reaches the plate an electron will be ejected. The quantum hypothesis predicts no time delay, since the photon either has the required energy and ejects electrons at once or does not have the required energy and thus never ejects electrons. Such an experiment on the photoelectric effect had actually been performed in 1902, but had lacked an interpretation. Its results were now completely explained by Einstein's application of the quantum hypothesis. Light indeed came in packages of a given amount of energy, not as a continuous wave-like front of energy. We must assume, Einstein argued, that an electron ejected from the metal was given energy by another particle, something like one billiard ball hitting another. The conclusion appeared inescapable, even if wholly paradoxical: in addition to behaving like a wave phenomenon, light was also composed of particle-like packets of radiant energy, called photons. The energy of a photon is directly proportional to its frequency (Riban, 1982, pp. 520–523).

The photoelectric effect, as interpreted by Einstein, demonstrated that light waves have particle-type properties. Could it not be that a particle, such as an electron, would have wave-type properties? By 1924, the French physicist Louis de Broglie had recognized the dual nature of *all* moving objects. He reasoned that photons were capable of transferring "momentum" (mv) upon impact just as a particle would. The momentum transferred was *inversely* proportional to the photon's wavelength, l . [The wavelength is inversely proportional to the frequency or energy of the photon; thus, the higher the frequency (and the higher the energy), the shorter the wavelength.] Why should not the moving electron have a wavelength associated with *it* which was inversely proportional to its momentum?

By equating the energy of a moving particle as derived by Einstein ($E = mc^2$) with the energy expression of Planck ($E = hf$), de Broglie derived a simple but revolutionary formula. His reasoning was as follows:

$$E = hf \text{ (from Planck)}$$

$$E = mc^2 \text{ (from Einstein)}$$

Setting these two expressions for energy equal to one another,

$$mc^2 = hf$$

which can be written—$c/f = h/mc$;
de Broglie also knew that the wavelength (l) of a given frequency of light (f) could be written as

$$l = c/f$$

Substituting this last expression in the one above:

$$l = h/mc$$

Then, recognizing that "c" is the velocity of a photon, de Broglie merely allowed "c" to be replaced by "v," the velocity of an object. This yielded:

$$l = h/mv$$

as the wavelength to be associated with a particle moving with momentum "mv." Simply put, elementary units of matter possess wave properties. Like light, matter has a double character, sometimes appearing wavelike in composition, sometimes particlelike.

Using this expression, de Broglie could compute the wavelength associated with any moving object. It may be asked why we do not observe a wave form in large objects of the kind we ordinarily encounter. Using de Broglie's equation, it is clear that objects with large mass, such as a stone, will have computed wavelengths which are remarkably minute. With a wavelength as short as that, we will likely go on thinking of a stone—for all practical purposes—as a particle rather than a wave. But now consider another entity we usually think of as a particle, namely, the electron. How does the de Broglie hypothesis influence our view of electrons in atoms?

Without going into the details, suffice it to say that we can compute the de Broglie wavelength of an orbital electron (around the nucleus of an atom). Significantly, the stable orbits of electrons around the nucleus are whole-number multiples of the de Broglie wavelength of an electron. This was precisely the conclusion that the Danish physicist Niels Bohr (1885–1962) came to when he proposed his theory on the properties of the hydrogen atom in 1913. For this achievement, he was awarded the Nobel Prize in physics in 1922.

Bohr's Model of the Atom

Bohr's model visualized the hydrogen atom as having various specific energy levels. He pictured the atom as having a central mass (nucleus) carrying a positive charge, called the "proton." Moving about that proton was a single electron, carrying a negative charge (Cohen, 1985b, pp. 427–430). The electron would normally be found at a certain orbital distance from the proton, called the first energy level or "ground state" of the electron. The electron, however, could be "excited" (given extra energy, say by an electric current or by heating) to a higher energy level. Bohr's crucial point was that the electron could assume only specific (excited) orbital states. That is, an electron could exist only at specific energy levels (and at specific orbits) and never in between those permitted, discrete levels (Blaedel, 1988, p.54). Suddenly, de Broglie had provided an explanation for Bohr's 1913 model. Again, matter in motion displayed wave properties. Why are electrons confined to certain given orbits only? According to de Broglie's new interpretation of the wave-like properties of the electron, these are the only positions where a "standing wave" of the electron's wavelength may be formed. At these positions, the electron is self-reinforcing, while between these positions its wave nature makes it self-canceling.

Now, for a huge object (by the tiny standards of an atom) such as a bacterium, the mass is so great that the observed behavior is dominated by those properties we ascribe to particles. For a tiny object, such as an electron, the wave properties can never be negligible. In certain circumstances, the particle properties will dominate the observed behavior, and under other conditions the wave properties will dominate. De Broglie's interpretation of matter as a dual "wave-particle" is fascinating, but is it real? [Recall, that a similar question was asked of Einstein's relativity theory.] If electrons are—what do you call them? "Wavicles?"—they should show the standard wave properties, such as diffraction, under the correct conditions.

Very promptly, the conclusion of the experimental laboratories regarding de Broglie's hypothesis came in: electrons do display wave properties as well as particle properties. By implication, all matter displays wave properties. Similarly, light (and by implication all radiation) displays quantum or particle behavior. Once again nature had revealed one of its subtleties. Old laws and ways of viewing things in classical physics were not wrong. But they were correct only for a restricted range of masses and motions. [Again, note the similarity to relativity theory's implications. Newtonian physics was shown to be valid only within a certain range of velocities. As speeds approached the speed of light, relativistic explanations take over.] Once the atomic realm was entered, the wave nature of particles could no longer be ignored. The science of physics would have to be reshaped for a *wave mechanics*, or *quantum mechanics* as it came to be called (Riban, 1982, pp. 531–532).

The new science of quantum mechanics was drafted independently mainly by two individuals. The German physicist Werner Heisenberg (1901–1976) and the Austrian physicist Erwin Schrödinger (1887–1961) had both been extending the quantum description of the atom. In 1925–1926, they blended their individual ideas to form the quantum-mechanical model of the atom. Schrödinger had developed a wave equation (which grew out of the classical theory of wave motion), based upon the assumption that the way electrons behave is governed by their wave nature. As a direct consequence of the development of his wave equation, he was able to predict exactly the various energy states that an electron can possess. For his theories, Schrödinger shared in the Nobel Prize in physics in 1933 (W. Moore, 1992).

Heisenberg used a purely mathematical approach independent of earlier theory. He had decided that it was impossible to construct visual analogies for atomic structure and proceeded to describe successfully the energy levels, or orbits, of electrons purely in numerical terms. For this system of *matrix mechanics* Heisenberg received the Nobel Prize in physics in 1932 (Cassidy, 1992, pp. 226–235, 324–325). The merger of Heisenberg's approach with Schrödinger's theories yielded the new, and highly mathematical, theory of quantum mechanics. It must be emphasized that there is simply no such thing as nonmathematical quantum mechanics. It is very complex and requires the precision of mathematics at every step. However, this does not imply that its conclusions are of interest only to mathematical physicists. Every day, the typical North American uses quantum mechanical devices that were completely beyond the power of science to understand in the 1920s. Today, you can carry more calculating power around in your hand, with the pocket computer, than the largest computers on earth possessed in the 1950s. This ongoing miniaturization of computers is part of the quantum-mechanical revolution. The successful quantum techniques for describing the situation in single atoms were later extended to crystalline aggregates of atoms in *solid-state physics*. Practical devices resulting from this include solar cells, transistors, lasers, and light-emitting diodes (LEDs) as found in calculators and watches (see section 5c).

Uncertainty Principle

Basic to quantum physics is the idea that there is a *fundamental* uncertainty which exists at the scale of the atom. No matter how good our instruments and regardless of how good our techniques, there are certain aspects of a submicroscopic body such as an electron that we can *never* know with certainty. Almost at the outset of quantum theory, Heisenberg showed that nature may have built in its own way of foiling our ability to find out certain atomic measurements precisely. This is called the "Heisenberg uncertainty principle." Basically, this principle states that as we measure one property—such as an electron's position—with greater and greater precision, another property—such as that electron's momentum—becomes fuzzier and fuzzier. Thus, if we really tried to pin down the electron's wavelength (by measuring "mv"), we would lose all knowledge of where it was! Precisely because an electron is *both* particle and wave, its position and momentum cannot be known to high accuracy simultaneously. Quantum physics tells us that the electron does not have a specific position and a specific momentum at any given moment. The uncertainty of its position and momentum is inherent in its "matter-waves." Heisenberg's reasoning makes this clear (Cassidy, 1992).

After having introduced matrix mechanics, Heisenberg went on to consider the problem of describing the position of a subatomic particle. How can one determine where a particle is? The obvious answer is: Look at it. Well, let us imagine a microscope that could make an electron visible. We must shine a light or some appropriate kind of radiation on to it to see it. Actually, the wavelength of visible light is about 5000 times larger than the diameter of an atom. In the same sense that an ocean wave sweeping over a small pebble is not disturbed by the presence of the pebble, a light wave sweeping over an atom would not be noticeably affected by the presence of the atom. We cannot see any effect of the presence of the atom on the visible light wave because its wavelength is too long. One must use "light" with a wavelength which is as small as the atom or electron; in fact, the wavelength should be much smaller. Very short electromagnetic radiation, such as X-rays or even gamma rays, should be used to see the electron. But the X-ray or gamma ray photons have a very considerable amount of energy and momentum, according to the ideas of Einstein and de Broglie. Since an electron is so small, a single photon of electromagnetic radiation striking it, would move it and change its position. In the very act of measuring its position, we would have changed that position.

This is, to be sure, a phenomenon that occurs in ordinary life. When we measure the air pressure in a tire with a gauge, we let a little air out of the tire and change the pressure slightly in the act of measuring it. Likewise, when we put a thermometer in a bathtub of water to measure the temperature, the thermometer's absorption of heat changes the temperature slightly. However, in these and many other common measurements, the change in the subject we are measuring is so small that we can ignore it. The situation is radically different when we come to look at the electron. Our measuring device is at least as large as the thing we are measuring. Consequently, our measurement must inevitably have, not a negligible, but a decisive effect on the object measured. We could stop the electron and so determine its position at a given instant. But, in that case, we could not know its motion or velocity. On the other hand, we might record its velocity, but then we could not fix its position at any given moment (Asimov, 1984, p. 408).

Quantum Reality

Quantum physics has given us a new—and sometimes strange—picture of reality at the atomic and subatomic level (Davies, 1980, pp. 9–11). Most significant, quantum mechanics has forced us to abandon the previous notion of strict causality in classical physics. Instead, quantum mechanics allows calculation of only statistical probabilities for the outcome of any atomic or subatomic interaction. The introduction of the idea of probability waves leads to a number of interesting implications.

The use of probability in the analysis of a physical situation means that there is some uncertainty. Even if something is highly probable, it is, by definition, slightly uncertain. Often when something is said to be probable or uncertain, the statement is made only because there is not enough time or a good enough measuring instrument available to make the measurement precisely. In quantum physics, however, it is believed that uncertainty is *inherent* in the very nature of the world—and cannot be removed regardless of how sophisticated the measuring technique is. Simply stated, this suggests that if predictions are made based on past events and a complete, well-validated theory, the results may not be unambiguous. Most important, the direct and rigid connection between cause and effect is destroyed, because it is not certain that the cause will lead to the predicted effect.

The uncertainty principle has had a major impact upon discussions of metaphysics and fundamental concepts of knowledge. It destroys the idea, made plausible by the success of Newtonian physics, that the universe is completely determined by its past history (see sections 2c, 2d). A late eighteenth-century disciple of Newton, the famous French mathematician and astronomer Pierre-Simon Laplace (1749–1827), believed that probability was nothing real, nor was it a fundamental law of nature: it was merely an expression of our ignorance concerning the precise details of any situation. A strict determinist, Laplace stated that if the positions and velocities of all the bits of matter in the universe were known at a given instant, then the positions and velocities of all these bits of matter could be calculated and predicted exactly for any future time. All future effects would be the precise result of earlier causes. Even if the task of measuring all these positions and velocities were humanly impossible, nevertheless the exact positions and velocities *did* exist at a previous time and scientific laws *do* exist. For Laplace, the future is predetermined.

But Heisenberg's uncertainty principle says this is not so. It is, in theory, impossible to make the measurements with sufficient precision to know them, or to calculate future situations, exactly. There are, according to quantum theory, limitations on causality. This, however, does not mean that the future is completely unknown. We can calculate probabilities that things will occur in the future, and statistically these calculations will be borne out. It is only for the individual subatomic particle that we cannot predict behavior. Heisenberg's uncertainty principle was not easily accepted by all physicists. Einstein, for one, was severely troubled by its implications. It ran counter to his philosophical intuition that "God does not play dice with the universe." Nevertheless, the prevailing mode of thought amongst most physicists today is that the uncertainty principle is valid and useful, and there are indeed limitations on causality (Spielberg and Anderson, 1985, pp. 251, 254–255).

As with relativity theory, the accuracy of quantum physics has been confirmed in countless experimental tests during the course of the twentieth century. Taken together, relativity theory and quantum mechanics have produced a revolutionary interpretation of physical reality. We are only just now beginning to understand some of the (still sometimes controversial) scientific, philosophical, metaphysical and, even, theological implications of the new physics (Herbert, 1987).

What is clear, is that Nature itself operates discontinuously—or in jumps—at a fundamental level. The success of quantum theory thus contradicts the old adage of classical physics, "Nature makes no leaps." ■

C. Molecular Biology: Watson, Crick and the Discovery of the Structure of DNA

■ ■ ■

The second half of the twentieth century will surely be remembered by future generations as the Atomic Age. Einstein's theory of relativity and the development of quantum physics revolutionized not only science but society. Nuclear weapons and computers are but two of the significant innovations which derive (in part) from these two theoretical revolutions in atomic physics (see sections 4a, 4b, 5b, 5c, 6a, 6b). The same half-century will be remembered, equally, as the "Age of Molecular Biology." In some respects, developments in genetics since 1950 have the potential for affecting the destiny of the present and future generations more deeply than even the startling developments in physics (Watson, Tooze, and Kurtz, 1983). Just as nuclear weapons and computers have become part of the daily life and collective psyche of our times, so have genetic engineering and biotechnology (see section 5d) (Kevles & Hood, 1992, pp. 281–282, 320–328).

It was the discovery of the three-dimensional structure of DNA, announced by James Watson and Francis Crick in April, 1953, which formed the basis for the remarkable breakthroughs in molecular biology that characterize our age. As they stated in their paper (in the British journal Nature) on the genetic implications of the DNA structure they had discovered: "Many lines of evidence indicate that DNA is the carrier of a part of (if not all) the genetic specificity of the chromosomes and thus of the gene itself" (Watson and Crick, 1953b, p. 964). Watson and Crick's now-famous depiction of the genetic material (DNA) as the "Double Helix" ranks—with the Copernican sun-centered astronomy (see section 2a), the Darwin-Wallace theory of natural selection (see section 3b), and Einstein's theory of relativity (see section 4a)—as one of the milestones and major turning-points in the history of science and technology. By demonstrating that it was the molecular *structure* of the gene which determined its *hereditary* and *cellular functions,* Watson and Crick (in the opinion of many) finally uncovered the elusive "secret of life." Whether or not this claim needs some modifications or restrictions—e.g., from a philosophical or religious perspective—there is no doubt that Watson and Crick's discovery transformed the science of biology (Suzuki & Knudtson, 1988, pp. 114–116). For their work on DNA, Watson and Crick, along with Maurice Wilkins, received a Nobel Prize in 1962.

DNA as a Unifying Principle

The discovery of DNA's structure has emerged as a broad unifying principle in biology. We have seen, historically, that certain theoretical developments in science (on occasion) will link together several fields that were previously studied separately. Newton's theory of universal gravitation united the hitherto distinct domains of terrestrial and celestial physics in one grand synthesis (see sections 2c, 2d). In a similar way, the Darwin-Wallace theory of natural selection ties together the various data of embryology, heredity, comparative anatomy, paleontology, and geology into a broad and compelling evolutionary framework. Einstein's theory of relativity explains the fundamental relationship between gravitation and acceleration and, ultimately, provides a framework for uniting the seemingly separate categories of space and time.

In an equally fundamental fashion, the discovery of the structure of DNA permits us to see that biological concepts which were previously studied at the level of the cell, tissue, organism or species (i.e., population biology), have a common foundation. They all derive, ultimately, from the molecular architecture of the gene and other specific macromolecules. In particular, the work of Watson and Crick and their colleagues (most notably Wilkins and Rosalind Franklin) united three traditions in biology that had previously been kept relatively separate. It was their genius to bring together these separate strands to form a powerful new scientific synthesis. These three traditions are:

1. *Structural*–this concerns itself with the architecture of biological molecules;
2. *Biochemical*–this approach is concerned with how biologically significant molecules interact in cell metabolism and heredity; and
3. *Informational*–this approach is concerned with how genetic information is transferred from one generation of (particular) organisms to another; it focuses on how this information is translated or coded into unique biological molecules which produce, ultimately, one species rather than another. (Mendel's Laws are a brilliant, and typical, example of the informational approach to interpreting biological phenomena.)

The discovery that the gene is, in fact, a specific three-dimensional chemical molecule provides a complete model now for interpreting *all* the structural, biochemical and informational data of biology (Suzuki & Knudtson, 1988, pp. 52–55).

Before the significance of the structure of DNA could be understood, two factors were necessary. First, it had to be shown that DNA was, in fact, the active substance of heredity. And, second, it had to be shown that it was the *structure* of DNA that accounted for its remarkable biological *functions* (Tamarin & Leavitt, 1991, p. 212). We need, therefore, to understand a bit about two types of special chemicals: *nucleic acids* and *proteins*. Nucleic acids and proteins are the largest molecules produced in living cells. Their chemistry is intimately related to their biological functions in all animals and plants. It is the chemical relationships between nucleic acids and proteins that constitute, in essence, the genetic process. Ultimately, it is the action of nucleic acids and proteins at the cellular (and nuclear) level that produces the characteristic features of any organism (its *phenotype*).

Proteins

Proteins occur in all kinds of cells. All cells make their own proteins by linking together (polymerizing) small molecules called *amino acids* into various arrangements, producing many kinds of proteins. Thus, proteins are what is termed macromolecules. While plants are able to synthesize all the kinds of amino acids, some animals are not. Animals, including humans, must obtain certain amino acids from their diet (the so-called essential amino acids). There are 20 amino acids which are used to build up proteins. Such a "string" of amino acids is called a polypeptide because the kind of chemical bond that keeps the amino acids together is known as a peptide bond. The number and sequence of amino acids distinguish one protein from another.

The functions of proteins fall into two main categories: structural and enzymatic. Structural proteins strengthen or protect other materials in the cell, chiefly in *cell membranes,* in the *ribosomes,* and in the *chromosomes.* Enzymatic proteins facilitate chemical reactions such as those which break down (degrade) foodstuffs, synthesize cellular parts, transport molecules through membranes, and perform other biological services rapidly and efficiently. In the presence of an enzyme, a chemical reaction may occur a million times faster than in its absence. Enzyme catalysis of chemical reactions is essential to permit the cell to grow and divide, to remove waste products, and so on. Life (as we know it on earth) without enzymes is impossible. The most crucial enzymatic reactions are those which build more proteins, the primary building blocks of an organism's phenotype (Tamarin & Leavitt, 1991, p. 242).

Like proteins, nucleic acids are macromolecules. That is, nucleic acids are made up of certain (repeating) units called *nucleotides.* Each nucleotide, in turn, consists of three smaller molecules: a sugar, a phosphate group (PO_4), and a nitrogenous base. When linked together, the nucleotides constitute a chain called a polynucleotide or *nucleic acid.* There are two kinds of nucleic acids, DNA and RNA. These two macromolecules are differentiated by the kind of sugar molecule each contains. DNA contains a sugar called deoxyribose and, hence, is called **Deoxyribonucleic acid.** RNA contains the sugar called ribose—which contains one more oxygen atom than deoxyribose—and, hence, is called **Ribonucleic acid.** We now know that genes are composed of DNA, except in a few viruses where they are composed of RNA. Three kinds of cellular RNA, produced under the direction of DNA, function in the synthesis of proteins.

The DNA molecules in all organisms are structurally alike in their general plans (Suzuki & Knudtson, 1988, p. 63). They are long thread-like molecules built from the same three components:

1. *phosphate* (PO_4), which gives DNA its acidic properties;
2. *deoxyribose,* an unusual kind of sugar with five carbons per molecule; and
3. *nitrogenous bases,* which give DNA some basic properties.

DNA has four kinds of nitrogenous bases: adenine (abbreviated as A), guanine (G), cytosine (C), and thymine (T). The two bases A and G— called purines—have similar structures, but differ slightly functionally because of different side groups on their molecules. The other two bases C and T—called pyrimidines—have similar structures but also differ slightly functionally because of their different side groups. These three components are put together as DNA subunits called nucleotides. Each nucleotide has the following composition: one phosphate attached to one sugar, which in turn is attached to one of the four types of bases:

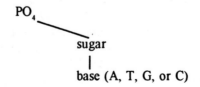

A chain of these nucleotides looks somewhat like a charm bracelet, with the bases in (seemingly) random sequence. One example, with an arbitrary sequence of bases (C, T, A, T, C, G...), looks like:

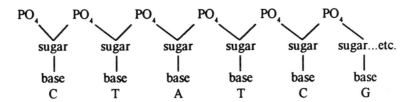

The overall architecture of DNA was worked out in the 1950s only after it became suspected that the gene was DNA. Structural studies on DNA were prompted by biological discoveries of DNA function.

DNA molecules are absolutely the largest ones made by cells. Some are nearly a billion times the weight of a hydrogen atom. Each bacterial cell of the microorganism called *Escherichia coli* has only one kind of DNA molecule. That molecule is its entire chromosome. Human cells, by contrast, with many kinds of DNA have 680 times the amount of DNA of an E. coli cell. Toads and other amphibians have even more DNA per cell than humans do. We now know that DNA is carried (or located) on the *chromosomes*. Although it had been known since the nineteenth century, that chromosomes (which carry the genes) in cells contain DNA, it was not until the early 1950s that the gene was conceded to *be* DNA. The reasons for this belated appreciation of DNA as the central molecule in biology are many, and they reveal much about how science works (Portugal and Cohen, 1977, pp. 156–158).

Narrowing Down the Choices

In the first place, chromosomes contain *proteins* as well as DNA. Since proteins are complexes of many (20) amino acids, most geneticists prior to the 1950s thought proteins were much more likely candidates for gene material than DNA. Before then, it was thought that DNA was a small (not true), simple (not true) molecule composed of only four kinds of nucleotides (true). It was argued that if genes did act as the information processors of heredity, then proteins were the most likely candidates to act as the gene language. Proteins with their 20 "letter" alphabet (their 20 amino acids) seemed a much richer "dictionary" of "words" (which would specify particular cell activities) than DNA with its four letter alphabet (the four different bases).

Secondly, the chemistry of DNA had been inadequately studied prior to 1950. Most biochemists had been spending their time unravelling the chemical form and function of what appeared to be far more important molecules: carbohydrates, lipids (i.e., fats and fatlike substances), and—most significant—proteins. The biological functions of these molecules were known before the functions of DNA and RNA were. Thirdly, the strong evidence developed from 1944 through the early 1950s suggesting that DNA was the gene material was comparatively unknown to a majority of geneticists of the day (B. Wallace, 1992, chaps. 6–8).

Most geneticists were then concentrating on patterns of gene transmission in *Drosophila*, corn plants and other complex organisms. *Drosophila* (commonly known as the fruit fly), in particular, was the favorite organism for laboratory studies in genetics because of its relatively short generation time (twelve days to produce a new generation). But the critical DNA investigations, in contrast, were being done on simple microorganisms, such as bacteria and viruses, whose DNA molecules were easier to study experimentally. These DNA studies were seldom published in the same scientific journals as genetic studies done on higher organisms, including *Drosophila* and corn. This is an example of how, sometimes, new information in science may not have the immediate impact it merits if it is not widely published. It is interesting to recall here that Mendel's own pioneering work in nineteenth-century genetics itself remained relatively unknown for more than thirty years because it had first been published (1865) in a central European scientific journal which did not have a wide international readership (Portugal and Cohen, 1977, pp. 114–115).

The discovery which first demonstrated that DNA did have genic properties was published in 1944 by the Canadian-born biochemist Oswald T. Avery and his co-workers, C.M. MacLeod and M. McCarty (Avery et al., 1944). They isolated DNA in the laboratory from a strain of bacteria with trait "A." They then showed that this DNA could enter cells of a strain lacking trait "A" and change, or "transform," them into a strain displaying trait "A." Avery and his colleagues proved that it was just the DNA in the donor bacterial cells—and not their RNA or protein—which had the power to transform the heredity of the recipient cells. They had tested different parts of the donor bacteria and showed that it was the DNA alone (with no other components of the original strain present or necessary) which could cause the bacterial transformation. This identification of DNA as the transforming agent was strong evidence that the genetic material was made of nucleic acids, not proteins or any other cell component. In fact, by showing that it was the purest and most protein-free preparation of DNA that was the active causative factor, Avery and his collaborators effectively discredited the then dominant view that proteins were the agents of biological specificity and cellular inheritance. The fact that the change (i.e., trait "A") was heritable, indicated that it was, in this case at least, a permanent genetic change (rather than some environmental factor) which produced the observed (phenotypic) trait.

Chargaff's Rules

Another crucial piece of information about DNA was developed in the late 1940s by the (naturalized) American biochemist Erwin Chargaff. He extracted DNA from many different organisms and analyzed its constituent bases chemically by a technique called chromatography. Chargaff showed that the DNA of organisms has the following common properties: (1) the number of purine residues in DNA approximately equals the number of pyrimidine residues (i.e., $A + G = T + C$); and (2) the number of A residues approximates very closely T residues (or, $A = T$), while G approximates very closely C (or, $G = C$). The significance of these experimental findings, known as "Chargaff's rules"—which showed that the amounts of the four bases did not vary independently—would become clear only with the development of the Watson-Crick model of the DNA molecule (Watson, Tooze & Kurtz, 1983, p. 16).

By the early 1950s, then, the stage was set for the rapidly ensuing elaboration of the structure, function and biological importance of DNA. Much of the credit for the discovery of the molecular nature of genes must go to people whose training was initially in physics and chemistry rather than in the biological sciences proper. For, they thought in terms of particles and molecules rather than in terms of the whole organism. They approached the analysis of genes as discrete molecules which must therefore have a definite physical structure. These novel biologists looked at cells as entities to be dissembled so that the component parts could be analyzed for both structure and function (Portugal and Cohen, 1977, pp. 204–229). (Their approach recalls Galileo's emphasis upon abstraction in the scientific method [see section 2c].) Techniques to do so without destroying biological activity of the component parts were developed around the same period of time (the 1940s) that geneticists discovered the advantages of studying genetic phenomena in microorganisms. The stage was thus set for the revolutionary combination of the three hitherto (largely) separate approaches—structural, biochemical, and informational—which ushered in the age of molecular biology.

A flurry of theoretical and experimental efforts to characterize the nature of DNA occurred throughout the scientific world at the start of the 1950s (Portugal and Cohen, 1977, pp. 263–264). For, only if scientists understood the molecular nature of DNA could they begin to understand how the gene determines the functions or structures of a cell. The significance of the quest was not lost on anyone, for what was being sought was the basis of all life. Since all matter is made of atoms and molecules, no understanding of the way in which living organisms function and reproduce would be complete unless one understood genetic processes at the level of molecules. The knowledge which has come from this approach is called molecular biology, which also includes molecular genetics. This knowledge has provoked so fundamental a reexamination of our concepts of biology as to constitute one of the major scientific revolutions of the twentieth century. The implications of molecular biology for society have been equally far-reaching (see sections 5d, 7b). Since the 1970s, Watson, himself, has been an active voice in the dialogue concerning the cultural implications of genetic engineering and bioethics (Tiley, 1983, pp. 197–199).

The excitement in the scientific community was great and the competition extremely keen to uncover the nature of DNA. In April 1953, in a paper (in *Nature*) scarcely two pages long, the solution was presented by the Englishman Crick, and the young American Watson (Watson and Crick, 1953a). Their analysis led them to formulate a model of the DNA molecule as a **double-stranded helical structure**, or what is now known as the Watson-Crick *double helix*. Avery's discovery of transformation in bacteria by DNA prompted Watson and Crick (and a number of other investigators) to look critically at what little was then known (in the early 1950s) about DNA structure. Specifically, they tried to understand how DNA could function as the central informational machinery for **gene replication** and **gene control of cellular functions**. They also sought to explain how DNA could be the basis of **gene mutations** (Tamarin & Leavitt, 1991, pp. 219–222).

The Architecture of DNA

Watson and Crick finally succeeded, after many blind alleys, in building a wire and metal model of the phosphates, sugars, and bases of DNA in correct 3-dimensional relationship to each other (Olby, 1974, pp. 98–99). Their model had two nucleotide chains running in opposite directions, with the bases of each chain on the interior and the two sugar-phosphate backbones on the exterior. A base on one chain is bonded to a base on the other chain by *hydrogen bonding* (that is, the two bases share hydrogen atoms between them). The overall shape of the Watson-Crick model of DNA resembles a ladder whose "rungs" are the so-called *base pairs*. The sides (or, supports) of the ladder are the alternating phosphate-sugar backbones, which are connected to the bases by *covalent bonds*. The DNA ladder is, however, not straight but twisted. Therefore, in three dimensions when upright it resembles a spiral staircase. This shape is technically called a double

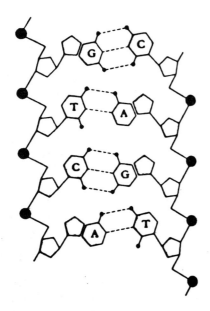

Figure 4.1. The structure of DNA, a schematic, flattened view of the molecule. Adenine (A) pairs only with thymine (T), and guanine (G) pairs only with cytosine (C). The dotted lines represent weak chemical bonds known as *hydrogen bonds*, which hold the two strands of the double helix together. A and T are held together by two hydrogen bonds; G and C, by three. From: *Human Genetics,* by Sam Singer. Copyright © 1985 by W. H. Freeman and Company. Reprinted by permission.

helix. Each specific gene is determined by its particular sequence of base pairs. Thus, these four "letters" (A, T, C, G) can code out an essentially unlimited number of distinct genes (Singer, 1985, pp. 56–60).

Recall that among the DNA bases (A, T, C, and G), the purines A and G are similar in shape and differ only in certain small side groups. Likewise, the pyrimidines T and C are also similar, differing from each other again only in side groups. These variable side groups are crucial to understanding base pairing in DNA. The fact is that the side groups of A are such that A can only "fit" the ladder rung if it is paired with T. A is said to be complementary *only* to T; both are "welded" into the DNA double helix on opposite strands. The same goes for G and C: they can also bond in complementary, dovetailing fashion between the two side strands in DNA. That is, if G is a "jigsaw" piece on one strand of DNA, it can *only* pair up with the complementary piece called C on the opposite strand. Likewise, C on one strand only pairs with G on the other strand. The only four kinds of base pairs between the two strands of the DNA backbone are thus: A:T, T:A, G:C, C:G. If an unaffiliated single strand of DNA existed that had the base sequence

T G C C T A A G C

it could pair up correctly with any available single strand of the complementary base sequence

A C G G A T T C G

but with no other sequence. The Watson-Crick model of DNA, therefore, at once explains Chargaff's experimentally observed rules.

The Genetic Code

Overwhelming experimental evidence has demonstrated that it is the sequence of just these four base-pairs in a DNA molecule that constitutes the chemical code, or message, for all the inherited information in cells. The elucidation of the *genetic code*—which determines the structures and activities of all living cells—is one of the triumphs of modern molecular biology (Watson, Tooze & Kurtz, 1983, pp. 31–44). In fact, one of the best tests of the significance of a scientific discovery is not only its immediate contribution but also its capacity to lead to further discoveries. This test is passed superbly by the Watson-Crick double helix. The deciphering of the genetic code in the 1960s by Marshall W. Nirenberg and H.G. Khorana—for which they shared a Nobel Prize in 1968—was a direct offshoot of the concept of the double helix. There have been a number of other Nobel Prizes awarded in the 1970s and 1980s for work which has contributed to our knowledge of the molecular nature of gene action (including one in chemistry in 1980 to Paul Berg, Walter Gilbert, and Frederick Sanger for their contributions to the experimental manipulation of DNA [see section 5d]). These, too, derive in one way or another from Watson and Crick's momentous 1953 discovery of the structure of DNA.

The helical shape, the sugar-phosphate side supports, the base pairs, and the kinds of bonds holding the overall structure together are common features of DNA in *all* organisms. DNA is common to all animals and plants in the sense that, say, a glucose molecule is the same shape in all organisms in which it is found. But DNA, unlike glucose, *is* different from one gene to the next in the same cell as well as being different from bacteria to pea plants to humans. Its *sole* difference in all these contexts resides in its particular sequence of base pairs for different genetic messages. This is the remarkable significance of the Watson-Crick model of DNA, which is at once beautifully simple and astonishingly versatile (Watson et al., 1987). That model has ushered in a revolution in molecular biology (Cohen, 1985b, pp. 384–385). As with relativity theory, quantum mechanics and some other notable scientific breakthroughs of the twentieth century, we are just beginning to comprehend the magnitude of the potential social implications of the revolution we associate with the names of Watson and Crick.

The story of the other participants in the DNA revolution—particularly Chargaff, Linus Pauling, Rosalind Franklin and Maurice Wilkins—must be skipped over in this brief survey (Stent, 1980, pp. 137–158). Watson's personal account of the discovery, *The Double Helix* (1968), describes in a controversial manner many of the complex social and psychological forces that motivated the various participants in the race to discover DNA's structure. Although biased, Watson's account does reveal the power of ambition and of a sometimes less-than-complete sense of fair play than the public generally recognizes in the pursuit of science (Stent, 1980, pp. 161–234). It remains clear, nonetheless, that the crux of the problem was solved by Watson and Crick. Picking up on Pauling's demonstration of the helical structure in proteins, and on the Wilkins-Franklin suggestion of exterior backbones and two or three helical chains in DNA, Watson and Crick finally put all the pieces of the genetic puzzle together (Crick, 1988).

Technological Revolutions of the Twentieth Century

5

A. Transportation: Railroads, Automobiles and Airplanes

■ ■ ■

Modes of transportation are crucial factors in daily life, local and national activities, and international affairs. Historically, most cities and towns were formed at the crossroads of overland caravan routes, at the strategic confluence of rivers, or at large, protected ports on seaways and oceans (generally as entrepots and trading centers). Almost all the major cities in the world, prior to the Industrial Revolution, have been located on rivers, lakes, and oceans since water transport—particularly waterways for heavy barges—was the principal means of commerce and distance travel. During the Industrial Revolution new modes of transportation challenged, and in some cases replaced, water and animal (including human) locomotion.

Railroads

The railways and international steam-maritime transport were the first technological innovations to revolutionize transport and travel in the nineteenth century (Gille, 1986, vol. 1, pp. 718–720). By 1870 the railways had altered the landscape in most major industrial nations. The effects of the railways were profound. When Alfred Russel Wallace, co-discoverer of the theory of evolution by natural selection (see section 3b), attempted to present a kind of balance sheet of nineteenth-century gains and losses—in his book *The Wonderful Century* (1898)—he cited "railways, which have revolutionized land-travel and the distribution of commodities" as the century's preeminent invention (Wallace, 1898, p. 150). In addition to their economic significance —Chicago's dramatic rise to civic importance, for instance, would scarcely have occurred had it not become a continental rail hub—the railroads exerted powerful social, political and cultural influences (Basalla, 1988, p. 195).

With its coupling of the symbols of speed and power, the railway, in some ways, set the pattern for most subsequent reactions to new technology in the nineteenth century—just as railway legislation set the pattern of legislation for telegraphy and wireless (Wrigley & Shepherd, 1991, p. 70). Railroads compelled the standardization of time and time-keeping with their (generally) rigorous schedules. They helped create and maintain national markets for both labor and produce, as well as for newspapers. The importance of such factors in the development of the modern concept of "the nation" was great. The railroads carried national "culture" as well as commodities (Marcus & Segal, 1989, pp. 96–97). They did much to break down local and regional differences in culture and language. Finally, the railroads allowed fast travel over long distances to an extent never before imaginable. And the effect of improved international maritime transport was hardly less dramatic: during the nineteenth century millions of Europeans were borne across the Atlantic Ocean, primarily to the U.S. and Canada (Bessel, 1989, p. 162).

Steam Railways

As more and more people came to live in large towns, the development of suburban railway services enabled people to live at some distance from their work and travel to and from it by train. This can be seen clearly in the London area, where the railway station in a suburban district provided a focus for housing development in that area. Also of great importance as a symbol of railway building was the construction of London's underground railways, which played a vital part in the swiftly growing passenger traffic of the capital. The first underground railway in the world had been the Metropolitan line opened from Paddington to Farringdon Street in 1863. In 1884, the Inner Circle line—which linked most of the main railway line termini—was opened. Both lines, of course, operated with steam engines with condensing apparatus designed to prevent smoke. In the year in which the Inner Circle was opened, Londoners were making four times as many journeys a year as they had made twenty years earlier. It wasn't until the railways were electrified, however, that daily urban transport was truly revolutionized (Buchanan, 1992, p. 140).

Indeed, horse-drawn transport was by no means eclipsed by the steam railway. It is true that coaches or other road vehicles running in direct competition with trains had no hope of competing with them, but it took time for the railway network to grow. The railways, in fact, by encouraging economic growth, generated short-distance horse-drawn transport to and from railway stations, as well as encouraging local traffic within rural areas. Above all, urbanization was proceeding apace and the rapidly growing towns relied almost wholly upon horse-drawn vehicles for the movement of passengers and goods, apart from London—and even there it is easy to exaggerate the importance of suburban rail services and the Underground until the close of the nineteenth century. Urban transport systems, such as they were, consisted primarily of horse-drawn omnibuses or, later, horse-drawn tramways (street railways), which began to spread in the U.S. during the 1850s, and in Europe and Great Britain in the 1860s and 1870s. Moreover, most people in the closing decades of the nineteenth century, even in the industrializing world, *walked*. They still did most of their moving about on foot and walked to and from work. The horse and the pedestrian remained familiar sights on the roads and streets of Europe and North America (Mathias & Davis, 1990, p. 100). Two technical developments were to radically transform this situation: electrification and the internal combustion engine.

The foundations of the international electrical industry were laid between 1880 and 1900. Electrical energy can be converted into heat, light, and mechanical energy (motion). Nineteenth-century developments in the science of electromagnetism prepared the way for the grand march of practical applications in all three domains. The first appeared with the telegraph and the telephone. It was the electric light which was probably the first *personal* introduction to the public of the marvels which electricity could perform. The mystery attached to such a feat, and the pleasing glow of the lamp, probably sold more lamps in the first months than did any evidence of the commercial significance of electric lighting. Although many contributed to its success, it is Thomas Alva Edison (1847–1931) who is associated in the public mind with electric lighting (Basalla, 1988, pp. 46–49).

Edison, the "Wizard of Menlo Park" (New Jersey), developed the first successful incandescent light in 1879. There is another form of electric lighting, namely, "arc lighting." It, too, was phenomenally successful. It truly lit the streets of late nineteenth-century Europe and North America (Marcus & Segal, 1989, pp. 143–145). But arc lighting is too harsh for smaller-scale places such as the home, office and factory. This is the market Edison brilliantly exploited. But his invention of the incandescent lamp was only the start of Edison's system. He also designed the wiring for houses, the underground cable system for the streets, a meter for measuring the amount of electricity used by the customer, and the details of generating electricity supply. Edison's genius lay in seeing that the commercial success of electric lighting depended equally on the means of its generation, transmission, and distribution (Millard, 1990). This is what is meant by an "innovation" in science or technology, as opposed to an "invention" (or discovery) only. Innovation refers to the first introduction of a new product, process, or system into the ordinary commercial or social activities of a country or region. Invention refers to the first idea, sketch, or contrivance of a new product, process or system (Staudenmaier, 1989, pp. 55–56).

Electric Traction

Edison's incandescent electric light was the sensation of the International Electrical Exhibition in Paris in 1881. Two years earlier, an equally sensational demonstration of the potential of electricity—this time to revolutionize urban transport—had been made at the Berlin Industrial Exhibition. In 1879, Ernst Werner von Siemens (1816–1892) built the first experimental "electric traction" streetcar line, or electric tramway, for the Berlin Exhibition (Gille, 1986, vol. 1, p. 704). Electric traction was the first serious alternative to horsepower in urban transport in the late nineteenth century. It proved more energy efficient, more flexible, cheaper and cleaner than the other alternatives such as steam street railways and cable cars (notably in San Francisco). It thus created the basis for a radically new concept of public transport.

The same electricity which was used increasingly for lighting from the 1870s also provided a new means of transmitting energy to drive motors. With the development of the dynamo—which could convert the mechanical energy of a steam engine (or hydroelectric power source) into electricity—electricity could be distributed from a single point throughout a transport system. It could then be reconverted by a motor (a dynamo operating in reverse) into mechanical energy to drive a tram. For traction purposes—moving a vehicle with a motor—however, a number of problems had to be solved. After various experiments in different parts of the world, including that of Siemens, in 1888 an able American, Frank J. Sprague, managed to provide all the answers at Richmond, Virginia. He demonstrated successfully the overhead trolley, the series/parallel controller and a method of mounting each motor, "wheelbarrow fashion," partly on the axle and partly by springs to the tramcar frame (Cudahy, 1979, pp. 21–22).

The early motors were of low horsepower but they made possible speeds twice as fast as were possible using horses, and were capable of serving longer routes; much faster tramcars were later developed. Lower fares, as well as better services, could be offered. This demonstrated that electric traction could indeed make possible clean, efficient, rapid mechanical forms of transport capable of carrying the masses. It liberated transport companies from the problems and expensive maintenance costs of horses. In so doing, it also made the streets and cities of urban Europe and North America smell much better than they did before (and probably better, and less noxious, than they would later in the twentieth century). Electrification of the tramcars, and the greater profits they offered, attracted American capital, and two large manufacturers eventually emerged—General

Electric and Westinghouse—to mass-produce standardized equipment at low cost. Cuts in journey times and lowering of fares encouraged further outward growth, as electric tramways were built beyond the existing limits of Boston and other American cities (Freeman & Aldcroft, 1988, pp. 155–157).

London's Underground

Electric traction was not limited to surface, urban transport. Electric elevated, underground and suburban railways soon followed. The first underground railway to use electric traction—the tube line between Waterloo Station and the Bank, in London—was opened in 1890. An underground tramway line was opened in Boston in 1897. In New York City, Brooklyn's elevated urban railway lines were fully electrified in 1900, Manhattan's in 1903. The first "subway" line (using a third rail to carry the current to the train rather than an overhead cable) in New York City opened in 1904. In Chicago, which was probably the world's fastest growing city in the last decades of the nineteenth century, electric traction was introduced on the city's elevated railways in 1897.

Electrification of city tramways now forged quickly ahead in many countries (McKay, 1976). Capital flowed into these enterprises, and manufacturing establishments were expanded and new ones launched. The German firm Siemens and Halske, also a principal manufacturer of telegraphic equipment, expanded at home and established branches in England, Austria, Russia, France, Italy, and Belgium. In one year, this firm received inquiries about installations of power and streetcar systems from thirty cities on three continents. By 1902, Siemens' company had more than eighty power systems under construction. The rate of building by all electrical power companies was such that by 1910 every large city in Europe and North and South America had been supplied with electric power for lighting and municipal transportation (Hughes, 1983). The stimulus to the European (particularly German) and North American economies was considerable. Electrification required vast quantities of steel, copper, cables, fabrics, steam engines, and construction materials. It gave work to thousands of men in mines and factories and on the construction sites. The electrical industry, indeed, operated like an enormous motor which moved the global economy forward at an increased speed (Buchanan, 1992, p. 76).

The building of these grandiose urban electric transport systems required great engineering efforts and massive amounts of capital. They also required—and depended for their continued existence upon—the promise of large enough numbers of *regular* passengers to make the projects economically feasible. Building New York City's first underground line (which ran the length of Manhattan), for instance, involved setting up a municipal "Rapid Transit Commission" to finance construction at the (then) enormous cost of nearly $38,000,000. Because of the staggering costs involved, these urban transport networks were often financed by international consortiums. Equally significant, as the size and the scope of the projects grew, so did the role of government, both locally and nationally (Colton & Bruchey, 1987, pp. 23–24). Public transportation, therefore, not only moved the public; it was regulated, if not directly operated, by public (municipal, regional or federal) agencies (Bessel, 1989, pp. 169–170).

Mass Transport Networks

By the turn of the century, the development of mass transport networks based upon the electric tram and railways had changed the face of cities in the industrialized world. It had also profoundly changed the way in which people lived in those industrialized countries (Gille, 1986, vol. 2, pp. 929–930). The most obvious way in which the new urban transport had created a novel daily environment was in the increased, and regular, mobility of people within, and beyond, the confines of the walking city. But there were other consequences of the new transport technology. In England, for example, the creation of a national railway network was one of the preconditions—together with technological changes in printing and the growth in literacy—for the establishment of mass circulation daily newspapers. Before the railway age the circulation of such daily newspapers as had achieved a national reputation was puny by modern standards. The coming of the railways, however, provided an unrivalled opportunity for greatly extending the radius of circulation. Towns and cities hitherto more than a day's coach ride from London could now be served in a few hours and newspapers could be distributed to all but the remotest parts of the realm within the day of publication (Bagwell, 1988, p. 117).

By the beginning of the twentieth century, electrified urban transport systems seemed the technological marvel of the future. As rapid and spectacular as their rise had been, however, the urban electric rail systems were soon eclipsed by an even brighter technological star: the motor car. Motorized buses on rubber wheels also started to attract passengers. By about 1920, the automobile was used for half the journeys made by Americans, with other countries approaching similar high figures for car and bus transport.

To be sure, electric railways and streetcars still continued as important means of urban transport. But they were under increasing pressure from the private car. In fact, today there are very few North American cities in which surface electric streetcars are still used. In the U.S., the only major cities which retain them are Boston and Philadelphia, and in both cases the streetcars go underground in the city center. In Canada, Toronto has an enviable surface electric transport system; its electric trolleys, still widely used, are, however, now somewhat unique in North America. Underground systems (subways), in contrast, still provide essential transport in many major cities worldwide, including Atlanta, Washington D.C., Toronto, Montreal, Paris, Moscow, Tokyo, and, of course, London and New York. For those who could afford them, however, (and even for many who could do so only by making other financial sacrifices) the private automobile exerted an almost irresistible attraction from the start.

Automobiles

As a social device as well as a technological one, the motor car differed fundamentally from the electric tram, the underground line, and the mainline train in a number of important respects. These are: (1) It is flexible. The route it follows is not fixed by rail; (2) It carries its own fuel supply. Moreover, a car's fuel supply can be turned on and off quickly; and (3) It provides *individual*, as opposed to only collective or communal, mechanically-powered transport. The motor car, therefore, provides a freedom to those who have access to it. It was destined to have a social and cultural impact far different from, and possibly more radical than, the electric railways. Car owners were no longer dependent upon where railway or streetcar companies chose to build their lines. They were no longer subjected to the regimentation of the railway timetable. Thus, car owners could travel when and where they wanted to, provided that adequate roads were available and not too congested.

At first, it appeared that electricity—in the form of large batteries carried on the vehicle—would power the car's motor (Marcus & Segal, 1989, p. 208). Electricity, as we have seen, had replaced steam as the prime energy source of industrialization because it was more flexible and versatile. It yielded, moreover, not only power but also heat and light. Compared to the steam engine the electric motor was a convenient miniature: it could be used as a small power plant wherever current was available. For municipal transportation and small workshops, for passenger and freight elevators, and for cranes, hoists, and ventilating systems the electric motor was an ideal power unit. It was, however, not ideal, not even practical, for the automobile. What *did* provide the answer to powering the individual motor car was, of course, the internal combustion engine (Bessel, 1989, p. 174).

Internal Combustion Engine

Internal combustion, itself, was not a new idea. Indeed, the first internal combustion engine was the gun. However, the gun's short, albeit powerful, explosive bursts of energy were not suitable for efficient motorized transport. What was needed was a way to put internal combustion energy to work with a smooth flow of power (Basalla, 1988, p. 198). A French engineer, Jean Etienne Lenoir (1822–1900), received a patent in 1860 for the first (gas) internal combustion engine that possessed practical value and provided the solution to the drawbacks of the electric car. Lenoir's patent was for a "motor worked by hot, expanding air created by the combustion of gas ignited by electricity and capable of replacing steam as a driving force" (Gille, 1986, vol. 1, p. 696). It was a "one-cylinder, two-stroke" engine, similar to the steam engine in this respect (see section 3c). The piston sucked in a mixture of air and illuminating gas for the first stroke. An electric spark then ignited the mixture, and the expanding gases drove the piston through the second stroke. A similar process on the other side then drove the piston back and the whole process recommenced. Lenoir initially used gas as a fuel but soon realized that petrol vapor could be burnt by using a carburetor. His engine was inefficient, however, and plagued by a number of serious technical problems, including frequent overheating which required large amounts of cooling water.

The Lenoir engine, nonetheless, was vigorously promoted as the "answer to steam." Distinguished engineers and professors visited the self-taught Lenoir. They measured the performance of his engine and published popular accounts and thermodyanimc analyses of it. These were picked up by the popular and technical presses of Europe and North America. Some journals confidently predicted that the development of Lenoir's engine would mean the end of the Age of Steam. Its major drawbacks, however, could not be ignored for long (Buchanan, 1992, p. 67). The result was that most Lenoir engines—eagerly purchased with great expectations—were soon scrapped or converted to steam. Lenoir did have one lasting achievement. His invention—and the large-scale technical and advertising campaigns to promote that new technology—stimulated a great deal of serious thought about internal combustion as an alternative to steam. Some of the massive propaganda efforts to introduce technologies today serve similar functions. Once again, we are reminded that it is innovation, not just invention, that is often crucial in the history of science and technology (Pacey, 1983, pp. 157–159).

The commercial history of the gas engine really began in 1876, when a German manufacturer, Nikolaus August Otto (1832–1891), patented a single-cylinder four-cycle engine. Otto's engine was the first "four-stroke" engine, the earliest recognizable ancestor of today's automobile engine. It worked quite differently from the familiar steam engine and the Lenoir engine. It first compressed a controlled mixture of gas and air (petrol was still considered too dangerous to use as a fuel in such an engine), which was then ignited. Instead of the Lenoir "two-stroke" process, in Otto's engine one complete cycle involved four strokes of the piston. These were:

(1) downwards, to draw in the fuel and air mixture through a valve near the top of the cylinder; (2) upwards, to compress the mixture; then after ignition (3) the power stroke downwards; and (4) upwards to expel the burnt gases through another valve. Otto's engine was more efficient than any contemporary steam engine or Lenoir engine, and operated far more smoothly and powerfully (Bessel, 1989, p. 175).

Otto and Langen

The new four-stroke engine of 1876 was a very flexible and versatile type of invention. The cylinders could be horizontal or vertical, large or small, and several cylinders could work on the same shaft, in various configurations. It could also be adapted to various fuels and to a wide variety of applications. Otto's engine proved to be a great commercial success. He had earlier formed a partnership with Eugen Langen, who brought capital and sound business judgment to the enterprise, as well as contacts with the international world of science and business. Together, Otto and Langen represent the same sort of fruitful combination of technical and business talent that made the partnership of Boulton and Watt so significant in the history of the steam engine (see section 3c). Their firm near Cologne (in Germany) quickly prospered as it became the world's largest manufacturer of internal combustion engines. The Otto & Langen company continued to be a fertile source of new talent and new ideas in the field, even as new competitors arrived on the international scene (Basalla, 1988, p. 203).

Within fifteen years of its invention, Otto's engine—or similar versions—was being manufactured in a dozen countries. Scores of competing firms sprang up to offer the same sort of engine to a rapidly expanding market. At the close of the nineteenth century, there were as many as 200,000 such engines in use, mainly in the U.S., England, and Germany. The Otto engines, however, were stationary and extremely heavy. They were thus used in providing power for machine shops, printing presses, pumping stations and similar large-scale operations. For such an engine to be used to drive private vehicles, they would have to be built in much smaller sizes and adapted to a liquid fuel. The only way to make an engine light *and* still powerful enough to drive a car was to make it run faster and more efficiently.

Daimler Engine

The detailed work necessary to develop a reliable small gasoline engine was carried out by many individuals in many countries during the last two decades of the nineteenth century (Gille, 1986, vol. 1, p. 721). Radical improvements were needed in such things as quality of fuel, fuel-air ratio, and timing of ignition. The most significant work was done in Germany in the 1880s, independently by Karl Benz (1844–1929) and Gottlieb Daimler (1834–1900). Both men were experienced professionals, driven by the still seemingly impractical idea of a small fast engine to drive a road vehicle. Interestingly, Daimler had started his career as a production manager for the Otto & Langen firm. When he left in 1882, to devote himself to developing the light fast engine, he took with him an inspired mechanic named Wilhelm Maybach. By 1900, Daimler and Maybach were responsible for the achievements in design, weight reduction, cooling, and carburetion that gave the automobile engine essentially its present form. In particular, it was Maybach who, in 1893, devised the small gasoline carburetor (which produced a fine jet spraying gasoline into the air-stream [being sucked into the cylinder] in precise and controlled amounts) which provided the "portable gas-generating plant" that made the automobile possible (Gille, 1986, vol. 1, p. 698).

The result by 1900 was a four-cylinder high-speed engine capable of 900 to 1,200 revolutions per minute, with an unheard-of weight ratio of 88 pounds per horsepower. Daimler had effectively opened up a field in which the steam engine could not compete. In 1885, Daimler patented his engine in France and his first motorcar in Germany. Six months later Benz of Mannheim also received a patent for a "gas motor driven vehicle." He developed a series of inventions which were equally crucial to the evolution of the motor car. Benz invented the steering system involving a fixed front axle with steerable stub axles, and (in 1899) a gear box for changing speeds. In 1901, the Daimler company unveiled the first of its Mercedes series, which outperformed all competitors in numerous test trials in succeeding years.

France was also an early leader in development of the motorcar, as its nomenclature reminds us—automobile, chassis, carburetor, limousine, etc. The French inventor and designer Emile Levassor developed the arrangement of units and driving mechanism that became standard in all motorcars—the engine cradled in the frame, the friction clutch, transmission, and power train. Levassor and his partner, the Parisian engineer René Panhard, acquired the right to use the Daimler patents in France in 1889. They completely reorganized their factory to concentrate on the production of automobiles. Two years later, their firm, Panhard et Levassor, began building its own cars in France. The firm of Peugeot also produced a car with a Daimler engine. The early history of the automobile, in fact, saw technology flow freely between countries as inventors sought to exploit or protect their patents by licensing them abroad (Ville, 1990, p. 175). In 1894, a Paris newspaper organized a trial run for motor vehicles of all kinds—steam, electric, gasoline—from Paris to Rouen and return. More than a hundred vehicles started , but only fifteen completed the race; all the best performers were gasoline-powered with Daimler engines. Organized automobile clubs and annual motorcar shows in principal French cities also served to propagandize this novel and seductive symbol of the age of technology. Even more so than the railway, the automobile seemed to answer to a deep-seated human desire for rapid mobility and an exhilaration in speed and power. The dominance of the automobile in the western way of life is not due to blind economic or technical imperatives, but rather to the fact that its usefulness is complemented by these two very considerable satisfactions (Pacey, 1983, p. 84).

Although Britain had pioneered the development of the steam locomotive, she lagged behind Germany and France in the development of motor transport. One of the main reasons for this was the existence, before 1896, of antiquated ordinances that prohibited self-powered vehicles on public roads. In addition, in many respects the British engineering industry was ill-equipped to meet the new challenge of motor-car manufacture at the start of the twentieth century (see section 3c). It was certainly less appropriately organized to this end than were its counterparts in Europe and the United States. The individual family firm still dominated the British scene. In the manufacture of motor cars as in the earlier manufacture of steam locomotives, individuality of design and excellence of workmanship was rated higher than the achievement of quantity production and cheapness (Bagwell, 1988, pp. 187, 192). Even as the use of the automobile spread in the first years of the twentieth century—Britain had the largest number of registered motor vehicles in Europe at the start of World War I—it remained largely the preserve of the wealthier classes. It was, to a large degree, fashionable to own a private motor car in Britain (Richardson, 1977). It was across the Atlantic, in the United States—where the utilitarian aspect of the automobile was emphasized from the outset—that the modern motor industry received its strongest encouragement.

Ford's Model T

Although the car made its appearance in the United States somewhat later than in Europe, it found a technological and cultural environment there ready to embrace it. The first motor car in North America was the "gas buggy" driven by the Duryea Brothers in Springfield, Massachusetts, in 1893. Another American engineer developing gasoline-fuelled cars at the time was Ransom E. Olds. He was the first mass-producer of motor cars (18,000 in 1901–1905), basing the early models of the "Oldsmobile" on a single-cylinder engine. Today, such engines are used in millions for driving light motor cycles, lawn-mowers, chain-saws, and a wide range of small machines. For motor cars, however, four cylinders were usual, as in the elegant Mercedes and the famous Model T Ford, which was to make motoring universally popular. The larger number of cylinders made for smoother running, and for more expensive models the principle was extended to six-, eight-, or even twelve- and sixteen- cylinder engines (Williams, 1982, pp. 158–159). But it was Ford's Model T which revolutionized automobile transport.

Originally a chief engineer for the Edison Illuminating Company in Detroit, Henry Ford built his first car in 1896. When the Ford Motor Company introduced its Model T car in 1908, its price was only $850. It was a serviceable, though hardly elegant, vehicle adapted to the vast network of rough country roads (Basalla, 1988, p. 202). The lesson that Ford taught America was quickly learned: the "auto" was a useful thing and something for everyone to own.

There are two important points which emerge from this consideration of the initial reception which greeted the private automobile at the start of the twentieth century. First, it reminds us that any invention of itself, no matter how brilliant, will never spread through society automatically. If it is novel, it must challenge many existing prejudices, both individual and social. New inventions or discoveries—in science as well as technology—generally must confront initial skepticism and/or opposition because they are new (Basalla, 1988, p. 143). Thus, the first automobiles were visualized as "horseless carriages," taking over all the conventional features of existing road vehicles except their motive power. Some inventions, like the typewriter, have been so novel that they have had to struggle to establish a regular form. In the case of the typewriter, once its form became established, the typewriter keyboard became a familiar feature of many later inventions—such as the computer (Buchanan, 1992, p. 200). Secondly, if a new invention does become adopted in a given society, it requires a network of supporting structures to ensure its wider use. Innovation—this transformation of a new technical or scientific concept (or process or device) into an accepted part of everyday social or industrial activity—requires a certain degree of political, economic, psychological, as well as practical restructuring of society. If those supporting structures are developed, then the invention will become an integral part of the social fabric. In doing so, certain inventions will alter that fabric considerably, even to the point of completely changing aspects of the social order (Reingold, 1991, p. 143). It was Henry Ford and his Model T which, more than anything else, created the modern —and revolutionary—social role for the automobile. Quite apart from its function in transport, Ford's Model T *created* a mass market for automobiles. To accomplish this, Ford (in 1913) introduced a moving assembly line. By this novel method, mass-produced components were put together to produce motor cars far more rapidly, economically and efficiently than hitherto had seemed possible. As a result of his new production methods, Ford was able to continually lower the price of his car: in 1924, its price reached a low of $295. By the time its production was halted finally, in 1927, 15 million Model T Fords had been sold—a record which stood until surpassed by the Volkswagen Beetle in the 1970s (Bessel, 1989, p. 177). Ford had opened up a new, truly mass, market and ultimately brought motoring within the reach of millions of people. Mass production methods also meant that a wide range of consumer products could now be provided in great quantity and with high quality. It is clear that the Ford style of mass-produced automobiles influenced, indeed altered, the whole structure of American society for decades. More and more people came to depend on the giant Detroit auto companies for employment, either directly or indirectly. The automotive influence—a technological innovation—spread to such related businesses as gas stations, motels, insurance companies, and drive-in stores (Staudenmaier, 1989, p. 196).

The Car Culture

Thus, the phenomenal success of mass-produced and mass-purchased motor vehicles in the 1920s and 1930s was as momentous a social revolution as it was a technological revolution. It effects are now felt worldwide (Flink, 1988). They include: (1) Many people have greater choice about where they can live, work, shop or spend their leisure time than ever before in history; (2) Urban housing markets have altered significantly. The rise of new suburban areas became possible as access by car became commonplace. Los Angeles is perhaps the most famous example of a city built by the automobile; (3) Travel on public transport systems has declined in many places, as people turned to the car to drive to work daily or to shop. In this sense, the automobile has not only replaced public transport for many. It has replaced walking; (4) With better roads and access to motor cars, the rural population—and rural society generally—became far less isolated than it had been; (5) Regional trading and shopping centers were able to draw customers on a regular basis from a much wider area. Shopping was no longer so geographically restricted and the nature of modern retailing began to change correspondingly. The suburban shopping plaza is a creation of the automobile (Jackson, 1985); (6) The motor car has ceased to be regarded as a luxury and has come to be seen increasingly as a necessity. (Relatively) cheaper car prices and the advent of the closed (and therefore all-weather) car in 1923 fundamentally changed the character and appreciation of private-car ownership. As a result, general private consumption patterns have altered considerably. Individuals and families now often devote considerable portions of their incomes to private motorized transport; finally, (7) People also managed to use their cars to kill and maim one another with increasing frequency. In the early days, with inexperienced drivers and often unreliable vehicles, the casualties were horrendous. In America at the beginning of the 1920s, one motorist in seven was involved annually in an accident which caused injury or death. The number of accidents in developing countries is particularly high in relation to vehicle registration (Barker, 1985, p. 15).

The revolution in transportation associated with motor vehicles, especially the private automobile, has had equally far-reaching impacts on the environment. Automobile ownership is practically universal in the U.S. and Canada and many other industrialized nations. Beyond the necessity factor, the automobile's popularity is due in part to the tremendous amount of freedom it gives the user. Perhaps no other technological innovation gives people at every socioeconomic level the power to overcome natural restraints on mobility. To appreciate this power, one need only reflect on the fact that we can travel at high speeds through some of the worst kinds of terrain in driving rainstorms, swirling blizzards, or intense heat. If a car has air and heat conditioning, this can be done at a comfortable temperature with stereo music, isolated from the external environment.

Pollution Problems

The price we pay, however, is high. Even if credit and the payment-by-installment options ease the monthly burden upon an individual or family, the "cost" to our environment is still enormous. For many years, pollution by automobiles has increased faster than the number of automobile miles travelled. Various design changes are responsible for this. Escalation in the power of internal combustion engines in the 1950s and 1960s was achieved through engineeering breakthroughs based on increases in engine displacement and in the compression of the gasoline-air mixture before ignition. While these technological advances result in more power per stroke, they also result in higher combustion temperatures and, consequently, greater quantities of nitrogen oxides and other pollutants.

In 1990, there were more than 500 million registered motor vehicles (cars and trucks) in the world, with close to 700 million projected by the year 2000 (*Scientific American,* 1990, p. 64). Three out of four of the world's motor vehicles are in North America and Europe. In the U.S., the car is now used for more than 90% of all urban transportation and more than 80% of all travel between cities. The figures approach similar—if not quite as high—levels in many other industrialized countries. The reduction in VIA rail service (announced in October 1989) in Canada typifies this trend. (It should be noted, however, that certain countries in Western Europe are beginning, at least tentatively, to attempt to reverse this trend.) In 1985 almost two-thirds of all Americans travelled to and from work *alone* in their own cars, with an average annual cost of $1,300 per person. Indeed, there is a strong incentive for an owner to use his/her car as frequently as possible so as to amortize its initial cost over a wide range of uses (Oppenheimer & Boyle, 1990, p. 116). It must be stressed, however, that in addition to their undoubted advantages, cars and trucks have increasingly cumulative harmful effects on human lives and on air, water, and land resources.

By providing almost unlimited mobility, automobiles and highways have been a major factor in urban sprawl, stimulating most North American cities to become decentralized and dispersed. The world's cars and trucks also kill more than 150,000 people, maim 500,000, and injure 10 million each year. Vast tracts of land are taken up by automobile traffic and parking. Roads and parking take up more than 60% of the total land area in Los Angeles and more than one-third of New York City (Miller, 1988, pp. 176–177). Similar figures apply to other major urban areas. Instead of reducing auto congestion, the recent emphasis on private as opposed to mass transit, particularly in North America, has compounded pollution problems. It has been argued that Americans abdicated control of their transportation policy in the middle decades of the twentieth century in favor of the economic agenda of the big automotive companies and their allies. In so doing, public mass transit was seriously weakened and the U.S. became almost totally reliant on the private automobile—with devastating pollution consequences (Thompson, 1991, p. 265). Internationally, cities such as Mexico City, Caracas (Venezuela) and Cairo (Egypt) have been forced to restrict severely the use of private motor cars. The full implications of the technological revolution created by mass ownership of private motor cars are still to be worked out (Mander, 1991, pp. 43–44).

Private vs. Public Transport

One point is clear. The private automobile must become a prime focus for society's efforts to deal with certain aspects of the environmental crisis. Just as the advanced industrial nations consume a disproportionately large share of the world's resources (see section 7g), so do they contribute a disproportionately large share of air pollution associated with motor vehicles. The U.S., for instance, with about only 5% of the world's population (1985) has about 35% of the world's total number of motor vehicles (cars and trucks). Compounding this problem is the fact that developing nations—in their desire to overcome massive debt and to become financially independent—are largely ignoring air quality and other environmental problems. The pollution emanating from their smaller number of automobiles per capita, therefore, may still constitute a major addition to global environmental impact owing to less stringent air quality regulations (Bridgman, 1990, p. 214).

A comparison of the various modes of transportation of people and commercial goods shows that motor vehicles account for most of the miles traveled. Far more passenger miles are traveled by automobile than by airplane. Automobiles account for nearly 90% of the miles traveled by people in the industrial countries. Airplanes garner a modest 9%. Each year, for example, Americans fly an average of nearly 600 miles per person in airplanes, ride about 150 miles per person in buses and trains, and travel about 120 miles on average on inland waterways. They travel an average of more than 6000 miles per person in automobiles. Similar relative percentages apply in many other industrialized nations. What this suggests is that the automobile is an obvious target in our battle to come to grips with our energy problems, particularly those relating to air pollution (Horton & Compton, 1984, pp. 587–593).

Human-generated air pollution sources can be divided into *mobile* and *stationary* sources. Mobile sources are automobiles, buses, trains, airplanes, and other fossil fuel-powered modes of transportation. Stationary sources include factories, power plants and various types of incinerators (such as those used in waste disposal). There is a practical reason for making such a division. It has to do with the differences in the pollution control problems presented by these two categories. Mobile sources tend to be much smaller, much more plentiful, and much more widely dispersed—and are therefore much more difficult to monitor than stationary sources.

Automobiles and trucks (highway vehicles) are the main mobile source problem with respect to air pollution. As one illustration of this, it is known that cars and trucks emit about six times as much pollution as railroads to carry the same load (of passengers or freight). Overall, highway vehicles generate roughly 10 times more air pollutants than other mobile sources (including air planes). Disregarding the relative *toxicity* of pollutants, automobiles alone produce about 2/3 of the *weight* of air pollutants that are generated by humans. This fraction can reach 90% in certain North American cities. As one example, automobiles continue to contribute most of the hundreds of thousands of tons of lead that are introduced into the earth's atmosphere each year. The average U.S. automobile also emits its own weight in CO_2 each year, a staggering 200 million tons per year for the country (Wyman, 1991, p. 261).

We have examined the reasons for the phenomenal success story of the private automobile in the twentieth century. The virtues and attractions of the private motor car are undeniable. Indeed, the appeal of the "freedom factor" is one of the major reasons why many people do not use less energy-intensive forms of transportation, like buses and bicycles. It seems inevitable, however, that buses, bicycles, and trains will have to assume an increasingly important role in the years ahead as the energy situation gets tighter and, especially, more expensive. Despite some discouraging trends at present, which place even greater emphasis on private motor cars (at least in North America), it seems fairly clear that the social role of the private automobile is now being reexamined (Lane, 1984).

A great truth may be emerging from the relatively poor results, thus far, of efforts to lure people away from their cars and onto buses and trains: nothing beats the private automobile in terms of convenience. Perhaps the solution to the problems created by the very success of the automobile lies in reversing some of the factors which facilitated this grand technological revolution in the first place. By making the private car less attractive—with such measures as sharply higher taxes, insurance and license fees, and severely limited parking options (including banning parking in some urban areas completely)—society may be able to reduce the negative environmental impact of this particular technology.

There are indications, also, that the development of highly fuel efficient prototypes by some European manufacturers (such as Volkswagen's VW E80 and Volvo's LCP 2000) may offer the prospect of emissions reduction (Eastwood, 1991, p. 31). Perhaps the most intriguing alternative to new cars or efficient cars is a new paradigm altogether: no cars, or at least less driving. Before dismissing this option out of hand, recall that most of the world has not yet been brought into the automotive culture completely. The United States' ratio of one car for every two people dwarfs India's ratio of one car for every 500 people, or China's ratio of about one car for every 1,000. The U.S. has developed a monoculture in transportation, and an entire socioeconomic framework has grown around it. The structure is extremely rigid. The car has no direct competitor so it can not be excised easily. The key to reducing dependence on the automobile is the gradual restoration of transport flexibility. Perhaps fortunately for China, India, and other Third World countries, their societies are in rapid transition but have not yet congealed around the private motor car (Oppenheimer & Boyle, 1990, pp. 126–127).

Airplanes

The airplane affects the lives of millions of people today. In some countries, such as the U.S. and Canada, air transport has almost completely replaced the railways as the chief means of long-distance travel. Air travel has largely supplanted ocean liners as the chief means of intercontinental journeys. In some areas of the world, such as remote parts of northern Canada and Siberia, air transport provides the major, sometimes the only, link between major settlements and the outside world. Of all the major transportation revolutions of the twentieth century, the development of the airplane owed most to military demands and the pressures of war, particularly World Wars I and II (Hallion, 1984).

At first, it seemed that the airplane might compete with the new motor car as the preferred means of personal transport. Many of those who were fully in the stream of scientific and technological optimism during the first decades of the twentieth century thought that soon they would have a "flying machine" that would carry them through the air as the automobile carried them over the roads. During the peak years of America's infatuation with aviation (1900–50), for example, there was much speculation about a family flying machine similar in price, safety, and reliability to the family car. For the new suburbanite this might mean an airplane in every garage. For the city dweller, some enthusiasts envisioned a helicopter on every apartment rooftop.

The engines developed for the motorcar, with their relatively high ratio of power to weight, made powered flight a realistic goal. This dream of a personal flying machine came close to realization in 1926 when Henry Ford began to manufacture an airplane that some called the "Ford flying flivver." In the 1930s, the U.S. Federal Bureau of Air Commerce made its contribution to this fad by financing the design of prototype aircraft that it hoped would be mass-produced like automobiles. One of these, the "Plymacoupe," was powered by a Plymouth automobile engine.

The dream of a private "air car" for the ordinary person, as we know, did not materialize. Personal aircraft remains an expensive, hazardous, and inconvenient means of travel compared with the automobile. Since World War II, people did take to the skies in increasing numbers—but not in privately owned planes. They fly as passengers in large aircraft, piloted and maintained by the professional crews of big corporations, both public and private (Basalla, 1988, p. 181).

Early Attempts

Although effective human flight became possible only in our own century, manned flight is not a new thing. During the Renaissance, the Italian scholar-artist Leonardo da Vinci (1452–1519) composed remarkable sketches of flying machines, for both powered and free flight (Hart, 1985, pp. 94–113). The first person to actually go aloft did so in a Montgolfier balloon in 1783. The Montgolfier brothers, Etienne and Joseph, were products of the Enlightenment (see section 2d). They had a remarkable vision of the technical and commercial potential of the future of aviation (Gillispie, 1983, p.87). The first successful human-carrying glider took flight in 1809. And the first trip in a motor-powered lighter-than-air craft was made near Paris in 1852, with a steam engine driving an airship. But the development of air transport into something that could alter people's everyday lives came somewhat later.

Already by the middle of the nineteenth century a great deal was known about the science of aerodynamics. The main design features necessary for airborne stability had been established, primarily through the work of Sir George Cayley (d. 1857), who was the first to fully understand the need for separation of the systems of lift and propulsion. He calculated, for example, the power required to achieve a given load and speed. The problem was how to power a flying machine. No engine then available had a sufficiently high power:weight ratio to make controlled flight possible (Williams, 1982, p. 260). What was required was a powerful but relatively lightweight engine—one that had a sufficient power-to-weight ratio to drive an aircraft without adding so much weight as to prevent it from getting and remaining aloft. As with the automobile, the solution was the gasoline-powered internal combustion engine developed in the 1880s, and patented by Daimler in 1889. Indeed, this development proved even more decisive for air transport than for motorized road transport. For, unlike the case of motor cars, which have also been powered by steam and electricity, mechanically powered air travel in heavier-than-air machines would have been impossible without the development of some form of reliable internal combustion engine (Bessel, 1989, pp. 191–192). Once these two separate lines of development met, powered flight became not only feasible, but inevitable. It was not until 17 December 1903, however, that the Wright brothers made their first historic flight at Kitty Hawk, North Carolina. Orville flew the aircraft from its launching ramp for the first gasoline-driven controlled flight in history. It lasted just twelve seconds.

The Wright Brothers

By the close of the nineteenth century, a number of pioneers had made significant scientific and practical contributions to the design of a heavier-than-air-machine that could take off, land, and be steered in the air. In 1900, the two active centers of interest and experimentation were Dayton, Ohio—where the bicycle makers Wilbur and Orville Wright were experimenting with gliders—and Paris, where an active Aero Club was sponsored and supported by many of the same men who were promoting the automobile industry. Free ballooning was a popular sport, and

French technologists and inventors fully expected that powered flight would also be a French achievement. In the event, although the automobile was Europe's gift to the United States, the airplane was America's first spectacular technological gift to Europe.

How the Wright brothers built and experimented with gliders and then proceeded to powered flight in 1903 has become a folk legend (Bilstein, 1984, pp. 10–17). Their patient and persistent work yielded high returns. They did everything the Europeans neglected. They built experimental gliders and thoroughly mastered the technique of flying them; they studied the principles of the air screw and built experimental propellers; they first used borrowed engines but finally constructed their own. After building several models the Wrights were able to make sustained circular flights of 20 minutes' duration at a height of 300 feet. Concerned about patents and the material rewards of their invention, the Wrights were quite secretive about their experimental flights. When press reports of their achievements began to appear, they gave up flying entirely between 1905 and 1908.

Rumors of their accomplishments were thus received skeptically in Europe—especially in France, where interest in flying was greatest and where numerous experimental machines were being constructed and tested. These were of all kinds, ranging from machines with some possibilities of flight to the utterly fantastic. However, the techniques and mechanisms of flight control developed by the Wrights were not understood or applied by the French pioneers. None of them became experienced glider pilots; they attempted to go direct to powered flight and they failed. They thought of the airplane rather as a machine which could simply be powered through the air and steered like an automobile or a motorboat.

In 1908, the Wrights made their first public flights, ending all doubts about their claims and achievements (Jakab, 1990). Wilbur made the first European flight at Le Mans, France on August 8; Orville gave the first public demonstration in the United States at Fort Meyer, Virginia, in September. What the spectators witnessed was amazing. They saw the Wrights take off, bank, circle, and return to the point of departure. Wilbur and Orville flew like birdmen, rather than as drivers of a powerful motorcar. In the spring of 1909, demonstrations were made in Rome, and in September-October Orville Wright made a series of flights in Berlin. The Crown Prince of Prussia was an eager passenger on one of the flights, and the Kaiser spoke enthusiastically about the possible military uses of the new invention.

While the Wright brothers' achievements in the United States faded into a welter of lawsuits over patents, European designers worked to put their revelations as to construction and control into practice, achieving now steady improvement. By 1909, with Louis Bleriot's flight across the English channel, the airplane can be said to have established itself as a viable practical invention.

Although the general public still viewed flying as too much of a novelty to be taken seriously, the world was well launched into the air age (Marcus & Segal, 1989, pp. 247–249). This early public cynicism may have stemmed from the flamboyant character of aviation at the time. As sensational mechanical contraptions, "aeroplanes" received their first wide public exposure as star attractions in aerial shows that featured various flying stunts. The attendant ballyhoo and publicity propagated the notion that airplanes were hazardous and their pilots were daredevils or fools.

Military Aviation

Once aircraft were flying it became logical to think of other forms of flight. Recall that during the first Scientific Revolution some three centuries earlier (see section 2c), as people were groping toward an understanding of the moon's motion in the heavens, the theoretical possibility of reaching the moon became a dream, explicitly stated by Kepler in 1609–1610. The rockets used by European armies in the first half of the nineteenth century provided an obvious model for technological visionaries in the first decades of the twentieth century. In Germany as early as 1923, Hermann Oberth published a book on rockets in space. He developed the theory of rocket propulsion and designed a spacecraft to be propelled by liquid fuel. This inspired the formation of a society for the promotion of space travel in 1927 (Neufeld, 1990). Two years later, this society was joined by a very keen member—a teenager named Werner von Braun. He became an active participant in the space society's very serious experimental work on rockets. When these were taken over by the German army in 1932, he chose to work for the army, because building weapons seemed to be the only available "stepping stone" into space. As is well known, the culmination of the army program was the V-2 rocket used to bombard British cities toward the end of World War II. After the first successful flight of V-2 in 1942, von Braun seemed to forget the war completely and enthused: "We have invaded space with our rockets for the first time. . . we have proved rocket propulsion practicable for space travel." In 1969, it was rockets designed by von Braun and his team, now working in America for the Apollo program, which made possible the first landing of men on the moon (Pacey, 1990, p. 175).

Closer to earth, both conceptually and practically, military and civilian interests between the two world wars conspired to make the airplane an integral part of the emerging global science/technology network. Armies and navies in many countries became interested in the airplane's possibilities as a military weapon. This in turn led to improvements in design and performance. In 1912, in Britain, the Royal Flying Corps was founded. In the first year of World War I (1914), aircraft were increasingly used for reconnaissance, though crews carried revolvers and rifles and dropped small bombs over the side of the plane. This led to the development of small, fast single-engined fighter planes by Britain, France and Germany. Larger multi-engined aircraft, with enclosed fuselages (carrying crew and cargo), were developed for use as bombers. Both types of craft contributed to significant peacetime technological developments of airplanes. In 1919, the British Royal Air Force operated a regular Hendon-Paris service, carrying delegates and mail to and from the Peace Conference. The French opened the first civilian international service, flying paying passengers between Paris and London in converted bombers.

Airplanes at this time were normally built with wooden frames which were covered with a treated fabric. The first all metal airplane was built by a German firm in 1915 for flight during the War. Nicknamed the "flying tank," it was the model for the first all metal civilian aircraft flown by a German airline in 1919. Just after the end of World War I, a number of long-distance flights were made. Pilots flying over deserts and oceans pioneered the way for later civil airlines flying with regular services over worldwide routes (Hudson, 1983, pp. 84–85). In 1919, the first nonstop flights across the Atlantic were made in wartime bomber types of planes. Within ten years, an American, Richard E. Byrd, had flown over the North Pole (1926), Charles Lindbergh had flown solo across the Atlantic from New York to Paris (1927), and the Pacific was crossed (from the United States to Australia). Finally, in 1931, the American Wiley Post flew around the world taking eight and three-quarter days. This episode dazzled public and press alike, and photos of Post, with his rakish eye patch, proliferated in tabloids across America. All these flights helped to demonstrate the reliability of the airplane over long distances. Commercial air services were established in many countries during the 1920s (Buchanan, 1992, pp. 152–153).

Civilian Aviation

The two countries that took a clear lead in civilian aviation during the 1920s and 1930s were Germany and the United States. German civil aviation benefited from the attentions of a government which had been prohibited, by the peace settlements of World War I, from developing military aviation. In the U.S., there were different reasons for success. The U.S. did not have a state airline, but because of its vast size there was a large potential market for airmail and passenger services (where air travel held clear advantages in time-saving over rail travel). Private airlines were able to expand rapidly, which in turn provided the demand for the development of new, larger, twin-engine, all-metal passenger airplanes. Companies like Boeing, Douglas, and Lockheed grew into the international giants they are today in part because of the orders for new passenger aircraft placed (first) by the large U.S. commercial carriers and, later, by airlines of other countries (Fearon, 1985, p. 31).

Since World War II, which witnessed a massive use of aircraft for military purposes, civilian aviation has continued to develop. Within a decade after the war, the airlines were boarding millions of passengers per year, in contrast to the mere thousands of the 1930s. From Presidents to vacationers, the speed and intercontinental reach of air travel introduced revolutionary changes in the cultural habits of the population, making air travel commonplace (Bilstein, 1984, pp. 174–177). Related developments in modern navigational technology (e.g., radio, radar, and direction finding apparatus) have enabled modern aircraft to fly day and night, in bad weather conditions, and at considerable heights, often above cloud cover. Sophisticated equipment now controls the landing automatically, permitting even greater reliability. Air travel today constitutes an integral part of the commercial transportation networks of most industrialized countries. Certain cities, such as Atlanta and Dallas in the U.S., have assumed major new importance because they are hubs of such aviation networks—as cities like Crewe developed rapidly as railway hubs in the nineteenth century. Airplanes have made the transition from technological oddity to social necessity relatively quickly. To be sure, this remarkable technological transformation of passenger transport has not been without its problems. Travel to and from airports on congested roads sometimes exceeds the time spent in the air itself. Airport security has become a matter of increasing domestic and international anxiety. And the financial status of airline companies causes major economic concern in most of the advanced industrial nations (Gille, 1986, vol. 2, p. 935).

Taken together, the railroad, the automobile, and the airplane constitute an utterly epoch-making transformation in the way people travel and live. In a deep sense, they characterize industrial society. But the twentieth century revolution in technology had its origins in the nineteenth century:

> Railways, together with steam-powered transport generally, developed much less as specified responses to the evolving transport demands of an industrial society, but rather as *manifestations* and *agencies* of much more fundamental social transformations, using the word *social* in its widest possible meaning. . . . Reservoirs of capital, accumulated from the first phases of industrialism, literally flooded in the wake of railway promotions [which] fired imaginations: the steam railway was an early and major representative of Victorian society's increasing fascination with mechanical contraptions. Once established, the railway became an agent of its own success.

To the surprise of many, it transformed travel into a consumer good in a way never known before . . . .Both railway and steamship played up to the symbol of progress that their intrinsic forms expressed. In a sense, the railway and the steamship were creating a world after their own image.

(Freeman and Aldcroft, 1988, pp. 30–31)

At the close of the twentieth century, we are still playing out the consequences of the industrial revolution in transport. ■

B. Microelectronics: Computers and Communications
Part I: Theory

■ ■ ■

The evolution of electronic technology over the past two decades has been so rapid that it represents yet another scientific revolution. Furthermore, the cultural impact of electronic technology—particularly in the form of computers—on social and economic change has been profound (Friedrichs & Schaff, 1982, pp. 273–274). Enough so, in the opinion of many observers, to warrant calling the period since the early 1970s a Second Industrial Revolution. Because many of the new major applications involve various kinds of computers, it is easy to gain the impression that the microelectronics revolution and computers are synonymous. As crucial as they are, however, computers are only a part of the broader transformation effected by electronics. Equally fundamental to many of the inventions which are changing the way we live as well as the way we think are the transducers or sensors. Transducers include the various devices or substances—such as photoelectric cells—that convert input energy of one form into output energy of another form. In fact, without electronic devices for sensing temperature, concentrations of chemical components, or various kinds of pressures, for example, computers would be of far more limited use than they actually are. They would not be able to exercise many of the control functions they presently do in various industrial processes. Clearly, microelectronics has inaugurated a new era in humanity's relationship to its machines (Turkle, 1985, pp. 271–305).

Early Computing Devices

Previously, machines functioned in essentially a physical manner. They harnessed energy, produced power, and acommplished physical work. The steam engine, the dynamo, the internal combustion engine, and the nuclear reactor all serve to augment the *physical* power available to people. In so doing, all these mechanical devices radically transformed our relationship to our environment. Microelectronic devices and computers are, however, radically different kinds of machines. They process and produce *information.* Specifically, computers now undertake work once performed only by the human brain (Dertouzos & Moses, 1979, pp. 190–191).

Humans, of course, have often created and used numerous devices to aid them in the formation and processing of data. Human history, in many respects, is the record of increasingly sophisticated mechanical inventions to aid our species in adapting to both its internal and external environments. In one sense, at least, "computers" have always been with us. When early humans first used their fingers and toes—then stones and notched sticks—to count, a revolution in human behavior was made possible. The Babylonian invention of place-value notation more than 3000 years ago, increased tremendously the potential use of numbers (Taton, 1963, p. 90). Counting with pebbles, called "calculi" in Greek, led to the invention of the abacus. In the seventeenth century, the slide rule was invented. An adding and subtracting machine, based on a gear mechanism, was invented by the French mathematician and philosopher Blaise Pascal (1623–1662). All of these mechanical inventions, however, required *constant human* intervention during their operation. It was the brilliant work of the British mathematician Charles Babbage (1791–1871), on his "calculating engines" during the period from 1812 to 1823, which prepared the way for the modern electronic computer. For Babbage had conceived of a computational device that would operate (to a limited degree only, in his time) *independently* of humans (Eames, 1990, pp.12–13).

Babbage's Analytical Engine

As a thinker living during the First Industrial Revolution in nineteenth-century Great Britain, Babbage was captivated by the potential of machine-power. He asked himself whether machines might not perform mathematical operations automatically. The French engineer Joseph Marie Jacquard (1752–1834) had earlier used punched cards to control textile machinery. Inspired by Jacquard's innovation in weaving, Babbage quickly saw the possibility of using such cards to code quantities and operations in an automatic computing system (Hyman, 1982, p. 166). His notion was to have sprung feeler wires that would actuate levers when card holes allowed them access. On this basis, he drew up plans for a machine of enormous vesatility and mathematical power. Especially remarkable was his incorporation of decision-making units of the logical type used in today's computers. Babbage also had a forward-looking view of science as an essential part of both culture and industrial civilization. He was among the first to argue that national governments have an obligation to support scientific and engineering activities, to help promising inventors, and to give scientists a broader role in public affairs (Hyman, 1982, pp. 122, 223–224) [see section 3a]. Ironically, financial support for Babbage's own invention, the "analytical engine," was not forthcoming, and it remained a "paper project" (Weinberg, 1990, p. 21). The advent of sophisticated electronics in the twentieth century was destined to change all that.

The early changes brought about by the electronics revolution were quite extraordinary, although they now seem commonplace. The telephone, which we take for granted, was invented more than 100 years ago. Nearly every decade since then, the quality and scope of service have steadily improved. Equally significant, the cost of telephone service (measured in constant dollars) is now but a fraction of what it was 50 years ago. Numerous other applications of electronics gradually, but dramatically, affected more and more individuals and permeated almost every aspect of society. Radio was a marvellous toy and a source of wonderment when it was introduced slightly more than 50 years ago. Now, North Americans listen to commercial radio an average of four hours daily, and radio is accepted as practically a natural phenomenon. Similarly, television created quite a stir when it was introduced about 30 years ago. Needless to say, it is an integral part of life in most industrial societies today (Martin, 1988, p. 11).

As rapid as developments in electronics have been during the twentieth century, it is the decade of the 1980s that witnessed the most striking advances. To understand the present significance and potential impact of this Second Industrial Revolution, some historical background is essential. It is the application of electronics—specifically *microelectronics*—to information processing that constitutes the core of the computer revolution (Friedrichs & Schaff, 1982, pp. 121–123, 190). As we have noted, prior to computers, machines transformed physical energy, to produce different types of work. The computer, however, processes and produces *information*.

Unlike previous machines, the computer can undertake work once performed only by the *brain*. It is this ability of computers to process, analyze and, now, create information that is the crux of the radical transformation now taking place in the workplace, the office, the factory and in most other aspects of economic, cultural, political and military activity. We are in the midst of a technological change that seems destined, for better or worse, to alter the very fabric of our lives (Nora & Minc, 1980, p. 129).

The world's first electronic digital computer, Colossus, was built in 1943 at Britain's secret wartime code-breaking center, Bletchley Park. Ten such machines were built, with the express purpose of reading German messages passed through their supposedly uncrackable code machine, Enigma. Throughout the rest of the war, the German high command continued to use Enigma, blissfully unaware that British intelligence was listening in. Some historians credit these computers with providing part of the reason for the Allied defeat of Nazi Germany (Hodges, 1984, pp. 198, 237). As with the first use of atomic energy (see section 6a), the first dramatic demonstration of the computer's practical utility was related to military applications.

ENIAC

At the same time, researchers at the University of Pennsylvania were working on a machine that could do more than just crack codes. John Mauchly and J. P. Eckert developed an "Electronic Numerical Integrator and Calculator," more commonly known as ENIAC. When finally switched on in 1946, ENIAC was capable of making the thousands of calculations per minute needed to assess the performance of new guns and missiles. (One version was later used in the development of the hydrogen bomb.) ENIAC's 9-ft.-high metal cabinets, bristling with dials, wires and indicator lights, weighed 30 tons and filled the space of a small gymnasium. It generated so much heat that industrial cooling fans were needed to prevent its circuitry from melting down. The machine contained no less than 70,000 resistors and 18,000 vacuum tubes, which failed at the rate of, on average, one every seven minutes. It cost over $2 million at today's prices and used so much electricity that, it is said, the lights of Philadelphia dimmed when ENIAC was turned on (Logsdon, 1980, pp. 35–36).

A handful of similar machines were constructed elsewhere in the U.S. and in Great Britain. But it seemed unlikely, at the time, that many of these bulky, cumbersome and temperamental monsters would ever be built outside of the universities, military installations, and government laboratories. Someone predicted that only four or five computers would be needed to fulfill the computing needs of the entire world. Indeed, in 1948 IBM itself decided, on the basis of market research, that there would never be enough demand to justify its entering the market for commercial computers. Nevertheless, the first commercial computer, UNIVAC 1 (Universal Automatic Computer)—another Mauchly-Eckert production designed for the Sperry-Rand Company—was installed at General Electric and IBM soon changed its mind. UNIVAC garnered priceless publicity by predicting, an hour after the polls closed, Dwight Eisenhower's 1952 presidential election (Marcus & Segal, 1989, p. 299). Within a decade, there were over 15,000 mainframe computers in the world. The 1960s and the early 1970s were the heyday of the mainframe and "data processing." Sales boomed and companies fell over themselves to install these new electronic brains. The most common of these was the IBM 1401, which cost the equivalent of $1 million (Forester, 1987, pp. 17–18).

Today, in sharp contrast, the same amount of computing power is contained in the average home personal computer. The very first microprocessor chip, the Intel 4004, introduced in 1971, was roughly equal in computing power to ENIAC. And by 1977, Intel founder Robert Noyce was able to claim, in *Scientific American*, that a typical microcomputer was much more powerful than ENIAC. As astonishing as the radical increase in power and decrease in size and energy consumption have been, the drop in the cost of computers has been equally remarkable. One can get some types of personal computers today for a few hundred dollars. Put another way, if the automobile and airplane businesses had developed like the computer business, a Rolls Royce would cost less than $3 and would run for 3 million miles on one gallon of gas. A Boeing 767 would cost just $500 and would circle the globe in 20 minutes on five gallons of gas (Nora & Minc, 1980, p. 16).

Second Industrial Revolution

There are several critical differences, however, between the First and Second Industrial Revolutions. The Industrial Revolution of the eighteenth and nineteenth centuries had a crucial but limited connection with contemporary scientific developments (see section 3c). In contrast, the microelectronics revolution is, essentially, a creation of science. Moreover, it owes its rapid pace and powerful societal impact to a constant harnessing of scientific knowledge and technical innovation. The First Industrial Revolution, furthermore, was (and continues to be) an enormous consumer of energy—mainly in the form of fossil fuels and nuclear power. The microelectronics revolution, again in contrast, requires far less energy to perform its miracles.

Whereas the First Industrial Revolution processed energy and power, the Second Industrial Revolution processes information (Weinberg, 1990, pp. 16–17). Information processing, as noted above, is not in itself a new phenomenon. The human brain has always been a supreme information processor. Humanity's fairly rapid evolutionary rise to the status of a dominant species owes much to the evolution of its powerful brain. There have been three seminal inventions, prior to the twentieth century, which have radically augmented the brain's scope and abilities. The invention of written (or painted or carved) language, some five or six thousand years ago, may be called the first great development by the human brain to aid in its handling of data and concepts. Some thousand years later, a second great advance was made with the Babylonian invention of simple arithmetic operations. Mankind began to use what would now be termed a digital representation of numbers. The invention of printing, about five hundred years ago, is the third great historical advance in humanity's information processing capabilities (see sections 1d, 1f, 1g).

These three momentous inventions, with minor modifications, characterized human ingenuity in handling information until the mid-nineteenth century. With written language, we gained the capacity to make a permanent record of information and also to convey messages across space and time; in other words, we mastered the techniques of *storage, retrieval,* and *communication.* With digital arithmetic, we gained the ability to perform accurate, repeatable *manipulations* of *quantitative data.* With printing, we gained the ability to make many identical copies of the same record and so *broadcast* a single message to a wide and continuing audience. These three inventions—which constitute, in effect, revolutionary breakthroughs for the human species—remained the basis for all progress and innovation in information handling until about a century ago. Brushes, pens, typewriters, calculating machines, and movable type and typesetting machines are all, essentially, faster, cheaper, more reliable and more efficient versions of the three seminal "information inventions."

It was the development of electromagnetic theory in the mid-nineteenth century which laid the groundwork for another—and potentially the most significant—revolutionary breakthrough in human information processing. In the last hundred years or so, we have witnessed the rapidly accelerating advent of a science-based technology so radical and novel that we may term it the fourth great advance in humanity's handling of data and ideas. This Second Industrial Revolution is rooted in electromagnetic theory and its many ramifications and applications. The following is only a partial list of electromagnetic devices which are transforming twentieth-century cultures: photography, photocopying, cinematography and holography; telegraphy, telephony, radio communication, radar, and sonar; sound and video recording and reproduction; vacuum tubes, transistors, printed circuits, lasers, fiber optics, and integrated circuits [large-scale integration of circuitry on a tiny semi-conducting "chip"]; and, finally, the bewildering variety of contemporary electronic digital computers (Martin, 1988, pp. 32–35).

The striking thing about the microelectronics revolution is that its advances appear to be occurring with increasing rapidity. As the information processing capabilities of computers become more complex and ever-more sophisticated, their production costs continue to fall. In fact, one of the reasons why computers and computer-related devices have become so pervasive is that they are so affordable. In particular, the cost of producing the silicon chips, which are the very core of most computers, has fallen sharply since the 1970s. Each year, scientists are able to pack more and more information components onto a silicon chip. Since making a complex chip costs only a little more than making a simple one, with each increase in complexity comes a corresponding decrease in price per function. Thus the incentive is always present to encourage the design of more sophisticated devices. The history of modern chip technology makes this quite clear.

Chip Technology

Chip technology began with the invention of the transistor in 1947, at Bell Laboratories in the U.S.. Transistors are basically small pieces of either germanium or (now almost exclusively) silicon [the main ingredient of beach sand] with wire contacts. They function as simple amplifiers and switches for electric currents and thus replace the cumbersome mechanical relays and valves which plagued ENIAC and other early computers. Transistors have gone through four main developmental stages: (1) In the 1950s, single circuits were mounted on boards; (2) In the 1960s, up to 100 circuits were built right into each board. This meant that large-scale computing could be had for the first time for less than $1 million; (3) In the 1970s, the boards got smaller and were replaced by silicon chips. Each year, engineers packed more circuits into the same size of chip—the so-called "integrated circuit." Now, whole circuits, consisting of many transistors, could be incorporated into a single silicon chip. Again, military orders helped firms to cover research costs and get their devices into mass production. Mass production meant that prices dropped and sales increased. The average price of an integrated circuit fell from about $30 to just $1, and the average number of components in a circuit rose from 24 to 64. This meant that powerful computers could be purchased for less than $100,000; (4) In the early 1980s, hundreds of thousands of circuits could be packed into a chip. A good computer could be bought for less than $10,000. Many personal computers for home or office now cost less than $2,500 and some rudimentary computers can be had for as little as $100. This trend toward miniaturization continues in the 1990s. The prospects for microelectronics as we approach the year 2000 are staggering (Nora & Minc, 1980, pp. 13–15).

Trends in miniaturization, which reduce cost and size and thus increase the applications of computers, may be illustrated by a street map analogy. Roughly speaking, in the 1950s information about just one street could be placed on a single chip or board. In the 1960s, the street map of a small town could be placed on the same size of device. In the 1970s, a chip could contain the street map of a smallish city, and in the mid-1980s the street map of the entire Greater Los Angeles area could be placed on a single silicon chip. It now appears possible to put the equivalent of a street map of the entire North American continent on just one tiny chip. By the end of the 1990s, it could be the whole world (Forester, 1987, pp. 20–23).

Computer Generations

Another useful way of comprehending the vast and rapid increase in the sophistication of computers is to describe the successive stages, or "generations," of computer development: (1) The so-called "First-Generation" computers of the 1950s still used the valves and vacuum tubes of the earliest computers, such as ENIAC. They performed their operations in "milliseconds" (thousandths of a second); (2) The "Second-Generation" of computers, appearing in the early 1960s, were based on transistors. Their operation time was in "microseconds" (millionths of a second); (3) The "Third-Generation" computers, which appeared in the early 1970s, are based on the "microprocessor." Invented in 1971 by Marcian "Ted" Hoff, a young engineer at a small American firm called Intel, the microprocessor houses the entire central processing unit (CPU)—the "brain" of a computer—on a single silicon chip. But the microprocessor is more than just a miniature version of an integrated circuit. An integrated circuit reacts in a fixed, pre-programmed way to an input signal to produce an output signal. In marked contrast, the response—the "logic"—of a microprocessor can be altered. In other words, the microprocessor can be programmed in different ways rather than react in one pre-programmed way only.

Hoff's invention was a tremendous breakthrough. By merely adding two memory chips—one to move data in and out of the CPU, the other to provide the program to drive the CPU—Hoff's chip became, in essence, a rudimentary general purpose (complete) computer. The microprocessor could do far more than a hand-held calculator. It could be used to control a set of traffic lights, an oven or washing machine, an elevator, or even a factory production line. The commercial potential was enormous. Moreover, the operation time of these microprocessors was now on the order of "nanoseconds" (billionths of a second). The Third-Generation computers provided access to data in so brief a time as to be scarcely conceivable a decade earlier. The computer on a chip had become a reality; (4) The 1980s witnessed the development of "Fourth-Generation" computers. These so-called "supercomputers" can perform 400 million or so operations per second! (By way of comparison, the average personal computer may perform "only" 500,000 arithmetic operations per second.) The "Fourth-Generation" computers cost between $5 million and $20 million to build. At the present time, only about 150 have been installed worldwide, mostly in government agencies and universities (Bloomfield, 1987, p. 87).

As powerful as the supercomputers of today are, they are still actually too slow for many potential tasks. For example, they can not perform the complex computer simulations which would enable designers in the automobile and aircraft industries to see how a planned product will behave under certain conditions. However, a new concept in computer architecture ("architecture" is the logical organization of a computer) called "parallel processing" seems destined to transform—improve—even the supercomputer. The problem with conventional computers using the dominant "von Neumann architecture" (named after the Hungarian-American mathematician

John von Neumann [1903–1957]) is that their tasks have to be broken down into a sequence of steps (Bolter, 1984, pp. 176–177). These steps are then laboriously executed by the computer one at a time. This means that the pace of computing is set by electronic circuit speeds, which in turn are limited by the agility of transistor switches, the speed of electricity, and the excessive heat generated by hard-working silicon chips (Aspray, 1990). Parallel processing, on the other hand, is much faster (and cheaper) because it enables the computer to execute the many different steps simultaneously (Raggett & Bains, 1992, pp. 166–167).

Fifth-Generation Computers

The application of parallel processing to Fourth-Generation computers resulted in an international race to build a Fifth-Generation computer. The competition is keen and governments and private industries—particularly in Japan, the U.S., and the European Economic Community (EEC)—are investing heavily. It is clear why these nations are devoting such vast intellectual and financial resources to the building of Fifth-Generation computers. The potential applications of such machines are extraordinary and the consequent demand for them will be great. Computer simulation seems poised to transform scientific research itself. More and more experiments in physics, fusion research, biology, and chemistry can now be simulated rather than actually performed. The potential applications of computer simulation to engineering, seismology, meteorology and bio-medical technology are equally profound. Complex problems of fluid dynamics and aerodynamics, for instance, can now be anlayzed by computer rather than by laborious calculations and costly re-creations. In one of the most exciting application areas of all—computer graphics—the newer supercomputers are revolutionizing the art of animation. Strikingly lifelike pictures of natural phenomena such as landscapes, surfaces and motions can now be created by computer and remarkable feats of visualization performed. This is transforming film-making and, for example, flight simulation, and will have a major impact on science and medical teaching and industrial training. At the same time, graphics chips are becoming more sophisticated as the demand for graphics software packages grows.

Of all the possible implications of the international race to build Fifth-Generation computers, the most controversial concern the subject known as "Artificial Intelligence" or AI. Academics have been studying and developing AI ever since a meeting which gave birth to the term at Dartmouth College in 1956 (Weinberg, 1990, p. 146). Early computer developments did little to justify the name given to the so-called "electronic brains" of the 1960s and 1970s. There was nothing, in fact, which could rival the human brain—which has 10 *trillion* circuits packed into an area the size of a cabbage. The recent advances of microelectronics during the 1980s, however, gave a powerful boost to AI research. Computers now exist which rival—if not mimic exactly—many of the functions that were once considered the unique property of the human (and higher primates') brain.

This latest phase in AI developments started when the Japanese announced in early 1981 that they had launched a massive 10-year project to produce Fifth-Generation supercomputers. Japan's Ministry of Trade and Industry (MITI) declared that country's intention to produce by 1991 the first of a new generation of what it calls "knowledge information processing systems" (KIPS). These—it was claimed—would rapidly supersede conventional computers. In particular, they would be capable of automatic language translation (an obvious priority for the Japanese in their effort to lead the international science and technology competition), document preparation by voice-activated "typewriters," expert professional advice on a wide array of subjects, and decision-taking on the basis of logical inference. Fifth-Generation computers will have to support very large knowledge bases, work at very high speeds, perform complicated logical inference operations as fast as current computers perform arithmetic operations, and develop a machine-user interface that allows significant use of natural speech and images (Ennals, 1990, pp. 15, 156).

The response to the Japanese challenge, particularly by the U.S., was swift. Two well-known authors on computers, Edward Feigenbaum and Pamela McCorduck, argued—in a 1983 book entitled, provocatively enough, "The Fifth Generation: Artificial Intelligence and Japan's Computer Challenge to the World"—that Japan's computer project amounted to a "technological Pearl Harbour." In essence, they said that the U.S. (and other advanced industrial nations) had better wake up before it was too late. Knowledge, they maintained, was the new "wealth of nations." If the Japanese succeeded in taking over world leadership in knowledge processing systems, they could dominate the world in every other way. Some skeptics responded that the Japanese plans were risky and over-ambitious. On the other hand, even if only 10 percent of the project's goals are achieved, it will probably have been worth it in terms of technological spin-off and new commercial products. It is indicative of the central role computers have come to play in most aspects of local, national and international affairs, that the U.S. could not dare *not* to respond to the Japanese challenge. During the 1980s, the U.S. and, in Europe, the EEC poured millions of dollars into research on advanced supercomputers and AI (Bloomfield, 1987, pp. 149–151). At the present time, the outcome of this intense research effort is unclear.

Expert Systems

Much of this scientific effort focuses on what are called "expert systems." To develop an expert system, AI researchers basically spend years picking the brains of human experts, such as doctors, geologists, and chemists. They try to extract their knowledge and to understand the way it is organized, so that it may be reproduced in computer programs. What differentiates the operation of an expert system from that of a conventional computer is its flexibility. A standard computer program specifies precisely how each task must be performed by the computer. An expert system, in contrast, tells the computer what to do without specifying how to do it. This is achieved by using special program languages, such as PROLOG, which allow a computer to manipulate symbols rather than only numbers. The "how" and "why" of the system are kept separate, allowing new data to be added at any time without altering the basic logic of the program (Bloomfield, 1987, pp. 220–222).

In an expert system, therefore, the computer exercises "judgment." It is able to do so by using certain intellectual rules of thumb, a process known as heuristics. Heuristics has also been described as the "art of good guessing." It enables experts—human or machine—to recognize promising approaches to problems and make educated guesses when necessary. Expert systems have been developed, with some notable successes, in a number of fields (Weinberg, 1990, p. 153). One of the most advanced is the medical system called CADUCEUS, developed in the mid-1980s at the University of Pittsburgh. CADUCEUS can diagnose diseases, using heuristics to narrow down the field and drawing on information in its large memory bank. Stanford has set up a national (U.S.) computer network called SUMEX-AIM to help AI work in medicine. In business, some commercial systems up and running include Xcon, developed by Digital Equipment Corporation (DEC) to help its sales force establish the exact needs of each customer, and Ace, a system devised by Bell Labs to help trace and analyze faults in telephone cables. In geology, an expert system called PROSPECTOR has been partly credited with the discovery of an elusive molybdenum deposit in Mt. Tolman, Washington. General Electric has a system for detecting faults in diesel locomotives. Finally, Teknowledge Inc. of Palo Alto (in the famous Silicon Valley at the south end of San Francisco Bay) and the French oil company Elf Aquitaine both have in use expert systems which advise oil rig operators on what to do when the drill bit gets stuck.

An expert system package is usually sold commercially as a general-purpose "shell." Its software can then be tailored to cover many different areas of expertise. The software has two parts. One represents the encoded knowledge of a human expert, and the other part helps the non-expert to use it. Initially, a "knowledge engineer"—as these researchers are styled—talked to an expert in the field of interest in order to try and structure the decision-making process into a set of rules (or model). The nonspecialist can then use the software by supplying the program with information about particular cases. The system consults its rules—actually guidelines—and supplies the advice requested. The early AI systems were often little more than programs demonstrating obvious decision procedures. But the recent breakthroughs in AI appear to bring computers to a new level of sophistication (Forester, 1987, pp. 45–49).

Can Machines Think?

The success of these expert systems, and the *pace* of research in AI generally, has rekindled a long-standing debate concerning computer science. Put simply, "Can machines think?" AI can be defined as that branch of computer science which aims to make computer systems behave intelligently, or at least demonstrate behavior that we might intuitively think of as intelligent. Programs already exist, as noted above, which show elements of intelligence. In fact, several programs can now outperform human experts at such tasks as diagnosing disease, matching up fingerprints, finding mineral deposits and—perhaps most significantly—controlling the manufacture and distribution of computers themselves. If research in AI continues to produce results at its present rapid rate, computers may start displacing humans from certain work requiring mental skills as completely as machines of the earlier Industrial Revolution displaced humans from physical tasks. Although it is too early to answer definitively the question of whether machines "think," AI research has already clearly illustrated that—at least in certain domains—there is no firm division between human and machine intelligence. The question "Can machines think?" should actually be rephrased to ask "What type of thinking do machines perform?"

The progress in AI is at once exciting *and* disturbing (Bloomfield, 1987, pp. 61–63). It is exciting because of its great scientific and technological potential. It is disturbing precisely because its very success seems to challenge traditional views of the human/machine distinction. Some modern philosophers have attempted definitions of intelligence that exclude machines. However, they are forced to revise those definitions each time AI makes possible computers of greater sophistication. It seems that we can no longer deny that intelligent machines exist. They do. What is required is an assessment of the likely impact of their large-scale introduction into society. For these supercomputers necessarily bring about new relationships between humans and their machines. The human/computer interface is likely to pose even greater, if more subtle, problems of sociopolitical and individual readjustment than did the Industrial Revolution of the eighteenth and nineteenth centuries (Leiss, 1990, pp. 138–140). What was once the province of philosophical speculation or literary discussion, now seems to be actually altering the very basis of our political, economic, cultural and even domestic arrangements.

The scenarios of science fiction—with respect to computers as well as many other areas such as environmental crises and biological engineering—are now assuming the substance of reality.

Arthur C. Clarke's *2001: A Space Odyssey* is perhaps the most famous expression of the ambivalent attitude toward the intelligent machine. "HAL"—short for "Heuristically programmed ALgorithmic computer—operates the spaceship, monitors the trip, and communicates with the astronauts in spoken words. HAL appears as a computer panel with a large TV eye. (Advances in robotics [see section 5c] promise intelligent computers that may one day possess mobility and form that may closely mimic that of human beings.) The computer begins to malfunction and the astronauts attempt to ascertain the difficulty. The climax of the most controversial part of *2001* occurs when HAL—the computer which was programmed to simulate human emotions—kills one astronaut and shuts off the life support systems of the hibernating crew members. The one remaining crew member performs a lobotomy on the brain of the computer, rendering it helpless. Thus, the human is able to disconnect the intelligence of HAL. Clarke appears to be suggesting that mankind will always be able to control his intelligent machines, if perhaps at a great cost. As computers become more powerful, however—as they assume more and more tasks formerly performed by humans and as they become more and more integrated into the fabric of society—the question of the possibility of ultimate human control becomes more complex, and to some, more troublesome.

The AI Debate

There are two extreme positions on the matter of machine intelligence, with many shades in between. At one extreme, many people assert that computers can only do what they are programmed to do. Hence they are not "creative" but are, philosophically speaking, "stupid." In any event, so this argument goes, if computers get out of hand, humans can always pull the plug. At the other extreme is the position which claims that there is no essential discontinuity between inorganic and organic structures. Advocates of this position maintain that organic life—including mankind—is just one stage in the development of more highly organized inorganic structures. Intelligent machines, so this argument goes, are just another phase in the evolution of matter. As such, they can evolve so as to become, ultimately, autonomous and independent of their original human creators. Current research in self-programming and learning computers is taken as support for this position. Many consider that the advent of learning computers—machines which "react" to the results of their own actions by modifying the way they "decide" to act in the future—answers the question of machine thinking. If computers can add to their own knowledge repertoires *without* additional human programming, then—so this argument concludes—machines can learn and think (Graubard, 1988, pp. 191–212).

The debate concerning machine intelligence actually has its roots with the French philosopher and mathematician René Descartes in the seventeenth century. Descartes maintained that the human mind was radically different from the body. This mind/matter distinction—known as the Cartesian dualism—placed the human mind, and thought, in a unique category. Descartes' position implied that machines could never be made to "think," even if they could be constructed to perform complex mechanical movements. Descartes further suggested that animals were also devoid of the capacity to think. In his terminology they were "beast-machines" (Bolter, 1984, p. 28).

Some years after Descartes' statements about the nature of humans, animals and machines, the mind/machine debate took an evolutionary turn. The eighteenth-century French philosopher Julien de La Mettrie (1709–1751), in a book entitled *L'homme-machine* ("Man the Machine," 1748), established the analogy of humans *as* machines. In combatting Cartesian dualism, La

Mettrie was denying that there is any sort of immaterial soul. Using the evidence from diet, disease, age and climate, La Mettrie attempted to show not only that mind or soul was dependent on body, but that mind and body were but different aspects of a single basic universal matter. Cleverly extending Descartes' own idea of animal automatism, La Mettrie argued that the human/ animal/machine distinction was one of degree only, not of kind. In principle, at least, one could construct a sophisticated machine that would function as a human being. Thought, according to La Mettrie's philosophy of *materialism*, was a property of matter just as, for example, electricity and motion are properties of matter. He further suggested that the human being could be compared to a large watch constructed with skill and ingenuity (Bolter, 1984, pp. 14, 205).

La Mettrie's version of materialism awakened renewed interest in the nineteenth century. Darwin and Wallace's theory of evolution by natural selection (see section 3b) proved that Descartes' absolute discontinuity between humans and other animals was no longer tenable in light of the evidence from biology. They demonstrated that *homo sapiens,* in its physical form, had indeed evolved from less complex living creatures. More to the point, Darwin argued that human intelligence had similarly evolved by the same process of natural selection. (It should be recalled that Wallace came to differ from Darwin on this particular issue.) Thus, following Darwin, it became possible to conceive of life, including intelligence, as being part of a gradual evolutionary process of inorganic matter being transformed into organic matter. Darwin did not resolve the mind/body debate. But evolutionary theory did place that debate on a new level of scientific investigation (Graubard, 1988, pp. 175–189).

One provocative entry into the human/machine debate was provided by the English novelist Samuel Butler (1835–1902). In a chapter called "Book of the Machines" in his famous utopian novel *Erewhon* (1872), Butler suggested that nineteenth-century machines were "improving" faster than people were. To emphasize this point, he noted that the industrial revolution was forcing more and more people to tend machines, to develop them and, ultimately, to reproduce them. Butler's depiction of machine evolution was intended to satirize Darwin, with whom he disagreed on a number of issues. In the twentieth century, however, the idea of machine evolution can no longer be considered simply a product of literary satire. Computers now can rival—in some instances surpass—aspects of human intelligence. Advances in AI and robotics have rendered certain phases of intelligent machine reproduction independent of human intervention.

Not only biology, but psychology and ethology (the scientific study of animal behavior) now provide new perspectives for analyzing the relationship between *homo sapiens* and other species. In a similar fashion, AI research has forced a rethinking of the human/machine boundary. The science of AI actually consists of two distinct—albeit closely related—approaches. The first area of AI research attempts to mimic human intelligence in a computer program. Here, scientists search for functional models that clarify our understanding of human cognition and language. But the second area of AI research focuses on attacking and solving problems without necessarily referring to models of human intelligence (Ennals, 1990, p. 30). The aim here is to exhibit the possibility of intelligent behavior outside the human cranium. From this perspective, AI is a science searching for principles underlying intelligent behavior in general—whether in humans, in animals, or machines.

Within the last few years a fascinating goal has captured the imagination of researchers across many scientific disciplines. Not only computer scientists, but psychologists, linguists, biologists, anthropologists as well as engineers and physicists have all taken up the question "Can mind arise from matter?" AI has already demonstrated that symbolic functioning—one standard definition of human intelligence—can arise from sophisticated combinations of computer hardware and software. The science of robotics has produced intelligent mobile machine systems which are either self-controlled (have their computers within) or remotely controlled (have their computer "brains" elsewhere). Medical research has produced "cyborgs," that is, entities built by joining mechanical and biological structures. (The word is coined from "cybernetic" plus "organism.") Examples of cyborgs would include people with, for instance, pacemakers or prosthetic (bionic) limbs. All these developments raise the possiblity of hooking up human beings to a sophisticated computer in order that the machine's capabilities might become directly and immediately available to the individual so connected. Clearly, AI research—and other aspects of microelectronics—have forced us to radically rethink our notions of the differences between humans and the new intelligent machines which they have helped to create (Thurd & Hansen, 1986, p. 26). While philosophers, theologians, moralists, and computer scientists (among others) ponder the status of these new creatures, society is already undergoing the effects of the impact of the microelectronics revolution (Martin, 1988, p. 53). ■

C. Microelectronics: Computers and Communications Part II: Applications and Societal Impact

■ ■ ■

We are now in the midst of a revolution in the processing of information which will have as profound—if not even greater—an impact on society and the individual than the earlier Industrial Revolution. The science and technology of information comprises a vast range of processes for storing information, for copying it, for transmitting it from one place to another, for displaying it, and for transforming it. Photography, motion pictures, VCR, and television gave us a whole new technology for storing and displaying pictorial information. Telegraphy, the telephone, the record (now the compact disc) player, and radio did the same for storing and transmitting auditory information (Levy, 1989).

The computer is unique among these techniques, as we have seen, because of its (seemingly unlimited) capacity for manipulating and transforming information. Alone among information technologies, computers rival the human brain in its versatility and autonomy. It is the computer's *intelligent* operation, coupled to its automatic functioning (increasingly free from human intervention), which poses the greatest potential—benevolent as well as pernicious—for the human species (Ennals, 1990, pp. 165–166).

As with the energy transformations associated with the First Industrial Revolution, the consequences of the information revolution spread out in many directions. First, there are the economic consequences that follow on any innovation which increases human productivity. These are perhaps the easiest effects of technological changes to predict. Second, there are consequences for the nature of work and leisure—for the quality of life. Some of these are immediately apparent—such as the automation of the factory—but other consequences are more subtle and slower to manifest themselves. Third, there are the consequences for political activity at the local, national, and international levels. The impact of microelectronics in this domain—from regulating traffic patterns to predictions of voting behavior to defense and armaments expenditures and uses—will surely be far-reaching (Roszak, 1986, pp. 187–193). Fourth, the information revolution—particularly as it concerns the computer—will have special consequences for privacy and individual liberty. Finally, there are the consequences for humanity's view of itself and its perception of the universe. Computers have entered the realms of philosophy, scholarship, art, music, literature and education. At a fundamental level, computers have challenged our traditional notions of human/machine distinctions (Menzies, 1989, pp. 56–60).

In each of these many directions, the immediate impacts of the microelectronics revolution are the most obvious. It is, however, the less readily perceived consequences that will be, in the long run, most significant. The different perspectives needed to assess the long-range as opposed to the short-range impacts of a new technology are, to be sure, not unique to the information revolution. It was not hard, for example, to foresee (at their appearance) that Newcomen's and Watt's engines would change the economics of mining in deep pits (see section 3c). It would have been far more difficult, perhaps impossible, to predict the chain of effects that would lead from the steam engine, to the internal-combustion engine, to the automobile and, finally, to the suburbs with their assorted social advantages and disadvantages (see section 5a).

Since we are still living, basically, at the start of the microelectronics revolution, it is the immediate consequences which are most obvious to us and which affect us most at present. About these, there is little disagreement as to their nature. There is, of course, much disagreement as to whether these early impact are "good" or "bad." The longer-term effects of the information revolution involve predictions, which afford greater scope for uncertainty and, hence, argument (Friedrichs & Schaff, 1982, pp. 25–26, 298). In this section, we can only mention briefly some of the more securely based predictions. We shall focus on four areas of impact: (1) Robotics and the automated factory; (2) Microelectronics in the home and office; (3) Microelectronics in commerce, banking, and shopping; and, last, (4) Computers, data networks and the threat to privacy.

Robotics and the Automated Factory

While the U.S. remains among the world's leader in production of goods and services, other advanced industrial nations are quickly closing that gap. In fact, certain of these nations—such as Japan, France, West Germany, and South Korea and other countries of the Pacific Rim—have annual manufacturing productivity growth rates significantly higher than the U.S. Japan has emerged as perhaps the leading industrial nation as we enter the twenty-first century. One of the most important aspects of this increasingly keen industrial competition at the international, as well as national, level is the growing use of computers and microprocessor technology in manufacturing. Today we are on the technological and sociological edge of a dramatic increase in the use of computers in our factories. This will have a major effect both on a nation's productivity and on the working conditions of many of its citizens (Brod, 1984, pp. 170–190).

The face of modern industry is being changed out of all recognition by cheap computing power. New techniques of automated production are bringing about a revolution in manufacturing greater than anything since the Industrial Revolution of the eighteenth and nineteenth centuries. Many of the concepts are not new. The idea of automation has itself been around for more than a century. What is making the difference today is the widespread availability of cheap, reliable and sophisticated control systems based on microelectronics. This—together with developments in "numerical control," which makes machine tools and robots more flexible and easier to use—means that highly complex automated factories can now be built at reasonable cost (Logsdon, 1980, pp. 260–264).

The McDonnell Douglas airplane parts fabrication plant in St. Louis (Missouri) provides an excellent example of the "factory of the future"—and one which is already here. The first impression when one views the McDonnell Douglas factory is the sheer size and loneliness of it all. Some two dozen acres of milling machines noisily grind grooves, slots and intricate patterns in airframe parts to a tolerance of 0.0025 inch. The machines, for the most part, work alone. They are watched by only a few workers, who glance occasionally at a control panel or sweep cuttings. Nor are these workers in charge here. The machine tools are directed by numerical controllers—minicomputers which control a particular phase of the manufacturing process. These numerical controllers are, in turn, directed by a whole hierarchy of computers presided over by a master computer. Some critics argue that computer-based monitoring available on factory floors may also be used to police the actions of workers, e.g., how long they are away from work-stations for breaks, trips to the bathroom, and so on (Hamlett, 1992, p. 93). This 750,000 sq. ft. aircraft parts fabrication plant is among the most advanced computerized manufacturing plants in the world. (Major and final assembly buildings containing nearly another million sq. ft. each are nearby.) But it is far from unusual, and will become even less so.

Highly automated plants elsewhere in the U.S., Japan, Canada and Europe now turn out automobiles, engines, oilwell equipment, elevators, electrical products and machine tools. These plants—particularly in Japan—are evolving into what had once been only an engineer's dream: the automated factory (Menzies, 1989, pp. 117–125). There are two major components to the automated manufacturing process. The first is called computer-aided design (CAD). With CAD, a user can define a part shape, analyze stresses and other factors, check mechanical applications, and automatically produce engineering drawings from a graphics terminal. These drawings can be three-dimensional designs which can then be examined, analyzed and even "tested" to simulated destruction without ever having been made. CAD leads, in turn, to computer-aided manufacturing (CAM). Here, the same design and prototype testing generates a common database about the product. From this database a set of instructions can be derived for actually manufacturing the product. Combining CAD and CAM makes possible a completely integrated, unmanned, automated and computer-controlled manufacturing process from concept to final product (Forester, 1985, pp. 262–266).

Computer-Aided Manufacturing

The advantages and potential of such CAD/CAM factories are many: (1) greater design freedom; (2) better management control; (3) shorter lead time [that is, the time needed, or available, between the decision to start a project and the completion of it]; (4) greater operating flexibility; (5) improved reliability [For example, a device using microelectronics can control a large number of variables in such a way as to achieve optimum operational conditions for the system as a whole. It is possible, for instance, to maintain heating and cooling at specified rates or to hold fixed temperatures for a specified time or until some measurement indicates that the temperatures should be changed.]; (6) reduced maintenance; (7) reduced wastage, scrap and rework [Microelectronics provides new scope for automatic testing, sampling and inspection. In chemical processes, metallurgy and food processing, where there is a need for sampling the product continuously, it becomes possible to fully automate analysis. In the manufacture of components, weighing, measuring and flaw detection can be carried out automatically. In a related context, the potential for monitoring the factory environment (both internally and externally) is enormously increased. The air of a factory can be continuously sampled for smoke or toxic hazards and the results of effluent analysis can be constantly fed back to the production process.]; and—as a result of all these—(8) increased productivity (Weinberg, 1990, pp. 136–137).

The basic methodology for a completely unmanned factory is now complete. Not only will such a plant automate the design, process planning, and fabrication functions, but it will also bring the entire assembly operation under computer control. The Japanese Ministry of International Trade and Industry (MITI) has announced that unmanned factories will be commonplace, at least in that country, by the end of the 1990s. One characteristic of such factories, of course, poses fundamental social as well as economic questions. The unmanned plants the Japanese are considering need employ only 1% of a conventional plants's labor force. In other words, 20 people would operate a factory that employed 2000 workers in pre-automation days. Certain critics contend that CAM is intended not merely to replace some workers, but also to control others by dictating the pace of operations. These critics cite General Motors' heavily computerized and automated Saturn division as an apt example of things to come (Marcus & Segal, 1989, p. 340). This would indeed be the epitome of scientific management or Taylorism (see section 3c). In any event, the trends converging towards completely automated factories—the most dramatic breakthrough since Henry Ford harnessed a conveyor belt—are unmistakable. Only the timetable is in dispute.

Central to the discussion of the societal impact of the automated factory is the development of the science of *robotics*. Basically, robots are microprocessor-controlled mechanical devices that perform a function or provide an intelligent interface between machines and processes. Robots have been talked about and tinkered with ever since the appearance in 1921 of the Czech author Karel Capek's play "Rossum's Universal Robots" or—as it is commonly called—R.U.R. Incidentally, it was this play which introduced the word "robot" into the English language. The word is derived from a Czech expression for work, implying drudgery or serf labor. Capek's robots were androids (that is, human-like creatures synthesized from biological materials, such as Frankenstein's monster), made by a secret process. They were living, intelligent creatures, but totally devoid of feeling and the ability to make value judgments. Their purpose was to provide cheap, flexible, undemanding labor, willing and able to work for long hours. Capek's robots became a favorite theme of science fiction writers for several decades but evoked little other interest. It was the advance of the microchip in the 1970s that changed all this and made robots a reality. The enormous advances in microelectronics made possible equally impressive advances in robotics.

The first generation of computer-controlled robots in the 1970s were little more than mechanical arms. They were also "deaf, dumb and blind" and very inflexible. They were used primarily for such tasks as spot welding, paint-spraying, loading and stacking. Advances during the 1980s, however, have vastly increased the sophistication and applications of robots. Today, robots can duplicate human manipulative skills with accuracy and precision. Their flexibility and versatility, as opposed to "hard" automation, make robots ideally suited to the kinds of small batch jobs that constitute the bulk of industry's manufacturing activity. They can free people from jobs that present serious health hazards (such as certain repair operations in nuclear power stations), are mundane, or highly repetitive. What is the merit, robot enthusiasts ask, in having people work in dirty, noisy, dusty and dangerous jobs? Perhaps most significant for the future will be the role played by robots in those environments which pose extreme difficulties for human activity, such as outer space and the ocean floor.

Robots today are no longer deaf, dumb, and blind (Forester, 1985, pp. 266–270). Japanese researchers have created robots with human-type hands and legs, TV-camera "eyes," artificial "ears" and "mouth," and touch and joint sensing. At the present level of robotics, these technologies are combined to provide the robot with some of the capabilities of a two- or three-year-old child. For example, when ordered to fetch an item in the room, the robot looks around the room and finds the article, walks to it, picks it up, and brings it back. If the robot does not understand a command, it "speaks up." The intensive research in robotics—particularly in Japan but also in the U.S. and Western Europe—seems certain to add to these sensing capacities. Many predict that the Fifth-Generation computers will endow robots with intelligence and massive computing power. These "super-robots" will be able to "infer logically"—that is to work out for themselves how to do something. The advent of the intelligent robot will challenge human perspectives as no machine has done before (Bolter, 1984, pp. 194–196).

Smart Robots

Even before such "smart robots" appear, however, the societal impact of already functioning industrial robots is apparent (Menzies, 1989, pp. 147–154). Certain of these impacts are beneficial. In some firms, employees displaced by robots normally move up to better, more challenging work. Engineers and draftsmen use CAD/CAM to enhance their creativity and productivity in ways scarcely imaginable a decade ago. Scientists can use robots to assist their research and experiments in novel ways. Robots can assist factory managers in routine measurement and inspection. Other impacts have been more ominous.

In Japan, Fujitsu Fanuc already has a plant where robots are helping make other robots. In another Japanese factory, a robot recently crushed a human worker to death, causing the world's first high-tech murder (Forester, 1987, p. 173). On a more general level, robots will likely have a disproportionate impact on the status of unskilled workers, who are often female or members of racial minorities. Some unions are now demanding that industry and government should plan for the changes ahead by putting more money into education and retraining schemes to ease the transition to the factory of the future. Some of the more skeptical unions leaders ask whether there will be any skilled jobs left for the workers to be retrained for. Their fear is that intelligent robots will soon be capable of replacing humans from not only the dangerous or menial jobs but from more sophisticated tasks as well. Machine vision, for example, offers the prospect of totally reliable and tireless robot eyes on the production line. Such efficient managerial robots may replace human quality controllers who, all too often, possess human fallibility (Engelberger, 1989).

Factory of the Future

On the whole private industry is doing very little to prepare workers whose jobs may be eliminated or substantially changed by the use of robots. To ease the transition and ensure optimal productivity and working conditions, there are a number of fronts on which the combined efforts of the public and private sectors will be needed: (1) affected industries should identify vulnerable categories of workers well before their jobs are actually eliminated; (2) education and training facilities should be established to retrain workers, caught in shrinking skill categories, in more marketable skills. Otherwise, unemployment is likely to become pervasive, especially among the least-skilled workers; (3) industry and government (separately or jointly) should create facilities to locate suitable jobs for displaced workers and to help pay the costs of relocation; and (4) industry, government and labor unions should cooperate in planning for long-range employment needs and publicizing new job-skill requirements (Shaiken, 1984).

The transition to the factory of the future is occurring now. The gains in productivity, cost efficiencies and greater flexibility for skilled workers are potentially enormous. Unfortunately, the need to upgrade the skills of the workers in an industrial society increasingly permeated by microeletronics is not always recognized clearly. Some critics argue that the increasing trend towards computerized and automated factories is a management tool to replace troublesome and expensive human workers by cheap and uncomplaining machines. If appropriate measures are not taken, each industrial nation will experience labor distress and worsened conditions of life and work for some segments of the population. It will take enlightened and cooperative strategies to steer a middle course between the extremes of a computer-aided management conspiracy against the human workforce and a naive belief that *all* technological changes are introduced with the interests of the workers at heart. It is crucial that our industrial societies understand the complexities and contradictions of, as well as the great potential for redesigning jobs in, the factory of the future.

Microelectronics in the Home and Office

A visitor to a typical office today would see much that would have been apparent thirty years ago. The visitor would see people reading, writing on paper, handling mail, talking with one another face to face and on the telephone, typing, operating calculators, dictating, and filing and retrieving documents from metal cabinets. But this visitor would observe some strikingly new behavior too. One would see a surprising number of people working with devices that have a typewriter-like keyboard but also have a video screen or an automatic printing element. In 1960, the odds were still overwhelming that someone working at an alphabetic keyboard device was female and either a typist or a key-punch operator. No longer. The keyboard workers are now both female and male, and the typewriter devices now accomplish an astonishing variety of tasks (Forester, 1985, p. 300).

This changed aspect confronting our visitor reflects a fundamental change in the concept of work for a large proportion of the population of advanced industrial societies (Menzies, 1989, pp. 69–82). Owing to the convergence of the new trends in processing information—the revolutionary advances in microelectronics, most specifically in computing and telecommunications—a major transformation has occurred in the place where white-collar workers work: the office. This fundamental change marks the transition from traditional paperwork to the "electronics office"—the office of the future (Friedrichs & Schaff, 1982, pp. 165–167). Such a change would scarcely have been conceived of as a real possibility even as recently as just ten years ago. For, it was in 1976 that the first personal computer, the "Apple I," appeared on the market. In less than a decade, Apple Computer had grown from a two-person shop into a $1 billion international corporation. In fact, it qualifies as one of the fastest growing industries in history. The remarkable rise of Apple, one of the phenomenal success stories of Silicon Valley, is central to the wider societal impact brought about by the advent of the personal computer.

In the 1960s, computers could be afforded only by the largest organizations and corporations, including national military establishments. Sharp reductions in cost made computers available, by the 1970s, to smaller corporations and individual departments of large organizations. Finally, by the early 1980s the success of Apple and its many competitors (such as IBM's PC model launched in 1981) and clones enabled personal computers to be owned and operated by the smallest offices and, even, in the home.

The purchase of personal computers for the home has been extraordinary. Sales have boomed and personal computers are now aggressively mass-marketed in practically the same way as soft drinks and are sold off the shelves in the proliferating stores of retail chains like Computerland and Tandy's Radio Shack. Publishers of magazines and books jumped onto the personal computer bandwagon soon after it got rolling, and in doing so started a publishing sensation. In 1981 there were less than a dozen computer magazines. By 1986 over 800 were available worldwide. Newsagents devote large portions of their display space to personal computer magazines. The top five of these boast circulations around the 500,000 mark (Weinberg, 1990, pp. 48–49, 51–53).

Home Computers

The rise of the home personal computer market has been one of the big surprises in the information technology revolution. It has placed considerable computing power in the hands of individuals—particularly secondary school and university students (Dertouzos & Moses, 1979, pp. 73–86). PCs have enabled millions to tinker with computers and analyze such things as financial problems and inventories in their own homes. PCs are changing many of the aspects of education and revolutionizing the very concept of homework (Logsdon, 1980, pp. 205–215). Furthermore, homework now means both school work done at home and, literally, bringing one's business activities into the home. People have also taken their PC's to work. Ironically, this has upset the grandiose plans of certain corporations to sell fully integrated automated office systems.

Few home users of personal computers are likely to be capable of operating machines that require sophisticated scientific and technical knowledge and skills. Thus, the development of a mass-market for PCs was dependent upon advances in microeletronics and programming which made "user-friendly" computers possible. Software packages now marketed by companies like Apple, AT&T and IBM—heralded by the appearance of menus, pictograms and windows on the screen—enable more people to use computers than ever before. A new generation is being brought up amidst computer video games such as Atari's "Video Computer System." In the near future, all personal computers are likely to become even more user-friendly. The keyboard will remain the dominant input device for many years to come. But in an effort to overcome the keyboard or terminal phobia which afflicts many people, personal computer manufacturers will make greater use of the hand-held mouse, touch screens and touch pads. These allow users to draw pictures or graphs on the screen. Voice recognition, although still bedevilled by technical obstacles, may become a standard option for personal computers in the not-too-distant future.

As prices tumbled and personal computers became more powerful, their home purchase accelerated. The world market, which was worth $1.5 billion in 1983, had grown to $4 billion by 1986. The creation of the personal computer means that individuals can for the first time keep powerful computers in their own homes. Like TVs and telephones before them, home computers have rapidly become part of the domestic furniture. Soon, it is claimed, every home will have one (Pagels, 1984).

Who buys them? One typical owner of a home computer is male and in his teens. Ownership is high in households with school-age children. Since PCs are now comparatively cheap, many have been bought by young people in order to play games (Brod, 1984, pp. 142–148). But many others have been purchased by concerned parents, anxious that their children do not "fall behind." There is also a significant market among adults who feel they need to learn about computing. In Great Britain—which proportionately has more computers in homes than almost any other country—a 1984 survey found that two-thirds of purchasers had bought home computers simply to learn about computers and computer programming.

In the U.S., surveys in the mid-1980s confirmed that between half and three-quarters of households used their computers primarily for playing games. But a sizable proportion said they were using them for word processing or to do office work at home, as a learning tool for children and parents, and for balancing checkbooks and the household budget. A few were using them to store recipes and addresses and to count calories. These surveys, moreover, found that interest in purchasing a PC by those who do not presently own one was greatest in the below-30 group and decreased sharply with increasing age. Only a tiny fraction of those over-60, less than 3%, expressed any interest. Strenuous efforts are being made by the industry to make home computers more useful and easier to use for everyone, not just hobbyists. One suggestion is that home computers could become the core of sophisticated home control systems, which would handle security and monitor heating, lighting and ventilation.

Another significant trend is the merger of home computers and the telephone—thanks to new, low-cost *modems*. Modems convert a computer's digital information into analog signals for transmission over the telephone lines. Thus, home computers will be used more and more for on-line information retrieval, especially financial information, by tapping into databases (like "CompuServe"). They will also be used for home banking and shopping.

Hackers

Computers have not been welcomed into every home, however. Easy access to hardware has created the new social category of "hackers" (Turkle, 1985, pp. 196–238). These are compulsive and obsessive programmers (sometimes called computer "junkies" or "computerholics") who get hooked on computers and spend all their waking hours in front of the flickering screen. There are fears that the new machines might inhibit or distort the social development of the young. Wives whose husbands have fallen in love with their computers have become self-described "computer widows." There have even been reports of families actually breaking up in the face of the computer invasion. As one divorcee put it, "Who would have ever thought that I'd lose my spouse to a machine?" A British hacker "broke into" the Duke of Edinburgh's secret electronic mailbox (on "Prestel") and left a rude message. With so much cheap and accessible computer hardware and software around, almost anything could happen (Forester, 1987, pp. 151–153).

In the office, some of the new keyboard workers are still secretaries, preparing or correcting conventional correspondence on word processors. But many other categories of office personnel are at similar keyboards that serve as computer terminals for significantly different purposes (Thurd & Hansen, 1986). In one office they may be managers checking the latest information on production performance, which is stored in a corporate data base in the company's mainframe computer. Economists are doing econometric modelling, perhaps calling on programs and data in a commercial service bureau across the continent. Librarians are working at terminals connected to a national network that merges the catalogues of thousands of participating libraries (Roszak, 1986, pp. 172–176). Attorneys and law clerks are at terminals linked to a company whose files can be searched to retrieve the full text of court decisions made anywhere in the country. Airline personnel and travel agents make reservations at terminals of a nationwide network. Some of these devices are self-contained personal computers that engineers and scientists, business executives, and many other people depend on for computation, data analysis, scheduling, and other tasks. Others are terminals connected to mainframe computers (Garson, 1988).

Many of the users of mainframe terminals and personal computers can communicate with one another and with their central offices through one of the half-dozen "electronic mail" networks now in existence in North America. A surprising number of people are doing these things not only in the physical office but also at home, on the factory floor, and even while travelling. By using a portable personal computer, for example, one can draw on information from files in a company's mainframe computer and communicate with colleagues via electronic mail. What all this adds up to is a radical shift from traditional ways of doing office work (based mainly on paper) to a reliance upon a variety of keyboard-and-display devices, or so-called personal work stations (Weinberg, 1990, pp. 74–77).

Computer Work Stations

A work station may or may not have its own internal computer. Technically speaking, a personal computer is essentially a small computer which has its own central processing unit (CPU). The CPU supervises the operation of the personal computer's entire range of functions. Other chips provide memory for the storage of instructions and data. Still other external storage devices, such as cassette decks and floppy disk drives, provide further memory capacity which can be transferred from one personal computer to another. Information is entered into the computer by means of a typewriter-like keyboard or is transferred from disks or tapes. Output is diplayed on a TV screen or the computer's own monitor. It can also be printed out on paper or converted from digital to analog signals by a modem for transmission over telephone lines. When we speak of an office computer work station, then, we mean both actual personal computers as well as terminals attached to a mainframe computer. The impact on the working conditions of personnel who use them are essentially the same (Forester, 1985, pp. 322–325).

Until recently, most computer work stations, and their supporting devices and database resources, were designed to serve a single purpose. These might be such specific uses as accessing stock market information or making air travel reservations. Now the capabilities of the work station have been greatly enhanced by incorporating the latest advances in the technology of information processing and telecommunications. A far wider variety of resources and functions have become accessible from a single work station. For example, the stock broker can not only check current prices with his/her terminal. He can also retrieve a customer's portfolio from the brokerage company's database or retrieve (from a distant data base) information on stock-price trends over many years. Literally millions of current and historical news items can also be called up on the screen. The stock broker can then issue orders to buy or sell stock, send messages to other brokers, and generate charts and tables. Such information can then be incorporated into a computer-generated newsletter addressed to customers ("desktop" or "electronic publishing") (Compaine, 1988, p. 41).

It is not only in large corporations that such devices are found. Low-cost personal computers and telecommunications-based services available to individuals or small offices are now common. Interestingly enough, many professionals and office workers in small offices now have work station resources superior to those in large corporations where the pace of introducing microelectronics technology may have been slower. As more and more word processors and other types of computer work stations are equipped with telecommunications capabilities, the impact on business and all types of offices (including those in government agencies, in schools and universities, in the media) will be correspondingly greater. Computer networks linking local and international offices are already in operation or will be shortly. Clearly, the accelerated pace of introducing microelectronics into the office milieu, which has characterized the 1980s, will have major consequences for most aspects of office work in the 1990s and beyond (Strassman, 1985).

Not all predictions for the impact of microelectronics on office work and organization are optimistic (Menzies, 1989, p. 203). There remains the significant question of just *who* will be using the sophisticated technology of computers and telecommunications (and how effectively)? There is serious evidence to suggest that employees writing and reading documents in the office today have measurably lower reading and writing skills than the generation that preceded them. According to some surveys conducted by the Educational Testing Service in Princeton, New Jersey, reading comprehension scores achieved by college-bound high school students have dropped slightly over the past decade. It cannot be substantiated that television (or any other single factor) has damaged the reading and writing abilities of children in the advanced industrial societies. But it seems clear that, for whatever reason, the average office worker and middle manager is somewhat less articulate than the average office worker of the preceding generation. It may be that the probable user of the new, vastly more sophisticated office information systems now, is likely to be less competent in constructing and interpreting messages. He or she will talk longer, say less, make more copies of what is said, and not read the electronic mail as quickly or comprehend it as well. One can even imagine that compensating filters will have to be erected to knock junk mail out of the computer networks.

Once again, we are reminded of the fact that the remarkable advances in science and technology—including those of microelectronics—can be used well, badly, or not at all (Brod, 1984, pp. 84–100). It is certain that office information systems based on computers and telecommunications will continue to evolve. Many of the advanced components are already available at reasonable cost, and current users are reporting that the benefits increase as familiarity with the information systems grows. The efficiency of our messages may decline as their number rises, but information technology contains the promise for new, more structured formats, far faster transmissions, lower costs, and easier access to complex files. The office of the future may soon be with us. In many respects, it already is (Kraut, 1987). It remains to be seen whether our social and managerial skills are commensurate with the scientific and technical expertise which produced the revolution in microelectronics. It may also be that society, for a host of noneconomic or nonmanagerial reasons, chooses to lessen the impact of this technology on certain aspects of traditional employment roles and practices.

Microelectronics in Commerce, Banking, and Shopping

Commerce encompasses most of the economic interactions among the members of a society. It is preeminently an information-intensive activity. Modern commercial transactions require that information on goods and services be made available quickly—sometimes almost instantaneously as on the floor of a stock exchange. The modern means of paying for goods and services, moreover, requires that financial information be transmitted between the parties involved, often acting at a distance from one another. When someone writes a check, for instance, no physical money changes hands. What happens is that information on a check simply causes the respective banks to alter their customer accounts. Even a banknote only contains the information, "I promise to pay the bearer" a specified amount. On its own, it is essentially worthless. Thus, modern money is really *information* about wealth or debt. Indeed, the whole of commerce is based on information.

We require information about the price of goods and services, about their storage and transportation, and information about payment or debt.

It is hardly surprising, therefore, that commerce in its various forms—primarily banking and finance, retailing, and distribution—has been deeply affected by the microelectronics revolution. Commerce, in fact, has been among the quickest sectors of society in adopting the new electronic technology. It is of some interest that ancient clay tablets found in the Middle East furnish strong evidence that writing itself may have originated with commercial records. Much more recently, the sales history of computers shows that the large-scale industrial applications of computers began in earnest with commercial functions. It is likely that the adoption of computers and telecommunications on so broad a scale by financial institutions encouraged, if not necessitated, similar moves by other institutions. The postal services, telephone systems, transportation companies, wholesalers and others all depend on the wheels of commerce and finance to function properly. The need for cooperation among the various sectors of an industrial society implies that a particular technology adopted in one sector will likely spread to other sectors. It is because of this multiplier effect that computers and telecommunications have displayed such explosive growth patterns in so brief a period (historically speaking).

Automated Teller Machines

Among financial industries, banking offers an excellent case study for assessing the impact of the microelectronics revolution (Menzies, 1989, pp. 97–98). Banks were among the first commercial users of mainframe computers back in the 1950s. This was because routine financial transactions were particularly amenable to automation. The whole notion of "electronic funds transfer" (EFT) actually predates the microchip by almost two decades. But predictions in the mid-1960s about the imminent EFT revolution and the "cashless society" being just around the corner did not then materialize. The high cost of electronic equipment like Automated Teller Machines (ATM), plus early resistance to payment with cards by consumers—who feared errors, fraud, and loss of privacy (see next section)—militated against an early electronic takeover in banking functions. A lack of cooperation between banks, and a mass of legal problems concerning what branches could and could not do, meant that the introduction of electronic technology was delayed further (Logsdon, 1980, pp. 315–317).

In the late 1970s and the 1980s, however, the situation changed. Once again, it was the invention of the microchip and allied devices which accelerated the pace of change. The costs of equipment such as cash dispensers and ATMs came down sharply. Over 50,000 ATMs had been installed in the U.S. by the end of 1985. By that time, Japan had more than 40,000 ATMs and France, 10,000. There has also been a rapid spread of ATMs in Canada in the past several years. Consumer resistance to EFT also waned as plastic cards and affiliated techniques became more familiar and apparently more reliable. The microchip continues to increase the power of computers behind the scenes in banks and other financial institutions. At the same time, the coming of countertop computer terminals and ATMs moved bank automation out of the back office and into the front office—indeed, onto the very streetcorners of many cities (Forester, 1987, p. 219).

The ATMs illustrate a characteristic of much of the automation of commerce. In an ATM transaction the customer himself punches a set of codes into a terminal and thereby provides the bank with machine-readable data. In effect, he/she is doing work for which the bank previously had to use its own staff. This type of indirect labor sharing is, in fact, characteristic of much of the modernization of industries. In the 1930s, for example, self-service in supermarkets began to replace what used to be the function of store clerks. In this sense, new technology can be used to save on space and staff. The implications of this for traditional employment categories are not entirely clear. What is clear, is that the microelectronics revolution is rendering some of the occupations of traditional society obsolete, for better or for worse.

A logical next step in the more complete automation of such commercial practices will be the introduction of electronic banking and shopping at home. Payments for all types of goods and services can be made by means of a computer terminal in the home. Potentially even more revolutionary than nationwide EFT would be the widespread use of TVs and telephones in conjunction with personal computers. To take advantage of home banking facilities, customers need a personal computer or similar device and a modem that enables them to hook up via the telephone line to their bank's computer. After punching in their PIN (Personal Identification Number), customers can then display their current balances and account details on their TV or personal computer screen, pay bills, transfer money from one account to another, call up statements and ask the bank questions. Home shopping or "teleshopping" systems work in much the same way. After the customer has viewed the goods and made a selection, payment is authorized by tapping in a credit card number (Compaine, 1988, pp. 202–203).

The benefits of microelectronics when applied to commerce, banking, and shopping are the familiar ones. They include increased efficiency, greater speed and convenience, greater reliability, and overall reduction in certain of the costs traditionally associated with many transactions. Home banking and shopping would be particularly useful to otherwise disadvantaged groups like the elderly and the disabled. The drawbacks are also clear. Some of them are related specifically to commerce and financial transactions; others belong to broader concerns about the impact of microelectronics generally on society. In the first category are concerns about loss and/or improper use of credit cards, fraud, theft, and actions required when errors in billing are found. Perhaps the biggest drawback is that when plastic cards are lost or stolen, there is as yet no easy way of preventing their illegal use by a third party. Some estimates have put the worldwide annual cost of card fraud as high as $1 billion. Banks and credit card companies have experimented with new types of cards—such as the "smart" ID card which contains the digitized fingerprints of the user—in the search for new, more secure systems.

Electronic commerce also figures in many of the controversies about the pervasive social impact of technological innovation (Logsdon, 1980, p. 327). Invasion of privacy is always a possibility. Another commonly voiced concern is that the quality of life is being eroded by the depersonalization associated with many kinds of automation. Often the "human touch" now seems too expensive a luxury for many cost-conscious modern businesses. There are certain situations, however, when automated systems are superior to (obsolete) personal interaction. For example, ATMs are extremely useful after ordinary business hours or for individuals who do not speak the language of a foreign country in which they are travelling. A broader concern arises from the fact that highly automated systems are often subject to major malfunctions. Their very sophistication becomes a liability in certain crises, such as power failures. Lastly, there is always the fundamental concern about the displacement of labor by microelectronic devices. Who is to be displaced, and how is the displacement to be handled? Efforts to retrain workers displaced by advances in automation generally have a poor record, even when an economy is growing rapidly. The least skilled workers will suffer most and are the ones whose educational and employment needs will require the greatest attention in an increasingly automated and computerized society. The immediate challenge, and a difficult one, is to manage the restructuring of the newly (but rapidly) emerging information/ microelectronics society in a humane way. Hopefully, we may then be spared the harsh social readjustments that characterized the early decades of the First Industrial Revolution (Ennals, 1990, pp. 102–105).

Computers, Data Networks, and the Threat to Privacy

One of the most significant consequences of the microelectronics revolution is the vast potential of computer data networks to gather, store and quickly access enormous volumes of information. The immense scale of information collected by government agencies, private corporations, and institutions such as hospitals and universities would not be possible without large centralized computers and their data bases (Nora & Minc, 1980, p. 113). Linkages of smaller computers serve a similar purpose. It is true that governments and certain private institutions did in fact collect some of this information before the advent of computers. With armies of meticulous clerks, there were a few industries and a few countries (like Germany in the 1930s) which did compile massive handwritten records about the lives of a great number of people. The power of the computer, however, far transcends that of human scribes—no matter how numerous and how well-trained—to gather and process information about individuals in a society. This will constitute one of the most far-reaching impacts of the microelectronics revolution (Hoffman, 1980).

One way to get a sense of the enormous change brought about by computers in so brief a period of human history is to compare the records that documented the life of a North American before the turn of the century with the records that document our individual lives today. One hundred years ago, the few records that existed could tell us when a child was born, when a couple were married, when a person died, and what the boundaries of the land purchased by a family were. In those days, moreover, only a handful of North Americans went to secondary school or (rarer still) to college or university. Social security or social insurance, income taxes, and life and medical insurance did not exist. Many people were self-employed or worked for other persons who did not desire or require personal information on them.

Today, fewer than 5 percent of North Americans work for themselves. And of the remaining 95 percent, almost half are employed by large corporations which collect detailed information about the education, health, family, and work habits of their employees. Today, most North Americans are covered by some kind of life and health insurance plans. Insurance companies routinely collect large amounts of information about their customers—revealing information such as whether they are seeing a psychiatrist, what drugs they use, or whether they have a drinking problem. Today, most children and many young adults are enrolled in schools, colleges and universities which generally collect detailed personal and financial histories about the student and his/her parents. Police and criminal information systems contain similarly extensive records about individuals, including criminal convictions, data on wanted persons, data on drug offenders, and data on traffic violations (Weinberg, 1990, pp. 101–102).

Concerns arise about the use and possible misuse of these computerized personal data systems. Certainly, there are numerous situations in which such data collecting practices seem reasonable and even desirable. Our modern societies could scarcely function without the data collected and processed by insurance agencies, school and university systems, medical agencies, banking machines and credit organizations and similar institutions. Such data collection and utilization is clearly necessary and probably beneficial to the individual in a technological society. The problem arises when one considers the potential for misuse or abuse of such information (Friedrichs & Schaff, 1982, pp. 283–290).

Two categories of misuse/abuse of information are possible. The first category includes the prejudicial or inappropriate use of information by the agency that actually collected the data from an individual. Thus, potential employers may use information extracted from potential employees—such as facts about medical or psychological histories—to deny employment. Far more serious, however, is the second category of potential abuse of information. This arises when two or more separate data collection systems are linked together in computer data networks. With the advances in computing storage and retrieval capacities and in telecommunications and transmission functions—such as we have witnessed in the 1970s and 1980s—the linking of computers in a massive communications network is now possible. A new—and to many, frightening—potential arises for combining data from completely separate sources into one centralized data network. Like the pieces in a puzzle, the (originally) separate pieces of data could be used to construct a fairly complete, but probably also distorted, image of the personality or character of an individual (Martin, 1988, pp. 54–55).

Transactional Information

The revolution in information technology now makes it possible to store, retrieve, and analyze masses of "transactional information." These include records of phone calls, credit card payments, air travel, reading habits as recorded by computerized library lending systems, and donations to particular political and religious groups. The sheer quantity of such transactional data on personal habits and histories is now extensive (Roszak, 1986, pp. 181–187). Given the computerized filing systems now available, many different organizations in our societies routinely collect and store vast quantities of this transactional information. The easy exchange of information between different data bases was technically not feasible at the start of the computer age. The potential for abuse, correspondingly, was not considered seriously. The sophistication of microelectronics and telecommunications has altered all that. There exists now a truly astounding maze of electronic "highways" that can move transactional information across a nation in a matter of seconds and at a trivially low cost. These giant data repositories now can "talk" to each other. Think of what it means that some 10,000 merchants in the U.S. are able to obtain a summary fact sheet about any one of nearly 90 million individual citizens in a matter of three or four seconds from a single data base in southern California. What does it mean that a handful of federal agencies in the U.S., not counting the Pentagon, have at least three separate telecommunication networks stretching all over that country (Dertouzos & Moses, 1979, pp. 87–89)?

The uses to which the information supplied by these data networks can be put are not generally appreciated by the public, or even the courts. In some cases, the power of this data can be astounding. In the early 1980s, the U.S. Senate created a special committee to investigate a very sensitive and delicate subject: the relationship between former President Jimmy Carter's brother Billy and the government of Libya. After many months of embarrassed maneuvering, the Senate committee issued a report on the antics of the brother of the President. Almost every other page of the committee's 109–page final report contains a footnote to the precise time and day of calls made by Billy Carter and his associates from at least ten different telephones operating in three different states.

The report said, for instance, that on November 26, 1979, Billy Carter and an associate began driving to Washington, D.C., from Georgia. Shortly after beginning the trip, the report said, the two men stopped to telephone the Libyan embassy and request a meeting with a high-ranking official. This assertion was supported by a footnote to telephone company records showing that a five-minute call at 3:43 was charged to Billy Carter's telephone from a pay telephone in Jonesboro, an Atlanta suburb. Another footnote said that calls were made from Carter's office telephone in Georgia to the Libyan embassy in Washington on March 7, March 10, four times on March 11, twice on March 12, three times on March 13, three times on March 14, March 15 and March 17 (Forester, 1985, pp. 546–550).

The investigations of the special Senate committee were publicly announced and caused political embarrassment to President Carter. The telephone (computer) records that documented the report, it must be noted, were obtained by a formal legal process. But this is not always the case. Obviously, investigators of all kinds are terribly interested in obtaining such transactional information—legally or otherwise. Such information can be extraordinarily revealing. Investigators can pinpoint the location of an individual at a particular moment, ascertain his/her patterns of work and travel, and identify his/her friends, business connections and political associations. Furthermore, investigators can obtain this transactional information months, even years, after the instance when the particular event documented by the computer records actually occurred. This computerized ability greatly enhances the scope of any investigation, whether overt or covert. Before the computer age, it was extremely hard to develop concrete evidence about the activities and whereabouts of an individual unless someone had been previously assigned to follow him/her (such as a private detective). In most cases, investigators were limited to pursuing the handful of persons they believed might undertake a forbidden or illegal act in the future. Now they can move back in time, easily gathering concrete evidence about any individual of interest long after the act in question occurred. The implications for the employee of any large corporation or for the citizen of a nation are potentially ominous.

Computer Crimes

The ability to obtain information from data networks by legal means is now extensive. The methods used to obtain, or disrupt, such information by less respectable means are also impressive. With access to a computer's operating system, anyone may copy, change, or delete data without authorization. In fact, computer criminals now have a variety of techniques at their disposal. The ability to access information illicitly has brought forth a whole new jargon of software sabotage. Examples include: (1) "The Trojan Horse"–this involves the insertion of false information into a program in order to profit from the outcome, such as a false instruction to make payments to a bogus company; (2) "Piggy Backing"–this entails tapping into communications lines and riding into a system behind a legitimate user who has obtained password clearance; (3) "The Salami"–this technique involves spreading the haul over a large number of small transactions, like slices of salami. For instance, a bank clerk might shave a trivial sum off many customer accounts to make up a large sum in his or her own account; (4) "Worms"–this process involves deleting specific portions of a computer's memory, thus creating a "hole" of missing information or shutting down the system's operation completely; and, lastly, (5) "The Virus"–this is a program that instructs the host machine to summon up its stored files. It then mixes them up, turning the computer's memory into a mass of confusion. "In fifteen years' time," said one Scotland Yard investigator recently, "almost every crime will involve a computer." One might add, given the extensive police use of data networks, that every crime *solved* will involve a computer. Even so, unless computer security is taken much more seriously—and the theft of information made strictly illegal and prosecuted diligently—computer crime and software sabotage could cause chaos in the 1990s (Forester, 1987, pp. 264–268).

The point is clear. There exists a tremendous potential for abuse of information in modern, sophisticated computer data networks (Nora & Minc, 1980, pp. 79–81). Private companies, for instance, can now have access to criminal data bases. Studies have shown that employers are unlikely to hire people with a criminal past. Although that is the prerogative of a prospective employer, at least two information abuses now occur routinely. First, the information about the criminal history is collected without the knowledge of the job applicant. This constitutes an invasion of privacy. Secondly, studies of the accuracy, and hence legitimate value, of criminal history data contained in many federal and local police agency files have demonstrated that some of the information is incomplete, inaccurate or ambiguous. For example, FBI computer files in the U.S. often display arrests and investigations that did *not* result in a conviction—or that related to minor offences in the dim and distant past—with the same data status as more serious offenses. The individual in question may thus be denied a job without knowing why or without the opportunity to challenge the validity of the transactional information used against him/her.

In the great rush towards the microelectronics society of the 1980s and 1990s, insufficient attention has been paid to potential information abuses such as these. Civil liberties organizations and similar groups are campaigning for adequate legislative safeguards to prevent or mitigate such computer invasions of privacy. These would include legislation granting an individual the right to access all information about him/her held in data networks, of whatever kind. When such information is found to be inaccurate or false, or if an unauthorized access to that information can be documented, the law should afford the aggrieved individual the right to have the information corrected (or deleted from the databank). There should also be legal remedies for unauthorized access and other computer crimes, such as software sabotage, theft of computerized information, and illegal hacking (Compaine, 1988, p. 219). Hacking covers a variety of legal and illegal activities. Essentially, it means using a personal computer and modem to enter other people's computer systems over the telephone wire by finding the right password. Famous examples include the students of Manhattan's (New York) Dalton High School, who, in 1980, used their classroom terminals to enter a Canadian data communications network, destroying key corporate customer files in the process. In 1984 young West German hackers caused chaos when they broke into their country's videotex network. Some French hackers actually gained access to the secret files of France's nuclear program. Hackers—sometimes called "modem maniacs"—have become increasingly controversial and common in recent years. Some steps, though far from completely adequate, have been taken to deal with such problems in the advanced industrial nations. Sweden led the way in data privacy legislation, but Canada, the U.S. and some countries in Western Europe have now enacted some (modest) computer-related laws. Societies in the microelectronics age will either pass legislation limiting collection, storage and access of personal information *or* adapt to a new situation of technologically induced reduction (or infringement) of privacy. Hopefully, a computerized version of George Orwell's *1984* will not be in our future (Bolter, 1984, p. 225). ■

D. Biotechnology

■ ■ ■

Of all the sciences, biology—the science of life and life processes, including the study of structure, functioning, growth, origin, evolution and distribution of living organisms—has always had a direct impact on human society and the environment. Human evolution was dependent on the growing biological knowledge which enabled early humans to domesticate and breed animals and plants. The history of medicine is, in many important respects, the history of humanity's increasing ability to control or mitigate the diseases afflicting our species. The theory of evolution by natural selection, developed by Darwin and Wallace in the nineteenth century (see section 3b), provided a comprehensive framework for the understanding of living organisms and their development and functioning. Finally, the discovery of the double-helix structure of DNA by Watson and Crick (announced) in 1953 (see section 4c), provided a radically new and powerful insight for biologists. The twentieth century will probably be remembered above all for two epoch-making scientific accomplishments: the knowledge of the structure of the atom and the knowledge of the structure of the gene.

The discovery of the structure of DNA was important not only for its theoretical implications, significant as these are. Since the gene is the basic unit of biological inheritance, it is the medium through which biological information of any given species of animal or plant is passed from generation to generation. It is the organizing principle by which lifeless raw materials are, with truly awe-inspiring efficiency, transformed into living entities. Thus, any insight into the structure and function of the gene affords humans the capability of influencing and altering these basic instructions of life. *Genetic engineering* is the manipulation of heredity or the hereditary material. Genetic engineering is a broad term which covers all human attempts to influence the course of evolution and alter its products. In the past decade, the dramatic advances in direct gene manipulation have given rise to the new field of *biotechnology*.

Definitions

Biotechnology is the application of scientific and engineering principles to the industrial exploitation of biological systems or processes, in order to provide new (or improved) goods and services. These applications range from the long-established technologies which are based on the commercial use of microbes (such as yeast in brewing) through to the more strategic research on genetic engineering of plants and animals (Persley, 1990, p. 1). Thus, biotechnology leads to the commercialization of the new techniques of genetic engineering (Higgins et al., 1985, pp. 1–3). Genetic engineering creates critical issues for ethics, philosophy and science policy (see sections 7a, 7b). Biotechnology shares in all these controversies and possibilities of genetic engineering. In addition, because it translates basic research into explicit commercial applications, biotechnology raises new questions for business, law, medicine and health care, agriculture and—even—biological warfare.

Humanity has tampered with heredity for as long as people have cultivated crops and bred livestock. Humans are responsible for countless alterations of the inherited properties of life forms on this planet. Traditionally, such genetic engineering was limited to artificial selection and hybridization. Artificial selection influences the inherited properties of future generations by carefully choosing their progenitors. Those subjects (animal or plant) with "desired" traits are selected for breeding while those considered "undesirable" are excluded, by one means or other, from the breeding population. Darwin regarded the tangible small-scale evidence of inherited change brought about by breeders and farmers through artificial selection of naturally occurring variations as support for the theory of evolution by natural selection. Hybridization is another genetic engineering technique. It is used to broaden the range of genetic traits from which to select those deemed desirable. Traditional hybridization, in which the inherited traits of different species or varieties are combined by interbreeding, was a well-established practice by the eighteenth century (Kohn, 1985, pp. 521–522).

The science of genetics, originating with Mendel's theory in the nineteenth century, has transformed the ancient craft of genetic engineering into a modern science-based technology. The basic principles of classical genetics, which were developed between 1910 and 1940, changed the study of biological inheritance from a descriptive, anecdotal account of various hybrid crosses, to a rigorous science (Tamarin & Leavitt, 1991, pp. 18–40). In the early part of the twentieth century, geneticists developed artificial mutagenesis. This was a novel method for generating new inherited traits. Artificial mutagenesis induces structural damage to the genetic material of living organisms by exposing them to chemical and physical mutagenic agents, such as X-rays and ultraviolet light. Applications of these principles of classical genetics had a profound effect on crop plant and domestic animal breeding. Rule-of-thumb breeding procedures were replaced with scientific regimes of artificial selection and hybridization. Artificial "in vivo" [that is, within the living organism] mutagenesis was used to generate additional genetic variation. Certain of these procedures were also applied to human populations, with often controversial results. It was Charles Darwin's cousin Francis Galton (1822–1911) who proposed that the human race might be improved in the manner of scientific plant and animal breeding. Galton's program for human improvement—which he termed "eugenics", from the Greek root meaning "good in birth" or "noble in heredity"—aimed to rid society of so-called biologically undesirable persons and to encourage the reproduction of so-called desirable people. Galton's ideas had a significant, in some instances tragic, impact on twentieth-century politics, notably in the brutal Nazi eugenics schemes prior to and during World War II (Kevles, 1985; Lifton, 1986).

Recombinant DNA Technology

The revolution in molecular biology made possible by the discovery of the structure of DNA created the conditions for an entirely new level of genetic engineering. Coupled with scientific breakthroughs in microbiology and biochemistry since World War II, molecular biology now affords humanity the opportunities for direct genetic manipulation of plants and animals (Farrington, 1989, pp. 29, 43). The massive funding poured into research on the functioning of DNA has generated a number of wholly novel techniques for microgenetic engineering. Preeminent among these is recombinant DNA technology. Recombinant DNA is a hybrid DNA molecule which contains DNA from two distinct sources. Scientists now have at hand a number of techniques for creating recombinant DNA *in vitro* [literally, "in glass"; the term refers to the study of biological processes outside the living organism, such as test tube research]. Recombinant DNA technology is the uniting of *in vitro* genetic recombination techniques with techniques for the insertion, replication and expression of recombinant DNA inside living cells (Watson, Tooze & Kurtz, 1983, p. 106). Microgenetic engineering enables the genetic engineer to decode, compare, construct, mutate, excise, join, transfer and clone specific sequences of DNA. It is now possible, therefore, to manipulate the inherited characteristics of cells and organisms through precise modification of the hereditary material itself at a molecular level.

At long last, we can look beyond the most visible manifestations of genes—physical traits ranging from hair or eye color to the texture of seeds—and gaze at the more revealing landscapes of genetic molecules themselves. This mid-twentieth century shift in focus has already paid rich dividends. It has enabled geneticists to identify and monitor the movements of individual genes directly, instead of relying exclusively on the indirect evidence of their "phenotypic footprints."

At the same time, this shift has given geneticists enormous new powers to intervene in hereditary processes and to manipulate individual genes to satisfy real or perceived human needs. Until now, the power to determine the fate of individual genes in living things has, with rare exceptions, resided in nature. Evolution tends to rid populations of organisms possessing detrimental genetic traits, albeit at a ponderously slow pace. But today we are rapidly assembling the technological tools to render our own quick judgments on the "genetic worth" of DNA sequences. We can also now impose those judgments by modifying the information stored in genetic molecules. As David Suzuki and Peter Knudtson put it: "Recombinant DNA technologies have transformed us from passive observers of the global hereditary scene to active choreographers of genes—for motives that could range from simple scientific curiosity or altruism, to profiteering or political demagoguery" (Suzuki & Knudtson, 1988, pp. 139–140).

In addition to its ethical and political dimensions, the commercialization of genetic engineering brings with it a higher order of risk than is ordinarily associated with biological research (Olsen, 1986). As the transition from research to commercial production occurs, so the sheer scale on which genetically manipulated microorganisms are used will increase. This alone increases the potential societal and environmental impact considerably. Moreover, large-scale industrial processes are operated under conditions quite different from those of scientific research.

The costs and economic impact of biotechnology are central to its very purpose and motivation (Antebi & Fishlock, 1986, pp. 191, 217). In this, it differs sharply from our traditional concept of pure scientific research. This distinction between pure and applied research is becoming blurred in many other fields of science as well. Microelectronics, for one example, provides ample confirmation of this (see section 5c). Furthermore, the large-scale industrial processes associated with biotechnology are operated by technicians and other personnel who do not possess the same level of knowledge as highly trained and qualified researchers. A similar situation characterizes many other fields of applied science and technology, such as the operation of nuclear power plants (Perrow, 1985). The potential risks associated with the commercialization of genetic engineering require specific attention.

Risk-management in biotechnology falls into two parts. The first is an assessment of the hazards, potential or actual, posed by the genetically manipulated microorganism. This deals with questions of its survival, multiplication, dissemination, transfer and pathogenic properties. This first phase of risk assessment provides the basis for the second aspect of risk-management, namely evaluation of the physical containment measures surrounding the biotechnology operations. Physical containment measures and industrial safety practices must be designed so as to reduce, as much as possible, the probability of the escape of genetically manipulated micro-organisms or vectors. [Vectors are self-replicating entities used as vehicles to transfer foreign genes into living cells and then replicate and possibly also express them; examples of vectors are plasmids and viruses.] This second aspect of risk-management is dependent on the guidelines governing large-scale industrial operations. The establishment of such guidelines is a difficult and often controversial task. Because of this, regulatory procedures must be in place to enforce the guidelines. Biotechnology is, therefore, at the interface of academic science, industry, and government activities (Kenney, 1986). The large-scale use of genetically manipulated micro-organisms poses new risks to workers and the environment. These must be dealt with effectively if the ominous scenarios predicted by some scientists, environmentalists and science fiction authors are to be avoided (Nelkin, 1992, pp. 219–222).

Plasmid and Virus Vectors

Recombinant DNA techniques were pioneered by research teams headed by molecular biologists Stanley Cohen and Herbert Boyer at Stanford University in California (Yanchinski, 1989, p. 67). Their experiments, performed in 1973 and 1974, used plasmid vectors. A *plasmid* is a small circle of DNA which replicates independently of the main chromosome(s). They were first discovered drifting in the cytoplasm of bacterial cells. Plasmids are small compared with a cell's central gene-bearing loop of DNA. They measure in length on the order of hundreds of base pairs, rather than millions. The genes of plasmids are not usually essential to normal bacterial metabolism. Thus, plasmids can be readily passed from one cell to the next—independent of the mainstream passage of genes during cell division—without disastrous consequences to cell activities. However, plasmids are also capable of fusing with the main chromosomal loop of bacterial DNA. If they then break free again, they can "tear away" a few neighboring mainstream genes. This means that during the course of their nomadic journeys, plasmids—like viruses—can transport genes throughout a population of suitable bacterial hosts (Tamarin & Leavitt, 1991, pp. 306–309).

Viruses are the other most important natural vehicle, or vector, for inserting foreign, "passenger" genes into a target cell. A virus is little more than a bundle of genes wrapped in a protective protein package for delivery. Existing on the biological boundary between the living and the nonliving, a virus is incapable of carrying out its own replication or metabolism. To do so, it must inject its nucleic acids into the interior of a host cell and genetically parasitize it. Unlike plasmids, viruses are not native residents of cells. However, since the early 1960s, geneticists studying "phages"—viruses that prey on bacteria—have known that viruses are capable of carrying bits of bacterial DNA from one host to the next. It is this natural gene-shuttling ability that has earned viruses and plasmids so prominent a place in recombinant DNA experiments (Watson, Tooze & Kurtz, 1983, p. 189).

The Boyer-Cohen research efforts at Stanford in 1973 and 1974 were crucial to the development of genetic engineering and biotechnology. These experiments used plasmids of the bacterial species *Escherichia coli,* commonly abbreviated to *E. coli.* This cigar-shaped microbe is quite common in nature and has been exhaustively studied. It inhabits the intestinal tract of most vertebrates, including humans. The Stanford experiments proved that it was possible for genes to be transferred into, cloned and then expressed in bacteria using transformation with recombinant plasmids (Suzuki & Knudtson, 1988, pp. 127–128). For example, in one set of experiments, two different antibiotic-resistant plasmids of *E. coli.* were cleaved and then recombined together. The hybrid plasmid thus formed carried genes for resistance to the two different antibiotics (in this case tetracycline and kanamycin). The hybrid plasmid was then injected into solutions of normal *E. coli.* Some of the *E. coli* cells that were infected with the hybrid plasmid then grew into colonies of *E. coli* that were resistant to both of the antibiotics.

Other sets of experiments by the Cohen-Boyer research teams demonstrated that recombinant DNA techniques made it possible for plasmid genes from one species of bacterium to be transferred into, replicated and expressed in *another* species of bacterium. A final set of experiments, the most dramatic by far, demonstrated that it was possible to transfer a gene from a higher animal—in this case, the African clawed toad, *Xenopus*—into *E. coli* bacteria. A hybrid plasmid was created by splicing some toad DNA to an *E. coli* plasmid. Colonies of bacteria descended from *E. coli* transformed by the hybrid plasmid were found to be expressing a gene that hitherto had only been expressed in toads. These experiments demonstrated the successful insertion, cloning, and expression of a gene from a higher animal into a bacterium. The remarkable success using plasmids as vectors in recombinant DNA technology has led to a veritable research industry centered on them. Plasmid vectors constructed for gene cloning and gene expression uses (in research laboratories and in industrial processes) constitute a significant portion of the commercial products of the genetic engineering industry (Nossal & Coppel, 1989, pp. 37, 125–126).

These recombinant DNA techniques were heralded as a new technological revolution. It was believed that these techniques would provide new benefits for society. These might include: (1) greater understanding of the causes and treatment of cancer; (2) more effective pharmaceutical products; (3) a second "green revolution," producing a greater abundance of food crops for less economically developed countries (Farrington, 1989, pp. 38–40); and last, but by no means the least exciting prospect, (4) new approaches to energy production and pollution control (Forster & Wase, 1987, p. 441). Moreover, the use of recombinant DNA techniques opened up new opportunities for scientific research into the mechanism of gene expression in higher organisms.

These new recombinant DNA techniques—and the biotechnology industry based on them—did, in fact, constitute a technological revolution. Prior to the advent of recombinant DNA techniques, the range of products and services provided by biotechnological processes was quite limited. Biotechnology was largely confined to the natural enzymatic capabilities of those biological agents amenable to large-scale culture, principally certain microorganisms. Many types of animal cells, however, can not be easily cultured on a large scale. This has severely limited their exploitation as a potential source of animal cell products. Using recombinant DNA techniques circumvents this natural obstacle. These techniques now permit the genetic resources of cells which are not amenable to large-scale culture to be tapped by inserting their genes into cells of organisms which *can* be cultured on a large-scale.

Genentech and Biogen

The first human gene to be expressed in bacteria by recombinant DNA techniques—and then synthesized on a reasonably large-scale— was the gene for somatostatin (Antebi & Fishlock, 1986, p.55). This is a small hormone that controls the release of other hormones from the pituitary gland. This was accomplished in 1977 by scientists at Genentech in the U.S. (Nossal & Coppel, 1989, pp. 40–41). Genentech is also the company which synthesized the hormone insulin in microbes in 1978, and human growth hormone in 1979 (Yanchinski, 1989, p. 67). Scientists at the Swiss genetic engineering company Biogen, engineered microbes to synthesize human alpha-interferon in 1980. The importance of the Biogen work on interferon was that it demonstrated that it was possible to use recombinant DNA technology to clone and express a gene about whose structure nothing was known and which ordinarily produces only a very small amount of product. Significantly, immediately after Biogen announced its success at a Boston press conference in January (1980), Biogen stock made a paper gain of $50 million (Antebi & Fishlock, 1986, pp. 81–82).

Emboldened by these early successes, other biotechnology companies have entered the search, and race, for other suitable human protein molecules to synthesize in microbes. There are believed to be over 50,000 different proteins in the human body (excluding antibodies), of which very few are currently used in medicine. In fact, fewer than 2% of these proteins have even been identified. Human proteins which have been indentified as targets for microbial synthesis using recombinant DNA technology include: (1) hormones and drugs, such as interferon, which are too complex to be made economically by traditional chemical methods; (2) blood-clotting factors, as alternatives to extracts from blood, for use in the treatment of hemophiliacs; (3) anti-clotting agents to stimulate the breakdown of blood clots which may precede strokes; (4) endorphins for the treatment of addiction to morphine drugs, for depression, and for pain relief (Antebi & Fishlock, 1986, p. 100); and (5) nerve cell growth stimulators.

It is certainly understandable why recombinant DNA technology was at first greeted with such widespread enthusiasm. Biotechnology, it was widely claimed, placed the genetic resources of the entire biosphere, including those of humans, at the disposal of the genetic engineer. The potential of this new technology is that it can take these genetic resources and use them, or alter them, in wholly novel ways. Moreover, the range of target molecules is not restricted to protein molecules. Yeast cells, for example, have long been used in brewing and fermentation to produce alcohol by promoting certain biochemical reactions. Other cells can be genetically engineered to perform similar biochemical functions in other processes. Recombinant DNA techniques can alter the biosynthetic pathways of cells, microbes and, possibly, even entire organisms. These altered biological agents might then combine and break down molecules in their immediate environment, thereby producing marketable nonprotein molecules.

The range of product molecules which can potentially be produced by recombinant cells—or organisms—encompasses virtually any organic molecule. Organic molecules are molecules which are produced by living organisms. Biotechnology may provide products that are currently available only by extraction from natural sources, such as certain flavor and perfume materials. Other potential commercial products include vaccines, pesticides, industrial solvents, oils, and lubricants. In this way, biotechnology may provide an alternative source of products now extracted from dwindling nonrenewable resources such as petrochemicals. It is this great versatility, and hence widespread applicability, of biotechnology, however, that caused some scientists, environmentalists, and public policy makers to feel uneasy. Amid the chorus of enthusiastic support for rapidly intensifying research and support of recombinant DNA technology, certain more pessimistic voices could be heard. They were concerned with the risk of conducting recombinant DNA experiments on a broad scale, fearful of potential biohazards.

Asilomar Conference

Significantly, it was a group of scientists who made the first serious effort to address the issue of the potential hazards of recombinant DNA research (Krimsky, 1982, p. 373). In February 1975, 150 participants from all over the world convened at Asilomar in the U.S. to make recommendations concerning the regulation of applying recombinant DNA techniques. One of the chief reasons for this act of "scientific self-control" was the concern that, as Stanley Cohen put it, "if the collected wisdom of this group doesn't result in recommendations, the recommendations may come from other groups less well qualified." Also influencing the decisions of the conferees was the knowledge that their recommendations were going to be scrutinized outside the scientific community, as well as within it by other colleagues. With some few notable exceptions, the Asilomar conferees concluded that recombinant DNA research should continue (Wade, 1979, chap. 5).

The recommendations of the Asilomar Conference appeared to provide adequate guarantees for conducting safe genetic engineering research. One almost immediate positive consequence of the Conference was that the National Institutes of Health (NIH) adopted many of the Asilomar recommendations. The NIH is significant because it is a major U.S. federal agency which funds and regulates federally funded research proposals. Any guidelines it adopted would have a major impact on the fortunes of recombinant DNA technology in the U.S. and, by example, also on any research undertaken in other nations. The first NIH "Guidelines for Research Involving Recombinant DNA Molecules" were issued in 1976 (Nelkin, 1992, pp. 227–238).

NIH Guidelines

Under the NIH guidelines, each of the various sorts of experiment employing recombinant DNA techniques was classified according to an estimate of the level of *risk* of *potential* biohazard it constituted. In addition, certain classes of experiments were considered to pose a potential hazard so great that they were prohibited outright. These included: (1) experiments involving the use of known pathogens or tumor viruses; (2) experiments requiring the deliberate release of recombinant organisms; and (3) those that required the use of recombinant DNA techniques on a large-scale. These last two points are extremely important. The NIH guidelines—and similar ones in other countries pursuing genetic engineering research—address the difficult problems associated with scientific research. Such research is usually conducted on a small-scale and laboratory conditions are generally (extremely) controllable. If such operations were to become commercial, and conducted on the far broader scale characteristic of biotechnology industries, there is no guarantee that operating conditions governing recombinant DNA technology could still be made secure. The NIH guidelines, then, really do not apply to commercial biotechnology (Yanchinsky, 1989, pp. 107–111).

For those classes of scientific experiments which were considered permissable, the NIH guidelines defined combinations of physical and biological *containment measures*. These correspond with estimated levels of biohazard presumed to be attached to each class of experiment. Physical containment measures are designed to prevent or minimize the escape of recombinant organisms. The 1976 NIH Guidelines prescribed four levels of physical containment, designated P1, P2, P3 and P4—in order of increasing rigor of containment procedures. Physical containment level P1 is required for what is perceived as the least hazardous class of experiments. In actual fact, this turns out to involve little more than the ordinary precautions taken in good microbiological laboratory practice. At the other extreme, a P4 laboratory is a maximum isolation installation. P4 containment procedures are deemed appropriate for handling the most dangerous pathogens, both actual or potential.

Biological containment is, essentially, an example of what is called a "technological fix." Technological fixes are attempts to solve an environmental problem arising from the use of a particular science or technology by devising a scientific or technical remedy—in other words, a further scientific or technological development. In this case, biological containment is intended to solve the problem of risk through the use of *enfeebled* microbial host strains and vectors. The purpose of biological containment is to reduce the potential hazard *were* the escape of recombinant microorganisms to occur. Microbial hosts are genetically enfeebled so that they are dependent on laboratory conditions for their survival and are less likely to survive were they to escape into the environment. Vectors are enfeebled so that they are less able to move to a new host strain. They are thus less likely to transfer foreign genes to nontarget microbial hosts. The biological containment levels in the 1976 Guidelines are classified from EK1, the lowest level of biological containment, to EK3, the highest level of precaution (National Institutes of Health, 1976).

There are a number of important criticisms of guidelines such as those adopted by NIH and those adopted in other countries, including Canada and the UK. Some critics feel that representatives of the general public—who would be most exposed to the risk of escaped pathogens—were not given an active enough role in the debates concerning recombinant DNA technology. Others argue that the question of the social morality itself of undertaking genetic engineering research and development had not been fully discussed. Concern was also expressed that the physical and biological constraints of the NIH and similar guidelines *might* work in general. But what if they failed in any one case? How would such a science-induced epidemic be controlled? (Nelkin, 1992, p. 230) All such criticisms turn on a dissatisfaction, justifiable or not, with the prevalent use of technological fixes to solve all our science/technology problems (see sections 6c, 7g).

The concerns expressed during the 1970s relating to the accidental escape of recombinant microorganisms from the laboratory were generally addressed in a satisfactory way by NIH and similar guidelines. A consensus developed that the main argument advanced to respond to the critics was valid: the microbes employed in scientific research *would* always be weakened laboratory strains, which could never establish themselves in natural ecosystems outside the laboratory. However, in the new era of biotechnology of the 1980s and 1990s, the situation is quite different. Commercial exploitation of microgenetic engineering aims to create biological products which are designed to perform specific tasks in the environment. These new genetically manipulated organisms—animals, plants, microorganisms, and live viral vaccines—have been engineered not only to survive, but to actually *flourish* in the biosphere. Their deliberate, as opposed to accidental, release creates problems which were not anticipated by the earlier guidelines.

Environmental Applications

One of the fastest growing areas of applied microbial engineering is in environmental applications for resource-recovery, waste-recycling, and environmental control (Higgins et al., 1985, pp. 280–281). Many of these applications exploit the extraordinary potential of naturally occurring microbes, such as those that tolerate high temperatures, high pressures, and high levels of radioactivity. Genetic engineering is being applied to create a new, more efficient order of microbial environmental control and resource-recovery agents. There is considerable commercial interest in genetically modifying microbes to digest oil slicks and recover oil from oil shale and tar sands. Acid-producing bacteria are being engineered to produce and withstand higher acid concentrations to improve their metal-leaching capability. Such bacteria can perform large-scale leaching of uranium from low-grade ores, for example. Other microbes can be used to remove sulfur from high-sulfur coal, to reduce sulfur dioxide pollution when the coal is burned. There is active research to genetically engineer strains of microbes which will be capable of detoxifying dangerous molecules in waste-treatment, such as the toxic chemicals from many modern industrial practices which now defy breakdown by naturally occurring microbes (Forster & Wase, 1987, p. 313).

However, the release of the new microbes presents new hazards. The expansion of the host range (and therefore applicability) for microbial pesticides, or the addition of new metabolic capabilities (such as nitrogen-fixation or pollution control) to a microbe, are genetic modifications. These same modifications may also alter some of the factors normally limiting microbial growth. Such limiting factors would include specific nutrient requirements or nonnutritional growth-regulators, such as acidity, alkalinity, salinity, and oxygen concentration. Any genetic manipulation that enhances the survival chance of a microorganism with respect to one or more of these limiting factors will alter its ecological relationships compared with those of its parental strain. Furthermore, because microorganisms actively exchange energy and nutrient elements with one another, a major metabolic change in a genetically engineered microbial species may have effects that extend well beyond that species. There may be unpredictable effects on the habitat and growth properties of other microbes in the same environment. There is also the potential for unpredictable effects arising from the transfer of vectors containing novel genes to other organisms in the environment.

Clearly, the ecological consequences of the deliberate release of microorganisms with major and novel metabolic capabilities into the biosphere are extremely difficult to assess. Risk-assessment, and risk-management, of the commercially produced microbes of the 1980s and 1990s will be a far more complex task than the risk-assessment of the 1970s (Krimsky, 1991). Fears concerning the release of novel, genetically engineered species into the biosphere assume a greater urgency now than they did when the original guidelines governing recombinant DNA technology were established. In biotechnology, as in many other exciting and promising areas of scientific research and technological development, the best course appears now to be one of proceeding cautiously (Imperato & Mitchell, 1985).

Recombinant DNA Debates

These debates about recombinant DNA techniques and biotechnology reflect the more general controversies on the appropriate role of science and technology in society (Ravetz, 1990, pp. 63–65). Uncertainties about the reliability of containment procedures in industrial recombinant DNA operations exist and must be faced. Risk-assessment for contained use and planned release of genetically manipulated organisms must be broadly based. It must include the very real possibility that, under commercial pressures, not all adequate safeguards (particularly if they are expensive or delay production) will be employed. There is also the risk that some genetically manipulated organisms may be stolen, or otherwise released from the containment facilities, without proper safety precautions. Arguments about the unreliability of purely technical safeguards to control recombinant DNA industries are not, as we have seen, unique. At the very least, there should be an independent inspectorate to monitor the standard of physical and biological containment procedures and industrial practices in operation at large-scale commercial biotechnology facilities.

Similarly complex situations arise with other instances of technological fixes. These include: (1) such devices as higher smokestacks to disperse pollution emanating from a specific local source; and (2) the use of sophisticated police computer surveillance and data banks to control computer crimes. In all these instances, the technological fix is employed more as a way of controlling symptoms of scientific and technological problems, rather than attacking their causes. The use of technological fixes, quite widespread in our advanced industrial societies, tends to focus our attention on piecemeal remedies. In so doing, we often neglect, or ignore, the possibly more deeply rooted social reasons for such problems or their symptoms. It is becoming clearer, to some groups and individuals at least, that by focusing on technological fixes—by throwing ever more scientific and technical resources into problem-solving for environmental concerns—our societies may be missing the point. What seems to be called for, now, is a truly multidisciplinary effort to address our numerous environmental concerns. Policies for regulating and controlling the applications of modern science and technology should now become the focus of informed public discussion and active public participation (Jasanoff, 1991) [see chapter 7].

Many writers and public figures now emphasize that exclusive, or undue, reliance upon technological remedies may not be the most effective way of dealing with our growing set of environmental problems. By accepting proliferating pollution, hazardous wastes, and climate malfunctions, for example, as a fact of "social life" we don't always search for the reasons as to why those problems exist to such a marked degree in the first place. Perhaps the best solution to environmental pollution owing to our massive use of fossil fuels and nuclear energy is to use less energy in the first place. The conserver society may be the best antipollution device available. Technological fixes, from this perspective, often act to discourage attempts at human negotiations and the altering of underlying social attitudes. In this light, the debates on biotechnology are actually debates about the direction our societies, and we as individuals, will be taking in the 1990s and beyond (Douglas & Wildavsky, 1982).

With respect to the specific issue of biotechnology, the political and economic climate is now favorable to more intensive research and development. The intrinsic scientific interest in recombinant DNA research, coupled with the powerful economic inducements for industry, have propelled companies to invest heavily in biotechnology. Significantly, soon after the discovery of recombinant DNA in the early 1970s, NIH altered its own patent policies to encourage some of the best NIH-supported scientists to participate in the commercial exploitation of their discoveries by forming startup firms (Alic et al., 1992, p. 384). It is advisable, nonetheless, that the scientific community and genetic engineering firms exercise restraint in pursuing microbial release experiments. Ideally, we should wait until such time as the science of ecology has matured sufficiently to provide the methodology adequate to the task of biotechnology risk-assessment. However, the pressures to forge ahead are powerful. There exists, for example, the potentially great social promise of gene therapy for disease, of new reproductive technologies, and of resource-recovery and waste-management possibilities.

Gene Therapy

Recombinant DNA technology empowers us to manipulate the genetic material of living cells more precisely than has previously been possible. The techniques were pioneered using microbial cells, but there are various ways in which the recombinant DNA technology can be applied to the genetic material of human cells. Of all the many implications of genetic technology, none is more controversial than human genetic engineering. The pace of development of new medical genetic technologies often is so rapid, that a full understanding of their potential social and moral consequences is not always possible. In any event, once a new medical genetic technology has been developed, there is a tendency—owing to perceived commercial as well as medical benefits—for its applications to be explored. There are then strong pressures to implement that technology (Kevles & Hood, 1992, p. 138). Such is the case with the medical use of genetic engineering. A wide range of techniques are being developed for the microscopic manipulation of human cells.

In the past decade, scientists have successfully injected foreign DNA sequences directly into the reproductive cells or developing embryos of a host of animal species, including frogs, rabbits and pigs. These pioneering experiments have generated considerable excitement among geneticists because they open new avenues for exploring the genetics, physiology and future development of these species. At the same time, they have also stirred great interest in possible practical applications of genetic manipulation in higher animals. Among these applications is the creation of novel, genetically enhanced "superlivestock" harboring foreign DNA sequences. Such genetic manipulations are designed to spur the growth of the animals or improve milk or meat production.

It may even be possible in the very near future to transform farm animals into "genetic factories" for the commercial production of hormones, antibodies and other valuable proteins. In the human sphere, these recent experiments in manipulating the genes of reproductive cells and developing embryos create truly revolutionary options (Persley, 1990, pp. 30–37).

One of the most exciting, albeit controversial, potential applications of human microgenetic engineering is that we may one day be able to intervene directly to correct genetic errors underlying a number of hereditary diseases. By demonstrating that foreign DNA can be directly introduced into animals as complex as mammals, recent studies have hastened the day when gene therapy—the medical replacement or repair of defective genes in living human cells—will become a reality. Even the most optimistic of these researchers realize that gene therapy will not be a panacea for all of the human species' ills. Of all diseases, only a portion have, up until now, been traced to specific genetic abnormalities—defects in one or more genes or chromosomes. Of these, only a smaller fraction still seem to be monogenic, or traceable to the activity of a single gene (and thus transmitted in simple Mendelian fashion). The majority of human diseases—from cancer and viral infections to mental illnesses and dietary deficiencies—seem to be the result of more complex interactions involving more than one gene *and* a multitude of environmental factors. Yet the ability to cure even one genetic disease is a goal that few would argue is not worth intensive research efforts and government and/or private funding.

Among the diseases which are known to arise from common single-gene disorders are Tay-Sachs disease, Sickle-cell anaemia, Cystic fibrosis, hemophilia (the blood-clotting disorder that afflicted Queen Victoria's royal pedigree), Huntington's chorea (which eventually crippled folksinger Woody Guthrie), Lesch-Nyhan syndrome, and Duchenne muscular dystropy. Typically, though not always, these single-gene disorders afflict babies and young people. Many of them are associated with chronic and distressing mental or physical handicap, or with both. Duchenne muscular dystrophy is a form of progressive wastage of the muscles which affects one in 3,000 male births. Apparently normal at birth, unusual clumsiness due to muscle lapse is apparent by 3 to 4 years of age, leading to wheelchair confinement by the age of 10, and death by about the age of twenty. Cystic fibrosis is a devastating childhood disease caused by the malfunctioning of mucus-producing glands in the body. Lesch-Nyhan syndrome is a devastating neurological disorder that can cause cerebral palsy, mental retardation, and even a bizarre form of behavior involving self-destructive biting of the lips and fingers. It affects about one person in 10,000, most of them children. Obviously, many single-gene diseases cause distress and suffering for afflicted children and their families. They also place a considerable burden on healthcare and other social services.

Most disorders caused by single-gene abnormalities are what are called inborn errors of metabolism. The defective gene usually cannot produce—or produces a defective version of—a critical enzyme. The absence of the enzyme in a particular person effectively blocks an essential biochemical reaction needed for normal functioning. In some cases, the absence of the biochemical reaction results in the buildup of toxic levels of unprocessed intermediate chemicals within nerve and other body cells. In the case of Lesch-Nyhan syndrome, there is a toxic buildup of uric acid. By correcting the single-gene defect, appropriate enzyme production is made possible and normal bodily functioning occurs. This is why such diseases are deemed to be appropriate candidates for gene therapy (Singer, 1985, pp. 130, 133–135).

There are several possible strategies for human gene therapy:

1. Gene Insertion–The most straightforward approach to gene therapy would be *gene insertion*. This would involve the simple insertion of one or more copies of the normal version of a gene into the chromosomes of a diseased cell. The defective gene would still remain in place. Once expressed, these supplementary genes could produce sufficient quantities of a missing enzyme or structural protein, for example, to overcome the inherited deficit.

2. Gene modification–A more delicate feat is *gene modification*. This would entail the chemical modification of the defective DNA sequence right where it lies in the living cell. An effort would be made to recode its genetic message to match that of the normal gene. In principle, this approach would be less likely to disrupt the intricate geographical layout of genes on chromosomes. This method would thereby reduce the possibility of unwanted side effects.

3. Gene surgery–The most radical approach would be actual *gene surgery*. This would involve the precise removal of a faulty gene from a chromosome. A replacement (normal) gene would then be introduced into the exact location of the original DNA sequence on the chromosome. The notion of transplanting freshly synthesized DNA sequences to replace defective ones is the ultimate dream of gene therapy. But it would demand a mastery of human genetics that, for the moment at least, simply exceeds the geneticist's grasp (Suzuki & Knudtson, 1988, pp. 184–185).

Eventually, all three approaches may prove medically feasible. But only the first—gene insertion—appears to be technically feasible for the immediate future. In any event, the costs of such procedures would likely be staggering, rivalling the required costs of heart transplants with all the pre- and post-operative patient care (Nossal & Coppel, 1989, p. 83). There are, of course, other available methods of treating genetic diseases, each with its attendant advantages and disadvantages. These include: (1) dietary supplements or avoidance (which circumvent the affected metabolic step and may prevent the onset of damage); (2) organ transplants to replace defective organs (Smith, 1989, pp. 93–113); and (3) behavioral strategies such as avoidance of drugs and environmental stimuli known to trigger the condition. But with a number of prominent research groups increasingly eager to begin clinical trials of gene-transfer techniques—on human volunteers suffering from incurable genetic diseases—reliance on the more traditional therapies may soon diminish (Kevles & Hood, 1992, pp. 128–135).

The attractions of gene therapy are powerful. The promise of ameliorating, or possibly curing, hereditary diseases by altering or replacing defective genes to overcome specific defects in the genetic program is an irresistible lure to continued research. It certainly represents an entirely novel approach to certain aspects of the broader questions of human disease and suffering. If genetic knowledge and technology are applied wisely, there may be little reason to fear the remarkable new conceptions of disease and cure now emerging from genetics research (Nossal & Coppel, 1989, pp. 150-151). At the same time, these novel techniques of human genetic manipulation call for society's utmost vigilance and public debate to ensure that genetic manipulation of human health does not foster a revival of dubious eugenics programs. The current and massive effort to map the human genome renders the need for social and individual responsibility more acute still (Kevles & Hood, 1992, p. 320). Having accepted gene therapy, the next issue will be whether the same techniques should be used to bring about changes other than the cancellation of genetic abnormalities. For many people, this is the frontier we must not cross. Correcting medical defects is one thing, but starting to choose the genetic characteristics of people with normal genes is another (Yanchinski, 1989, p. 119). Medical biotechnology affords one of the most complex examples of the risks and benefits associated with advances in science and technology.

There exists also the potential for ecological disruption, even disaster. At the present time, for instance, biotechnology is making a significant contribution to biological warfare. Microgenetic engineering permits the construction of microbes with previously unattainable combinations of characteristics. Biotechnology is thus revolutionizing both defensive and offensive biological weapons research. It is imperative that the public become fully aware of this new biological dimension to the arms race. Through public opinion, pressure should be brought to bear upon governments to ban the use of biotechnology for military purposes in order to avert the ensuing, potentially catastrophic, consequences (Wright, 1990). Biotechnology—and genetic engineering in general—confronts us with powers and perils. Some of these are unprecedented in human history. It is only by recognizing the necessary constraints on biotechnology and its manifold applications, that our societies—indeed, the biosphere—will avoid certain of the pitfalls that await the overly optimistic. ∎

Science, Technology and Global Affairs

6

A. Science and Social Responsibility: The Atomic Bomb and World War II

■ ▪ ■

In November 1945, just three months after the first atomic bombs were dropped on Hiroshima (6 August 1945) and Nagasaki (9 August 1945) in Japan, J.Robert Oppenheimer declared: "We have made a thing, a most terrible weapon, that has altered abruptly and profoundly the nature of the world" (Oppenheimer, 1946, p. 7). Oppenheimer, one of America's most brilliant physicists, was then the director of the Los Alamos (New Mexico) laboratory where the first atomic bombs were designed and assembled. Many others—including other scientists, but also politicians, diplomats and ordinary citizens—expressed similar views. Oppenheimer voiced what many recognized at once, namely, that the destructive power of the new weapon was without precedent in human history. With its dramatic appearance on the political scene, the first atomic bomb called into question some of the basic assumptions governing the conduct of international relations. Science had entered the world of power politics in a cataclysmic way. We have seen that science and technology have exerted considerable sociopolitical impacts throughout history. However, in 1945 it seemed that the relationship between science, technology and society had entered a new, and deeply disturbing, phase (Malcolmson, 1985, pp. 7–9, 27–31).

The atomic bomb is a supreme example of how the abstract researches of scientists, such as Einstein and his generation of physicists, can quickly become applied in ways that could not have been foreseen originally. The history of the atomic bomb constitutes a critical case study for the contemporary social context of science and technology at the local, national, and global levels (Rhodes, 1986). Science and technology today are an inextricable part of our culture. Even the most esoteric discoveries can soon be translated into applications that prove both beneficial as well as gravely dangerous. Oppenheimer's statement poses the dilemma facing modern society clearly. Nuclear energy, genetics, chemistry—the list goes on—provide us with technologies and products without which modern society would be unthinkable. Yet in the very process by which new developments in science and technology serve and satisfy particular societal appetites—or create them—our environment, both physical and cultural, becomes transformed in often unexpected and unintended ways. There exists a gap between what we perceive our social, political and philosophical issues to be, and the actual conditions which modern science and technology create. It seems that we still live, in our thoughts and actions, in a sociopolitical age that science is rendering obsolete in some crucial respects (Jervis, 1989). In perhaps no area is this paradox more acute than in the relationship between science and military affairs.

Nobel's Legacy

The beginnings of the modern arms race may be traced to events toward the close of the nineteenth century. Up until that period, manpower—numbers, training, and discipline—had been of decisive importance in determining a nation's military strength. It was with the Franco-Prussian War of 1870–71 that the importance of sophisticated armaments began to rival personnel in providing the measure of military might. Expenditure on these new armaments, including improved transport and delivery of weapons and communications signals, grew dramatically. By the start of World War I, scientists had become critical actors in the development of new materials and methods of warfare. The invention of dynamite in 1866 by Alfred Nobel may be seen as one of the earliest examples of the tight modern relationship between scientific discovery and military matters. In retrospect, Nobel's legacy establishing prizes for scientific achievement and for contributions to world peace might seem a symbolic recognition that scientific advances made war more dreaded than ever. In the light of subsequent history, Nobel's gesture appears a rather utopian prelude to the assertion of the political responsibility of scientists of the present age. Nobel believed that universal possession of so destructive a weapon as dynamite would in itself cause war to be avoided, or even eliminated, as an instrument of international competition. Clearly, a similar belief is held by some today regarding the possession of nuclear weapons. In any event, by the start of World War I, science and technology had come to play a dominant role in military preparations (Olby, 1990, pp. 939–943).

Scientists and engineers could, with some justification, begin to envision themselves as rivals to the professional soldier. During World War I, new weapons were introduced which owed all or part of their genesis to science and technology. In strictly military terms, the most significant technical innovations were those that greatly increased mobility on land and through the air. The technologies associated with the internal combustion engine—the motor car, the tank, the warship and, above all, the airplane—both stimulated and were stimulated in turn by the preparations for, and conduct of, war (see section 5a). But, though it claimed fewer casualties, it was poison gas more than any other development which brought to light the changing relationship of science to warfare. The employment of chlorine gas by the Germans in April 1915 opened the path to the fateful scientific involvement in war which characterizes the twentieth century. Indeed, World War I is called by some historians the "chemists' war." Like chemistry, but on a much smaller scale, biology also was found to have military application during World War I. German agents are said to have secretly infected horses shipped from the Unites States to Europe.

Indisputably, the science which figures most significantly in war and peace in the twentieth century is physics—specifically atomic and nuclear physics. With the development of the atomic bomb and the decision to use that bomb against Japan in August 1945, the full implications of science for war became evident. When Albert Einstein affixed his signature to a two-page letter to President Roosevelt six years previously (on 2 August 1939), the process which led to the famous Manhattan Project of World War II commenced (Grodzins & Rabinowitch, 1963, pp. 11–12). Einstein later regretted signing this letter—which may be taken as symbolically and actually inaugurating the Nuclear Age—and spent much of the remainder of his life in campaigning for world disarmament and peace. The steps which led to Einstein's letter—recommending that atomic bombs could, and should, be made—constitute a crucial background to the complex contemporary issues regarding the social responsibility of science and scientists. This tale begins innocently enough with some brilliant advances in theoretical physics during the last few years of the nineteenth century.

Discovery of Radioactivity

Primarily through the researches of Marie (1867–1934) and Pierre Curie (1859–1906) and Antoine Henri Becquerel (1852–1908), it was established that certain "radioactive" substances spontaneously emit subatomic particles and high-frequency electromagnetic radiations. Becquerel made the first discovery of natural radioactivity in the element uranium in 1896. Two years later in 1898, the Curies announced their discovery of two new radioactive elements: radium and polonium (named after Marie's country of origin, Poland). They concluded that the immense strength of this "ray activity" within the atom exceeded that of any known chemical or mechanical forces. All the chemical reactions or application of heat to which these substances were subjected did not seem to affect their capacity to give off these peculiar and powerful rays. Marie Curie in particular believed that some new force of nature was involved. Unlike the processes that normally generate heat and light around us, this radiation was not the consequence of ordinary chemical changes. It was Marie who gave the name of radioactivity ("ray activity") to the power of uranium, radium, polonium and other substances which displayed a similar property.

During the last two years of the nineteenth century, radioactivity itself was analyzed further. The New Zealand physicist Ernest Rutherford (1871–1937) found in 1898 that there are at least two components in radioactive emanation. He called the first type "alpha rays." These were the least penetrating, being stopped by a few centimeters of air or thin sheets of paper. Rutherford called the second, more penetrating type, "beta rays." A third type of ray was discovered by the Curies' colleague Paul Villard in 1900. They were later called "gamma rays" and are the most penetrating. In September 1898, Rutherford became professor of physics at McGill University in Montreal. His laboratory there was one of the best in the Western Hemisphere. (It was financed by a tobacco millionaire who himself considered smoking an awful habit.) In collaboration with the British chemist Fredrick Soddy (1877–1956), Rutherford advanced the still-accepted explanation of radioactivity. Their theory, announced in 1902–1903, was called the disintegration or transformation theory. Although alchemy had long be excised from scientific chemistry (see section 2b), Rutherford and Soddy declared that radioactive atoms emit rays as a by-product of their transformation, or decay, to another more (relatively) stable species of atom. This theory, with its emphasis on the transformation of radioactive elements was to prove crucial in the development of atomic physics during the first decades of the twentieth century (Allibone, 1972).

For his achievements at McGill, where he remained until he moved to the University of Manchester in England in 1907, Rutherford received the Nobel Prize for Chemistry in 1908. (Marie and Pierre Curie had shared the Nobel Prize for Physics in 1903 with Henri Becquerel.) In 1911, Rutherford proposed a model of the atom. He demonstrated that an atom consisted largely of empty space, with a very tiny and very dense positively charged nucleus at the center and oppositely charged (negative) electrons arranged somehow around it. Rutherford's model of the nuclear atom was refined by the Danish physicist Niels Bohr (1885–1962). Bohr demonstrated that the electrons, each with a negative charge, orbited the nucleus at specific, fixed distances (see section 4b). Bohr's atom as a whole is, therefore, electrically neutral. His now famous model depicts the atom as a tiny solar system. However, whereas the planets revolve about the Sun at various distances during their orbits, Bohr's electrons can orbit the nucleus only at certain fixed distances.

Rutherford's demonstration of the atomic nucleus focused the attention of scientists on the central nuclear core, rather than the whole atom, as the source of radioactive decay. Much research in physics was done on the structure of the atom and the nucleus in the two decades following Rutherford's announcement. It was shown theoretically that the spontaneous transformation of one radioactive nucleus into another follows the law for the conversion of mass to energy claimed by Einstein's theory of relativity (see section 4a). Investigation of the nucleus received a new impetus in 1932, with the discovery of the *neutron* by the British physicist James Chadwick (1891–1974). Because the neutron is not electrically charged, it would not be repelled by the highly charged (positive) nucleus. The neutron was seen thus as a "magic bullet" in experimental studies in atomic physics. The discovery in 1934, by Irene (Marie's daughter) Joliot-Curie (1897–1956) and Frederic Joliot-Curie (1900–1958), of artificially induced radioactivity opened further vistas. They demonstrated that radioactivity could be induced in substances which were normally nonradioactive. Their work stimulated further investigations of nuclei with neutron probes. The culmination of these experiments was the study of the effect of neutron bombardment of uranium atoms in 1938 by two German scientists, Otto Hahn (1879–1968) and Fritz Strassman (1902–1980) (Hartcup & Allibone, 1984, pp. 119–120).

Nuclear Fission

Hahn and Strassman expected to find the formation of uranium isotopes with atomic weights slightly higher than that of ordinary uranium (owing to neutron capture). Instead, to their great surprise, they found that the sample of bombarded uranium contained nuclei with roughly half the charge and mass of the original uranium nucleus. This mysterious result was soon cleared up by the Austrian-Swedish physicist Lise Meitner (1878–1968) and her nephew Otto Frisch (1904–79). They suggested that in Hahn and Strassman's experiment the uranium nucleus was actually split by incident neutrons into two smaller nuclei, with the attendant release of some free neutrons. It was also noted that the combined mass of the fission fragments was appreciably less than the mass of the original uranium atoms. It was rapidly realized by some physicists that this process of *nuclear fission* should produce an appreciable amount of energy. For, in accordance with Einstein's conversion formula $E=mc^2$, the decreased mass of the fission products should appear in the form of energy.

Frisch and Meitner's interpretation of Hahn and Strassman's experimental findings as nuclear fission opened up a radically new path in physics. For, instead of just "chipping off" small pieces of a bombarded nucleus, as was the case in all previous experiments, here was the complete break-up of an atomic nucleus. The Hahn-Strassman experiment (at the Kaiser Wilhelm Institute in Berlin) was thus the first laboratory demonstration of the theoretical prediction of nuclear fission (Weart, 1979, pp. 55–59). But it was just that: a laboratory experiment using only small samples of uranium. The path was now open for scientists to investigate the dynamics of nuclear fission on a broader scale. In particular, the attendant release of neutrons as fission by-products implied the possibility of a *sustained* fission process. If somehow the free neutrons released during the initial fission reaction could themselves initiate further fission of surrounding atoms, a "branching" or "chain reaction" might be possible. *All* the nuclei in a given uranium sample could, theoretically, break up with the liberation of a tremendous amount of energy.

In fact, when news of the German work reached the United States in January 1939, a few American scientists quickly duplicated the experimental procedures of Hahn and Strassman. In September of that same year, Niels Bohr and the physicist John Wheeler published a major article in the *Physical Review* on the theory of nuclear fission. It was now clear to scientists throughout the world that it was theoretically possible—although in practice very difficult—to produce a chain reaction that would lead to an uncontrolled release of energy. In other words, an atomic explosion was a scientific possibility (Weart, 1979, pp. 108–109). It is highly significant that the article of Bohr and Wheeler was both the first and last comprehensive article on the theory of nuclear fission which appeared as open literature in an international scientific journal. The curtain of secrecy was soon imposed on free exchange of ideas on that subject. Such a restriction of discussion is, ideally, alien to the pursuit of scientific knowledge. But the efforts to produce an uncontrolled atomic explosion—in effect, an atomic bomb—had become embroiled in the opening phases of World War II (Pais, 1991).

Einstein's Letter

It is at this point that Albert Einstein's famous letter to President Roosevelt enters into the picture. A group of European émigré scientists—including refugees from Hitler's Germany and fascist Italy—had resettled in, among other countries, the United States (Fleming & Bailyn, 1969). Familiar with the brilliant advances in physics during the late 1930s—particularly the experimental work of Hahn and Strassman in Berlin—these émigré scientists worried that Nazi physicists might soon succeed in providing Hitler with the ultimate weapon: an atomic bomb (Weart, 1979, p. 185). They believed that only if the Allied powers beat the Germans in this scientific race would a Nazi victory in World War II be averted. They further believed that the Allies would not use such atomic weapons except defensively. Ironically, their basic fear proved unjustified. As it turned out later, German scientists started only very slowly on nuclear research for a bomb. The Nazi nuclear program never made significant progress. Some historians suggest that certain German physicists deliberately stalled in their research because of distaste for Hitler's aims (Walker, 1989). And when, finally, Allied bombing and relentless military pressure on Germany's eastern front strained the capacities of the Nazi regime, the scientific work there came virtually to a standstill. However, that could not have been known, or even foreseen, in 1939.

Thus, a group of notable physicists—including Leo Szilard, Enrico Fermi, Eugene Wigner and Edward Teller—urged the most famous "new American" of them all, Einstein, to write personally to President Roosevelt. They believed that Einstein, then living in Princeton, New Jersey, could (and should) use his international fame to secure the power and assistance of the United States government in the scientific investigation of the problem of producing a viable chain reaction. Einstein agreed and his letter to Pres. Roosevelt, dated 2 August 1939—about the potential implications of atomic energy—is a crucial document in both the history of physics and in the modern relationship between science, technology, and government.

To understand the symbolic as well as practical importance of the Einstein letter, it is necessary to recall that the United States government offered at that time virtually no funding for atomic research. Much of the American scientific community itself, and all of the military establishment, scoffed at even the idea of the possibility of creating such a weapon. Fermi, one of the few scientists then deeply absorbed in research on a chain reaction, made negligible experimental progress because no pure uranium was available to him. He and Szilard tried by themselves to secure the support of the U.S. government but were unsuccessful. They thus turned to Einstein to press their case to Roosevelt. Einstein was a logical choice. He was the most famous scientist in the world, a bitter foe of Hitler, and known personally to Roosevelt. His letter was brought to the President in October 1939 by Alexander Sachs, an amateur follower of scientific affairs and a personal friend of Roosevelt (Jungk, 1958, pp. 85–86). In it, Einstein clearly informed the President of the potential significance of atomic research and urged the Administration to establish an official contact with the group of physicists then working on chain reactions in the United States.

Roosevelt, preoccupied with the war and other matters of state, seemed at first uninterested in Einstein's letter. Sachs—because he was, unlike the President, familiar with scientific matters—reiterated the urgency of Einstein's comments. The crucial point here is that only a scientist or a scientifically knowledgeable person would have even been aware of the experimental work of Fermi and Szilard. At that time, the prospect of uranium being turned into a new and important source of energy in the immediate future would scarcely have seemed likely. That experimental research in atomic physics would also lead to the construction of extremely powerful bombs of a new type would have appeared as mere science fiction. Roosevelt could hardly have been expected to regard the letter as a significant item on the agenda of a wartime leader. Einstein's final point, that Germany had stopped the sale of uranium from the Czechoslovakian mines she had recently taken over, makes sense only if one were aware of the significance of the experimental work at the Kaiser Wilhelm Institute in Berlin. Sachs was in a position to understand the full implications of Einstein's letter, and he finally convinced the President of its importance (Sherwin, 1987, pp. 26–27).

Manhattan Project

Roosevelt agreed to set up a government advisory group to evaluate the issues raised by Einstein. The project to develop an atomic bomb—which would later evolve into the **Manhattan Project**—was begun officially by the U.S. governement with a grant of $6000 for uranium research. When measured against the final total of $2 billion consumed by the Manhattan Project—the largest scientific undertaking in history up till that time—the scientists' disappointment at Roosevelt's initial response may be imagined (Sherwin, 1987, p. 42). In fact, the atomic project proceeded only slowly during 1939–42, for a number of reasons. There was nearly complete incomprehension, if not opposition, to the proposal to fund atomic research both in scientific and governmental circles. There seemed little justification for funding such research when so many other, more proven, enterprises were pressing their claims on a wartime budget. Moreover, the growing atmosphere of uncertainty and secretiveness among the Allies augmented the countless administrative and technical obstacles facing coordinated energy projects. That these obstacles were overcome is largely due to the sustained efforts of émigré scientists like Einstein and Fermi and certain of their colleagues in the U.S., the U.K. and Canada. These scientists repeatedly took the initiative in bringing atomic weapons into the world. As one historian has stated, their initiative was perhaps the most important "raw material" used in the rapid achievement of atomic power (Jungk, 1958, p. 113). The definitive role of scientists in initiating the Allied efforts to build atomic bombs in World War II poses, in dramatic fashion, the question of social responsibility in science.

It is clear that the concerned scientists had made a positive moral decision to encourage the development of a potentially devastating weapon. Most of them, to be sure, labored under the belief that Germany might be engaged on just such a project. In the early years of the War, they believed that an Allied counterprogram was essential to avert disaster. Einstein declared, however, that at the time he took the fateful step of writing to Roosevelt, he assumed the U.S. would never use such a bomb except for self-defense against a similar weapon. But when, six years later (1946), the first atomic bomb was used against Japan—an enemy which did not possess such a weapon—Einstein felt that the scientists had been politically naive, perhaps, in 1939. He said with deep regret after the war: "If I had known that the Germans would not succeed in constructing the atom bomb, I would never have lifted a finger" (Jungk, 1958, pp. 86–87). The irony of the decision taken by the pacifist Einstein only renders the sociopolitical dilemmas facing scientists when they, or their ideas, enter the political realm more acute (Galison & Bernstein, 1989). In any event, the situation passed out of Einstein's and his scientific colleagues' hands in 1942.

In one important sense, the scientists had finally achieved their goal. Roosevelt and British Prime Minister Winston Churchill agreed in 1942 to concentrate the work of Allied scientists in North America (in laboratories in the U.S. and Canada). Even this concentration of work almost immediately proved itself too uncoordinated for such a massive and urgent project as the wartime atomic program. Oppenheimer suggested that U.S. and Canadian research efforts should be united in one location (Badash et al., 1980). Otherwise, he argued, duplication of proceedings and confusion of directives would inevitably result due to the strained atmosphere of war preparations. Oppenheimer further suggested that the entire Allied research and development effort be put under the direction of a single individual. His views were accepted and a super laboratory was set up, under his direction, at Los Alamos in New Mexico. Thus began the Manhattan Project, out of which was to come the first atomic bomb in 1945 (Sherwin, 1987, pp. 53–58).

The Manhattan Project is crucial in history for several reasons. First, it did achieve the goal of producing an atomic weapon based on the theory of a sustained nuclear chain reaction. But there were a number of other aspects of the Manhattan Project which were equally momentous (Stoff, 1991). It signalled the definitive entry of government into its modern large-scale involvement with basic scientific research and development. Up until the 1930s, much of the support for basic research came from the funds of wealthy individuals such as the Rockefellers, the Mellons, and (as we have seen) the Canadian McGill. The decision to develop the atomic bomb, however, initiated a project which was beyond the means of even the wealthiest private benefactors. Government funds—those of the U.S., Canada and the U.K. primarily—were committed on a massive scale. Scientific talent from many nations was assembled at Los Alamos. Backed by the support of Churchill and Roosevelt and the enormous organizational capacity of American industry, the Manhattan Project rapidly grew into a multibillion dollar enterprise. Major industrial plants to implement the atomic technology went up simultaneously with, or sometimes before, the laboratory testing of prototypes. The conduct of basic research and the development of new technologies—as well as the steps leading to the political decision to use the bomb against Japan in August of 1945—all involved scientists and engineers, in largely unprecedented ways, with the complex workings of government, military planning, and the politics of funding. The Manhattan Project may be taken, then, as symbolic of the coming of age of modern science as a major, if not the dominant, force in twentieth-century society (Kevles, 1977).

For science and scientists, perhaps the most critical outcome of the Manhattan Project has been to focus the issue of their social responsibility more sharply than ever before in history. To put the question bluntly, but simplistically, it may be asked: "Were the scientists responsible for Hiroshima and Nagasaki?" The answer, at once equivocal and true, is "yes and no." In at least two senses, certainly, scientists such as Einstein and Fermi were directly responsible. It was the theoretical and experimental work of physicists and chemists which led to the possibility of developing an atomic bomb. Moreover, it was the scientific community itself—or rather, one segment of it—which informed and convinced political and military leaders of the (perceived) urgency of actually developing such a weapon. But the final decision to fund the Manhattan Project was a political one. And the decision to deploy the developed technology—the bomb—was ultimately a political and military one (Sherwin, 1987, pp. 202–210, 224–228).

Even if the question posed above can not be given a simple answer, the very fact that it may be asked reveals a critical aspect of modern science and technology. History is replete with examples of the often crucial role science and technology have played in cultural matters. However, the political role of scientists and engineers, although always present, was largely incidental or minimized. To be sure, there are notable historical exceptions. In the seventeenth century, Galileo assumed an explicitly polemical public stance in his struggles with the Roman Catholic Church (see sections 2a. 2c). During the French Revolution, scientists and engineers were pressed into direct political and military state service (see section 2d). The professionalization of science during the nineteenth century further deepened the scientist's involvement in social issues (see section 3a). But it is the Manhattan Project which most clearly, and irreversibly, established the modern sociopolitical context of science (Kaplan, 1983, chaps. 1–3).

In speaking of the political role of scientists, we are not referring to the political role that each scientist may exert as an individual citizen of a particular society. Rather, we are referring to the role that scientists, either individually or as a group, exercise as members of their profession. Each profession, ideally, confers a degree of expertise upon its members. Whether in the case of scientists that technical expertise extends to their sociopolitical pronouncements is another matter. Indeed, as the conflicting opinions among the scientific community itself (concerning the decision to build and drop the atomic bomb) revealed, the scientists had no unique or unambiguous political advice to offer in the early 1940s (Sherwin, 1987, pp. 210–215). Einstein himself had contradictory attitudes about his role in those fateful years. What *is* clear is that scientists were decidedly unprepared to assume the functions of statemen and strategists. Nothing in their scientific training had prepared them for these broader sociopolitical tasks. Equally clear, however, was the fact that scientists had specific areas of expertise which were directly relevant to political decision-making. The enormity of the Manhattan Project and its consequences for war—and peacetime—demonstrated at the very least, and in a most striking and fearful manner, that significant new links had to be formed between the scientific community and the world of political and social action. Science's age of innocence—if indeed there had ever been one—came abruptly to an end on 6 August 1945 (Malcolmson, 1985, pp. 67–68, 107–110).

The Military-Industrial Complex

As events record, the dropping of the atomic bombs did mark a clear turning-point in the relationship between science and society. The notion that science was in some way a politically neutral activity was banished irrevocably. The internationalist tone of science and its professional bodies, which was (more or less) a characteristic feature of the pre–World War II landscape, vanished during the war and its Cold War aftermath. Both individually and in groups, some scientists became forceful advocates of national nuclear development for military purposes. This foreshadowed what President Dwight D. Eisenhower would later call, in his now-famous farewell address to the nation in January 1961, the "military-industrial complex" (Eisenhower, 1961, pp.

1038–1039). Eisenhower was referring to that linkage between scientists, engineers, politicans, and the military which came to influence the direction of much of U.S. government spending on research and development (R&D) since World War II. Briefly put, in the U.S.—as in many other nations—scientific progress, the demands of the armed forces and political decisions came to affect each other intimately. This resulted in the modern arms race (Mandelbaum, 1981, chap. 1).

The arms race rendered explicit one set of ideological forces operating in science and technology. Certain scientists and engineers work in government or industrial laboratories with the explicit aim of developing new weapons systems. Many of these offer new possibilities in, for example, accuracy, destructiveness, or ability to penetrate enemy defences. The various branches of the armed forces (army, navy and air forces) often compete with one other for the best and most up-to-date weapons system. Politicians and their advisors try to resolve the competing claims of the armed forces. In the process, they try to devise effective defense policies using the weapons systems that exist, or that were ordered by a previous government. They also encourage continued weapons research so as not to fall behind other countries in military technical developments. This once again brings in the scientists and engineers in defense-related laboratories (Rosenthal, 1990). For some researchers, the military-industrial complex means jobs, money, excellent career opportunities and, on occasion, access to the corridors of political power—as in the controversial career of Edward Teller (Teller, 1991).

The scientists who emerged from the Manhattan Project had great prestige and became a significant political force with vested interests of their own (York, 1989). They were persuaded of the limitless potentialities of nuclear energy and intrigued by the research questions that were associated with it. The increasingly expensive and arcane explorations of the nuclear physicists, in turn, were protected by the government support given to the defense industry to finance the practical results achieved by nuclear engineers. In an important sense, the U.S. Atomic Energy Commission (AEC) inherited the operating patterns and attitudes of the Manhattan project, with its ties to the military and industry and its emphasis on large-scale mission-oriented megaprojects (Morin, 1993, p. 62) Nuclear physics became the handmaiden both of post-war commercial nuclear technology and sophisticated weapons development programs.

Many other scientists, however, interpreted—and continue to interpret—their social mission differently. In the United States, after World War II, scientific lobbies succeeded in mobilizing the political support that established civilian, as opposed to the threat of military, control of atomic energy (Smith, 1965). Many scientists have worked conspicuously, as did Einstein, to further the peaceful uses of the atomic energy they made possible. They contributed significantly to agreements on technical aspects of international control of atomic energy. They were pioneers in the vast task of educating laymen in the facts and implications of the new energy source. The founding in 1945–6 of the *Bulletin of the Atomic Scientists* (which remains an influential international forum for debate on nuclear and other environmental issues), and the establishment of the Pugwash Conferences on Science and World Affairs, testify to that new, or reactivated, sense of social concern (Grodzins & Rabinowitch, 1963).

The experiences of scientists involved in the Manhattan Project presaged the intimate involvement between science, technology and political power that characterizes our time. The links forged by the atomic bomb between science and war have changed the nature both of science and war in the latter decades of the twentieth century (Olby, 1990, pp. 941–943). Scientists, especially those prominent in their disciplines, have acquired an unprecedented degree of access to the highest councils of decision-makers in every industrialized society (Frangsmyr, 1990, pp.

270–291). Never before has the geopolitical power of a country (or any autonomous political entity) been so largely a function of its scientific and technological achievements (or shortcomings). Never before have the great world powers depended as they do now on the regular contributions of science and technology to the making of war and peace. Indeed, never before have the economic, social and ecological consequences of scientific discovery and technological innovation been so decisive for the fortunes of particular nations and for the global system (see sections 7c, 7e). Reciprocally, the advance of scientific knowledge and research and the achievement of new technological objectives have become more and more heavily dependent upon public subvention (Herman, 1990). Governments in technological societies have acquired a powerful role in the production of scientific knowledge (Galison and Hevly, 1992). By controlling funding and legislation, governments can direct research and development toward certain priorities (see section 7a). These same political tools may be used also to prevent certain types of research or at least minimize their impact (Spiegel-Rosing & Price, 1977, pp. 355–391).

For all these complex reasons, then, the contemporary scientist or technologist can be described—as was first done by Mary Shelley in her 1818 novel *Frankenstein*—as the Prometheus of the modern world. Like Prometheus, the scientist's gifts may be regarded as benevolent, evil, or some mixture of the two. For some 200 years since the time of Newton, science and technology came gradually to be regarded—particularly in the industrialized countries—as the basis for social progress. Science promised to many an improved condition on earth and, in the minds of certain visionaries, the indefinite perfectibility of the human species (see section 2d). Scientists were regarded as benign, if indirect, servants of humanity. Events of the latter half of the twentieth century, symbolized clearly by the development and use of the atomic bomb, have provoked a more sinister image. Science and technology now are frequently vilified as the causes of actual or impending catastrophes. Scientists are regarded by some with great suspicion. They are thought of as intellectual perpetrators of environmental or moral crimes (see section 7b). Both images of science, benevolent and malign, are provocative and serve a useful function in focusing public controversies concerning the use of science and technology (Nelkin, 1992). But each image alone can easily incite one form of fanaticism or other. What is required, instead, is a more comprehensive understanding of the social context in which science and technology actually operate. We may then be in a more informed, and hopefully stronger, position to see how our increasingly fragile and vulnerable modern societies can best—and with the least environmental damage—absorb all the unsettling changes which science and technology now produce in such relentless profusion. ■

B. Nuclear Politics: CANDU;
Reactor Safety and Hazardous Wastes; Proliferation

■ ■ ■

Since the close of World War II, nearly fifty years ago, humanity has lived in a nuclear age. The most dramatic signal that a new age had begun was the dropping of the first atomic bombs on Hiroshima and Nagasaki in August, 1945. Equally significant, however, was the science and technology which made those very bombs a possibility. Nuclear reactors, which play so dominant a role globally and domestically today, are the twins of nuclear weapons (Lovins & Lovins, 1980). Since the 1950s, nuclear reactors and allied technologies have afforded significant benefits in electrical power generation, medicine and scientific research. They have also created certain devastating environmental impacts. Both the military and nonmilitary uses of nuclear energy raise complex political, economic, social, and ethical issues. As with many other advances in science and technology, applications preceded full awareness of social and environmental consequences.

Nuclear Dilemmas

In many respects, the nuclear dilemmas confronting us in the 1980s and 1990s derive from decisions shielded from public scrutiny made in the 1950s and 1960s. At first, the new nuclear science and technology were to some degree esoteric and not fully comprehensible to the non-specialist (Balogh, 1991). The citizen could merely gaze in wonder at nuclear developments. However, there was another, and more overtly political, reason for the lack of public participation in nuclear decisions then. Nuclear matters, almost inseparable from the arms race of the Cold War, were viewed at the highest political and military levels as issues of national security. Again, the public was excluded from discussion (Morone & Woodhouse, 1989, pp. 39–42, 89). Those decisions made in the 1950s and 1960s have created a world which is today embedded in a nuclear framework. Whatever the visions—either military or domestic—of the early proponents of nuclear energy may have been, it is clear that the world shaped by those decisions arouses fear or distrust of nuclear energy today. It is not merely the huge weapons arsenals of the U.S., the Soviet Union, China, France, or the UK which arouses public (and private) unease. We now also recognize the enormous, and in some respects unforeseen or unforeseeable, environmental and social consequences of nuclear energy. There is, thus, a two-fold task facing us in the 1990s. First, we must deal with the environmental and sociopolitical consequences of nuclear decisions taken decades ago. But second, we must set policies and priorities today that will ensure that our nuclear predicament will not mortgage the future irreparably. Both these tasks require fuller public participation in nuclear debates than has hitherto been the case (Mansfield, 1984). The prerequisite for such participation is a citizenry informed, not misinformed or ignorant, of the basic elements of the crucial controversies today. This section will look first at how the nuclear debates manifest themselves in one country, Canada. The Canadian situation provides an excellent case study for comparison with the pattern of nuclear debates in other countries (Nelkin & Pollak, 1981). We will then examine two particular aspects of the nuclear debates from a global perspective. These are: (1) reactor safety and hazardous wastes and (2) the politics of proliferation.

Nuclear Politics in Canada: CANDU

The analysis of Canadian nuclear policies affords an insight into the intricacies of national nuclear politics worldwide for several reasons. First, the sheer dimension of the subject in Canada is daunting. Nuclear questions touch on practically every aspect of domestic politics. Second, nuclear questions seem particularly emotion-charged. Reports of possible health effects of radiation released during the operation of nuclear generating stations such as that at Pickering, near Toronto, provoke the bitter controversies surrounding the siting of such plants near any major population center. Similarly, the bombing of the Toronto plant of Litton Systems Canada in 1982 was a particularly graphic depiction of the mixed feelings that surround any nuclear-related industry. Litton produces the guidance system for the U.S. Cruise missile, which is designed to carry nuclear weapons. Supporters of the Litton contract point to the impressive economic benefits which accrue to its employees. Opponents argue that this is further evidence of the complicity of Canada in the U.S. nuclear military complex. The bombing, which caused $5 million damage, was a violent example of confrontation. Indeed, one can say that conflicts over Litton are symbolic of the contending values inherent in modern industrial society (Giangrande, 1983, pp. 11–44).

The third reason why examining nuclear policy issues is so complex is their long-range dimension. Even if a moratorium on nuclear development were to be declared tomorrow, Canada—and any nuclear nation—would still need sensible and detailed policies for at least the next half century. It will take at least that long to deal with the issues raised by the past forty years of nuclear development. Moreover, Canada is now facing major policy choices which, once made, will commit the nation to certain economic, environmental, and political paths for the next several decades. The decisions regarding Ontario Hydro, for example, will have a profound political and economic impact on that province. The fortunes—good or bad—of the uranium industry in Saskatchewan and Ontario will affect the economies not only of those provinces but of the entire country. The long-range prospects of international exports of CANDU have political and military, as well as economic, significance. Clearly, of all the scientific/technological issues confronting us today, nuclear policy is one of the most crucial, and one demanding the most informed and critical public discussion and debate (Babin, 1985).

Origins of CANDU

Although it is not widely recognized by the public, Canada's contemporary nuclear status has its roots in the development of the first atomic bombs during World War II. Together with the UK and the U.S., Canada contributed significantly to the Allied efforts to produce a viable nuclear weapon. The Manhattan Project irrevocably committed the three nations principally involved to a nuclear destiny. Canada's own wartime research effort, culminating in the CANDU reactor, provides a concrete illustration of how technology is shaped as much by political and economic forces as by decisions arising from within the specific knowledge base of science and engineering (Hartcup & Allibone, 1984, pp. 119–135).

Within the broader Manhattan Project, Canadian researchers were assigned the task of producing plutonium for possible use in atomic bombs. They successfully developed a process by which plutonium could be produced from the bombardment of ordinary uranium with neutrons, using heavy water [deuterium oxide] as a moderator. The method chosen for production of plutonium necessitated the development of a prototype of a heavy water-moderated/natural uranium reactor. The technology thus acquired would later become the basis for Canada's commercial nuclear reactor, the CANDU. CANDU stands for CANada Deuterium Uranium.

All commercial nuclear reactors are producers of heat, which in turn is used to produce electricity (Roberts, 1990, pp. 111–121). They do the same job as coal, oil, or natural gas in the generation of electricity: producing heat to convert water into steam, which then spins a turbine-generator to make electricity. In Ontario, the power of the atom supplies more than 40% of the electricity consumed in homes, schools, businesses, and industries. (Coal-fired and water-power stations supply the rest.) Because of the radioactive nature of the fuel and the reactor products, however, commercial nuclear reactors pose their own unique environmental and health hazards. Ontario's commitment to nuclear energy, as in Canada generally, is thus more than simply an economic matter. CANDU reactors constitute a technology which is the result of an intricate web of scientific, historical, political, military, as well as industrial factors. The genesis of the CANDU system, thus, tells us a great deal about the social context of science and technology both in Canada and globally (Bothwell, 1988).

It is significant that the origins of CANDU were in the military preparations for World War II. To be sure, at the conclusion of the war, Canada officially and publicly announced her decision *not* to use her nuclear know-how for the development of nuclear weapons. Yet it was precisely her wartime experience which led to the commissioning of the earliest nuclear reactors (NRX) at Chalk River (in 1947). This was the prototype of what eventually was to become the CANDU reactor. Thus, the production of plutonium—which was the original motive for developing heavy-water reactor technology—is an inseparable part of CANDU's commercial operation. Moreover, Canada supplied the U.S. with much of the uranium for the development of its first atomic bombs. After World War II, Canada continued to supply substantial quantities of uranium for the nuclear weapons programs of the U.S. and the UK. One of the incentives, in fact, for Canada to embark on a full-scale commercial development program for CANDU in the late 1950s and early 1960s, was tied to the U.S. decision at that time to place an embargo on any importation of uranium.

During World War II there was a perceived shortage of uranium in the U.S. There had been little need to prospect for uranium before the war, so there were few verified deposits and almost no data for estimating the domestic supply of uranium ore. The known reserves of uranium in the early 1940s in the U.S. were quickly depleted in the first phases of the Manhattan Project. Thus, the U.S. turned to Canada's extensive uranium resource base (Morone & Woodhouse, 1989, p. 30). When the actual extent of America's vast uranium reserves became evident during the 1950s, the U.S. barred further imports in order to force domestic reliance on its own supplies. Canada had, by then, a well-established uranium industry producing large supplies of good quality ore. The development of an indigenous commercial nuclear reactor industry seemed the appropriate, perhaps logical, course. At the same time, successive Governments have reiterated Canada's decision not to use her technology or her resources to become a nuclear weapons-producing nation.

The critical stages of CANDU development began in earnest in 1952 with the formation of a new Crown (Federal) agency, Atomic Energy of Canada Ltd. (AECL) (Bothwell, 1988). Meanwhile, in the early 1950s, Dr. J.R. McKenzie, President of the NRC, had already entered into a dialogue with the powerful provincial public utility Ontario Hydro. The growth orientation of Ontario Hydro matched the enthusiasm of the small but vocal Canadian nuclear establishment of scientists, engineers, and certain political officials. Ontario's hunger for electric power—in the post-war boom years of the late 1940s and early 1950s—together with the massive capital endowments of Ontario Hydro, provided just that opportunity the nuclear advocates required. By 1953, Ontario Hydro had made the decision to go nuclear. The wartime Chalk River Laboratories became the center for the massive development of the CANDU commercial reactor system. Although not a nuclear weapons nation, Canada had entered upon the global nuclear stage as a major player. All the controversial nuclear issues confronting the world since the 1960s—commercial sales of reactors, reactor safety, hazardous wastes, weapons conversion from commercial reactor technology, nuclear proliferation, the arms race—would affect Canada decisively. In this sense, the origins and development of Canada's nuclear program provide an instructive introduction to the torturous world of nuclear politics.

CANDU Exported

One of the central issues concerning nuclear technology in Canada is government policy toward sales of CANDU reactors abroad.

The CANDU reactor has a proven track record as being among the safest and most efficient of the many different types of commercial reactors available worldwide. CANDU represents one of Canada's most successful entries into the international competition of high-technology. There is great pressure from the nuclear industry and the pronuclear lobbies, such as the Canadian Nuclear Association (CNA), to encourage exports of CANDU. Yet Canada's very success in this high-tech field has raised controversial matters. Since commercial nuclear reactors can be diverted to uses other than just the production of electricity, concerns have been expressed about the efficacy of safeguards and inspection rights the Canadian Government imposes upon CANDU sales to foreign nations.

In 1974, Canada's nuclear policy received a startling shock. India exploded a plutonium bomb with plutonium extracted from the spent (used) fuel from a CANDU research reactor (near New Delhi) it had purchased (Giangrande, 1983, pp. 146, 155–156). Now, one of the great advantages of the CANDU as opposed to other commercial reactors is that it can be refuelled while still operating. The ingenious on-load refuelling mechanism developed by Canadian technology—which removes the need for shutting down reactors during refuelling—is one of the major selling-points of CANDU reactors (Patterson, 1983, p. 65). At either face of the reactor is a refuelling machine in a shielded vault. One machine rams fresh fuel bundles into one end of a reactor tube, while the other collects used ones as they emerge from the other end. The full machine then feeds the used fuel down a conveyor to eventual storage in a large water-filled cooling pond under the reactor station. Ideally, the spent fuels—which are highly radioactive and contain plutonium produced in the reactor (from U-238 conversion)—are then disposed of safely and securely stored. The advantage of this on-load refuelling is that costly and long plant shut-downs, which are necessary for many other types of commercial reactors, are avoided. However, since spent fuel can be removed without any obvious interruption of ordinary reactor activity, it is especially vulnerable to theft or diversion to other purposes. India did just that. It accumulated sufficient plutonium extracted from spent fuel bundles to provide the material necessary for a nuclear bomb (Finch, 1986).

As a result of this incident, Canada did strengthen her CANDU inspection rights (to prevent such covert activity) after 1974. These safeguards were outlined in the House of Commons in 1974 and 1976. They require any country making nuclear purchases from Canada to ratify the Nuclear Non-Proliferation Treaty (1968) or to accept "equivalent international safeguards." But in the extremely poor economic climate of the late 1980s, there was intense pressure to ease these tighter safeguards to promote sales to such potential buyers as Mexico, Argentina (it would be the second sale; Argentina purchased a CANDU in the 1970s), and Brazil. Canada's success in commercial nuclear technology is linked, therefore, to her controversial role as a potential supplier for weapons production (Giangrande, 1983, pp. 140–170).

A similar dilemma was posed by Ontario Hydro's plan to export tritium. Tritium is a radioactive form of hydrogen, and is a by-product of the process for making the heavy water used in CANDU reactors. It can also be used in certain types of nuclear weapons. Ontario Hydro says it will sell its tritium only for fusion research purposes to those nations which are committed to the nonproduction of nuclear weapons, such as West Germany and Japan. Once again, the potential diversion of tritium to nonpeaceful uses, or its theft by groups committed to terrorism, raises the specter of Ontario Hydro as a contributor to the arms race. Even if such fears prove groundless or are exaggerated, they still point to a fundamental dilemma at the core of Canadian commercial nuclear policy. On the one hand, there are those groups such as AECL (which sells CANDU), Ontario Hydro, and the CNA who believe that any extension of nuclear technology is desirable. Other groups, such as the Canadian Coalition for Nuclear Responsibility (CCNR) and Energy Probe take a different stance. They maintain that any economic arguments for extending such technology only entrench an industry which should come under greater public scrutiny than has been the case. The status of Ontario Hydro is central here. As the purchaser of 21 of the 29 Canadian-made CANDU reactors built or under construction, it is the bulwark of the Canadian nuclear industry. To many critics, Ontario Hydro's decision to go nuclear, and its subsequent enormous growth as a public utility predicated upon nuclear-generated electrical power, have not been open to adequately unbiased public information or debate. These critics charge that alternative energy sources have not been given sufficient attention owing to Ontario Hydro's powerful political and economic position (McKay, 1983).

It is clear that domestic debates about nuclear energy are intense in Canada. The above controversies about CANDU sales and energy production are but two of the issues confronting the nation's nuclear policies. A third concerns the so-called "American Connection." In a number of ways, Canada is tied directly or indirectly to the nuclear activities of the U.S. Canada exports uranium to the U.S. CANDU-generated electric power is sold to the U.S. The Cruise missile has been tested in the Weapons Range in northern Saskatchewan. Canada has been a member of the North American Air Defense Command (NORAD) since 1957. Under this agreement, all major military decisions affecting North America would be made from NORAD headquarters in Colorado. Canada is thus implicated, at least indirectly, in U.S nuclear weapons policy. These three issues are fairly specific to the history and development of nuclear energy in this country and its sociopolitical context. Other issues in nuclear policy facing Canada are reflective of more widely shared global dilemmas (Jasper, 1990). These include reactor safety, hazardous wastes, and the politics of proliferation, to which we now turn.

Reactor Safety and Hazardous Wastes

One of the most controversial questions deriving from the commercial use of nuclear reactors is that of safety and/or potential hazard to the environment. The field of risk-assessment attempts to weigh the expected beneficial uses of a given technology against the potential risks associated with its use. Nuclear reactors pose two distinct categories of risks. The first arises from the normal operation of the reactor as it performs its task of generating energy. The nuclear reactor releases radiation in a variety of ways. Generally, the design of a reactor has been executed to ensure safety to the workers and to persons living in areas adjacent to the reactor site. The ordinary operation of a reactor also necessarily results in the production of waste products of varying degrees of radioactive hazard. The on-site storage and ultimate long-term management of these radioactive wastes constitutes a massive industry in itself. The second broad category of risks associated with nuclear reactors arises from the possibility of malfunctioning. The accidents at Three Mile Island (near Harrisburg, Pennsylvania) in March 1979 and at Chernobyl (in the former Soviet Union) in April 1986 radically transformed the context of analyzing potential hazards of civilian nuclear power plants. They served to sharpen dramatically the public dread associated with the possible catastrophic effect of reactor malfunction. The unthinkable had become the actual (Starr & Pearman, 1983).

Radiation Biohazards

It was the American geneticist Hermann J. Muller (1890–1967) who first demonstrated the biological hazards posed by radiation. Muller won the 1947 Nobel Prize in medicine and physiology for his work on the genetic effects of radiation. Muller showed that gene mutation rate is directly proportional to dosage. He worked specifically with X-rays but his conclusions were soon shown to apply to other types of ionizing radiation, including the alpha and beta particles and gamma rays produced in nuclear fission. Unless radioactivity takes place in a vacuum, the radiation emitted must pass through a surrounding substance. In some cases, it is stopped by the material barrier of its container from proceeding further. In other instances, it passes through the shielding material and continues on its path. The consequences depend on the substance, on the type of radiation, on its energy and on its intensity (Hurley, 1982). Neutrons are also emitted in the fission process. Some of the nuclei in the surrounding air absorb neutrons and become radioactive. This process is called neutron activation.

When ionizing radiation passes through a substance it causes changes in the structure of the constituent material. Sometimes the changes may be permanent, at other times they may be temporary. More significantly, the changes may be useful or they may be destructive. The effects of ionizing radiation depend roughly on how much energy the radiation releases into a given amount of material: the more energy, the more disruption (Upton, 1982). The original unit of radiation exposure was the roentgen, named after the German physicist Wilhelm Roentgen (1845–1923), discoverer of X-rays. The effects of ionizing radiation become particularly important if the radiation is passing through living matter. The delicate and intricate molecular arrangements of living matter can be easily upset by radiation. There are several units used to measure radiation effects on living matter. The most common are the "radiation absorbed dose," or "rad," and the "roentgen equivalent man," or "rem." The rad is a delivered (absorbed) unit of radiation energy equal to 100 ergs per gram of tissue. The rem is a rad adjusted for relative biological effectiveness (RBE) of the radiation source. One rem is one rad times the RBE of the radiation in question. RBE is the term used to compare the effectiveness (severity of damage) of different kinds of radiation to the effectiveness of beta particles as the standard. Beta particles have an RBE of 1. Alpha particles by contrast have RBEs of 10–20. Thus, one rem of any kind of radiation does an equivalent amount of biological damage as one rem of any other kind. After large doses (1,000 to 1,000,000 rads), effects are easily seen and there is a high incidence of death. Moderate doses are known to increase the likelihood of cancer and birth defects. Lower doses may cause temporary cellular change, but it is difficult to demonstrate long-term effects (Enger et al., 1986, p. 197).

Clearly, one of the greatest debates concerning the ordinary operation of nuclear reactors focuses on the health risks of exposure to radiation (Wagner & Ketchum, 1989). This question affects the issue of occupational health, since the workers in a nuclear plant are the persons most directly exposed to radiation during routine functioning. Because radiation is also emitted into the surrounding air and through ground and water release, residents in neighborhoods near nuclear reactors must be included in this particular aspect of risk assessment (Pochin, 1985). Added to this man-made radiation is the ionizing radiation from natural sources, to which we are normally, and continually, subjected. This includes cosmic rays, uranium and thorium in the earth, and certain radioactive isotopes of substances in our bodies, particularly Potassium-40. This "background" radiation varies considerably from place to place on the earth, and according to height above sea-level. The complex question of permissible doses of radiation in the workplace and in surrounding neighborhoods has generated considerable controversy (Bertell, 1986). These debates are made more contentious because the scientific study of the biological effects of radiation is itself the subject of vigorous disputes. Suffice it to say that it is known that a dose of perhaps 450 rem of radiation over the whole body will kill half the human beings exposed to it (Miller, 1988, p. 51). Very much smaller doses will produce cell damage that may lead to leukemia and other kinds of cancer. Furthermore, radiation damage to the complex molecules in the reproductive cells, which contain the hereditary information, may produce mutant offspring. Even a single gamma ray can disrupt a gene. It may produce unforeseeable effects if this particular gene should be in the reproductive cell which subsequently helps to form a child. It can be appreciated, then, that the scientific study of the effects of ionizing radiation on living organisms (radiobiology) is both challenging and open to widely differing interpretations of data (Gofman, 1981).

Radioactivity Release

The issue of permissible radiation exposure directly affects the question of the production and storage of the fuels and wastes normally associated with nuclear reactors. Throughout the nuclear fuel cycle, the materials involved share one common property: they are all to some extent radioactive. Natural radioactive materials, such as uranium ores, are encountered in mining and milling. These substances remain radioactive throughout enrichment, fuel fabrication, and transport. But their emissions are not particularly intense, nor do they add substantially to normal background radiation. This, however, changes markedly once they find themselves inside an operating reactor. Bombarding neutrons from reactor cores tend to make the fuel bundles, and their entire neighborhood, intensely radioactive. So long as the materials in this neighborhood remain within the biological shielding all is well. But radioactivity inevitably finds a number of escape routes from the confines of reactors, however well buttoned up they may be. The most important escape route is via refuelling, when much (or all) of the radioactive inventory of the spent fuel is removed from the core of the reactor. It is significant to recall that CANDU reactors, which permit on-line refuelling, minimize this particular radiation hazard.

Radioactivity is also released outside the biological shield of a nuclear reactor (Roberts et al., 1990, pp. 139–144). Any radioactivity released into the surrounding environment during routine operation is called a running release. Reactor coolant, for example, may carry radioactivity out of the biological shield. If the coolant is heavy water, neutron absorption by deuterium can turn it into tritium, which is radioactive. Similarly, sodium, which is used as the coolant in liquid metal fast breeder reactors, absorbs neutrons to become the intensely gamma-active isotope Sodium-24. Because coolant may leak, or actually flow, into the environment (depending upon the particular coolant and reactor design involved), it is essential to decontaminate the cooling circuits of a reactor to minimize running release. Furthermore, in the course of everyday business in a reactor plant a certain amount of solid material also becomes contaminated with radioactivity—floor mops, paper towels, broken glassware from sampling labs, etc. These contaminated solids, at present, are usually simply buried in designated ground sites or dumped at sea in specially prepared containers. It is clear that any such methods for safe disposal or decontamination of running release are prone to defects or accidents.

Permanent Storage

In contrast to these low-level wastes, the spent fuel of reactors is highly radioactive. The temporary storage, permanent disposal, and possible reuse (including, for example, diversion of plutonium to weapons production) of high-level wastes present some of the most challenging problems posed by the operation of nuclear reactors (McCuen, 1990). To give some indication of the magnitude of the problem, by the early 1980s more than 10,000 tons of spent fuel had been produced by commercial nuclear reactors in the U.S. alone. This spent fuel is currently stored primarily in water-cooled basins at reactor sites. Such a method, to be sure, is merely temporary. Effective methods for long-term storage, such as placing the spent fuel in geologic repositories, must be developed. The permanent and safe storage of reactor wastes, including those now being generated, represents one of the most formidable technological challenges to nuclear scientists. The uncertainty as to whether such methods can be developed—or will be available quickly enough to deal with past radioactive wastes—provides the critics of commercial nuclear power with some of their most powerful arguments against the use of reactors. Nuclear wastes, moreover, constitute only one part of the broader problem of hazardous waste management of all toxic substances (Harthill, 1984).

Waste management systems must be designed and operated not only for active reactors. Just as reactor fuel becomes no longer usable, so too the reactor itself will in due course, for one reason or another, have to be shut down permanently. Unlike a fossil-fuelled power station, however, a reactor cannot simply thereafter be dismantled and the ground cleared for future use. Many parts of the reactor plant—such as the concrete biological shielding which encases it and the spent fuel cooling pond—may have also become contaminated. The shut down plant will have to be "decommissioned." The operation of nuclear waste management systems extends far beyond the lifetimes of the components of the nuclear fuel cycle, for the biosphere must be protected from these wastes for centuries to come (Roberts et al., 1990, pp. 155–161). Unfortunately, no nuclear reactor has as yet been successfully decommissioned. More significant, even the theory as to how to achieve that goal has not been completely worked out. The prospect of many aging nuclear power stations spread over the global landscape in the early twenty-first century is, obviously, discomforting to many critics of commercial nuclear power.

Such are the complex issues—political as much as scientific—attending the use of nuclear reactors to generate power commercially (Walker, 1992). These issues become far more contentious when the possibility of an accident at a nuclear plant arises. The risk-benefit analysis is difficult enough when dealing with commercial nuclear reactors which are operating effectively. One must weigh the real social and environmental costs, such as genetic damage or higher incidence of cancers, against the equally real (although sometimes disputable) economic benefits attached to nuclear-generated power. In the case of a nuclear accident, ordinary risk analysis becomes the analysis of catastrophe.

By the end of the 1960s, there had been major reactor accidents in Canada, the UK, the U.S., and Switzerland. In December 1952, an accident in the core of the NRX (a research reactor and precursor of CANDU) at Chalk River disgorged radioactivity to the surroundings. In October 1957, a raging fire occurred at the Windscale Number One plutonium-production reactor on the Cumbria coast of England. The Windscale reactors were air-cooled and the accident caused a major malfunction of that cooling system, spreading radioactivity over Westmorland and Cumberland. In October 1966, a valve malfunction created the preconditions for a core meltdown in the breeder reactor at the Enrico Fermi-1 plant south of Detroit (Patterson, 1983, pp. 45–6,

119–22, 135–137). The nuclear industry stressed that none of these accidents posed a significant danger to the public. That argument—although critics dispute it—was shattered, in any event, with the accident at Three Mile Island in 1979. TMI was a devastating shock to an already beleaguered nuclear industry both within the U.S. and outside its borders. Whatever the prospects for an expanded commercial nuclear policy in any given country after 1979, the accident at TMI would henceforth always loom in risk calculations. Then came Chernobyl.

Chernobyl

The nuclear accident at Chernobyl eclipsed all previous problems with civilian nuclear plants (G. Medvedev, 1991). The reactor released more than 6 million times the amount of radioactivity released at Three Mile Island. The Chernobyl accident occurred because of a series of problems: (1) A test was being conducted under the jurisdiction of electrical experts not thoroughly familiar with nuclear safety; (2) The operators withdrew all but six of the 215 control rods from the core, although at least 30 are required to be in place according to the operating manual for the Chernobyl reactors; (3) Operators turned off the automatic equipment designed to shut down and cool the reactor in an emergency; (4) Operators kept the unit running in spite of a computer printout warning several minutes before the accident that the reactor was in serious danger and should be shut down. Soviet scientists and officials who investigated the accident concluded that the operators had lost their "sense of vigilance towards safety." One author of the report of the International Nuclear Safety Advisory Group on the Chernobyl accident said that the "operators got swelled heads" because the reactor had enjoyed the best operating record of any reactor in the Soviet Union. As a result, "they thought they could do anything to this reactor."

A number of experts have pointed out that the design of the Chernobyl reactors was inferior to some Western ones, such as CANDU and those in the U.S. They point out that it was easier for the Soviet operators to override the automatic safety mechanisms than would be the case with other reactor designs. They point out, further, that the Soviet reactor had far less complete containment shielding than those of most Western nations (which can better withstand an explosion and still keep the radioactivity from being released into the environment). Whatever the particular defects of the Soviet reactor, however, the Chernobyl disaster had a devastating impact on public perceptions of nuclear risks worldwide. Where Three Mile Island was a reminder that something might happen, at Chernobyl something did happen. The potential for catastrophe that is always a part of the public dread or rejection of nuclear power was fully realized. The effect on public opinion polls was sharp. Even before Chernobyl, in early 1986 only a third of those interviewed in the U.S. considered nuclear energy a desirable source for additional commercial expansion. After the accident, nearly ¾ of those polled expressed opposition to building additional nuclear plants. The same was true in Europe, where 83% of those interviewed in West Germany and the UK opposed increased reliance on nuclear power. 70% or more had such sentiments in Canada, Yugoslavia, and Italy. In France, where the government is heavily committed to further expansion of nuclear power, slightly more than half the public was opposed by late 1986 (Morone & Woodhouse, 1989, pp. 98–101).

The occurrence of nuclear accidents, some of them catastrophic, has served to strengthen the opposition of those members of society who consider nuclear energy entirely inappropriate as a source of commercial power production (Park, 1989). These protests have become increasingly vocal and, sometimes, violent. Public demonstrations against the expansion of commercial nuclear power—dramatically reported in the media—are becoming common in the U.S., the UK,

Canada, France and West Germany, among other nations. When the links between civilian nuclear activities and the potential aggravation of global nuclear weapons proliferation are considered, the protests become more strident still.

Nuclear Proliferation

Clearly, commercial nuclear reactors are a fact of both domestic and international life. One of the major worries associated with commercial reactors, aside from their environmental hazards, is the link between nuclear reactors and plutonium production (Patterson, 1983, pp. 193–210). In addition to generating electricity, commercial and research reactors generate substantial quantities of plutonium. As we have seen, plutonium is a principal component of one class of nuclear weapons. It has been estimated, for example, that for each year of operation of a typical 1000 megawatt nuclear electric plant, enough plutonium is generated to equip 20 to 25 nuclear bombs. Historically, none of the original nuclear weapons nations—the U.S., the UK, the Soviet Union, France and China—acquired their weapons as a direct result of existing commercial nuclear technology. (Recall that Canada, which was one of the major contributors to the theory and technology which led to the production of the first atomic bombs during World War II, renounced from the first any attempt to develop its own nuclear weapons arsenal.) However, the widespread use of commercial nuclear reactors today (they are in operation in more than 20 nations) creates the potential for misuse. The conversion of commercial nuclear power facilities to weapons production, directly or indirectly, is a distinct possibility.

To be sure, conversion of commercial technology to weapons production is not the only means of acquiring nuclear military capability. Direct military production, or the sale and/or theft of weapons or weapons-grade material, are also significant possibilities. Nuclear proliferation, therefore, remains one of the gravest threats to world peace. There are actually two components to the global spread of nuclear weapons. The first is called vertical proliferation. This refers to the development of increasingly sophisticated nuclear weapons by those nations already possessing a nuclear arsenal (Alic et al., 1992, pp. 135–136). The second component is called horizontal proliferation. This refers to the potential or real acquisition of nuclear weapons by additional nations.

Horizontal Proliferation

Horizontal proliferation, as generally understood, consists of several steps toward a full-fledged, operational nuclear force. The first actual explosion—such as India's test explosion in 1974—is the most visible step in the process. But the initial decision by any state to embark upon a series of steps leading to that first explosion is the most significant step. It is agreed that any effective international policy to prevent proliferation should be directed at dissuading or preventing nonnuclear states from taking even the first step (Vance, 1989). Unfortunately, the risk of several additional countries acquiring weapons is particularly acute in some of the world's most volatile areas. In such cases, the addition of nuclear weapons to regional conflicts already inflamed by ideological tensions and conventional warfare could be disastrous—both locally and globally. As one example, Pakistan's obvious pursuit of a nuclear weapons capability may cause India to revive its nuclear explosives program (apparently dormant since 1974). This could lead Pakistan to go even further, and a regional nuclear arms race would be underway. Any possible intervention by the Chinese (on either side) would further exacerbate the danger. Future hostilities in the region might then result in the actual use of nuclear weapons, with horrific consequences—including the possible involvement of the superpowers in a conflict of global dimensions. Such a nuclear escalation is perhaps a more likely possibility in the Middle East. Israel's nuclear capabilities are currently unmatched in that area. They seem likely—if not inevitable—in the long run to provoke the acquisition of nuclear weapons by her Arab adversaries. Once again, any Arab demand for Russian or Chinese nuclear backing could provoke a global nuclear escalation of a local conflict.

For all these reasons, it appears that the possession, or absence, of operational nuclear weapons for any particular nation is more a function of political will than of technical know-how. The mere possession of nuclear weapons capability does not imply that a nation will develop such an arsenal. In fact, many of the advanced industrial countries which clearly have such capabilities—including Canada, Sweden, Japan, and the European NATO countries other than France and the UK—have thus far determined that it would be against their interest to acquire nuclear weapons. They and many other nations, including some which already have nuclear arsenals, such as the UK and the U.S., have joined in international efforts to curb or prevent entirely any further spread of weapons. Such efforts to achieve nonproliferation reflect the growing awareness of the local and global risks of recourse to nuclear war. This, in turn, is linked to the perception that nuclear weapons have questionable military utility. Hopefully, it is no longer considered self-evident that "going nuclear" enhances a nation's political security or political standing (Spector, 1990).

Nuclear Non-Proliferation Treaty

The most significant of these attempts to curb the spread of nuclear weapons is the Treaty on the Non-Proliferation of Nuclear Weapons (NPT) signed in 1968. Altogether, over 100 countries formally have renounced their intention of acquiring nuclear weapons by ratifying the NPT (Article II). Three major nuclear weapons states—the U.S., UK, and the former Soviet Union—agreed, under Article I of the NPT, not to transfer any of their own weapons to another country's uses. Finally, under Article III, all signatories agreed to accept international safeguards for the explicit purpose of preventing diversion of nuclear energy and material from peaceful use to the production of nuclear weapons. The adequacy of these safeguards is subject to much debate. They most likely would not deter a nation, intent on deception, from obtaining the nuclear material and technology necessary to manufacture nuclear explosives. Moreover, a new proliferation concern—obviously not covered by any treaty—has developed. Subnational or transnational groups, including terrorist organizations, could attain the capability to manufacture independently a nuclear explosive from stolen plutonium or highly enriched uranium. This possibility would become more troublesome if reprocessing and recycling of plutonium is introduced as a major part of the commercial nuclear fuel cycle in certain types of reactors. This is one of the fears expressed by those opposed to the commercial development of a plutonium-dependent breeder reactor program. Much of the requisite technical knowledge for bomb design, it should be noted, is available in the public scientific literature (Bailey, 1991).

In an imperfect world, however, the NPT is justly regarded as a possible deterrent to proliferation. Even France and China, which are not parties to the Treaty, have declared that they would abide by most of the guidelines. However, five countries which have nuclear capabilities are not parties to the treaty at all. They are South Africa, Brazil, Agentina, Pakistan, and Israel. These countries either have, or can soon be expected to have, nuclear power reactors in operation—each capable of generating enough by-product plutonium annually for over a dozen nuclear weapons. Clearly, the often seemingly urgent incentives for certain nations to go nuclear must be countered by equally potent political, moral and military disincentives to do so. If nonproliferation is to become an effective international nuclear policy, it is up to individual countries to guarantee adherence to treaty commitments and to international safeguards and inspection guidelines. The challenge is formidable from a technical as well as political standpoint. The breakup of the former Soviet Union—and the attendant uncertainty over the control of its vast nuclear arsenal (Glynn, 1992, pp. 215–216)—has only accentuated the dilemma posed by nuclear proliferation. ■

C. Acid Precipitation

■ ■ ■

The phenomenon of acid precipitation is one of the gravest environmental problems facing us. It has been called an invisible plague of the industrial age. As an issue with both scientific and political dimensions, it ranks in urgency alongside contemporary concerns like the global increase in carbon dioxide in the atmosphere (the so-called greenhouse effect), the spread of toxic chemicals in the environment, and the possible environmental consequences of commercial and military nuclear facilities. The term acid precipitation (or deposition) refers mainly to the dilute sulfuric and nitric acids which are created in the smelting of certain ores and when fossil fuels are burned in power stations or motor vehicles. (It may also involve hydrocarbons and ozone, acting alone or together.) These chemicals then fall to the earth, often over areas at great distances downwind of the possible sources of the pollutants (Schmandt, 1988, pp. 278–279). Acid precipitation—often shortened conveniently, but somewhat misleadingly, to "acid rain"—can be wet (rain, snow, mist) or dry (gases, particles, smog). Acid rain will be used hereafter to refer to both dry and wet acid deposition (Bridgman, 1990, p. 115).

The effects of acid rain elicit a now familiar litany (Regens & Rycroft, 1988, p. 52). Trees are being damaged, and soils left too acid to support plants. More than half of West Germany's forests are affected, and the German fir is close to extinction. In most other European countries forests are damaged. In parts of Europe and in the U.S., acid pollution has cut crop yields. Lakes are being acidified by acid water flowing off surrounding land. In Sweden, one lake in five has turned acid. In Ontario, Canada, nearly 50,000 lakes are already affected. Fish and aquatic plants are dying. In parts of Poland, railway tracks have been so corroded that trains cannot travel faster than 40 kph (25 mph), and the gold on the roof of Cracow's cathedral chapter is dissolving. Acid rain is cited as a possible cause of much of the corrosion to cars in urban centers (Roberts et al., 1990, pp. 64–69).

International Dimension

The dilemma is not confined to Europe and North America (Wyman, 1991, p. 147). China is the world's third biggest emitter of acid-forming sulfur dioxide, after the U.S. and the former Soviet Union. It has an enormous acid rain problem, and winds may be blowing the pollution to Japan (Bridgman, 1990, pp. 133–134). In India, the Taj Mahal is dissolving in an acid wind. Acid deposition has been found downwind of the Zambian Copperbelt in Africa. In Johannesburg, buildings are corroding. Soil samples from Sao Paulo state in Brazil have shown unusually high acid levels. In the Arctic, atmospheric haze has turned experimental filters grey or sooty black. Because fossil fuel emissions in one country are often converted into acid deposition in another, acid rain has become a major transboundary and international issue. Scandinavian governments, for example, are critical of Britain's inability, or unwillingness, to curb its acid emissions. Acid rain is a notoriously sensitive matter in Canada-U.S. relations (Schmandt, 1988).

There are two broad classifications of environmental pollutants. First, there are manmade materials such as persistent synthetic chemicals like DDT. These are not part of natural environmental cycles and therefore do not readily break down when released into the environment. A subset of this group would include some nuclear waste products that are, strictly speaking, parts of natural cycles (radioactive decay); but these cycles operate so extremely slowly over such long-time spans that those particular nuclear wastes, such as plutonium, are effectively nonbiodegradable. The second category of pollutants comprises materials that already exist naturally in the environment. When these materials occur in normal concentrations, natural environmental processes can cope with them by neutralizing them, breaking them down, dispersing or recycling them. Pollutants of this second type are not necessarily harmful in themselves. They create problems only when they overload natural biogeochemical cycles (Forster & Wase, 1987, pp. 442–443).

Acid rain falls in this second group. Its basic ingredients—sulfur dioxide, nitrogen oxides and ozone—do appear naturally in the environment, although ordinarily in small concentrations. In fact, the natural acidity of rainfall provides free supplies of valuable nutrients for plant growth. Some areas (such as parts of Scandinavia) with mineral-deficient soils are happy to receive the sulfur because otherwise costly artificial fertilizers would be required. It is the *increased* acidity experienced locally and globally in recent years that appears to produce serious environmental problems, and which is the true focus of the acid rain debate.

It is important to realize that all precipitation normally is slightly acidic. This is due to the fact that carbon dioxide, which is an ordinary by-product of many biochemical activities, occurs naturally in the atmosphere. When carbon dioxide combines with moisture it forms carbonic acid (a very weak version of soda water). However, precipitation may also become acidic when other substances, notably sulfur dioxides, nitrogen oxides, and chlorine, have been released into the air. Each of these compounds reacts chemically with water vapor and oxygen in the atmosphere to produce acids. Again, there is nothing unusual about any of this. Over the ages, without any assistance from humans, nature has made acid rain from the oxides of sulfur vented by volcanoes and from other gases vented into the atmosphere from natural sources. Acidic soils have also been around since before there were terrestrial plants.

What is new, and what is the crux of the acid rain problem, are the sources of atmospheric acidity due to human activities (Roberts et al., 1990, p. 56). Again, since earliest times humanity's agricultural and technological endeavors—as well as the very process of respiration—have contributed to acid precipitation. At the present time, however, it is the burning of fossil fuels (such as coal and oil) rich in sulfur, nitrogen and, in some cases, chlorine, and the smelting of sulfur-rich ores which are the major sources of acidity in the atmosphere. More than 75% of sulfur dioxide in the atmosphere above Eastern North America is put there by human technologies. For example, in the smelting of sulfide ores of copper, such as at the vast INCO operation at Sudbury, Ontario, the sulfur is oxidized to sulfur dioxide. This gas may be carried over long distances in the atmosphere before being deposited with rain or snow. It is during this period of transport that sulfur dioxide is further oxidized by the action of ultraviolet light and ozone. The sulfur trioxide thus formed becomes hydrolyzed to sulfuric acid which dissolves in the precipitation. The result is acid rain. Nitric acid and hydrochloric acid are formed in the atmosphere in analagous processes.

Fossil Fuels

Since the entire world is now dependent upon the burning of fossil fuels and the smelting (processing) of primary ores (such as copper sulfides), it is not surprising that acid rain has become an issue of global dimensions. In the U.S., the largest source of such oxides is the coal burned for electricity consumption. In Canada, the smelting of sulfur-rich ores as well as the burning of coal used in thermal electric generating stations are major sources. It is useful, in these matters, to distinguish between two kinds of pollution sources. The first kind is called a "point source" (Wyman, 1991, pp. 187–192). Examples of point sources are smokestacks in a large fossil fuel power plant or the smelters for refining nickel and copper ores. The second kind of pollution source is called a "non-point source." Examples of nonpoint sources would be the collection of automobiles in any large city, such as Los Angeles or Toronto (Macdonald, 1991, pp. 241–244).

Historically, the earth's atmosphere has been capable of absorbing and rendering harmless—by dispersion or biochemical degradation—the pollutants produced by the human species. But with the accelerated industrialization characteristic of the nineteenth and twentieth centuries, the atmosphere's ability to absorb pollutants has been severely taxed. In some instances, the environment appears to be reaching, or surpassing, its viable pollution limits. Although acid rain is an ancient phenomenon, it is one which nature always seemed capable of handling. Until recently, that is. Descriptions of acid rain appear in certain written accounts as early as the eighteenth and nineteenth centuries. It was known then that certain smogs and rains could damage factories and plants in London, England. The first modern published reference to acid rain is generally considered to be that made by an English chemist in 1872. Robert A. Smith discovered a link between acid in rain falling near Manchester and the sulfur dioxide given off when coal was burned (Regens & Rycroft, 1988, p. 38).

It was not until the second half of the twentieth century, however, that the full extent of the environmental problems caused by acid rain became apparent. Part of the reason for this tardy recognition of the problem arises from certain characteristics of acid rain. As a form of pollution, acid rain has some unusual properties. It is invisible, with no discernible taste or smell to humans. It has remained largely undetected even in areas where it has been falling for many years, because its effects on the environment are not readily noticeable in their early stages. It is a silent, creeping form of cumulative pollutant. Only in advanced cases are its effects sufficiently quantifiable to be convincing in any statistical sense.

Forests in North America and Europe may now be receiving as much as 30 times more acidity than they would if precipitation fell from, or through, clean air. In terms of sulfur alone, eastern North American rainfall has been shown to have 2 to 16 times the sulfate content of rainfall downwind of less populated regions of the continent. Because of the direction of prevailing winds, a significant proportion of the acid rain affecting Ontario probably has its origin in the northeastern U.S.. In any event, the Canadian acid rain problem is most acute east of the Manitoba/Ontario border. Of course, Canadian-generated acids also fall in precipitation over the U.S. Acid rain is absolutely a joint U.S.-Canadian dilemma, requiring bilateral action if it is to be dealt with effectively. Beyond North America's borders, acid rain is equally problematic. Wet deposition of sulfate in China, for example, has been shown to be 7 to 130 times that of remote areas of the southern hemisphere. It is only very recently, however, that such massive amounts of acid rain have begun to cause obvious damage to the animals and plants in even the most susceptible soils and waters where rain falls most heavily (Kupchella & Hyland, 1989, pp. 329–330).

The acidity of any chemical solution, including acid rain, is measured by the pH scale. Without getting involved in the complicated derivation of the pH scale (it is logarithmic), it is important to know that the scale runs from 0 to 14. The pH of any solution is actually an *inverse* measure of its hydrogen ion concentration, the active component of acids. Thus, the lower the pH, the more acidic the solution—pH values go down as the acidity, or hydrogen ion concentration, goes up (gets stronger). The positively charged hydrogen ions influence chemical processes by reacting with negatively charged groups of organic and inorganic chemicals. A pH of 0 represents the most highly acidic solution. A pH of 7 implies a neutral solution, that is, one that is neither acidic nor basic. Finally, a pH of 14 represents the most highly alkaline (basic) solution. For example, battery acid has a pH approaching zero. Lemon juice has a pH of 2, while vinegar has a pH of around 3. Distilled water has a pH of 7; it is neutral. Alkaline substances include baking soda (pH = 8), ammonia (pH =11), and most common household bleaches (pH = 12–13, on average). "Normal" or unpolluted rain has a pH (on average) of 5.6; normal rain is, thus, slightly acidic. Some acid in rainwater is useful in helping water dissolve soil minerals, making them available to plant and animal life. Such acidity is often neutralized by the soil itself, for example by the alkaline carbonates in limestone. But higher levels of acidity become destructive (Regens & Rycroft, 1988, pp. 35–37).

A crucial point concerning the pH scale is that a change of only one unit of pH represents a *ten-fold* change in acid concentration. For example, rainfall having a pH of 4.5 is ten times more acid than normal rainfall (pH of 5.6). In the Muskoka-Haliburton area of Ontario, as in a number of other regions in North America, the average pH of precipitation is less than 4.5. This rain with a pH below around 4.5 is the "acid rain" on which the debate centers, and from which the acrimony stems. But rainfall or snowfall measuring a pH of 3.5 (which contains 100 times the acid of ordinary rain) has been recorded on some occasions in parts of eastern Canada and the northeast U.S.. An even lower pH was unofficially recorded in rain during a 1978 storm in Wheeling, West Virginia. The pH of the rain fell below 2, making it as acidic as lemon juice. Some ground waters and soils, it should be noted, are naturally acidic. Small pools in upland *Sphagnum* (a species of moss found in swamps and fens) bogs commonly have a pH of 3–4; but only a fraction of this can be attributed to pollution. There are some naturally acidic lakes in Sweden with a pH of 4.5, but they are exceptions to the rule. Surface water (lakes, streams, seas) normally has a pH from 6 to 9. Lakes in areas with bedrocks that do not weather easily, or where the surrounding soils are low in lime content, can have a "natural" pH of 6. Such lakes are also low in nutrients for aquatic species. In favorable summer conditions, on the other hand, the pH of nutrient-rich lakes in lime-rich areas can be as high as 9 (McCormick, 1985, p. 18).

There are three major stages in the acidification of surface water. These represent the progressively more damaging environmental effects of acid rain. In the first stage, bicarbonate ions present in the surface water neutralize acids by reacting with hydrogen ions to produce carbon dioxide and water. Lakes have varying concentrations of negatively charged bicarbonate ions, the levels depending largely on the surrounding bedrock and soil. Where the soils have a high neutralizing capacity, few hydrogen ions will reach the lake, which will therefore have high and stable levels of buffering bicarbonate ions. But lakes and watercourses in poorly buffered areas must use—and may exhaust—their bicarbonate ions. The natural formation of new bicarbonates (via carbonic acid from the air, weathering from the land, and decomposition of water plants) can be overwhelmed by continuous inputs of acid. As long as the bicarbonate content is maintained at a critical minimum level, the pH value of the water will remain stable, and plants, animals and microorganisms will be unaffected. But a lake or watercourse subject to major acid inputs will be vulnerable.

In the second stage of acidification, the bicarbonate content drops below the critical level, and large influxes of hydrogen ions can no longer be neutralized. The pH value becomes unstable and begins to decrease faster than before. Acid surges can dramatically upset the delicate balance that remains. A sudden release of huge amounts of acidic water into the lake or watercourse—after the first thaw of spring in the northern hemisphere, or when heavy rains follow a period of drought—can be deadly. This danger is especially great if the organisms are at the most sensitive part of their life-cycle (for fish, when they are young, i.e., at the fry stage). The third stage comes when the pH value stabilizes around 4.5, regardless of new influxes of hydrogen ions. Almost all the original life (including snails, crustaceans and many insects) disappear, and a small number of resilient animal and plant species predominate. An entirely new ecosystem emerges. The acidified water becomes abnormally clear because the tiny plants that normally float on the surface, and the organic matter normally suspended in the lake, are both greatly reduced in density. Natural sources of acidity can contribute to a background acidity as low as pH=5 in some lakes. But these are not by themselves enough to account for the recent marked rises in acidity measured in many parts of the globe (McCormick, 1985, pp. 24–5). It is human-produced acid rain, invisible but potent, which is the culprit.

The invisibility of acid rain accounts not only for the difficulty in detecting it. It also accounts for the difficulty in attributing specific consequences to its action. Thus, even when we suspect acid rain is causing severe environmental damage, it is often hard to pinpoint the connection between damage and specific sources of emission. A famous historical example of an air pollution disaster—albeit one involving much more than acid rain—is instructive here.

Disaster at Donora

In the small industrial valley town of Donora, in Western Pennsylvania, on an exceedingly calm day in 1948, the valley held the emission products from factories and trains. The toxic "soup" was incubated together with people for several tragic days. Nearly half of the people of Donora were stricken with severe eye, nose, and throat irritation, chest pains, and labored breathing. Twenty people died over and above the number expected during that period. Here, too, animals as well as people got sick. Here, too, people with preexisting conditions—most asthmatics, nearly everyone with heart diseases, and most others with diseases like chronic bronchitis and emphysema—suffered seriously. But a world then caught up in the post-World War II recovery had little room for air pollution in its order of priorities. Air pollution and acid rain were obviously not yet social concerns whose time had come.

The Donora episode is important for several reasons. First, it demonstrates that environmental problems can only be addressed if they are deemed to have a high public priority. At the close of the War, industrial growth and economic recovery eclipsed environmental concerns as the most important social issues. Equally crucial, however, even if a particular pollutant (or pollutants) is suspected of causing environmental and health dysfunctions, it is a complex task to demonstrate that in a scientifically conclusive manner. Some scientific investigators stated that sulfur dioxide was one of the main—if not the major—ingredients in the Donora disaster. Others think that zinc ammonium sulfate may have been the major cause. The most generally accepted conclusion about the Donora episode is that *several* toxic agents were responsible.

Establishing the specific cause or causes of environmental damage is, therefore, often a complex and controversial scientific problem. When we try to relate the specific pollutant, such as acid rain, to more long-term environmental effects—such as death to aquatic life in affected lakes or human illness or death—the issue becomes far more complicated. In the Donora case, it was difficult for scientists and doctors to identify the cause of disasters involving a large number of *sudden* deaths. It was even more difficult to identify particular pollutants as the cause, or one cause, of illnesses that are *chronic*—diseases like cancer, lung disease, and heart disease. These chronic diseases develop gradually and insidiously, with vague, often inconspicuous symptoms at first. Then, at some point, respiratory and cardiovascular systems are compromised to the extent that any extra stress can push them beyond their limits of physiological compensation. When death finally occurs, it may have no apparent connection to air pollution even though such pollution was possibly a major factor (Kupchella & Hyland, 1989, p. 284).

The Donora disaster, because human health was dramatically affected, generated some public response to the scientific issues involved. Even so, the response to pollution was ambiguous and, finally, forgotten in the wake of more immediately pressing social concerns. When the effects of pollution are less dramatic or less obviously related to human health, the public and governmental response is often even more ambiguous and less prompt. Acid rain affords, unfortunately, a supreme example of such inadequate social response to an environmental crisis. It has caused, as yet, no dramatic episode involving human death. Its principal effects appear for the moment to be on aquatic and forest communities. However devastating these are—and they represent an environmental crisis of global proportions—they fail to impart the same sense of urgency that more visible crises impart. Even when the visible impact of acid rain is dramatic, society's response may still be inadequate. Perhaps the most infamous example of a specific point source for acid rain pollution is the International Nickel Company's (INCO) smelter in Sudbury. The INCO smelter complex holds the dubious honor of being the Western world's largest single source of sulfur dioxide emissions. It generates more sulfur dioxide in a single year than was blown out by the May 1980 eruption of Mt. St. Helens.

Canadian Involvement

Serious Canadian interest in—indeed, awareness of—acid rain began in the early 1970s. Two environmental scientists, R. J. Beamish and Harold Harvey, published a report in 1972 which documented the decrease in fish life in lakes in the Killarney Park wilderness region in northern Ontario. Beamish and Harvey had studied the region since 1966, when they tried stocking the lakes in order to reestablish the level of sport fishing for which the area had once been acclaimed. When none of the four thousand pink salmon that Harvey and Beamish introduced survived the first year, they decided to measure the acidity of the area's lakes.

During the summers of 1969–71, Beamish and Harvey tested 60 lakes in the region and discovered that the pH level averaged 4.4. This was a profound drop from the 6.8 pH measured ten years earlier. The ten-year pH change in the Killarney lakes represented a more than hundredfold increase in acidity. Although Harvey's and Beamish's report concentrated on their observations of declining fishlife in the Killarney lakes, they also referred to a 1971 Swedish government report linking the acidification of Swedish lakes with pollution from industrial sources upwind in England and other parts of Europe. According to the Swedish study, pollutants could remain airborne much longer, and thus travel much farther, than had previously been believed. Since the Killarney lakes are located downwind from the INCO smelter, Harvey and Beamish suspected that airborne pollutants from the Sudbury complex could be responsible for the increased acidity of, and declining fish life in, the Killarney lakes. Thus Harvey and Beamish, effectively, introduced the term acid rain into North American terminology. Despite Harvey and Beamish's predictions of potentially dangerous damage to the Canadian environment, few Canadians were roused into action. Not until 1976, when Ross Howard, a reporter for the *Toronto Star*, wrote articles on acid rain based on conversations with Harvey, did public reaction begin to force government officials and industry leaders to rethink environmental policies. This public activity was, in large part, due to the increased activity of Canadian environmental groups. The most important in this regard is the Canadian Coalition on Acid Rain (CCAR). Founded in June 1981, CCAR represents more than 50 groups, mostly from eastern Canada. It does not advertise itself solely as an environmental group. Less than one-third of the member groups, in fact, are primarily environmental groups. The others come from a broad spectrum of political and social bases. Funding for its Canadian (as opposed to U.S. and international) activities is provided in part by the Canadian government, although it is not officially linked with the government. CCAR is mainly interested in informing the public and government leaders on both sides of the border of the dangers of acid rain. By remaining independent and disseminating information, CCAR believes it remains credible and convincing. The activities of CCAR reflect the broader issues of policies and politics concerning acid rain and other environmental problems (Macdonald, 1991, p. 70). By virtue of its role as public educator, CCAR is able to achieve part of its goal of increasing awareness of the scope of the acid rain dilemma. This it does by an efficient organization and sophisticated media campaigns. It also lobbies for acid rain legislation in Canada and the U.S. In the last analysis, effective environmental action with respect to acid rain depends on cooperation—voluntary or enforced—between industry, government and the public (Schmandt, 1988, pp. 129–130).

One of the major policy problems in dealing with acid rain stems precisely from the fact that the "acid" in acid rain often comes from far away. Airborne sulfate originating in England and elsewhere in northwestern Europe has been linked, as noted above, to increased acidity in the rain coming down in Scandinavia. Some of the acid rain in New England and New York is believed to originate in coal burned along the Ohio River. American oxides of sulfur and nitrogen end up in Canadian acid rain. To a lesser extent, Canadian oxides end up in American acid rain. Up until now the connections between acid rain and its sources have been derived primarily via computer models and by correlations between emission and deposition. Only recently have atmospheric scientists begun to follow tracer substances put into the atmosphere to see just how they travel. Most of these studies are still in the evaluation stages, and some are in the planning stages. But those that have been completed tend to support computer models—qualitatively if not yet quantitatively. But even as we wait for direct confirmation, the time for action is now. This need for effective measures to control acid rain, and transboundary pollution generally, has already raised some delicate international political issues. To be sure, the Canadian-U.S. acid rain dilemma is as urgent, complex, and—at times—bitter as anywhere else in the world (Schmandt, 1988, pp. 253–263).

Transboundary Pollution

In August 1980, the U.S. and Canada signed an agreement to work on transboundary pollution, but the U.S. balked at following through (Wetstone and Rosencranz, 1983). The Reagan administration was, and was perceived to be, antienvironment. The disarray of the Environmental Protection Agency (EPA) under Anne Burford Gorsuch, and the highly publicized and flamboyant activities of then Secretary of the Interior James Watt, alarmed a public now sensitized to environmental issues. With such key appointments, the Reagan administration showed itself at first unwilling even to concede that acid rain was a problem. It was, moreover, reluctant to impose the cost of emission control on industry. Although a bilateral scientific working group was formed, the group released its report a year late and with considerable disagreement as to the degree of emission control needed. Canadian officials accused the American government of stalling and even blatant interference with the work group.

Critics of the Canadian position, on the other hand, point to certain weaknesses in the state of environmental legislation in Canada. They cite loopholes in the legislation mandating emissions controls (Macdonald, 1991, pp. 178–187). Such loopholes have afforded Canadian industry and public utilities lobbyists a means of negating or delaying the implementation of effective antipollution policies. These critics point out, moreover, that Canada—with its sale of CANDU (and other sources of) generated electricity—has an economic stake in driving up the price of American electricity. It remains a fact, also, that the Sudbury smelting complex is still the largest single generator of sulfur dioxide in the world. Finally, Canada's sulfur dioxide emissions per capita are greater than those of the U.S. Clearly, any effective solution to Canadian-U.S. acid rain problems will require a concerted political, economic and public response (Kupchella & Hyland, 1989, p. 337). In any event, the costs of cleaning up the environmental problems resulting from acid rain have been estimated in the billions of dollars. Previously, such vast sums of money have usually been made available for defense and wartime activities. Only if the various national governments commit equal resources, both human and financial, to environmental problems can we hope that dilemmas such as acid rain will be adequately addressed.

Future Prospects

The recent history of national and international interest in acid rain reveals some major areas of agreement and disagreement (Macdonald, 1991, pp. 246–252). Few today can disagree with the verdict that acid rain is one of the greatest environmental problems of our time. Neither is there any doubt now that upper air wind systems blow oxides (and other pollutants) vast distances, across national boundaries and even wide oceans. There is, however, a smaller measure of agreement over *what* has specifically caused any particular acidification of lakes, rivers, forests, or buildings and other structures in different countries. There is even less agreement over the most appropriate measures for solving the problem. The lack of unanimity in national views on acid rain is not from want of trying. Since the mid-1970s, scientific and political meetings on the subject have been held in many countries. The scientific community has devoted much research to assessing the key ingredients in the acid rain dilemma.

There are, to be sure, certain critical areas of scientific uncertainty still remaining (Park, 1987, pp. 186–187). Recognizing that such elements of scientific uncertainty exist, however, must not be taken as an excuse for delaying implementation of responsible environmental policies. The scientific literature is now immense on subjects such as emission, dispersion, deposition in ecosystems, biological consequences, and the devising and testing of various control strategies for reducing sulfur dioxide and nitrogen oxide emissions at source. The technology to diminish the adverse environmental impact of acid rain now exists (Mohnen, 1988). The proposed solutions fall into two groups: cure and prevention. Curative measures can be applied where the problems actually appear, such as the treatment of acidified lakes. Preventive measures can be applied at the source, that is, at points of emission of the sulfur and nitrogen oxides. Clearly, the latter measures

Technology	Some Associated Environmental Problems	Mitigatable?
Photovoltaics, Solar Thermal	Landuse Competition.	No, but tolerable amounts involved.
	Pollution during Production of Materials.	To some extent.
Biomass (Solar energy Collected in the Form of Biological Material).	Destruction of Habitat and Loss of Biological Diversity.	To some extent.
Wind.	Aesthetic.	No.
	Noise.	Yes.
Hydro (Big and Small).	Loss of Key Wildlife Habitat and Recreation Opportunities.	Only by scaling number of projects way down.
Geothermal.	Water Pollution.	Yes.
Ocean Thermal.	Interference with Ocean Cycles.	?

Figure 6.1. List of solar-related and geothermal technologies, associated environmental problems, and whether the environmental problems can be mitigated. From Richard L. Wyman, ed., Global Climate Change and Life on Earth, Copyright © 1991 by Routledge, Chapman and Hall, Inc. Reprinted with permission.

are generally preferable. They are more effective, more sustainable and, in the long run, environmentally more sound than merely curative measures.

Examples of such preventive measures include the following: (1) burning less fossil fuel. Since all fossil fuels contain some sulfur (coal having a higher sulfur content than oil and gas), any reduction in the consumption of coal and oil in conventional power stations would markedly reduce sulfur dioxide at source. Substitutes would include generating electricity by renewable energy sources such as the sun, wind, tides, falling water (hydroelectricity), and natural heat in the earth's crust (geothermal energy). There are many research initiatives underway into these so-called "alternative" or "soft" technologies. Although they are often expensive and limited by geographical and climatic factors, alternative energy technology is seen by many scientists and most environmentalists as the most permanent solution to reducing acid-producing emissions at source (Wyman, 1991, pp. 227–241). Nuclear power is also often cited as an alternative to fossil fuels. But there are equally severe environmental hazards associated with it; (2) reducing the sulfur content of fuels before combustion; (3) reducing emissions of sulfur dioxide after combustion but before exhaust gases are emitted from power station chimneys (stacks) into the atmosphere. Many new power stations now are required, for example, to have some form of "scrubbing" devices; (4) reducing emissions of nitrogen oxides from motor vehicle exhausts. Since the private automobile is (collectively) one of the greatest sources of such emissions, much research has focused on either removing or treating the nitrogen pollutants within the automobile exhaust systems. This can be done by either installing appropriate technical devices (such as mufflers and after-burn systems) or redesigning petroleum engines to minimize the production of pollutants in the first place; (5) providing mass transit alternatives to the private car. Obvious examples include the transit systems in such cities as San Francisco, Boston, and Toronto, the heavily used commuter trains in London, England, and limited-stop commuter buses to/from many major cities in Europe and North America.

Adoption of any or all of the above policies to reduce the dimensions of the acid rain problem will encounter enormous obstacles. These obstacles will, ultimately, be due more to economic or sociopolitical hindrances than they will be to scientific uncertainties or technological incapacities. Money is inevitably an important factor, because pollution control on the scale favored by some policy makers would require vast investment in control technologies. That money has to come from somewhere. Many politicians, and segments of the general population, argue that we simply can't afford such costly clean-ups, either because the money is not there or—more realistically—because it is earmarked for uses deemed of higher social priority (like defense or industrial expansion). Political factors are also influential (Rosencranz, 1986). Some nations, such as those of eastern Europe, do not see pollution control as an item demanding as urgent attention as other forms of east-west economic cooperation. The U.S. and the UK, two of the world's largest producers (and "exporters") of acid rain, have repeatedly found reasons for remaining relatively uncooperative in this critical area of international politics. At a more individual level, old habits die hard. Commuters often prefer their private cars for comfort and convenience, despite their heavier relative environmental cost. Antipollution devices also boost the purchase cost of a new car. Many of us practice energy conservation measures far less diligently than we should.

In the final analysis, political mobilization for the battle against acid rain will come from a combination of forces (Bridgman, 1990, pp. 138–39, 219–20). Public opinion (which is becoming gradually more supportive of acid rain control measures) and pressure from environmental and other interest groups can influence government policies. International pressures may also encourage—force?—delinquent nations to comply with emission standards. Economic factors will also play a part. Governments can encourage the use of certain technologies, and the decreased reliance on others, by appropriate tax incentives and pollution fines. Such measures can be directed at both the corporate sector and the individual consumer. The scientific verdict on acid rain, while not completely unanimous on certain details, is clear and compelling. It is unlikely that many freshwater and forest ecosystems—on which we rely for resources and thus survival—can continue to function if acid rain persists at today's levels. It is not a question of whether acid-forming emissions *should* be controlled. It is rather a question of *when* our political determination(s) will be mobilized to effectively control them. Perhaps effective policies will be instituted in time to avert irreversible environmental degradation. However, as with the issue of ozone depletion, indications suggest that acid rain and other environmental concerns will remain difficult to address quickly at either the national or international levels (Nelkin, 1992, p. 75). ■

Planning for Science and Technology

7

A. Science Policy

■ ■ ■

We have seen how integral a part of society science and technology are today. Obviously, the question arises as to whether we are guiding the powerful forces of scientific and technological change and development properly. We want to know, that is, whether there are adequate policies shaping the applications of science and technology, both nationally and at the global level. This leads us into the new, exciting, but complex field of science policy (Inose et al., 1991).

There is one obvious meaning of science policy. This is associated with the self-proclaimed mission of scientists and engineers during the Scientific Revolution: science for the public good. Ever since the inception of modern science in Western Europe during the sixteenth and seventeenth centuries, scientists and technologists have conceived their activities in terms of noble aspirations. Francis Bacon was the most eloquent of these propagandists for the scientific method. By linking their work to an increase in society's welfare—first of their own nations, but ultimately of the entire human race—the pioneers of the Scientific and Industrial Revolutions sought to reduce suffering due to disease, to satisfy material wants, and to alleviate degrading labor (see sections 2c, 2d, 3a, and 3c).

In this sense, science policy would mean providing those resources by which scientists and engineers could best advance their disciplines. What Francis Bacon and his peers had in mind were such things as government support—financial and political—for doing science and technology (Alic et al., 1992, pp. 380–390). The social status of those engaged in scientific and technological activities had to be raised in comparison with such elevated professions as medicine, the clergy, and law. During the course of the eighteenth, nineteenth, and early twentieth centuries this is, in fact, what happened. It became possible for individuals, more and more of them, to earn their livings by doing science and technology. Governments turned to their scientists and engineers for advice—at first on technical matters but then on broader social and political issues (see sections 2d, 3a, 6a). Until World War II, it seemed that the collective purpose of science and technology had hardly changed since the seventeenth century.

Policy Concerns

Scientists and engineers still contributed to a standard list of fundamental human and social needs: food and energy supply (see section 6b), health needs, transportation (see section 5a), shelter, and personal comfort and security. Two factors associated with World War II and the immediate post-war period (the early 1950s) seemed, however, to challenge the general assumption that science and technology, if given sufficient encouragement, would almost automatically lead to social progress. The first was the role of the atomic physicists in developing the atomic weapons which were used against Japan in August 1945 (see section 6a). The second was the growing realization that our technological interaction with the environment was producing unanticipated and often disastrous consequences. It became clear that science for public policy could no longer concentrate on accelerating the pace of innovation as an aim in itself. Rather, it became apparent that science policy would have to deal, if not become entirely preoccupied, with the unwanted and (often) unintended effects of science and technology's desired contributions (Lester, 1989). Recent anxieties about the deterioration of the global environment have had the effect of intensifying the ambiguity that surrounds the social role of scientists and engineers. Today, these experts are treated in a paradoxical fashion by the public. They are, to be sure, still treated with the highest respect as society's most knowledgeable analysts of the physical environment. At the same time, however, scientists and engineers almost as often seem to be charged with complicity in, even responsibility for, environmental degradation (Marx, 1992, pp. 449, 467).

From the 1950s onward, there have been a variety of ways in which the controversial issues of science policy have come to the attention of governments and, increasingly in recent years, to the general public (Morin, 1993, pp. 37–46). These include: (1) the role of "scientific publicists." One of the first of these was the noted biologist Rachel Carson. Her book *Silent Spring*, published in 1962, indicted the widespread use of chemical pesticides and other industrial chemicals as having a devastating effect on animal and plant species. Carson was much attacked by industrial and private interests, but has since come to be honored as one of the pioneering environmentalists who brought environmental problems to the forefront of the public agenda (in North America); (2) the occurrence of random events of low statistical probability but high social and environmental consequence. This would include such famous nuclear disasters as Three Mile Island and Chernobyl and the Valdez oil spill in Alaska; (3) expression of public sentiment. This would include the increased public concern for such things as endangered species and forest destruction; and (4) media attention, sometimes instigated by dissident scientists. Such individuals as David Suzuki and Ralph Nader have been able to use the media to focus attention on urgent scientific and technological concerns.

This list is by no means exhaustive. It does serve to indicate how policy issues concerning science and technology actually find their way onto the public policy agenda (B. Smith, 1990). Of course, once the issues are raised, the next question is how public policy may be formulated to deal effectively with the concerns expressed by different groups and institutions within society. Given the undoubted role that scientific and technological developments play in modern society, some observers feel that scientists themselves are the best group to establish guidelines for science policy. These observers, by no means restricted to the scientific community itself, argue that scientists and engineers by virtue of their professional expertise bring a certain objectivity and rationality to the political process. It follows, on this view, that society can best entrust its science policy to a sort of technoscientific elite of experts (Hamlett, 1992, pp. 36–43).

As science and technology become more heavily dependent on computers and information processing, it is felt (by some) that scientists alone command the intellectual technology so vital to decision-making on intricate scientific and technological issues. Utilizing the power of mathematics, statistics, computers and simulation techniques, for instance, scientists and engineers—so this argument runs—are the best equipped members of our society to deal with the many issues raised by scientific and technological advance. Scientific knowledge (and information-processing) itself is thus seen as the key for managing a society that seems increasingly threatened by technical interventions made in the past or quite recently (see section 5c).

Expertise

Science policy as formulated by the technical experts has certain advantages (Thompson, 1991, pp. 275–290). These include: (1) identifying clearly hazards arising from science and technology. Scientific analyses and studies have contributed greatly to our understanding of such complex environmental effects such as acid rain, ozone depletion, and the so-called "greenhouse effect"; (2) promoting research that is directly relevant to policy. Biologists themselves, for instance, were among the first members of society to consider the potential hazards of Recombinant DNA research (see section 5d); (3) assessing the consistency of standards involving environmental hazards. This would include setting up standards for measuring, e.g., radiation doses or air and water pollution; (4) scientific analyses may often organize and summarize technical details in a form that allows systematic updating as new facts emerge; and, finally, (5) even a flawed scientific analysis, if it is explicit and clear, may provide a good point of departure and help focus broader policy debates.

As important as these advantages of scientists as policy makers are, there are a number of serious flaws in relying upon experts alone to make science policy decisions (Jasanoff, 1986, p. 10). These include: (1) although scientists and engineers are trained to be (relatively) objective, there is always a subjective element which enters into their role as advisers to industry or government. Scientists, when they act as lobbyists for one scientific program rather than another, often are motivated by the same financial, psychological, and political considerations that affect any group of lobbyists; (2) overconfidence in current scientific knowledge. Almost by definition, many scientists and engineers encourage the application of a new technology or procedure before a full study has been made of possible side-effects or environmental consequences. DDT—to cite one famous example—came into widespread, and practically uncontrolled, use before scientists had even considered the possibility of the side effects that today make chemical pesticides look like a mixed, and irreversible, "blessing" (Hamlett, 1992, pp. 156–158); (3) tendency to invoke scientific and technological "solutions" to environmental or ethical problems. Such "technical fixes" sometimes aggravate the very situation they are intended to rectify (see sections 5c, 5d, 6b); (4) failure to anticipate the human factor in many large-scale scientific and technological undertakings. For example, owing to inadequate training and control room design, operators at Three Mile Island and Chernobyl repeatedly misdiagnosed the problems of the reactors and took inappropriate actions (Medvedev, 1991, pp. 13–14, 32–35, 57–61) (see section 6b).

In the past few decades, this view of science policy by technical experts has come under severe criticism. As long as public trust in science and technology was still high—as it was until the 1960s—the public could rest content in the belief that a small circle of a scientific elite was functioning as the best advisers to governments, industry and other public and private institutions. However, looking back now from the early 1990s to the science policy formulation of the 1950s and 1960s seems almost like looking back at a bygone age (Branscomb, 1992, p. 317). Science and public policy have long since ceased to be bound by a relationship consisting of a few scientific experts and a few highly placed government and military officials. There are a number of reasons why we now find ourselves in need of new guidelines for science and technology policy formulation. The most significant of these is that the "public" has intruded into public policy in many areas, not least in those areas concerning science, technological change, and the environment.

It is, to be sure, not always easy to define who the public is or what the public wants. But most contemporary observers would probably agree that a new set of political actors and new social movements have come to the forefront in an altered public awareness of the impact of science and technology. They have done so, first, by questioning what has been taken for granted so far—namely that science *always* works for social progress. The next step was to protest that the public's concerns were not taken into account properly when making social decisions about science and technology (Lester, 1989). Finally, the new actors in the science/technology debates of our day are claiming (often with great force and persuasiveness) that the science for public policy consideration should be subject to participatory scrutiny like other inputs into the political process. Since it has become obvious that science and technology sometimes have negative side effects, and even cause great harm, the assumption valid from the seventeenth century onward—that science and technology would inevitably produce results for the public good—is no longer tenable.

Precisely what form this new science policy will take is not yet clear. Certain aspects, however, are beginning to emerge. Most significant is that *controversy* seems to erupt over nearly every aspect of science and technology (Nelkin, 1992). Decisions once thought to be only technical—and thus within the province of experts—are now seen to be intensely political. Each of the following applications of science and technology, for example, has implications that far transcend its (initial) avowed purpose: (1) drugs to stimulate the growth of beef cattle may cause cancer; (2) more efficient industrial processes may threaten worker safety and health; (3) biomedical research may be detrimental to human (experimental) subjects and may pose critical ethical questions (see section 7b); (4) a new airport may turn a previously peaceful residential neighborhood into a sonic dump; and (5) biotechnology research may be diverted to purposes of biological warfare (Yanchinsky, 1989, pp. 88–96). The above is a mere sample of the controversial political, ethical, legal and environmental concerns that arise from any actual or potential application of science and technology today.

Risk Assessment

The difficult process of weighing the perceived benefits of any new scientific or technological innovation against potential disadvantages (or social/environmental "costs") is known as *risk assessment* (see sections 5d, 6b). The minimal scope for any adequate risk-benefit analysis would include at least the following points: (1) a preliminary clear and exhaustive description of the proposed science or technology and its intended benefits. It is at this point that the traditional expert role of scientists and engineers is most appropriate: they are probably the best informed members of society to predict the *intended* outcome and consequences of a given innovation; (2) an equally clear and comprehensive description of the probable (or even possible) *adverse* consequences, both social and environmental, to be expected if the particular science or technology is implemented; and, perhaps most important but difficult of all, (3) a complete consideration of all the sources of *uncertainty* involved in making a decision concerning the particular science or technology. Uncertainties arise in a) scientific and technical knowledge itself, b) determining society's (or a particular group or individual's) values, c) the decision-making process, and, finally, d) the actual (as opposed to the desired or intended) implementation of the scientific/technological innovation (Nossal & Coppel, 1989, pp. 137–140).

The point is that even if we are aware that there may be unwanted and detrimental consequences attached to science and technology, it is by no means a simple task to add them into the risk-benefit equation. Even assuming that the outcomes of a particular scientific or technological process (such as the installation of a nuclear power plant or the use of a new pesticide) are known with a fair degree of accuracy, the question of perceived risks involves a political, even individual, dimension (Rosenbaum, 1985, pp. 88–91). For example, how are we to weigh the perceived advantages (to transportation and the economy) of a new airport with the negative consequences (including destruction of agricultural land, increased ground traffic congestion, and sonic booms) to the people who live in the area of the proposed site. There is an inherent uncertainty in any risk-benefit determination. This uncertainty arises primarily from the fact that different groups or different individuals have different perceptions of benefits and risks. A new nuclear plant may be viewed as a sign of progress to a public utility. It may, however, be viewed in quite the opposite way by local residents or environmental action groups (Nelkin, 1992, pp. 97–111).

This difference in perceived risks/benefits is further complicated when we consider short-term vs. long-term consequences. A given drug may have dramatically beneficial immediate results but result in long-term adverse effects. How does the biomedical policy-maker balance the two? Or, to cite another possibility, diversion of a river or lake to provide water for irrigation and other purposes may cause severe ecological disruption in the long-term. Again, how are the technological policy-makers to decide? Finally, the construction of an industrial plant (lacking the often expensive pollution controls that would be mandatory in many advanced industrial nations) in a developing country may bring short-term economic returns but create long-term environmental hazards (see section 7e). All these uncertainties must, somehow, become part of the newly emerging concept of a comprehensive science/technology policy (Bryner, 1987, p. 45).

There are, as yet, no unambiguous answers to the knotty questions posed by any honest risk-benefit analysis. Nor is there even a guarantee that we can construct an effective science policy. At the very least, there will be increased public participation in science policy-making. Although experts will still play an essential role in policy formulation, they will become one actor in the public debates concerning science and technology. There are obvious advantages to, indeed a necessity for, involving the public. It is clear that the public does know something about the social/individual consequences of science and technology: the quality of life is determined as much by perceptions as it is by physical or medical innovations. It is, for instance, the patient (or the family?) who must ultimately decide whether a radically new life-extending technology is "worth it" (see section 7d). More often than not, the public has good reasons for skepticism concerning many new and highly touted applications of science and technology. Finally, since it is the public who will be most affected by the implementation of any new science and technology, surely it is the public's right to be included in the science/technology policy process.

Public Participation

This right to be included, however, presupposes certain conditions if the public is to play a productive role in science policy decisions. Members of the public—including politicians!—must be prepared to become as fully informed as possible on the technical aspects of the scientific or technological process under deliberation (Davis, 1992). There are educational obligations that accompany the right speak out effectively in policy debates. In line with this freer flow of information, there must be strict efforts—on the part of government, industry, as well as public interest groups—to avoid secrecy, lip-service testimony (by biased or financially involved experts), superficial public-opinion polls, or other manipulation of public opinion. Concerning this last point, the media will come to play an ever-increasing role in science popularization and debate (Nelkin, 1987). It is essential that safeguards are put in place to secure against unintentional, or intentional, misuse of the powers of the mass media in our society. Finally, once a policy decision has been taken to go ahead with a particular science or technology innovation, every effort must be made to ensure that all perceived risks are avoided or minimized as completely as possible. To this end, there must be effective cooperation between governmental regulatory agencies and industry and public interest groups at all levels—local, state (or provincial), federal and, in certain cases (such as acid rain) international—to monitor risks and impose *effective* penalties for hazardous activity (Macdonald, 1991, pp. 172–192).

The basic point concerning our modern, and hopefully more sophisticated, attitude toward science/technology policy is that we must face the impossibility of a risk-free existence. Many of the science policy decisions made in the past have already created environmental and social hazards with which we will have to learn to cope, if not live comfortably. A forceful example here is the massive quantity of highly toxic radioactive wastes stored, properly or otherwise, in sites across the globe. Equally important, many scientific and technological innovations of the present (or future) will entail certain risks alongside their perceived benefits. There must be fuller disclosure of these risks to workers and consumers. Such knowledge would enhance their ability to negotiate fair compensation for hazardous work and fair prices for safety devices. This may be particularly important when workers serve as guinea pigs for the rest of society (Nelkin and Brown, 1984). Substances that workers handle in concentrated doses often reach the public in weaker doses (e.g., PCBs). Processes that prove themselves first in industrial applications, with insufficient attention having been paid to possible health hazards, often find domestic uses (e.g., microwaves). Because health effects can be most easily detected when large doses are given to a readily defined population, every effort should be made to learn the most from this bitter lesson in which workers (and, often, their supervisors) partake (Nelkin, 1992, pp. 130–146). Hopefully—to be sure—technologies or scientific processes that are dangerous or poorly understood will not be implemented in the first place.

A new approach to science policy may not offer our society complete guarantees that science and technology will always serve the public, or individual, good (Morin, 1993, pp. 156–172). In some situations, better information and more open policy debates may lead the public to decide that certain risks are, in fact, less important or likely than they thought. Thus, an informed public policy debate may encourage science or technology innovation in certain cases—with ultimately uncertain consequences. In other situations, the public may demand increased wages or safer products, leading in turn to increased prices that more accurately reflect the full social costs of the product—while they increase the economic burden. One beneficial side effect of better information would be that people are at least aware of the risks in the machinery or substances and consumer products they choose (or are compelled) to deal with. Science and technology by their very nature can not be risk-free. In an age as permeated by science and technology as our own is, it is far better to be alerted to those risks than to be blissfully unaware of them, or deliberately misled by industry or government. Public awareness and informed participation will, if nothing else, contribute to a more open and politically-sensitive science policy than has hitherto been the case (Dickson, 1988). ■

B. Science and Ethics

■ ■ ■

Just as the latter decades of the twentieth century are witnessing a new approach to the field of science policy, so also is there a major reexamination of the relationship between science and ethics (Wiseman, Vanderkop & Nef, 1991, pp. 7–11). This reexamination focuses on two major areas. First, the broad and complex issue of ethics *in* science is undergoing important revisions. As science becomes a more intricate social activity, so do the ethical issues confronting the scientist in the performance of his/her professional work become more pressing. Secondly, the wide-ranging impact science and technology have upon both society and individuals provokes a wide range of (often unanticipated) ethical and legal controversies *about* science.

Science and technology—for so long believed to be either automatically benevolent or, at the least, ethically neutral—now excite growing suspicion, sometimes fear, among many sectors of society (Thompson, 1991, pp. 249–264). The ethical activities of scientists and engineers in the conduct of their work are coming under scrutiny. As well, the ethical *implications* of certain types of research and their practical applications are being subjected to a new and critical analysis (Antebi & Fishlock, 1986, pp. 217–219). Significantly, a growing number of scientists and engineers themselves feel that questions about the ethical and social responsibilities of researchers and their research must be faced more directly than has previously been the case. In short, our traditional view that scientists and engineers have a bargain with society by which they produce ideas and devices with few or no constraints on their research has been shaken (Spiegel-Rosing & Price, 1977, pp. 79–82).

Attempts to impose certain types of restraints or regulations—ethical, legal or financial—on research have been particularly apparent in the biomedical disciplines. In a very real way, the new biology has given humans powers which force us to go back to the drawing board for a reconsideration of the very notions of birth, life and death. Human experimentation, life-extending technologies, fetal research and medical euthanasia, to name but a few recent areas of research, have extended enormously the ethical implications of developments in the life sciences (Nelkin, 1992, pp. 3–25). In fact, a new field of study called *bioethics* has emerged which attempts to examine explicitly the relationship of biological knowledge and technology to human values (G. Smith, 1989, pp. 9–13).

This does not mean, of course, that the links between science and social and ethical values have not been discussed and argued about—often with bitter controversy—before in history. The conflict between Galileo and the Catholic Church in the seventeenth century, over the Copernican theory, is one of the major historical examples of the potential for conflict between science and religion (see sections 2a, 2c). The often acrimonious debates concerning the ethical and social implications of the Darwin/Wallace theory of evolution by natural selection—debates which began more than a century ago and continue in some circles unabated today—constitute another notable historical example of the broader controversies created by scientific advances (see section 3b). However, in both these celebrated cases, attempts to crush the scientific theories ultimately failed.

Galileo, Darwin and (to a lesser degree) Wallace were hailed as brilliant and courageous seekers after truth. Indeed, Galileo came to symbolize the figure of the noble scientist, pursuing knowledge for the good of humanity against the forces of religious and philosophical dogmatism and obscurantism. Galileo's brilliant (if not completely innocent) polemics against his ecclesiastical opponents argued eloquently for the *autonomy* of science. He fervently believed in the freedom of scientists from external restraints, including theological ones, on the conduct of their research. From the seventeenth century to the mid-twentieth century, Galileo's view of science (and scientists) as ethically neutral searchers after "objective truth" gained fairly complete acceptance. Most scientists and many lay persons came to regard science as an activity (largely) free from the political, ethical, social, and legal problems and questions that seemed an inevitable adjunct to all other human activities (Ben-David, 1971, pp. 85–87).

Norms of Science

Such a purist view of science was not merely wishful thinking. Up until the twentieth century, and particularly until World War II, science and scientists appeared to act in a fashion which seemed almost to guarantee ethical neutrality. A special "code of ethics" seemed to envelop science and safely guide scientists in their research. This traditional code of ethics, which owes its clearest formulation to the American sociologists Robert K. Merton and Bernard Barber, includes the following characteristics:

1. **Universalism**—this implies that empirically verified knowledge knows no national boundaries. Thus, the truth of a scientific statement should be independent of a particular scientist's nationality or political or social opinions;

2. **Organized skepticism**—each scientist is *obligated* to subject his own research and results, as well as the findings of other scientists, to the most rigorous scrutiny. Thus, no data can be accepted "on faith" or because of the eminence of the researcher presenting the data, but must be critically examined and retested. Moreover, a scientist is obligated to make public his/her criticisms of the work of other scientists when he/she believes it to be in error;

3. **Communality**—a scientist must share the results of research freely with others, since scientific advance is predicated on the free flow of ideas;

4. **Disinterestedness**—a scientist pursues science for "its own sake." This implies that science should not be used to enhance a scientist's prestige or authority in the nonscientific affairs of the general population. Knowledge and discovery should primarily be ends in themselves and not pursued (solely) for financial motives. In this context, it should be noted that most scientists, at least prior to the nineteenth century, did not earn their living primarily from doing science. However, the professionalization of science during the course of that century produced a radically changed situation by the start of the twentieth century (see section 3a);

5. **Rationality**—this is the trust in the virtue of scientific reason. Accordingly, theory formulation and empirical testing and criticism are considered superior to tradition, authority, or moral beliefs in "scientific matters";

6. **Emotional neutrality**—this enjoins the scientist to avoid so much emotional involvement with his/her research that he/she would be prevented from exercising objectivity. Thus, the scientist should willingly reject an existing theory (even his/her own!) when new evidence makes that necessary. (Storer, 1966, pp. 76–80)

This code of ethics is (was), to be sure, an *idealized* set of norms for behavior, rather than a description of the way actual scientists always operated (Barbour, 1993, p. 29). After all, scientists are human beings. The remarkable fact, however, is that most scientists during the seventeenth to nineteenth centuries could attempt to act according to the (unwritten) code. For instance, prior to World War I, scientists did form an international community of scholars. Research and ideas did flow (more or less) freely across national borders. Science was not pursued *primarily* for motives of financial gain or political influence. Finally, (documented) instances of fraud or deception in science seemed notably rare or infrequent (Ben-David, 1991). As a general picture of scientific activity and scientists' behavior, then, this somewhat idealized code of ethics seemed fairly accurate. It should be emphasized, that this code operated not because of any particular moral superiority of scientists themselves. Rather, the *social context* of modern science during the seventeenth to nineteenth centuries permitted (or did not place tremendous obstacles for) such behavior to constitute the norm (Spiegel-Rosing & Price, 1977, pp. 357–358). It was the social context of twentieth-century science (and technology) which changed the nature of the scientists' pact with the public.

Since the advent of nuclear power and the contemporary biomedical revolution (see sections 5d, 6a, 6b), among other major theoretical and technical developments, the traditional code of ethics for science has come under increasing challenge. Since World War II, the scale of government and industry funding for science-related research and development has grown tremendously. Before the twentieth century—and even, in some cases, as late as the 1930s—science was conducted (generally) by individuals or small research groups. An individual scientist, moreover, could probably have a fairly complete grasp of his/her particular field and related fields. Thus, a scientist was probably fully aware of the potential applications of his/her own and related research. Indeed, because public funding was relatively small-scale up to the twentieth century, links between "pure" research and technological ("practical") application were often slow to manifest themselves, or were indirect. Of course, the history of science and technology shows many significant examples of the rapid and sometimes major social impact of ideas and inventions throughout all periods. Galileo himself, on some occasions, received financial remuneration from various governments for practical aspects of his work. The French state directly employed scientists in many important capacities during the Revolution of 1789 (Olby et al., 1990, pp. 1015–1016). On the whole, however, a rapid translation of science into public impact was infrequent or relatively small-scale.

With the rise of "big science" and "big technology"—as symbolized most dramatically by the Manhattan Project of World War II (see section 6a)—the traditional role of scientists (and technologists) altered in important ways (Spiegel-Rosing & Price, 1977, p. 96). First, science is now massively funded by governments and private industry for specific social and political purposes. Since much research is now mission-oriented, the scientist is more likely to be aware of the potential practical or ideological applications of his work than in the past. Also, as science itself becomes a more expensive activity, the competition for available public and corporate funding becomes much keener. In order to obtain grants to keep their laboratories operating, senior scientists now frequently must conform to the desires or whims of administrators of foundations, corporate boards, or government agencies to a somewhat greater degree than previously. Competition for "start-up" funding (to commence research) is especially acute among younger, less well-established scientists. There is, moreover, the time constraints imposed by tighter deadlines to produce "results" more quickly. For all these reasons, there has been some erosion in the traditional concept of science as an activity governed by the open and free exchange of ideas and by the lengthy process of peer evaluation and critical review of theories and experimental data (Huber, 1990). Some observers point to an increase in the proportion of papers published in scientific journals which are incompletely verified, shoddy, or (in some instances) even fraudulent (Broad & Wade, 1982).

Industrialization of Science

What has been called the "industrialization of science," therefore, has created new ethical and social conditions and problems for science and scientists (Ravetz, 1971). As science and technology become more directly tied to specific corporate and government objectives, there is an inevitable decline in the free exchange of scientific and technological information. Secrecy in science is not only characteristic of military research and weapons development. Secrecy—and espionage—have come to permeate some of our most glamorous high-tech research enterprises. The international high-tech race between the giant industrial labs of Japan, the U.S., and Europe affects scientists not only in those places but in other countries, including Canada (see section 7c). As individual scientists now perform as workers in a large-scale research institute or government project, any single individual comes to know less of the total picture. His/her own quite specialized area of research may not have any obvious connection to the broader economic or political purpose of the total project. For these and similar reasons, the image of the scientist as always seeking objectively for truth and working automatically for the public good seems no longer valid (Iannone, 1987, pp. 178–182).

The view of science (as it was created during the seventeenth and eighteenth centuries) as being ethically neutral—or divorced from overt sociopolitical concerns—is no longer adequate to describe the activities of modern scientists and technologists. Science is now often supported to further specific sociopolitical and ideological agendas (Rouse, 1987). The time lag between the actual performance of research and its practical applications is short, in some cases almost instantaneous. Scientific and technological breakthroughs often have immediate societal, ethical and legal consequences. Microelectronics (including computers) and biomedical developments (including those in reproductive technologies) are two of the more striking examples of how research and theory now make the transition from science fiction to social fact in astonishingly short time (see sections 5c, 5d). Finally, the growing awareness in the 1970s and 1980s of the devastating environmental impact of much of our science and technology, has destroyed permanently the idea that scientific research is value-free, ethically neutral, or divorced from standard political or economic interests or motives.

The need to consider the ethical and environmental implications of even the most abstract scientific research is now recognized (Wiseman, Vanderkop & Nef, 1991, pp. 36–40). If scientific research was ever divorced from its societal, ethical and legal consequences—and history is ambivalent on this point—it certainly cannot be today. We no longer can afford the leisure of centuries, decades, or in some cases even years or months, to witness the full implications of scientific activity. There are increasingly urgent demands to consider the social and ethical implications of science and technology *before* the research is undertaken or the technology is implemented. Full public controversies, it seems, should occur prior to the large-scale applications of a particular scientific development or technological breakthrough. Public participation—and sometimes bitter controversy—in the formulation of science and technology policy is one indication of the new ethical dimension of science (see section 7a). Among scientists themselves, however, a new ethical code is also being articulated (Webster, 1991).

A New Code of Ethics

The new code of ethics, although incomplete and by no means accepted in all circles, has the following features: (1) *Refusing* to do certain research—this implies that, if a certain type of research or experimentation will (or might) have harmful consequences or if it would harm its human or animal experimental subjects in some way, the scientist(s) should refuse to conduct such research. This is, however, not always an easy ethical decision. During World War II, as we have seen, the scientific community itself was split on the research involved in the Manhattan Project. Some scientists chose gladly to participate, others refused to cooperate, and still others—notably Einstein—participated in the research leading to the development of the first atomic bombs but later were consumed by guilt and remorse (see section 6a). Even in those cases where research and experimentation are obviously evil or misguided—such as the research on human subjects conducted by the Nazis—there may appear to be overriding political or ideological reasons for some scientists to participate. But the refusal to do certain types of research (particularly in such matters as chemical and biological warfare or biotechnology) is becoming more common among certain scientists (Ravetz, 1990, pp. 278–283); (2) *Choosing* to do certain kinds of research or experimentation—this implies that, if a certain avenue of research appears to have a high social priority, the scientist(s) should elect to do it. Furthermore, even if such research might not bring the individual scientist(s) greater rewards in earnings or professional prestige than other types of research, the scientist will be guided by "higher" motives. Examples might include research on alternative technologies (see section 7g), or publicizing research results which demonstrate environmental hazards or moral problems associated with new, or established, scientific or technical processes (Rabino, 1991, p. 85).

For the scientist(s) following the above two guidelines, there is the obligation to (3) *Influencing* other scientists and engineers—this implies that a scientist concerned about the sociopolitical or ethical implications of a particular avenue of research and development should communicate those concerns to other scientists. A notable example of this was the founding of the journal called *Bulletin of the Atomic Scientists* after World War II. A group of scientists concerned about the spread of atomic and nuclear weapons, and other implications of the Atomic Age, sought a forum to broadcast those concerns to other scientists and to the public. The *Bulletin* remains today one of the most respected voices for social and ethical concern in science on nuclear and many other environmental matters; and, finally, (4) *Informing* the public—if a particular area of research or experimentation (however esoteric or specialized) might have a significant social or ethical impact, the scientist(s) should make the relevant issues public. This is, without a doubt, one of the most sensitive and challenging of the new ethical responsibilities being urged upon scientists and engineers (Iannone, 1987, pp. 323–325).

Traditionally, scientists were (to some extent) shielded from direct involvement in social and ethical controversies concerning the implications of their work. As long as the time lag between research and its broad social application was relatively extensive, the scientist could, with some justification, claim that the ultimate use of his research by government or commercial corporations was not his/her concern. Even if there were negative consequences, society would have sufficient time to resolve the social or ethical dilemmas. At the present time, with the often immediate impact of any new science or technology, the luxury of neutrality is no longer an option. Because scientists *do* possess expert knowledge about certain aspects of research or development, they are now expected to participate in various public debates concerning the social impact of their work. Scientists also have an ethical obligation to educate the public on scientific and technical issues. Clearly, there are some pitfalls awaiting the scientist who enters the (for him/her) comparatively uncharted territory of political involvement or the mass media (Nelkin, 1987). Yet, there is a growing consensus among the scientific community that such a public role is part of the professional duties of being a scientist. Once again, the scientist and technologist today is being asked to assume a political and ethical posture that would have been unexpected, indeed considered inappropriate and resisted strongly, before.

For these reasons, science and technology can no longer be considered ethically neutral or politically (or culturally) value-free (Wiseman, Vanderkop & Nef, 1991, pp. 27–31). The scientific community is now witnessing—indeed, contributing to—a critical change in certain of the principles governing its professional conduct. Ethical, political, and ideological debates, to be sure, have not been absent in the history of science. Such debates, however, seem to be an integral, rather than unusual, aspect of scientific and technical developments today. In addition to these controversies *within* the professional community of scientists, there exist the critical public and private sector controversies concerning science and technology. They are as complex and unpredictable as any other ethical and political debates. The concerns relating to science and technology, however, fall into well-defined general categories.

Ethical Concerns About Science

The major categories of ethical concerns *about* science and technology include: (1) "Slippery-slope" science and technology—this relates to the fact that advances in science and technology sometimes blur ethical boundaries that previously seemed clear-cut. Examples would include biomedical technologies such as life-extending machines, prenatal diagnosis (and operations upon the fetus), and reproductive engineering (Barbour, 1993, p. 197). Such new techniques seem to force a reexamination of the basic concepts of "life" and "death." Some critics argue that if such technologies are not closely regulated—or banned entirely except in the most extraordinary circumstances—society and individuals will find themselves on a "slippery-slope" of relativistic ethics on which traditional moral guidelines may tumble away (Iannone, 1987, pp. 128–131); (2) Research using human (and animal) experimental subjects—this relates to the fact that much research, especially in the biomedical and social sciences, often relies (necessarily or unnecessarily) upon humans and the higher animals for experimentation and theory validation. Most of us would likely condemn outright the types of "research" performed by the Nazis prior to, and during, World War II as unethical (Lifton, 1986). Yet, we may not be aware that much current scientific research often subjects humans and animals to unusual, cruel, or painful treatment. Examples would include physical or psychological "deprivation experiments," use of "involuntary subjects" such as prison inmates and hospital patients, and use of animals in pharmacological and cosmetics testing. These concerns raise the urgent need to develop satisfactory ethical guidelines and controls on living subjects research or, when such controls are impossible, to restrict or ban such research; (3) "Prejudicial science"—these concerns center on the fear that scientists may present hypotheses or data which can be used to buttress a particular, and socially pernicious or unethical, ideology. Examples would include eugenics, some types of genetic counselling, and the recent controversies about the legitimacy of using IQ data to support racial prejudices. As with the previous two categories, it does not appear feasible to place a ban on pure research. Rather, one would look to effective public scrutiny, panels of experts, or government and university watchdog agencies to monitor how controversial data is presented or interpreted (Olby et al., 1990, p. 895); and finally (4) "Subversive science"—these issues deal with the fears that certain areas of fundamental scientific research and their findings may somehow demean humanity. History, as well as our own time, affords numerous examples of scientific theories or experimental findings inciting bitter ethical controversies. Galileo's conflict with the Roman Catholic Church concerning the Copernican system, the ongoing debates between evolutionists vs. creationists, and the biomedical controversies of today (such as those relating to the rights of the fetus or the terminally ill) are all evidence of the powerful impact of science and technology upon ethical systems. Some critics argue that science and the scientific method occupy too authoritative a role in modern society. These critics emphasize that science is only one mode of knowing and does not have an exclusive claim to objective truth or certainty—ethical, religious and other kinds of knowledge have equally important status. Such concerns, while legitimate, have always been present in the history of science. Each age attempts to find the proper mix of science and other fields of knowledge and values. In general, society will deal with the ethical concerns about science and technology by establishing guidelines and regulations (ethical, political, legal) to govern research and development, rather than placing outright bans on such research (Graham, 1978).

Science and technology can no longer be regarded as ethically neutral or value-free. Much of contemporary scientific and technical research and development raises immediate ethical problems (Barbour, 1993, pp. 211–212). We now know, in a way earlier generations could not, that what is called pure science or innocent knowledge can easily have significant, sometimes harmful, societal and environmental impacts. There is simply too much knowledge and technical ingenuity to discharge even basic scientific research from its moral and social obligations. Part of the burden for the ethical consequences of scientific research must rest on the individual scientist or technologist. An equal, if not greater, ethical burden rests upon those who use science and upon the people science and technology are presumed to serve. A new ethics for science can only arise from a determined and cooperative effort between the scientific and technological communities, the government (at all levels), corporations, and the public. The growing awareness of the ethical and cultural complexity of science and technology represents perhaps the most fundamental challenge, and opportunity, of our time. ■

C. Science, Technology and the Economy

■ ■ ■

There are three major types of economic systems found throughout the modern world. These are, with numerous national and regional variations: (1) **subsistence**; (2) **capitalist** or "commercial"; and (3) **centrally planned** (usually communist or state socialist). Subsistence economies characterize many of the less-developed countries of the globe. These economies rely upon modern science and technology in only very limited ways. The other two economic systems, which characterize the nations of the developed world, rely in major respects upon modern science and technology. Most capitalist and centrally planned economies are based on increasing economic growth by a combination of a larger population and greater (average) per capita production and consumption. Such growth—as measured by "gross national product" (GNP) and "average per capita GNP"—is generally assumed to: (1) raise the industrial and economic level of a country and assist its performance in global science/technology competition; (2) provide for full employment and control inflation; (3) increase the general standard of living and provide for a better quality of life for all citizens; (4) help eradicate poverty; and, lastly, (5) provide funds for environmental protection and improvement (Griffin, 1989, p. 29).

Events of the past decade have called into question some of these assumptions concerning the consequences of continued industrial expansion (Adams & Solomon, 1991, pp. 122–128). It is not entirely clear that continual economic development is possible or even desirable. Many industrialized nations face periodic crises of inflation and unemployment. The quality of life in many industrialized countries appears in some significant ways to be deteriorating. Pollution of all kinds (toxic chemicals and hazardous wastes, industrial and photochemical smog, ocean and groundwater contamination, ozone layer depletion, noise, and the list goes on) is on the increase globally (see section 6c). Although life expectancies are lengthening, our health care systems appear to be in crisis (see section 7d). And the costly efforts to transfer science and technology to the developing nations often results in negligible or adverse consequences (Griffin, 1989, p. 144) (see section 7e). The interrelation between science, technology and the economy differs greatly between the developed and the developing worlds, between various nations in the industrialized world itself, and between different regions and sociocultural groups within any given nation (Grindle & Thomas, 1991, pp. 97–99).

In general, there are two major aspects to national economic policies, in most industrialized countries, with respect to science and technology. The first deals with the various measures and incentives, of both the public and private sectors, which may better prepare a nation to deal with the highly competitive science/technology industrial climate of the 1990s (Crane, 1992, pp. 165–193). The second general area treats the environmental consequences of the aggressive industrial growth of the past few decades. We are entering an era of increased ecological awareness and sharpened environmental debates, both locally and globally. As we have seen, economic and environmental concerns are not always compatible. The U.S. and Canada, as two of the world's richest countries, will face significant challenges in trying to reconcile the demands of continued economic growth and rising expectations of living standards with the equally pressing concerns of environmentalists (see section 7g).

Science-based Industries

North Americans have been fortunate in confronting past economic challenges, in large part because their considerable endowment of natural resources has served them well. But while the U.S. and Canada remain affluent, their advantages globally are diminishing. Indeed, the prime factor in the new international economic climate will be science and technology-based industries (Yanchinsky, 1989, pp. 55–56). In order to retain the competitive edge needed in the 1990s and beyond, North Americans will have to use science and technology to develop new knowledge-intensive activities and sectors while—at the same time—maintaining their position in those knowledge-intensive industries in which they have already demonstrated successful capabilities, such as biotechnology and telecommunications (Forster & Wase, 1987, p. 285) (see sections 5c, 5d). The Canada-U.S. free-trade agreement, for instance, may provide both opportunities and threats for both nations. But the real threat lies in the rate of scientific and technological progress elsewhere, notably in East Asia.

To prepare for the intensely competitive science/technology world of the 1990s, it is necessary for the U.S. and Canada to act quickly and decisively. Both nations face an enormous challenge to develop and harness science and technology for industrial renewal. They can thus become more competitive in global markets in a period of fundamental changes to the world economy. But although governments (at all levels) are increasingly working with the private sector to improve performance, the pace and scale of such efforts still fall short of what is required. There is much that can be done to improve the federal-local partnerships in science/technology developments. There are still many issues and controversies about policy to resolve, barriers to overcome, resources to reallocate, new links between government, industry and university-based research to forge, and opportunities to grasp.

One way by which the U.S. and Canada might address these problems is through science/technology "networks." These networks would enable scientists and engineers in industry and universities to communicate more effectively with each other and with their peers abroad (Crane, 1992, pp. 108–109). Some policy analysts suggest that there should be closer links between universities and industries, especially with small companies. These companies could also be encouraged to make greater use of professional environmentalists and engineers. Universities are also being encouraged to consider how they can most effectively provide first-class scientific, environmental, and technological knowledge and expertise to industry. It must be recognized, however, that all such links between the academic and commercial sectors pose new problems as well as opportunities (Kenney, 1986).

To improve export performance in science and technology-based industries, boards of directors might be strengthened by members with scientific and technological expertise. Science/technology issues must receive higher priority attention—than they do at present—within corporations at board and senior management levels. Industry's efforts at self-help (in both developed and developing nations) will need to be reinforced by positive government programs (Fransman, 1986, pp. 129–130). A program that warrants support would be one to raise the standards of industrial and engineering design. As the Japanese have shown so dramatically, it is less basic inventions which create social wealth than the ability to transform R & D (research and development) quickly into world-class goods by integrating design with manufacturing. Universities can also assist industry by developing broader education—particularly so-called "continuing education"—in science and technology management. Students in engineering and science should be encouraged to take courses in environmental and health issues and in business administration (and conversely). All these various strategies should be integrated in defining coherent national science/technology targets and priorities. Once the key industrial strategies are identified, business must collaborate more closely with universities and governments to ensure that the knowledge generated in laboratories and research institutes is translated effectively to domestic customers and suppliers—and, ultimately, exported abroad (Mowery & Rosenberg, 1989).

Canada presents particular challenges to the formulation of effective economic policies relating to science and technology. Canada's resources for science and technology research and development are limited, and are now spread too thinly across too many areas. Most advisers strongly recommend that Canada focus her efforts on a few science-based industries, where there is a greater chance of becoming a world leader. Canada clearly does not have the population resources nor the economic potential of the U.S., Japan or the European Common Market, and can not hope to challenge those industrial giants across the boards (Freeman, Sharp & Walker, 1991). Instead, Canada should aim to develop more world-class companies (or indigenous multinationals) focused on a few, strategic science and technology-based industries. Two fields which are frequently mentioned are (1) the design of home-based and other health and social care systems, and (2) environmental technologies. The first field could be driven by public and private funding and by university and industry generated innovation and development. Home-based and other care systems would address the serious problems emerging for the care of an aging population—surely a large market and a worthy challenge. Canadian efforts here would also serve a potentially large market in other advanced industrial countries (see section 7f).

Sustainable Development

Domestic and global concerns to clean up and restore the environment present another set of highly significant opportunities for both the U.S. and Canada. In the growing movement toward sustainable domestic and global development, environmental and economic policies must go hand in hand (Adams & Solomon, 1991, pp. 96–107). The U.S. and Canada can build on their existing expertise in certain areas such as waste disposal and recycling as well as environmental clean-up and enhancement technologies (Antebi & Fishlock, 1986, pp. 162–163). One way to achieve that goal would be through major government and private programs to fund advanced ecological research in various sciences (including environmental toxicology and ecosystem health) and to develop environmentally sound technologies. This science and technology research could contribute toward the newly emerging holistic approach (in the industrial world) to the environment (Harrison, 1992, pp. 301–303). The U.S. and Canada could thus be at the forefront of the global effort to incorporate the human species as an integrated (rather than intrusive or disruptive) part of the total ecosystem. Such programs could also foster industry-university networks to encourage diffusion of environmental technology and provide recognition to successful performers. It is in every nation's long-term interest to respond to the global ecological crisis by cleaning up its own backyard, while also addressing global issues through international organizations (Gupta, 1988, pp. 73–74). Even in the short term, concern for the global environment could be rewarding. The early development and export of ecologically sound technologies could bring immediate profits to North American entrepreneurs.

Most important, by integrating environmental and economic decision-making, the U.S. and Canada could demonstrate world leadership in *sustainable development*. North American industries should adopt so-called "preventive technologies." Unlike "remedial technologies" which attempt to treat adverse environmental consequences *after* their occurrence, preventive technologies would aim at completely eliminating or minimizing environmental degradation (Crane, 1992, pp. 59–62). To be most effective in this science/technology leadership role, North Americans must, of course, set a good example at home. If Americans and Canadians are not prepared to tackle environmental problems that are solvable through their actions alone—such as reduction or elimination of the pollution of ground and surface water caused by resource-based industries—then who will (or should) pay attention to them when they speak to problems that require international collaboration for their solution (Macdonald, 1991)? As two of the world's most advanced industrial societies, the U.S. and Canada have contributed to the global ecological crisis created (in part) by the inappropriate use of science and technology. There are a few positive signs that they now may be ready to take a leading role in reversing the world's environmental degradation and in encouraging an appropriate use of science and technology (see section 7g). It is essential that all advanced industrial countries adopt patterns of science and technology use for the 1990s and beyond which will be both industrially competitive and ecologically sound. Our global future depends on the effective implementation of such policies. ■

D. Health and Medicine

■ ■ ■

Of all the modern impacts of science and technology, none have been more dramatic and controversial than in the areas of health and medicine. Developments in biology and related sciences have transformed many fields of medicine (see sections 4c, 5d). Medical technology—also called "health technology"—has further revolutionized both the practice of medicine and the daily lives of practically every citizen. Medical technology, which is far more than "hardware," is pervasive in our society and in our health care systems (Iannone, 1987, pp. 146–157). The drugs, devices and medical/surgical procedures which characterize this new technology have altered the way we live, the way we treat our illnesses and, finally, the way we die.

Great advances in public health and medicine have been made during the twentieth century and continue to appear with increasing frequency in the present decade. There are numerous statistics which attest to the achievements of medical science and technology. In the United States, pneumonia, influenza, gastrointestinal infections, diptheria, poliomyelitis, and other infectious diseases were among the major causes of death in 1900. Today, the death rate from those diseases is but a fraction of the total death rate. Similarly pronounced reductions in the fatality of infectious disease occurred in Canada and other advanced industrial nations. Yet there are a number of circumstances which cloud this positive picture.

For one, infectious diseases still plague much of the developing world. In those nations, average life expectancies at birth are notably shorter than in the developed countries and health (generally) may be a far more elusive state for much of the population. It must be noted, however, that there have been some impressive achievements in health in the less developed countries in recent years. Since 1960, the average life expectancy at birth has increased from just over 40 years to almost 60 years. Still, this must be compared to an average life expectancy of over 70 years in the more developed countries. Even in the developed countries, public health and medicine present problems of tremendous scope. The total costs of health care are staggering and continue to rise. Total national health expenditures in the United States, for example, have risen immensely from $27 billion in 1960 to over $650 billion in 1990 (World Almanac, 1992, p. 949). Roughly similar figures, proportionate to population, characterize Canada. It is widely agreed that health care systems in North America are in a state of crisis. The sheer costs of maintaining even our present health systems pose a monumental challenge to budgets at the federal, state (and provincial), and local levels.

"Diseases of Civilization"

Not only are the costs of medical care in the developed countries great. The very nature of health and disease has itself undergone a remarkable change during the twentieth century. The main disabilities that now consume budgets (both public and private) and fill the hospitals are the so-called "diseases of civilization." These include the chronic and degenerative diseases—such as strokes, cancer, mental illness, cardiovascular diseases, arthritis, cirrhosis, chronic bronchitis and emphysema—as well as injuries at work, at home, at play and, above all, while driving automobiles (Nelkin & Brown, 1984). A *chronic* disease lasts for a long time (sometimes for life) and may flare up periodically. The affected individual is, consequently, ill for much of his/her life.

In contrast, *acute* diseases are infectious diseases (such as measles, whooping cough, smallpox and typhoid fever) from which the victim either recovers or dies in a relatively short time.

The chronic and degenerative diseases are fundamentally different from acute infectious diseases. (Certain chronic diseases can also be infectious, such as malaria and tuberculosis. These generally are no longer a serious health problem in the advanced industrial societies.) They require different research priorities, different approaches to treatment, cure, and prevention, different institutions, different practitioners, and different policies and financing. Most of the information now available indicates that the causes of degenerative and chronic diseases lie mainly in factors such as social, economic and—above all—environmental conditions (Gorman, 1979). This, however, does not deny that, in certain chronic diseases, heredity often plays a role. Individual behavior—whether from ignorance, carelessness, or social conditioning—also plays an important role. Unhealthy behavior may take the form of poor eating habits, overweight, careless driving, smoking, abuse of alcohol or drugs, or poor physical maintenance (including lack of exercise). Moreover, the problem of infection in the developed countries is by no means a thing of the past. New (or recently activated) diseases—such as acquired immune deficiency syndrome (AIDS), Legionnaire's Disease, chlamydia, herpes and variant strains of influenza—have assumed (near) epidemic proportions in recent years. AIDS, in particular, poses fundamental challenges to our public health establishments (Arno & Feiden, 1992, pp. 236–246).

The causes of disease have always been manifold. This is especially true of the chronic diseases, whose causes are often subtle and extend over a long period of time. Ailments may be caused by combinations of (1) environmental stress and hereditary predisposition, (2) poor diet and low-level infection, or (3) diet and social conditions (smoking and asbestos dust, alcohol and lack of exercise, and so on). For many of our modern ailments, single measures like the quarantine of the sufferers or immunization are less likely to be the answer than something more complex, like living a "healthy life" (Brandt, 1987). In addition to detailed research on the human body to identify the causes and processes involved in disease, more extensive epidemiological statistics on populations are needed if the multiple factors are to be untangled. For example, an apparent correlation between cancer and high meat consumption is suggestive, but by no means conclusive. Since meat consumption rises with standard of living, something else that rises with standard of living might be the cause of the cancer, or one of the causes (Hilgartner & Nelkin, 1987).

Public Health Breakthroughs

For our new era of diseases of civilization, then, it is becoming apparent that some of the traditional scientific and technological approaches to health and medicine that proved so triumphant earlier are now no longer always the most appropriate. Certainly, brilliant achievements in such fields as bacteriology, surgery, and public sanitation revolutionized medical practice and public health in the nineteenth and early twentieth centuries. The discoveries of Louis Pasteur (1822–1895), Robert Koch (1843–1910), and Joseph Lister (1827–1912) are symbolic of medical advances which transformed public health during the course of the nineteenth century and after. Pasteur's experiments which demonstrated the connection between microorganisms (such as bacteria) and disease are justly famous. Koch proved, in 1876, that anthrax—a disease affecting mainly animals—was caused by a specific microorganism, the anthrax bacillus. Other bacteria were discovered in quick succession, and the connection between disease and a *specific* microbial cause was proven. Koch thereby established a model—the germ theory of disease—to explain many other illnesses and, consequently, methods of prevention and cure (Dolman, 1973, p. 422). Lister introduced the practice of antisepsis in operating rooms, thus reducing the rate of infection.

Another source for major advances in scientific medicine came with the increased sophistication of organic chemistry during the late nineteenth century. One consequence of this was the chemist's ability to synthesize new substances of use in pharmacology, as with the creation of "aspirin." Interest in the mechanism by which a dye is permanently fixed onto a colorless fabric led the German bacteriologist Paul Ehrlich (1854–1915) to speculate on the possibility of fixing a poisonous chemical onto target germs which had invaded the blood stream. This idea of a "magic bullet," or **chemotherapy** (as it is now known), had its first success between 1909 and 1911 when Ehrlich tested a synthetic organic arsenic compound on patients suffering from syphilis (Dolman, 1971, p. 298). Used successfully to fight the appalling increase in venereal disease during World War I, this drug also freed from lunatic asylums many inmates who displayed the general paralysis and other symptoms which eventually overcame those suffering from tertiary syphilis. In 1935, the German chemist Gerhard Domagk (1895–1964) found that a derivative of a synthetic dye cured mice infected with bacteria. Marketed rapidly under the trade name "prontosil," it was soon discovered that the active component was a sulfonamide. From this substance, a complete range of other bactericides, or "antibiotics," could be developed (Posner, 1971, p. 154). This alone created a revolution in the twentieth century treatment of disease. Domagk's discovery completely changed the prognosis of many dangerous and potentially fatal diseases such as puerperal fever ("childbed fever"), cerebrospinal meningitis and pneumonia. In a similar context, Alexander Fleming (1881–1955), Howard Florey (1898–1968) and Ernst Chain (1906–1979) shared the Nobel Prize for Medicine in 1945 for the discovery, and industrial process for the manufacture, of penicillin. The medical applications of the antibacterial properties of this mold constitute another revolution in twentieth-century treatment of disease.

Of critical importance in the prevention and cure of disease have been the striking achievements in genetics during the twentieth century (Higgins et al., 1985, pp. 298–302). The first 50 years of genetic research culminated with the discovery of the structure of DNA in 1953 (see section 4c). Molecular biologists and medical scientists have since made the second half of the twentieth century a brilliant era in the diagnosis, treatment and cure of genetic diseases (Nossal & Coppel, 1989, pp. 38, 55, 72–84) (see section 5d). The final decade of this century, however, seems to call for additional, sometimes novel, approaches to the questions of health and medicine.

Stress and Disease

Medical research today is placing greater emphasis on the role of stress in disease. This stress can be of two types. One is the psychological stress induced by events (deaths of loved ones, bankruptcies, professional crises or demands) and the mental and emotional response to it. Stressful events are now suspected to be factors in many chronic diseases. They have been observed to affect the immune system and render a person more vulnerable to disease, including cancer. Whether the interaction of the mind with the immune system occurs through the general stress reaction, or by more specific hormonal pathways, is currently under research. A new medical speciality, psychoneuroimmunology, has emerged. This is one of the most promising of the recent convergences of scientific disciplines (i.e., the behavioral sciences, the neurosciences, and immunology) which have evolved to achieve a more complete understanding of nervous system-immune system interactions and their influence on health and disease.

Not all stress is mental, however, and the human immune system is also under a second category of stress from the growing variety of "strange" molecules in the environment (Kupchella & Hyland, 1989, pp. 526–529). These molecules are strange in the sense that they have not been present at previous stages in human evolution and therefore they present new challenges to human adaptation (Bergin & Grandon, 1984). This applies to many of the tens of thousands of new chemical compounds introduced over the past 40 years, including insecticides, herbicides, plastics, glues, paints, cleaners, and food additives. This category also includes many of the by-products of industrial technology, such as nuclear and fossil fuel power plants and the processing of ores (see sections 6b, 6c). In the near future it may apply to new varieties of foods, flora, fauna, microbes and viruses introduced by genetic engineering or biotechnology (see section 5d). The net result of these kinds of stress seems to be the appearance of a new set of health problems—a troubling syndrome characteristic of overload, breakdown, or deficiency of the immune system (and sometimes the nervous system).

Sometimes termed "atopic allergy," sometimes "environmental illness," this "twentieth-century disease" (if it is a single entity) is characterized by a broad set of rather widespread but unspecific symptoms. These include fatigue, headaches, depression, poor concentration, mental confusion, dizziness, asthma, tension, and allergies to all kinds of things (foods, pollens, dusts, organic vapors, perfumes, synthetic materials and so forth). It deserves the name twentieth-century disease for two reasons. First, many of these environmental stresses have appeared only recently. And second, in former times, many people with deficiencies in their immune systems—whether from genetic or other causes—would have quickly died off from common infections. Today, paradoxically, we are protected against traditional infections, but are subject to new, often debilitating, environmental stresses (Allman, 1985).

It is partly because of the very growth of scientific knowledge that the medical field finds itself embroiled in controversy today. Even the best-intentioned doctors sometimes find themselves under attack from several directions. Many popular, as well as academic, writings reflect a disillusionment with standard medical practice. Critics charge that a health care system which continues to focus primarily on the "germ-and-antibiotic" approach to treatment is not appropriate for some of our modern ailments. Some critics claim further that doctors are forced to adopt an impersonal assembly-line approach by the very fee structure of our modern health care systems. Often, the most efficient way to deal with the increasing number of physical and mental illnesses is by (sometimes inappropriate) prescription of drugs. Other critics blame the pharmaceutical industry for "pushing" its products—often incompletely tested for effectiveness or safety—in medical schools, in doctors' offices, and, through the media, directly to the consumer (Arno & Feiden, 1992, pp. 142–146, 193–196).

Thus, the flux in knowledge, in practice, and in public awareness—what we have termed "science/technology controversies"—is creating a number of policy problems for medicine and health care systems in the developed nations (including the U.S. and Canada). The present health system is in a state of chaos or creative ferment, depending on how one looks at it. Health, everyone agrees, is more than the absence of disease. But no one seems capable of coming up with a good, socially equitable, and politically operational definition. Most thinking and funding on health focuses on hospitals and the medical profession. Yet the hospitals of our societies are, in the main, filled with the emergency "rescue" cases and the sufferers from chronic and degenerative diseases. As important as these functions are—our hospitals are marvels of modern medical science and biomedical technology—they do not really address the fundamental question of disease *prevention* or health *promotion*. For this, a broader social perspective, which includes health education, disease prevention, and reduction of environmental factors in disease, is needed (Faber & Reinhardt, 1982).

Challenges Ahead

There are many harmful conditions which require social action or government action to put them right. Toxins in water supplies, polluted air in public buildings, hazards in the workplace, and additives and contaminants in foods are only a few. The people who live around Lake Ontario, for example, may face serious problems if nothing is—or can be—done about the toxic wastes slowly seeping into the water from old chemical dump sites in the Niagara area (Macdonald, 1991, pp. 111–112). Already, fish in the lake contain traces of several highly toxic chemicals. Persons who regularly eat such fish risk serious health problems. Acid rain is another environmental problem that not only kills lakes, but has been observed to give human beings respiratory and other problems (see section 6c). Illness from the misuse of pesticides is becoming more recognized. In certain developing countries, for instance, deaths from pesticide use now approach the totals from malaria, tetanus, diphtheria, whooping cough, and poliomyelitis. The risk of cancer among welders, particularly of stainless steel, has become a concern of the World Health Organization. And these are but a few examples of the many environmental factors in disease that need public surveillance and remedial (i.e., regulatory) social and political action.

Even some of the most promising areas of medical technology need closer public scrutiny and open debate before they become implemented (Kevles & Hood, 1992, pp. 134–135). A (partial) list of recent, emerging, and predicted medical technologies is indeed impressive: (1) extensive computerized diagnostic programs, (2) laser surgery, (3) remote monitoring of heart rate and other functions, (4) automatic drug-release devices, (5) self-diagnostic kits for home use, (6) regeneration of nerves, brain tissue, limbs, (7) genetic analysis and screening, and (8) recombinant DNA. All of these technologies have great promise. They also raise serious ethical, legal, and economic issues (Draper, 1991) (see section 5d).

Techniques for overcoming infertility—artificial insemination, implantation, the use of surrogate mothers—pose new and often troubling ethical dilemmas (Nelkin, 1992, pp. 45–56). So, too, the use of life-sustaining technologies (particularly in cases of severe brain damage, brain death, or otherwise hopeless prognosis) raises difficult questions. Are such sustained lives "worth living?" Who makes the decision to institute or terminate such life-extending technologies (G. Smith, 1989, pp. 62–65)? These new medical technologies reflect, in a most poignant fashion, the manifold issues which surround science and technology generally. Risk-benefit analysis, public participation, and regulation against economic or political abuse must become an essential part of contemporary public health policies. Decisions concerning our massive and extremely costly health care systems should involve individual physicians, health policy-makers and the public. Full information on a particular medical technology's benefits, risks, and costs should be obtained before the decision to implement it is taken. In our society, where new medical technologies are often exceedingly expensive, consideration should be given to the system of financing health care so that all may benefit equally. The benefits of life-extending technologies or long-term custodial care, for instance, should be weighed against their social costs. As more sectors of society compete for a share of fixed or decreasing budgets, there will probably be more acrimonious controversies concerning medical technologies in the near future.

For all these reasons, large-scale changes in the character of health care systems in the U.S. and Canada (among other nations) are taking place (Naylor, 1992, pp. 220–226). These changes include: (1) new preventive and health-oriented therapies; (2) greater recognition by governments, professionals (not only doctors), and individuals, of psychological and lifestyle factors in health and disease; (3) research into, and regulation of, occupational and environmental factors in health and disease; and (4) design of more cost effective institutional structures. An urgent issue is to accomplish changes in these directions rapidly enough to head off escalating crises of funding as the aging bulge—the demographic shift to an older population—moves more of the population into the age-period of chronic diseases and retirement (see section 7f). Also, as the health establishment adapts, there will be inevitable struggles over who belongs to the establishment—i.e., what practitioners (acupuncturists? herbalists?) are legitimate from the point of view of public safety and eligible for reimbursement from insurance schemes—and who controls or directs health care (Nelkin, Willis & Parris, 1991).

Clearly, science and technology are key ingredients in this process of the evolution of health care systems. The large and rapidly growing volume of scientific and technical knowledge in the fields of health and medicine presents problems of assimilation, integration, access, and education. A holistic movement both within and outside the medical profession is symptomatic of some of these changes in emphasis, technique, and policy (Iannone, 1987, pp. 141–145). As in so many other fields, science and technology in health and medicine pose exciting prospects and crucial dilemmas at the close of the twentieth century. ■

E. Science and Technology in Developing Countries

■   ■   ■

The role of science and technology in developing countries is a complex one. Clearly, it is not simply a question of applying the patterns of science-based technology which have characterized the growth of the industrialized (developed) countries, such as Great Britain and the U.S., since the eighteenth century (see sections 3a, 3c, 3d, 5a). This is for two reasons. First, the nations which industrialized during the nineteenth and early twentieth centuries did so at a period when resources were relatively abundant and population problems not pressing. Thus, there were few impediments to a fairly rapid growth of science and technology (Griffin, 1989, pp. 100–102). The situation facing the developing countries of today is far different. Resources are scarcer (and not always availabe to the nations which require them most) and population problems are extreme. Second, and perhaps most important, there was (during the nineteenth and early twentieth centuries) a general and widespread faith in science and technology as powerful agents of social progress. Events of the last few decades have clouded that optimistic picture. The social and political malaise of the industrialized countries indicates that scientific and technological development are not necessarily automatic guarantees of collective (or individual) well-being. Furthermore, the environmental crises of the late twentieth century have revealed the significance of the destructive consequences of industrialization (see sections 6b, 6c). Thus, the use of science and technology by the developing nations today will occur in ways much different from those which characterized the nineteenth and early twentieth centuries (David, 1986, pp. 115–116). Nonetheless, because the goals of the developing countries remain those of raising living standards and feeding growing populations—as well as competing economically, to some extent, with the advanced industrial nations—science and technology will remain important agents of sociopolitical change (Higgins et al., 1985, pp. 305–306).

Technology Transfer

The role of science and technology is complicated by yet another factor. The "rich" industrialized countries, already far ahead, are drawing still further away from the developing nations. This gap between rich and poor nations represents a dangerously explosive global situation. For, not only are the peoples of the Third World aware that these differences in living standards exist and are growing; they are also perceived to be due, in part at least, to past and present exploitation. However, economic advance in the developing countries is dependent, to some extent, on the acquisition of scientific and technological know-how from the developed world—what is called *technology transfer*. Cooperation between advanced and developing nations, in the form of financial and technical assistance (foreign aid), is essential. Such cooperation is in line with the vital interests of all nations on this globe. Reducing the socioeconomic gap between developed and developing countries must be a priority concern of the entire world (Persley, 1990, pp. 135–141).

Throughout history, the assimilation of science and technologies invented elsewhere has been central in raising living standards of recipient countries or regions. And throughout history there has always been a gap in living standards between donor and recipient nations. In the past, however, certain regions have been able to resist or reject technology transfer and isolate themselves from scientific and technological developments elsewhere. Japan during the eighteenth and early nineteenth centuries is a notable example. Of course, when Japan did decide to embrace western science and technology during the twentieth century, the results were nothing less than astounding (Fransman, 1986, p. 66). According to many observers, Japan is now the world's leading scientific/technological power. Such isolation is not possible today. Not only is the world united in a global economic framework (however unequal the partnerships may be), but there is greater ease of communications and transportation. The images of western affluence reach even remote and rural corners of the globe via television and advertising. Technology transfer is thus embedded in a confusing mixture of real and perceived gains from acquiring foreign technologies (Norwine & Gonzalez, 1988, p. 34).

Technology may be defined as a *method* for doing something. Using a method requires three elements: (1) information about the method; (2) a means of carrying it out; and (3) some understanding of it. There is much confusion and controversy surrounding the concept of so-called "appropriate" technology transfer. Appropriate technology refers to the nature and level of technology (and science) most suitable to a particular country (or culture) at a given stage of development. The controversy surrounding appropriate technology arises from trying to identify only one or two of the above elements as *the* basic element of technology. For instance, information and means can be transferred, but understanding can only be acquired by study and experience. Information embodied in blueprints, operational manuals, and technical books *is* transferrable, as are physical means such as highly sophisticated agricultural machinery or power generating stations (including nuclear reactors). But both physical means and information are worthless unless the recipient knows how to use them. This should involve both the knowledge of a technology's potential (good and bad) and some experience in its use (Farrington, 1989, pp. 39–40, 65).

The transfer of information or means is not the same as the acquisition of an indigenous or native technological or scientific *capability*. The ability to use technology effectively comes from a nation's (or an individual's) understanding of both its function and its purpose. For example, full knowledge of the optical and chemical properties underlying photography is not essential to taking a snapshot with a camera. But the camera is useless without the developing and printing services required to develop the photo, or the technical know-how to repair the camera. The point is, that much of the technology transferred from advanced to developing countries often fails to take into account the necessity of developing the surrounding infrastructure to support the proper functioning of the technologies in question (Iannone, 1987, p. 280). Giving sophisticated tractors to a Third World country might, at first, seem an unalloyed blessing. However, if there does not exist a supporting network of services to maintain and repair the tractors, they may quickly become white elephants—rusting unused. Moreover, tractors commit a country to a long-term dependence on imported petroleum fuels (if it does not possess its own supplies). If there is an interruption in world petroleum supplies, or if the recipient nation can no longer afford to purchase petroleum, the tractors once more become symbols of expensive but unused or unusable technology (Fransman, 1986, pp. 14–16).

Hydroelectric Dams

This raises the central question of whether a technology developed and utilized in an advanced industrial nation is really appropriate for use in a Third World country (Drori, 1993, p. 212). Massive hydroelectric dams are characteristic energy-producers in many of the advanced nations, particularly Canada and the U.S. Among Canada's many foreign aid consultants are Hydro-Quebec and Ontario Hydro. Both are provincially owned electrical utilities that have received contracts worth millions of dollars over the years from the Canadian federal government to advise Third World governments on how to set up their own electrical systems. But these utilities are exceedingly large and exercise energy monopolies over larger territories than any other utility in the non-Communist world. Their directors and engineers thus think "big." Advice to Third World governments understandably tends to promote the adopting of big systems, like huge hydroelectric dams, to produce energy—whether or not bigness is required or appropriate. In this way huge and often wholly inappropriate technological systems have been adopted in Third World countries (Adams & Solomon, 1991, pp. 52–53).

Sometimes, the results of such technology transfer can be quite the reverse of beneficial; they are disastrous. In spite of their economic benefits, some giant hydroelectric projects have been highly problematic. The Aswan Dam on the Nile, built in 1971 by the Egyptians with Soviet assistance, is inefficient, has caused soil erosion, and has spread schistosomiasis in the irrigated areas (Gupta, 1988, p. 34). Their social and environmental costs—often underestimated or ignored altogether by advisers—turn out to be immense. For example, in Ghana, no one knows what happened to most of the 80,000 people who lost their livelihood when they were thrown off the land to make way for the Volta River Project's giant hydro dam. Some 10,000 were able to fish for their livelihoods in Lake Volta, which the dam created. Another 2,000 were employed by the Kaiser and Reynolds aluminum smelter made possible by the newly generated electricity. But the great majority became dispossessed farmers (Adams & Solomon, 1991, pp. 42–43).

Like similar peoples in many Third World countries, these farmers when evicted from their fertile valleys usually have two options. Either they move into nearby forests, which they clear to farm, or they move onto smaller or less fertile plots in more marginal areas. In either event, their activities are self-defeating and environmentally destructive. The results are deforestation or, because of careless or inappropriate farming practices, further land degradation. Eventually, the reckoning has to come. The forests are cleared and the land utterly exhausted in a futile attempt to satisfy food needs (Harrison, 1992, p. 83) As a final irony, the topsoil lost from the land because of deforestation and farming degradation, goes into the river basins and ends up filling the dam reservoirs, cutting their useful lifespans by up to one-half. Then, whatever industrial development depends on power from these dams will either have to stop or find some new (probably non-existent or unavailable) source of power. These dams were originally considered to be a means (virtually unlimited electric power) to an end (industrial development and economic prosperity). In actuality, however, they will no longer be a means, and neither will the ends be secured. But the river valleys on which thousands had depended for their livelihoods will have been destroyed, yielding no more harvests and providing no more power.

The Peligre hydroelectric dam in Haiti was hailed just one generation ago as a great boon to the Haitian economy. Thanks to this inexhaustible source of power, which would fuel industries in and around the capital city of Port-au-Prince, prosperity was just around the corner. What opposition this dam might have aroused among those whose valley was flooded would not have been taken seriously by the majority of the population. Here was a chance for Haiti to have lasting benefits: those who would put their own selfish interests ahead of progress and of the national interests must surely have been quickly dismissed. Today, because it is so rapidly filling up with silt, the Peligre dam is so incapacitated that cities are blacked out for as much as twelve hours daily. The enormity of this technological mistake is only now beginning to set in (Adams & Solomon, 1991, pp. 44–46).

Appropriate Technology

Clearly, technology transfer, as it has been usually conceived, is not always the transfer of "appropriate technology." It often imposes a technology which, although it may have performed well in an advanced industrial nation, is unsuited for a developing nation. Proponents of technology transfer also often assume that the cultural and sociopolitical traditions (which pose obstacles to the new technology in a variety of ways) of a recipient nation are merely "impediments to progress." In so doing, the question of alternative technologies is not addressed. Not only are traditional cultural and social patterns threatened or disrupted, but the potential utility of local capabilities and traditional craft practices in raising living standards are ignored (or minimized).

Technology (and the social context of science) is multidimensional. Many different capabilities are required to assess, select, assimilate, use, adapt, and create it. Elements of different technologies already exist in the developing world (Farrington, 1989, pp. 61–65). Sometimes a completely new technology is not needed. Rather, what is required is improvement on existing technological elements, or an addition of certain new elements imported from abroad and adapted to local conditions. Countries may follow many different paths towards the acquisition of the technology they need (Iannone, 1987, p. 285). In most cases, the wholesale importation of a foreign technology package will not bring the expected results—and may cause serious problems. Similarly, the view that technological aid should be a way station on the road to western-style development poses grave problems (Gupta, 1988, pp. 73–74).

An appropriate technology which is best suited to a developing country will probably be quite unlike the science-based technologies which characterize the advanced industrial nations (Iannone, 1987, pp. 286–298). The latter are technologies which are urban-based, large-scale, capital and resource intensive, and which are predicated on mass production and consumption (see section 3d). As we have seen, such technologies are not appropriate (or perhaps even possible) for developing countries. What seems to be needed is a view of society and technology (and science) which recognizes that different cultural and geographical groups will have different technologies appropriate to them. In this sense, the only wise technologies are those which seek to accommodate themselves to the biological and cultural environment within which they are to be used. Moreover, technological development makes sense only if it entails the development—not exploitation—of the people and skills of a region by and for those people. Technological development in the Third World which fills the coffers of multinational corporations or local authoritarian governments may make sense to those organizations; it will not make sense to the indigenous populations (David, 1986, pp. 166, 190).

To be sure, societies in most of the developing nations today are not small, idyllic communities which can exist in some paradise of self-sufficiency and environmental purity. The majority of people in developing countries already live in cities of substantial size. Global population rates ensure that many of these Third World cities will soon rank among the most populous urban centers on earth (Gupta, 1988, p. 57). The answer, then, is certainly not rejection of technology and science. Rather, the answer lies in technological development which draws upon existing cultural and environmental structures. An appropriate technology would attempt to stem the further flow of rural populations to the swelling cities. This could be done by providing tools, machines, and products for use in the villages that are of appropriate scale, well designed and well made, and cheap enough to be productive in the local context. Of course, modified aspects of western science and technology must be employed if the teeming populations of the Third World are to be housed, fed, and clothed (Antebi & Fishlock, 1986, pp. 130–131). Some type of mass production and mass consumption is inevitable. But these appropriate industries would be relatively labor-intensive and rely upon low-capital techniques and low-energy consumption. Finally, as far as possible, the technologies should use renewable energy flows and minimize environmental impacts.

The concept of appropriate technology and science for developing countries has implications for the developed nations also. Indeed, there are growing, and increasingly vocal and influential, groups in the advanced industrial nations (primarily in the U.S., Canada, and Western Europe) which argue that alternative—more appropriate—technologies are desperately needed there (see section 7g). Clearly, traditional notions of western science and technology—based on the idea of automatic sociopolitical and economic progress—do not seem suitable for many of the developing parts of the globe (Grindle & Thomas, 1991, pp. 56–57). Nor do they now appear, at least in some respects, the most suitable guides for our own society. It is to be hoped that the lessons now being learned—primarily through the severity of various environmental crises—by the advanced industrialized nations, will benefit both them and the other nations of the world. ■

F. Gerontology and Demography

■   ■   ■

The aging of human populations is a phenomenon associated with industrialized societies, particularly in the twentieth century (Olshansky et al., 1993). In Europe, North America and other developed regions, the aging of populations—that is, the greater proportion of a given population which is over a given age (usually taken, for statistical convenience, to be 65 or some figure close to that)—has come to dominate the social welfare and economic maintenance agenda of many nations (Lee, Arthur & Rodgers, 1988). A new science has been created to deal with the issues of aging: *gerontology*. Gerontology is the multidisciplinary scientific field devoted to the study of the biological, psychological, and social phenomena associated with aging. Thus, gerontology deals with such issues as retirement, leisure, health care systems and the spectrum of socioeconomic and psychological matters related to the increasing numbers of older people in our societies.

The questions associated with aging played a less important role in preindustrial times than they do today for two basic reasons (Bjorksten, 1987). First, few persons (relatively speaking) lived to advanced ages. For a number of reasons, owing mainly to health, diet, and the ravages of infectious diseases, the life expectancies in preindustrial societies were lower than at present. Secondly, the phenomenon we know as retirement essentially did not exist. Older people typically worked until they were no longer physically capable. At that point, the family—which was the basic unit of production and income—provided the necessary support and care. Most people were self-employed farmers, which allowed them to continue working as long as possible. Many others worked in small production or other work organizations characterized by flexibility and the ability to accommodate the declining work capacity of older workers.

Industrialization during the nineteenth century, especially in North America and Western Europe, brought about a great number of changes which profoundly transformed the character of the societies affected (see sections 3c, 3d). Most significant was the fact that retirement, as a general stage in life, became both possible and necessary for the first time in history. The most important reason for this was the decline in agricultural employment and the accompanying decline in self-employment associated with industrialization. Under the factory system, the family typically no longer owns its means of production. Few people are able to continue working as long as possible because few are self-employed. In addition, industrial employment is often less flexible and more demanding and taxing of older workers' physical and mental capacities.

Industrialization was also accompanied by the growth of labor unions. Many of these fought hard for the financial security of workers during illness and, particularly, old age. A few isolated private pension plans emerged in a number of countries during the middle and late nineteenth century. However, it was not until 1889 that the first large-scale public pension program was implemented by Chancellor Bismarck in Germany. Widespread "social security"—also called "social insurance"—systems developed during the twentieth century in most industrialized countries as a response to these pressures arising from the changing nature and organization of work. At first, social security was viewed as a necessary state measure to deal with the growing numbers of unemployed, and often destitute, elderly persons in industrialized societies. But with the increased levels of support provided by public or private pension systems, it became possible for the older people in society to *expect* to live at least moderately well (Ycas, 1987). Improved health and life expectancy during the twentieth century, coupled with provisions for economic support after employment, meant that more and more people could expect to be "retired." Retirement, both mandatory and voluntary, has created a number of prospects and problems that are unique to industrialized societies such as the U.S. and Canada.

Recall that demography is the "study of the characteristics of human populations such as size, growth, density, distribution and vital statistics" (Weller & Bouvier, 1981). "Population aging" may be defined as a series of increases in the percentage of older persons in the total population. "Older" may be defined in any number of ways; indeed, what constitutes "being old" varies both from society to society and from individual to individual within any given society. For sake of convenience, however, and for the sake of legal and economic matters, an arbitrary cutting point is often used to mark off the segment of the older population. In Europe and North America the common age has been 65, or in some cases 62. However, with the recent advent of early retirement and, conversely, the abolition of some mandatory retirement ages, the question of who—and what—constitutes being old is undergoing renewed attention and debate.

Population Age Structures

In the course of population aging, the age structure of a population may be said to achieve higher and higher levels of maturity. Age structure maturation and population aging are equivalent. The opposite of age structure maturation is rejuvenation, when a larger proportion of a population falls into a younger age group. This happened, for example, during the Baby Boom era from roughly 1946 to 1966. During that period, a marked increase in births (beginning shortly after World War II and continuing for some 20 years) contributed to a growing youthful proportion of the population for both the U.S. and Canada (Bouvier, 1980). Population aging practically stalled in the U.S. and actually reversed in Canada. A rejuvenation of a population also occurs periodically with the influx of (relatively) youthful immigrants, such as happened in Canada with the wave of immigration following the Hungarian revolution of 1956. Except for these breathing spells, however, population aging has been a steady, gradual process since the start of the twentieth century (Roadburg, 1985).

At the mid-1980s, the U.S. had a slightly more mature age structure than did Canada. Roughly 1 in 9 (i.e., nearly one-eighth) Americans were aged 65 and over, while just over 1 in 10 Canadians were similarly aged. Both populations, thus, have begun to show definitely mature age structures, in sharp contrast to the immature ones they had in 1900 when neither country had much more than 5% of its population above the age of 65. The latest U.S. Bureau of the Census and Statistics Canada projections suggest that both countries will see a further aging of the population during the remaining years of this century, with Canada drawing closer to the American level of maturity of population age structure (Rathbone-McCuan & Havens, 1988). By the year 2000, roughly 13% of Canada's population, and slightly more than that for the U.S., is expected to be at least 65 years old. During the twenty-first century, age structure maturation will probably increase even more rapidly. Population aging will likely accelerate sharply in both countries (but more rapidly in the U.S. for a number of reasons) when the Baby Boomers (those born between 1946 and 1966) begin to penetrate the current categories of ages for retirement after 2010. In 2030, according to current projections, more than 1 out of 5 Americans (21%) and just below that figure of Canadians (19%) could be 65 or older. In contrast with the slow growth of the *total* population, which is projected to rise at an average annual rate close to 1% in both countries, the population aged 65 and over will (barring a major environmental or medical catastrophe) grow more than twice as fast.

The size of the older segments of the senior population is projected to grow even more dramatically. The Canadian projections, for instance, anticipate a huge growth rate of 4% or more per annum for those aged 85 and over for the remaining years of this century. Continued strong growth is projected (above 3%) into the first decades of the next century. In consequence, the numbers of Canadians in this age group will jump from about 200,000 in the mid-1980s to more than 400,000 by the year 2000. Although such figures represent only a small fraction of the total population, they pose a radically new situation. Indeed, in the U.S., on any given day, 1.3 million seniors, or 4.5 per cent of all Americans aged 65 or older, may be found in nursing homes. In 1989, the total cost of nursing home care for the elderly was $47.9 billion, or 8 per cent of all health care expenditures in the U.S. This was a 12 percent increase from the year before (Wolinsky et al., 1992, p. S173). In other words, a veritable population explosion among seniors—particularly of quite advanced age—is underway in North America and will not end soon. The social-economic, political, medical and cultural implications of this gerontological revolution are, and will continue to be, wide-reaching. Among other things, the aging population will place new demands upon society's scientific and technological resources (Yanchinsky, 1989, p. 79).

Social Security

World War II operated as a watershed in the social policy formulation of both the U.S. and Canada regarding senior citizens. The period prior to World War II was essentially one of mainly private schemes of social insurance. In contrast, the postwar era has witnessed the transition to nearly comprehensive social security for old age. In the U.S., Congress had passed the Social Security Act in 1935, but it provided cash benefits only to retired workers in commerce and industry. In 1950, the act was amended to cover farm and domestic workers, and many state and municipal employees. Social Security coverage became nearly universal in the U.S. in 1956, when lawyers and other professionals came under the system. Canada's social security system, begun in 1940, is similar to the U.S. system. It includes the Old-Age Security Pension, which guarantees a minimum retirement income to all persons age 65 or older who have lived in Canada at least 10 years. Beneficiaries are paid regardless of their work records. A second major component of the Canadian social security system is the Canada Pension Plan. This went into effect in 1966 and provides additional monthly benefits to retired workers based on their earnings and their contributions to the pension plan (Markides and Cooper, 1987, pp. 43–75).

A major difference between the U.S. and Canada, however, is the universal publicly insured health care system in Canada. This has been assessed as adding the equivalent of one-third, on average, to the incomes of older Canadians. In contrast, the Medicare (established by Congress in 1965) and Medicaid provisions of the U.S. are neither universal nor as comprehensive (Marmor, 1973). Hence, they do not have a similar effect of supplementing the income of older Americans. The Canadian system of old-age support has three tiers, i.e., public, public contributory, and private (including e.g., trust-fund plans and group annuity plans). By contrast, the U.S. system relies only on the latter two tiers (Markides and Cooper, 1987, pp. 9–41). When this difference is further related to the differences in the health care systems, the two North American income policy approaches have created very different systems, structures, and benefits levels (Novak, 1985).

Central to the contemporary debates about the proper mix of public and private solutions to pensions and related issues are the competing claims about the relative merits of these programs (Naylor, 1992, pp. 104–124). For some, universal (i.e., without regard to economic status) social benefits are the foundation of the "just" and "good" society; to others, these benefits provide unneeded and unwarranted subsidies to the rich. An understanding of these issues is important for several reasons. In North America, as elsewhere in the advanced industrial societies, public programs for the elderly represent one of the largest single components in the budget of the modern welfare state (Rosa, 1982). As a result, old-age policies are a major political issue. They are, in fact, subject to those same key aspects of controversy which characterize many of the other science/technology-related debates we have studied (Nelkin, 1992). As the population continues to age, North American political life will be increasingly affected by what has been termed the "graying" of the state budget. As more and more members of society live longer and longer in retirement, greater financial and social burdens will be placed upon society to support and maintain seniors in health and dignity (Longman, 1987).

Health Care

One of the most significant areas of concern for the older segments of our society is, of course, health care. In some senses, the very possibility of an aging population is a direct result of the remarkable scientific, particularly medical, advances since the nineteenth century. As people live longer, however, they present a special set of health and medical—in addition to social and cultural—demands upon society. The formal health care systems in Canada and the U.S. are organized primarily around physicians and institutional services, such as hospitals and homes for the elderly. The medical-industrial complex of our society tends to focus the energies for health care on doctors, drugs, and hospitals (Chappell, Strain, & Blandford, 1986). However valuable these factors are—and they are essential—it is becoming clear that they are not the total answer to the needs of an aging population (Iannone, 1987, pp. 146–157).

For one thing, the formal health care systems have become, simply, too expensive. Some critics argue that the present health care systems for the elderly will soon bankrupt federal and local budgets already stretched to the limit (Davis, 1986). Some redirection away from formal institutional systems, toward community and family supportive and social services will be necessary. Signs of this redirection appear in the recent increase in such informal, local, and often volunteer, support mechanisms provided by meal services, transportation services, and home-maker and handyman assistance. Nonetheless, long-term care of the elderly, even of the relatively more robust seniors, will remain as one of the most challenging tasks on the agenda of any developed industrial society.

This population aging which has characterized the demographic outlook in the U.S. and Canada for most of this century is a consequence of declining fertility and increasing longevity. Birth rates have dropped steadily in this period, with the exception of the Baby Boom (evident in the 1951 and 1961 census years). The temporary upswing caused by the Baby Boom has been countered by a drop in fertility experienced by the Baby Boom daughters as they mature (Faux, 1984). This pattern—of increase in life expectancy coincident with declining fertility trends—is consistent with the general situation in the rest of the industrialized world. Average life expectancy for North Americans in the past fifty years increased from about 60 years for men and 62 years for women (a half-century ago), to slightly more than 70 years for men and nearly 80 years for women by 1989 (Naylor, 1992, p. 217). There are two significant trends to be noted in this context. First, the gender gap among the aged is striking: there are more elderly females than elderly males. Second—and perhaps more important—the older population is itself aging. In 1981, people aged 80 and over represented 19% of those aged 65 and over. By the turn of the century (the year 2000), they will make up 24% of that population (Bjorksten, 1987).

The aging of a population presents a relatively novel phenomenon in human social history. Scientific, medical, and technological advances have created the conditions for such a situation. Societies will, therefore, turn to those same forces to assist in dealing with the challenges and problems created by aging populations. Questions of retirement, pensions and other financial services, health care systems (both institutional—private and public—and informal, or community-organized), leisure, and, finally, the cultural and sociopolitical role of seniors will require a combination of many factors for satisfactory solutions (Whitehead, 1988). One of the most far-reaching, and probably unanticipated, consequences of the Scientific and Industrial Revolutions has been the graying of industrial societies. It is to be hoped that the science of gerontology, coupled with appropriate sociopolitical and economic measures, will permit industrialized societies to deal with this particular cultural impact of science and technology (Maguire, 1988). ■

G. Alternative Technology: "Green Politics"

■ ■ ■

The headlines travelled worldwide in March of 1983 when members of a new political party, known as the Greens, were elected to 27 seats in the West German national parliament. A few weeks later, newspapers featured photos of the new Green legislators in a colorful procession carrying flowers and tree branches. They were accompanied by representatives from peace and ecological movements from all across Western Europe. This was the first time most North Americans had ever heard of the West German Greens, or of the larger Green Movement that had by then spread all across Europe. In Belgium, Norway, Britain and the Netherlands, Green or Ecology parties have also begun waging campaigns for local electoral office. The Greens are a symbol of hope for a new kind of politics—the "new environmentalism" which emerged out of the political and cultural upheaval of the 1960s and 1970s (Spretnak & Capra, 1986). This new environmentalism is based on a philosophy in which human and ecological values outweigh the usual demands of power and industrial expansion. Like other kindred organizations, such as the international Greenpeace environmental movement, the Greens aim to create a human culture which will tend to preserve, not disrupt or destroy, the integrity of the entire biotic community—which includes humans and all other species of animals and plants (Hamlett, 1992, pp. 66–67).

Over the past several years, groups expressing a Green approach to social change and an ecologically sound way of life have been arising all across North America (Macdonald, 1991, pp. 38–41). The special aspect of the Green movement is its deep understanding of the links between social and ecological problems. The Greens—and other exponents of the new environmentalism—question many of the most deeply held assumptions of technological society. In this, they share the philosophy of earlier movements, such as "primitivism" and "pastoralism"—as embodied in the writings of Jean-Jacques Rousseau (1712–1778) and other Romantic authors of the eighteenth and nineteenth centuries. Henry David Thoreau (1817–1862), the author of the American classic *Walden* (1854), might stand as one of their patron saints (Marx, 1992, pp. 461–465). The Greens and their allies seek, in a similar fashion, to reorient both politics and economics away from the principles of unbridled industrial expansion and toward a more environmentally compatible paradigm (Tokar, 1987).

The Greens criticize the unchecked industrial growth that has characterized much of the world since the nineteenth century as bringing the earth to the brink of ecological collapse (Worster, 1985). Our industries release poisons that are altering the world's climate, disrupting food chains, destroying entire forests, and spreading radiation and toxic chemicals throughout the biosphere (Dahlberg, 1985). The catalogue of recent calamities attributable to the malfunctioning of science-based technologies is disturbing: Three Mile Island, Chernobyl, Bhopal, the Challenger explosion, and the Exxon oil spill are only the most notorious of a long list of disasters (Nelkin,

1992, pp. 80–96). New technologies also feed a relentless militarism, exacerbating the threat of nuclear, chemical, and biological warfare. Industrial economies, according to the Greens, create the illusion of affluence for a privileged few, while robbing people around the world of the most basic means of subsistence. It has become clear to many Greens that the hazards of further industrial development now outweigh any possible benefits to humanity.

Ecology

The science of ecology has inspired a new understanding of humanity as but one element in an intricate web of relationships that make up the natural world (Kupchella & Hyland, 1989, pp. 17–18). A close study of nature reveals the profound interdependence of all living beings. The plants, the oceans, the soil, and all living creatures are essential parts of a natural, living whole. Removing or damaging one piece of the whole makes life more difficult for all. The Greens see the rise of modern science as tending to set humanity against nature, rather than working within a natural framework. Science and technology, since the eighteenth century, have flourished within a framework which regards humans as essentially wielding complete power over a pliant, ever malleable nature. We now are beginning to see that this framework is flawed. As the growing magnitude of environmental crises indicates, humanity is starting to reap the rewards of its careless, conquering attitude toward nature (Ashworth, 1986). It was Francis Bacon who best epitomized the new scientific spirit of the seventeenth and eighteenth centuries. Bacon successfully popularized the idea of the manipulative power of science (see sections 2c, 2d). Understanding nature was not enough. For Bacon, "man's destiny" was literally to enslave nature. This aggressive literary style permeated his description of nature and was crucial to the conceptual transformation of the earth as a "nurturing mother" and womb of life into a source of secrets to be extracted for technological and economic advance. As an influential philosopher of emerging modern science, Bacon fashioned a new ethic sanctioning the exploitation of nature (Wormald, 1992). He forcefully reinterpreted the significance of the great technological discoveries of the middle ages: printing, gunpowder, and the magnet (see sections 1f, 1g). They did not, like former inventions, "merely exert a gentle guidance over nature's course; they have the power to conquer and subdue her, to shake her to her foundations" (Merchant, 1980, pp. 164–165, 172). These were the ideas that were to shape the course of the Industrial Revolution in Europe and North America, the rise of the factory system, and the emergence of modern scientific technology (see sections 3c, 3d).

The Green perspective on ecological problems and ecological politics aims to heal a world that has fallen out of environmental balance. In two centuries of industrial development, western civilization has come to threaten the very survival of the ecological relationships that have evolved on the earth over many millions of years (Seitz, 1992, p. 122). The most profound changes have occurred in just the past 30 to 40 years: a visible drop in the number of species of animals and plants; the wholesale destruction of forests; a marked increase in atmospheric carbon dioxide; seasonal holes in the ozone layer; the contamination of the atmosphere with radioactive fallout; and, finally, the proliferation of highly toxic and mutagenic chemicals spreading through our air, soil and water. People knowledgeable about ecology, geology, and the chemistry of the earth's atmosphere are beginning to wonder out loud how much further this civilization can go before permanently crippling the earth's ability to sustain life (Milbrath, 1984).

The Greens argue that we in the developed world have built a synthetic shield around ourselves—a shield of concrete, steel and plastic, of chemically-treated food and disinfected water. And despite the obvious signs that developed societies are showing serious signs of crisis, many

North Americans continue to promote the short-sighted notion that more industrial growth is the answer to the plight of poor people everywhere. This mania for industrial expansion, in the last 30 years, has spread the damage to far corners of the world previously considered too remote to be of use to us (McKormick, 1985). There is a constant search for more profitable sources of oil and minerals and for cheaper labor to run the machines that make our clothes and our computers. Industrialism has spread to the heart of Africa, to the Siberian tundra, to the Amazon jungles and to the frozen Arctic and Antarctic. Meanwhile, the search for more and more people to buy the vast quantities of often worthless goods that the machines produce pulls even more of the world's peoples into our throw away consumer culture.

Green politics is an attempt to stem the ecological damage brought about by industrial civilization (in both its Western capitalist and Eastern state socialist branches). It rejects the "throwaway ethical beliefs" upon which most industrial societies are built (Porritt and Winner, 1988). These usually assume that human beings are apart from, and above, nature and that their role is to conquer and subdue nature to further human goals. Matter and energy resources are assumed to be virtually unlimited because of human ingenuity. Endlessly rising production and consumption is considered to be the primary goal of most developed industrial societies. A strong technological optimism pervades these societies, perpetuating the myth that science and technology can always patch up any environmental problems they create.

Sustainable-Earth Ethics

In sharp contrast, the new environmentalism envisions a society based on "sustainable-earth ethics" or "deep ecology" (Devall & Sessions, 1985). Sustainable-earth ethics are based on the belief that humans are part of nature, and that our primary purpose is to share, not plunder, the earth's finite resources. Humans should interfere with nonhuman species only to satisfy vital human needs, and work with—not against—nature. Matter and energy resources are finite and must not be wasted. The Greens reject the notion that production and consumption of material goods must increase endlessly. Their rejection of the primacy of the economic criteria of ever-increasing production and consumption in framing social policies has parallels, again, with earlier rejections of unlimited urban industrial expansion. Thomas Jefferson (1743–1826), the third President of the United States, in his political emphasis on less tangible, qualitative social goods, put forward a late eighteenth century version of the "quality of life" argument (Marx, 1992, p. 464).

Achieving a sustainable-earth worldview involves working with nature. Such a view advocates selectively modifying small parts of the biosphere to meet human needs on the basis of ecological understanding and caring for the earth and all its species. Deep ecology calls for us to distinguish between our manipulated wants (created by the powerful forces of advertising and the media) and our "true" needs by making our lifestyles more harmonious with natural cycles. It urges adopting a philosophy of "voluntary simplicity" based on doing more with less. The Greens emphasize the need for a true commitment to working with nature, which requires not only an intellectual understanding of the general way nature works but also direct emotional involvement with nature. In this way, humanity may begin to defend the earth from further environmental damage and to heal its ecological wounds.

The Greens repudiate the maxim of industrial society which asserts that we need not adapt ourselves to the natural environment. The advocates of industrial civilization claim that we can "remake" nature to suit our own needs by means of the tools—both material and philosophical—provided by science and technology. Instead, the Greens insist that humans should work with, and not against, nature and the environment. They see the major function of the state as preventing individuals and corporations from exploiting or damaging the environment (Dorn, 1991, pp. 174–176). A sustainable-earth ethic means, simply, a desire to get the most out of what people use, and a recognition that the wasteful use of precious resources is harmful and detrimental to the quality of everyone's life. The Greens emphasize that we can never completely "do our own thing," without exerting some effect now, or in the future, on other human beings and on other living species. All past, present, and future actions have effects, most of which are unpredictable—as the unintended, and often disastrous, environmental consequences of two centuries of scientific and technological development repeatedly confirm.

The Greens reject our present sociopolitical framework which usually bases decisions on short-term (and short-sighted) planning and goals. Instead, they argue we must construct a new framework which bases society's, and each individual's, decisions on long-term planning, and goals embedded within an "ecological intuition." It should be noted, of course, that not all environmental groups adopt the radical politics of the Greens. The well-known Sierra Club, for example, objected to having its name associated with extremist political acts that characterize many Greenpeace protest events—such as sailing small boats into nuclear testing blast zones in the South Pacific. All such acts are, to be sure, carefully designed to provide gripping media images (Macdonald, 1991, p. 98)

The Green alternative operates at both the collective and individual levels. Each of us can start, it is suggested, by doing a number of small things to lessen environmental and resource problems. Examine your room, your home, your school, your street, your city and your country. What are your own environmental bad habits? Everyone doesn't need to be an ecologist, but you do need to "ecologize" your lifestyle. Try to minimize the number of high-energy, high-waste, or highly polluting things you do. Most important, the Greens insist, is the need to become politically involved on local and national levels (Tokar, 1988). Start or join a local environmental group. Become the "biosphere citizen" of your block, school, apartment building or dormitory. The environment would improve noticeably, the Greens assert, if each of us made an annual donation of money, time, or both to one or more politically active environmental organizations working for causes we believe in (Wolfe, 1983). Working to elect sustainable-earth leaders—and to influence officals once they are elected to public office—would also serve to further a new environmentalism.

Think Globally, Act Locally

A central maxim of the Greens is to "think globally and act locally." Individual acts of consumption and litter have contributed to the mess in which we find ourselves. When you are tempted to say "This little bit won't hurt," remember that hundreds of millions of others are saying the same thing. Picking up a single beer can, joining a carpool, or bicycling to school or work, writing on both sides of a piece of paper, and not buying overpackaged products can all be significant acts. Turning off a light when leaving a room, or not using more light than is necessary, ultimately reduces the need for nuclear and coal-burning electric power plants. Each small act reminds us of ecologically sound practices. Start now with a small, concrete, personal act, and then add more such acts. Individual actions help reduce pollution, give us a sense of involvement, and help us develop a badly needed ecological consciousness (Miller, 1988, p. 598).

Our awareness must then expand to recognize that large-scale pollution and environmental disruption are caused primarily by industries, governments, and big agriculture. The ultimate targets of ecological reform, therefore, are these large socioeconomic and political structures (Commoner, 1990, p. 179). Beginning at the individual level and working outward by joining with other similarly ecologically-minded people, is one potentially powerful way of stemming the destruction of the environment caused by much large-scale technology. The Green vision of politics and a peaceful world moving beyond industrialism is changing the terms of the environmental debates in many countries today. Even in Japan—today's leading symbol of technological achievement—a Green movement has developed. Greens are appearing in some Third World countries too. For increasing numbers of people, the Green alternative for an appropriate use of science and technology represents one path to an ecologically harmonious world (Berger, 1986). ■

H. Women in Scientific and Engineering Careers

■ ■ ■

It is by now a truism that women's careers in science and engineering pose particular difficulties compared to those of women in other kinds of work. We tend to think of the history of science and technology as a history of men. More than that, we often think of that history as the story of a very few men—Aristotle, Copernicus, Newton and Einstein—who revolutionized our view of the universe. But the history of science and technology is much more than that. It is the story of the thousands of people who contributed to the knowledge and theories that constituted the science and technology of their eras and made the dramatic advances possible. Many of these people were women. Yet their story remains virtually unknown. Except for names like Marie Curie (see section 6a), the history of science and technology often seems devoid of females. However, at the present time, when the pressures to educate more scientists and engineers is great, young women must be made more fully aware of their potential careers in science and technology. It is precisely because very few women had access to formal technical education prior to the twentieth century, that their contribution to the history of science and technology has been less significant than it might have been (Alic, 1986, pp. 1–10). Adding insult to injury, many women scientists and engineers have had their work suppressed or ignored. Their discoveries and inventions have often been attributed to others, generally husbands, brothers, or male colleagues (Cutliffe & Post, 1989, p. 195).

Historical Context

The reasons for this historical subordination of women in science and technology are exceedingly complex. Certainly, they have more to do with the cultural context of developing modern science than with any deficiency in aptitude for such careers on the part of women. Lately, feminist historians and philosophers have successfully produced new understandings of the Scientific Revolution, which examine the ways in which modern science in its historical origins was a highly gendered construction. The conception of nature which eventually emerged as dominant in the seventeenth century—and continued triumphant in western culture until only very recently—is a mechanistic, materialistic conception (see sections 2c, 2d). This mechanistic view of nature is a distinctly masculinized conception which replaced an older feminized view of nature (Olby et al., 1990, pp. 105–109). As Carolyn Merchant states: "The mechanists transformed the body of the world and its female soul, source of activity in the organic cosmos, into a mechanism of inert matter in motion. . . . Moreover, as a conceptual framework, the mechanical order had associated with it a framework of values based on power, fully compatible with the directions taken by commercial capitalism" (Merchant, 1980, pp. 192–195).

This important perspective elucidates the limitations imposed historically upon the role of women in science and technology. There are significant constraints created by such cultural characterizations of nature as feminine and science and technology as masculine. Other similar dichotomies traditionally used have been: subjective vs. objective, soft vs. hard, and dependent vs. independent. By so defining science and technology, women—by their presumed "nature" and "temperament"—have been by and large excluded from such careers. Consequently, females who did achieve some degree of eminence in those fields were considered unique or untypical of their sex. Women scientists involved in "conquering" nature were regarded as anomalous (Daston, 1992, pp. 229–230).

The development of modern science in its institutional structures paralleled this masculine perspective. The claim that science and technology were value-neutral served to render invisible the injustices in the system by sealing an already self-reinforcing gendered structure (Schiebinger, 1989, p. 266). The professionalization of science and engineering during the nineteenth and early twentieth centuries was largely a male-dominated enterprise (see section 3a). Scientific societies were primarily, though not exclusively, male preserves. In nineteenth-century Britain, as engineering institutions developed, they adopted a deliberate policy of excluding women (Carter & Kirkup, 1990, p. 9). Margaret Rossiter, in her study of women scientists in America in the nineteenth and early twentieth centuries, demonstrates how—despite an expanded female presence from 1880—trends in higher education and career options tended to restrict their permissable roles. Within the overall structure of male domination in American science, women took up subordinate positions—as assistants in laboratories and observatories, as junior professors, or confined to "feminine" scientific fields such as cosmetic chemistry (Rossiter, 1982). For all these reasons, modern science—until only very recently—is revealed as a largely patriarchal institution of limited adaptability, which, like the culture at large, operated gender stereotypes to the disadvantage of women (Olby et al. 1990, p. 103).

Future Prospects

Today, when science and technology are undergoing radical reassessments, women will assume a much greater role in those fields than previously in history. The fact that many countries are considering the merits of a more ecological, more holistic, approach to science and technology, suggests that women will assume a greater role in these areas. A revamped educational system will surely be essential in training more women for the scientific and engineering professions (Rothschild, 1988). Obviously, for both males and females, there should be more funding in the U.S. and Canada—and worldwide generally—for better laboratories, better classroom instruction in science and technology, and better development of spatial-visual skills (through activities and exercises) related to the sciences. But there must also be certain new attitudes in science and technology education to motivate girls (and women) to pursue such careers (Kirkup & Keller, 1992, pp. 178–187). Parents might be encouraged to suggest, or support, scientific inclinations in their young female (as well as male) children (Carter & Kirkup, 1990, p. 55). Schools, particularly at the elementary level, should use nonsexist language examples and include information on women scientists and engineers. Most important, society must avoid sex-stereotyped views of science (and technology) and scientists, which are fostered by texts, media, and many adults.

Such sex-role stereotyping affects females interested in pursuing education or careers in science and technology in two ways. First, the feminine stereotype of women as emotional, artistic, nurturing, and delicate, suggests that women are not suited for science and engineering. Second, the masculine stereotype—analytical, pragmatic, logical, and rigorous—which is commonly used to describe science as masculine, may dissuade young women from entering science. Sex-role stereotyping in either form is a persistent and subtle (but powerful) barrier to women in science and technology. These attitudes, both at home and at school, should be changed (Sorensen, 1992, pp. 5, 17).

Society's vision of the future must include the participation of more women in scientific and engineering careers. To achieve that end, more young girls should be stimulated to develop the prerequisite skills to do science and technology by "tinkering" with mechanical and electrical toys. Girls should also be encouraged to enroll in mechanical drawing, shop, and industrial arts classes. Within academic science and technology, teachers—especially at the elementary levels—must be encouraged to present a positive view of science and technology, accessible to all students—female and male. The image of science and technology should be presented as neither masculine nor feminine. These fields are egalitarian (Keller, 1985). Both young men and young women should be motivated to pursue such careers. If we are to deal adequately with the problems and promises generated by advanced industrial societies, women and young girls should be encouraged strongly to make their contributions.

From the beginning of recorded history, women have made significant contributions to almost every branch of science and technology. This has been accomplished despite generally held prejudices that either women are intellectually inferior to men or that their societal roles program them to be housewives and mothers. Many females have perservered in their intellectual and practical endeavors despite the numerous barriers that have been erected to confine their activities to the kitchen and the bedroom. The achievements of women scientists and engineers from Sappho to Marie Curie and beyond, must compel society to provide better education and more opportunities for young girls and women in those fields. Certainly, the statistics afford some hope. Women now comprise approximately half of all students of pharmacy and of veterinary medicine. Females comprise about one-third of all medical students. And about half of the students entering graduate school in biology are women. It is to be hoped that the status of women in science and technology professions will soon match those of men in these hitherto male-dominated fields (Carter & Kirkup, 1990, pp. 154–171). For, ultimately, our survival as a species depends on the contributions all can make to the most appropriate use of science and technology. ∎

Bibliography

Adams, Bill. *Green Development: Environment and Sustainability in the Third World*. New York: Routledge, 1990.

Adams, Mark B., ed. *The Wellborn Science: Eugenics in Germany, France, Brazil, and Russia*. New York: Oxford University Press, 1990.

Adams, Patricia, and Lawrence Solomon. *In the Name of Progress: The Underside of Foreign Aid*. 2d ed. Toronto: Energy Probe, 1991.

Adas, Michael. *Machines as the Measure of Men: Science, Technology, and Ideologies of Western Dominance*. Ithaca, NY: Cornell University Press, 1989.

Alic, John A., et al. *Beyond Spinoff: Military and Commercial Technologies in a Changing World*. Boston: Harvard Business School Press, 1992.

Alic, Margaret. *Hypatia's Heritage: A History of Women in Science from Antiquity to the Late Nineteenth Century*. London: The Women's Press, 1986.

Allibone, T.E. *Rutherford, the Father of Nuclear Energy*. Manchester: Manchester University Press, 1972.

Allman, W.F. "Staying Alive in the 20th Century." *Science 85* (Oct. 1985): 31–41.

Antebi, Elizabeth, and David Fishlock. *Biotechnology: Strategies for Life*. Cambridge, Mass.: MIT Press, 1986.

Apple, Rima D., ed. *Women, Health, and Medicine in America: A Historical Handbook*. New Brunswick, NJ: Rutgers University Press, 1990.

Appleman, Philip, ed. *Darwin: A Norton Critical Edition*. New York: Norton, 1970.

Arno, Peter S., and Karyn L. Feiden. *Against the Odds: The Story of AIDS, Drug Development, Politics and Profits*. New York: Harper Collins, 1992.

Arnold, Dieter. *Building in Egypt: Pharonic Stone Masonry*. New York: Oxford University Press, 1991.

Ashworth, William. *The Late, Great Lakes: An Environmental History*. New York: Alfred A. Knopf, 1986.

Asimov, Isaac. *Asimov's New Guide to Science*. New York: Basic Books, 1984.

Aspray, William. *John von Neumann and the Origins of Modern Computing*. Cambridge, Mass.: MIT Press, 1990.

Avery, Oswald T., C.M. MacLeod, and M. McCarty. "Studies on the chemical nature of the substance inducing transformation of *Pneumococcal* types." *Journal of Experimental Medicine* 79 (1944): 137–158.

Babin, Ronald. *The Nuclear Power Game*. Montreal: Black Rose Books, 1985.

Bacon, Francis. *The New Organon and Related Writings*. Indianapolis: Bobbs-Merrill, 1960.

Badash, Lawrence, et al., eds. *Reminiscences of Los Alamos*, 1943- 1945. Dordrecht: Reidel, 1980.

Bagwell, Philip S. *The Transport Revolution*. London: Routledge, 1988.

Bailey, Kathleen. *Doomsday Weapons in the Hands of Many: the Arms Control Challenge of the '90s*. Urbana: University of Illinois Press, 1991.

Baker, Keith Michael. *Inventing the French Revolution*. Cambridge: Cambridge University Press, 1990.

Balazs, Nandor L. "Einstein: Theory of Relativity." In vol. 4 of *Dictionary of Scientific Biography*, edited by Charles C. Gillispie. 16 vols. New York: Charles Scribner's Sons, 1971.

Balogh, Brian. *Chain Reaction: Expert Debate and Public Participation in American Commercial Nuclear Power*, 1945–1975. Cambridge, England: Cambridge University Press, 1991.

Barbour, Ian. *Ethics in An Age of Technology*. San Francisco: Harper, 1993.

Barker, Peter, and Roger Ariew, eds. *Revolution and Continuity: Essays in the History and Philosophy of Early Modern Science*. Washington, D.C.: Catholic University of America Press, 1991.

Barker, T.C. "The International History of Motor Transport." *Journal of Contemporary History* 20 (1985): 3–19.

Barrett, Paul, et al., eds. *Charles Darwin's Notebooks, 1836–1844: Geology, Transmutation of Species, Metaphysical Enquiries*. Ithaca, NY: Cornell University Press, 1987.

Basalla, George. "Science and the City Before the Nineteenth Century." In *Transformation and Tradition in the Sciences*, edited by Everett Mendelsohn. Cambridge, England: Cambridge University Press, 1984.

——. *The Evolution of Technology*. New York: Cambridge University Press, 1988.

Baumer, Franklin L. *Modern European Thought: Continuity and Change in Ideas, 1600–1950*. New York: Macmillan, 1977.

Beagon, Mary. *Roman Nature: The Thought of Pliny the Elder*. Oxford: Clarendon Press, 1992.

Beer, Gillian. *Darwin's Plots: Evolutionary Narrative in Darwin, George Eliot, and Nineteenth-Century Fiction*. London: Routledge & Kegan Paul, 1983.

Bell, Robert. *Impure Science: Fraud, Compromise and Political Influence in Scientific Research*. New York: Wiley, 1992.

Ben-David, Joseph. *Scientific Growth: Essays on the Social Organization and Ethos of Science*. Berkeley: University of California Press, 1991.

——. *The Scientist's Role in Society: A Comparative Study*. Englewood Cliffs, NJ: Prentice-Hall, 1971.

Benjamin, Marina, ed. *Science and Sensibility: Gender and Scientific Enquiry, 1780–1945*. Oxford and Cambridge, MA: Basil Blackwell, 1991.

Berger, John J. *Restoring the Earth*. New York: Alfred A. Knopf, 1986.

Bergin, Edward J., and Ronald Grandon. *The American Survival Guide: How to Survive Your Toxic Environment*. New York: Avon, 1984.

Berlin, Isaiah. *Karl Marx*. 3d ed. Oxford: Oxford University Press, 1963.

Bernstein, Jeremy. *Einstein*. London: Fontana/Collins, 1973.

Bertell, Rosalie. *No Immediate Danger*. New York: Women's Press, 1986.

Bessel, Richard. "Transport." In *Science, Technology and Everyday Life, 1870–1950*, edited by Colin Chant. London: Routledge/Open University, 1989.

Biagioli, Mario. "Galileo the Emblem Maker." *Isis* 81 (1990): 230–258.

Bijker, W.E., T.P. Hughes, and T. Pinch, eds. *The Social Construction of Technological Systems: New Directions in the Sociology and History of Technology*. Cambridge, Mass.: MIT Press, 1987.

——, and John Law, eds. *Shaping Technology/Building Society: Studies in Sociotechnical Change*. Cambridge, Mass.: MIT Press, 1992.

Bilich, F. *Science and Technology Planning and Policy*. Amsterdam: Elsevier Publishing, 1989.

Bilstein, Roger E. *Flight in America, 1900–1983*. Baltimore: Johns Hopkins University Press, 1984.

Bjorksten, Johan. *Longevity: Past, Present, Future*. Charleston, SC: JAB Publishing, 1987.

Blaedel, Niels. *Harmony and Unity: The Life of Niels Bohr*. Madison, Wisc.: Science Tech Publishers, 1988.

Bloomfield, Brian P., ed. *The Question of Artificial Intelligence: Philosophical and Sociological Perspectives*. London: Croom Helm, 1987.

Blume, Stuart S. *Insight and Industry: On the Dynamics of Technological Change in Medicine*. Cambridge, Mass.: MIT Press, 1992.

Boas, Marie. *The Scientific Renaissance: 1450–1630*. New York: Harper & Brothers, 1962.

Bodde, Derk. *Chinese Thought, Society, and Science: The Intellectual and Social Background of Science and Technology in Pre-modern China*. Honolulu: University of Hawaii Press, 1991.

Bolter, J. David. *Turing's Man: Western Culture in the Computer Age*. Chapel Hill: University of North Carolina Press, 1984.

Bookchin, Murray. *Remaking Society: Pathways to a Green Future*. Boston: South End Press, 1990.

Bothwell, Robert. *Nucleus: The History of Atomic Energy of Canada Limited*. Toronto: University of Toronto Press, 1988.

Bouvier, Leon F. "America's Baby Boom Generation: The Fateful Bulge." *Population Bulletin* (April 1980): 1–35.

Bowen, Alan C., ed. *Science and Philosophy in Classical Greece*. New York: Garland, 1991.

Bowler, Peter J. *Charles Darwin: The Man and His Influence*. Oxford/Cambridge, Mass.: Basil Blackwell, 1990.

——. *Evolution: The History of an Idea*. Revised ed. Berkeley: University of California Press, 1989.

Boxer, M.J. "Protective Legislation and Home Industry: The Marginalization of Women Workers in Late Nineteenth/Early Twentieth-Century France." *Journal of Social History* 20 (1986): 45–65.

Brandt, Allan M. *No Magic Bullet*. New York: Oxford University Press, 1987.

Branscomb, Lewis M. "America's Emerging Technology Policy." *Minerva* 30 (Autumn, 1992): 317–336.

Brantlinger, Patrick. *Energy and Entropy: Science and Culture in Victorian Britain*. Bloomington, IN: Indiana University Press, 1988.

Bridgman, Howard A. *Global Air Pollution: Problems for the 1990s*. London: Belhaven Press, 1990.

Broad, William, and Nicholas Wade. *Betrayers of the Truth*. New York: Simon and Schuster, 1982.

Brod, Craig. *Technostress: the Human Costs of the Computer Revolution*. Reading, Mass.: Addison-Wesley, 1984.

Brooke, John Hedley. *Science and Religion: Some Historical Perspectives*. New York: Cambridge University Press, 1991.

Brooks, J.L. *Just Before the Origin: Alfred Russel Wallace's Theory of Evolution*. New York: Columbia University Press, 1984.

Browne, Janet. *The Secular Ark: Studies in the History of Biogeography*. New Haven: Yale University Press, 1983.

Bruun, Christer. *The Water Supply of Ancient Rome: A Study of Roman Imperial Administration*. Helsinki, 1991.

Bryner, Gary C. *Bureaucratic Discretion: Law and Policy in Federal Regulatory Agencies*. New York: Pergamon Press, 1987.

Buchanan, R.A. *The Power of the Machine*. London: Viking, 1992.

Burchfield, J.D. *Lord Kelvin and the Age of the Earth*. New York: Science History Publications, 1975.

Burlingame, Leslie J. "Jean Baptiste de Lamarck." In vol. 7 of *Dictionary of Scientific Biography*, edited by Charles C. Gillispie. 16 vols. New York: Charles Scribner's Sons, 1973.

Butt, Nasim. *Science in Muslim Societies*. London: Grey Seal, 1991.

Calder, Nigel. *Einstein's Universe*. New York: Penguin, 1982.

Cantelon, Philip L., Hewlett, Richard, and Robert C. Williams, eds. *The American Atom: A Documentary History of Nuclear Policies from the Discovery of Fission to the Present*. 2d ed. Philadelphia: University of Pennsylvania Press, 1991.

Capra, Fritjof. *The Turning Point: Science, Society, and the Rising Culture*. New York: Simon and Schuster, 1982.

Cardwell, D.S.L. *Technology, Science and History*. London: Heinemann, 1972.

Carter, Ruth, and Gill Kirkup. *Women in Engineering: A Good Place to Be?* London: Macmillan, 1990.

Cassidy, David C. *Uncertainty: The Life and Science of Werner Heisenberg*. New York: Freeman, 1992.

Chalk, Rosemary, ed. *Science, Technology, and Society: Emerging Relationships*. Washington DC: American Association for the Advancement of Science, 1988.

Chandler, Tertius. *Four Thousand Years of Urban Growth: An Historical Census*. Lewiston, NY and Queenston, Ontario: St. David's University Press, 1987.

Chant, Colin, ed. *Science, Technology, and Everyday Life, 1870–1950*. London: Routledge/Open University, 1989.

Chappell, N., Strain, L., and A. Blandford. *Aging and Health Care: A Social Perspective*. Toronto: 1986.

Charlton, D.G. *New Images of the Natural in France: A Study in European Cultural History, 1750–1800*. Cambridge: Cambridge University Press, 1984.

Chatterji, Manas, ed. *Technology Transfer in the Developing Countries*. New York: St. Martin's Press, 1990.

Chubin, Daryl E., and Ellen Chu. *Science off the Pedestal: Social Perspectives on Science and Technology*. Belmont, CA: Wadsworth, 1989.

——, and Edward J. Hackett. *Peerless Science: Peer Review and U.S. Science Policy*. Albany, NY: SUNY Press, 1990.

Clagett, Marshall. *Ancient Egyptian Science: A Source Book*. Vol.1. Philadelphia: American Philosophical Society, 1989.

——. *Greek Science in Antiquity*. London: Abelard-Schuman, 1957.

——. *The Science of Mechanics in the Middle Ages*. Madison: University of Wisconsin Press, 1959.

Clair, Colin. *A History of European Printing*. London/New York: Academic Press, 1976.

Cline, Barbara Lovett. *Men Who Made a New Physics: Physicists and the Quantum Theory*. Chicago: University of Chicago Press, 1987.

Clutton-Brock, J. *Domesticated Animals from Early Times*. Austin: University of Texas Press, 1981.

Cohen, I. Bernard. "Benjamin Franklin." In vol. 5 of *Dictionary of Scientific Biography*, edited by Charles C. Gillispie. 16 vols. New York: Charles Scribner's Sons, 1972.

——. *Benjamin Franklin's Science*. Cambridge, Mass.: Harvard University Press, 1990.

——. *The Birth of a New Physics*. Rev. ed. New York: W.W. Norton & Company, 1985a.

——. *Revolution in Science*. Cambridge, Mass.: Harvard University Press, 1985b.

Cohen, M.N. *The Food Crisis in Prehistory: Overpopulation and the Origins of Agriculture*. New Haven: Yale University Press, 1977.

Coleman, D.C. *Myth, History and the Industrial Revolution*. London: Hambledon Press, 1992.

Coleman, James A. *Relativity for the Layman*. Rev. ed. New York: Penguin Books, 1969.

Colton Joel, and Stuart Bruchey. *Technology, The Economy and Society*. New York: Columbia University Press, 1987.

Commoner, Barry. *Making Peace with the Planet*. New York: Random House, 1990.

Compaine, Benjamin M., ed. *Issues in New Information Technology*. Norwood, NJ: Ablex Publishing Corporation. 1988.

Corsi, Pietro. *The Age of Lamarck: Evolutionary Theories in France, 1790–1830*. Berkeley: University of California Press, 1989.

Cotterell, Brian, and Johan Kamminga. *Mechanics of Pre-industrial Technology: An Introduction to the Mechanics of Ancient and Traditional Material Culture*. Cambridge: Cambridge University Press, 1990.

Cottingham, John, ed. *The Cambridge Companion to Descartes*. Cambridge: Cambridge University Press, 1992.

Crane, David. *The Next Canadian Century: Building a Competitive Economy*. Toronto: Stoddart, 1992.

Crick, Francis. *What Mad Pursuit*. New York: Basic Books, 1988.

Crombie, A.C. *Medieval and Early Modern Science*. 2 vols. New York: Anchor, 1959.

——. "Rene Descartes." In vol. 4 of *Dictionary of Scientific Biography*, edited by Charles C. Gillispie. 16 vols. New York: Charles Scribner's Sons, 1971.

Cronin, Helena. *The Ant and the Peacock: Altruism and Sexual Selection from Darwin to Today*. New York: Cambridge University Press, 1991.

Crosland, Maurice, ed. *The Emergence of Science in Western Europe.* New York: Science History Publications, 1976.

——. *Science Under Control: The French Academy of Sciences 1795–1914.* Cambridge: Cambridge University Press, 1992.

Cudahy, B. *Under the Sidewalks of New York. The Story of the Greatest Subway System in the World.* The Stephen Greene Press, 1979.

Curran, James. "Capitalism and Control of the Press, 1800–1975." In *Mass Communication and Society,* edited by James Curran et al. London: Edward Arnold, 1977.

Cutliffe, Stephen H., and Robert C. Post. *In Context: History and the History of Technology.* Bethlehem, Penn.: Lehigh University Press, 1989.

Cutliffe, Stephen H., and Steven Goldman, eds. *New Worlds, New Technologies, New Issues.* Bethlehem, Penn.: Associated Universities Press, 1992.

Dahlberg, Kenneth A., et al. *Environment and the Global Arena.* Durham, NC: Duke University Press, 1985.

Dales, Richard C. *The Intellectual Life of Western Europe in the Middle Ages.* 2nd revised ed. Leiden: E.J. Brill, 1992.

Darwin, Charles. *The Origin of Species and The Descent of Man.* 6th and 2d eds., respectively. New York: Modern Library, 1936.

——. *The Origin of Species by Charles Darwin: A Variorum Text.* Edited by Morse Peckham. Philadelphia: University of Pennsylvania Press, 1959.

Daston, Lorraine. "The Naturalized Female Intellect." *Science in Context* 5 (1992): 209–235.

Daumas, Maurice, ed. *A History of Technology and Invention.* Translated by E. Hennessy. 3 vols. New York: Crown Publishers, 1969–1979.

——, and Paul Gille. "The Steam Engine." In vol. 3 of *A History of Technology and Invention,* edited by Maurice Daumas. 3 vols. New York: Crown Publishers, 1979

David, Wilfred L. *Conflicting Paradigms in the Economics of Developing Nations.* New York: Praeger, 1986.

Davies, Paul. *Other Worlds: A Portrait of Nature in Rebellion: Space, Superspace and the Quantum Universe.* New York: Simon & Schuster, 1980.

Davis, Karen. "Aging and the Health-Care System: Economic and Structural Issues. *Daedalus* 115 (1986): 227–246.

Davis, Philip J. "What Should the Public Know about Mathematics?" *Daedalus* 121 (Winter 1992): 131–138.

De Beer, G.R. *Charles Darwin: Evolution by Natural Selection.* London: Nelson, 1963.

Debus, Allen G. *The English Paracelsians.* London: Oldbourne, 1965.

Dertouzos, Michael L., and Joel Moses, eds. *The Computer Age: A Twenty-Year View.* Cambridge, Mass.: MIT Press, 1979.

Desmond, Adrian. *The Politics of Evolution: Morphology, Medicine, and Reform in Radical London.* Chicago: University of Chicago Press, 1989.

——, and James Moore. *Darwin: The Life of a Tormented Evolutionist.* New York: Warner Books, 1991.

Devall, Bill, and George Sessions. *Deep Ecology: Living as if Nature Mattered.* Salt Lake City: Gibbs M. Smith, 1985.

DeVries, Kelly. *Medieval Military Technology.* Peterborough, Ontario: Broadview Press, 1992.

Dickson, David. *The New Politics of Science.* Chicago: University of Chicago Press, 1988.

Dijksterhuis, E.J. *The Mechanization of the World Picture.* Oxford: Oxford University Press, 1961.

Dixon, Robert T. *The Dynamic World of Physics.* 1984.

Dobbs, Betty Jo Teeter. *The Janus Faces of Genius: The Role of Alchemy in Newton's Thought.* Cambridge: Cambridge University Press, 1991.

Dolman, Claude E. "Paul Ehrlich." In vol. 4 of *Dictionary of Scientific Biography*, edited by Charles C. Gillispie. 16 vols. New York: Charles Scribner's Sons, 1971.

——. "Robert Koch." In vol. 7 of *Dictionary of Scientific Biography*, edited by Charles C. Gillispie. 16 vols. New York: Charles Scribner's Sons, 1973.

Donato, Clorinda, and Robert M. Maniquis, eds. *The Encyclopédie and the Age of Revolution*. Boston: G.K. Hall & Co., 1992.

Donnelly, J.F. " Science, technology and industrial work in Britain, 1860-1930: Towards a new synthesis." *Social History* 16 (1991): 191-201.

Donovan, Arthur. "Lavoisier as Chemist and Experimental Physicist." *Isis* 81 (1990): 270–272.

Dorn, Harold. *The Geography of Science*. Baltimore: Johns Hopkins University Press, 1991.

——. "James Watt." In vol. 14 of *Dictionary of Scientific Biography*, edited by Charles C. Gillispie. 16 vols. New York: Charles Scribner's Sons, 1976.

Douglas, Mary, and Aaron Wildavsky. *Risk and Culture*. Berkeley: University of California Press, 1982.

Doyle, William. *Origins of the French Revolution*. 2d ed. New York: Oxford University Press, 1988.

Drake, Stillman, ed. and trans. *Discoveries and Opinions of Galileo*. New York: Doubleday, 1957.

——. *Galileo at Work: His Scientific Biography*. Chicago: University of Chicago Press, 1978.

——. "Galileo Galilei." In vol. 5 of *Dictionary of Scientific Biography*, edited by Charles C. Gillispie. 16 vols. New York: Charles Scribner's Sons, 1972.

——. *Galileo: Pioneer Scientist*. Toronto: University of Toronto Press, 1990.

Draper, Elaine. *Risky Business: Genetic Testing and Exclusionary Practices in the Hazardous Workplace*. New York: Cambridge University Press, 1991.

Dreyfus, Hubert L. *What Computers Still Can't Do: A Critique of Artificial Reason*. Revised ed. Cambridge, Mass.: MIT Press, 1992.

Drori, Gili S. "The Relationship between Science, Technology and the Economy in Lesser Developed Countries." *Social Studies of Science* 23 (1993): 201–215.

Duffy, John. *The Sanitarians: A History of American Public Health*. Chicago: University of Illinois Press, 1990.

Durant John R. "The Ascent of Nature in Darwin's *Descent of Man*." In *The Darwinian Heritage*, edited by David Kohn. Princeton NJ: Princeton University Press, 1985.

——, ed. *Darwinism and Divinity: Essays on Evolution and Religious Belief*. Oxford: Basil Blackwell, 1985.

Eames, Charles and Ray. *A Computer Perspective: Background to the Computer Age*. Cambridge, Mass.: Harvard University Press, 1990.

Eastwood, Penny. *Responding to Global Warming*. New York and Oxford: Berg, 1991.

Edelstein, Sidney. "William Henry Perkin." In vol. 10 of *Dictionary of Scientific Biography*, edited by Charles C. Gillispie. 16 vols. New York: Charles Scribner's Sons, 1974.

Einstein, Albert. *Relativity: The Special and the General Theory*. London: Methuen, 1983; rept. of 1920 ed.

——, and Leopold Infeld, *The Evolution of Physics*. Cambridge: Cambridge University Press, 1971.

Eisenhower, Dwight D. *Public Papers of the President of the United States: Dwight D. Eisenhower, 1960–61*. Washington, D.C.: Government Printing Office, 1961.

Elkana, Yehuda. "Transformations in realist philosophy of science from Victorian Baconianism to the present day." In *Transformation and Tradition in the Sciences*, edited by Everett Mendelsohn. Cambridge: Cambridge University Press, 1984.

Ellis, Derek. *Environment at Risk: Case Histories of Impact Assessment*. New York: Springer-Verlag, 1989.

Emerson, Roger L. "The Organization of Science and its Pursuit in Early Modern Europe." In *Companion to the History of Modern Science*, edited by R.C. Olby et al. London: Routledge, 1990.

Engelberger, Joseph F. *Robotics in Service*. Cambridge, Mass.: MIT Press, 1989.

Engelhardt, H. Tristram, Jr., and Arthur L. Caplan, eds., *Scientific Controversies: Case Studies in the Resolution and Closure of Disputes in Science and Technology*. Cambridge: Cambridge University Press, 1987.

Enger, Eldon D., et al. *Environmental Science*. 2d ed. Dubuque IA: Wm. C. Brown, 1986.

Ennals, Richard. *Artificial Intelligence and Human Institutions*. London: Springer-Verlag, 1990.

Ewen, Stuart. *Captains of Consciousness: Advertising and the Social Roots of the Consumer Culture*. New York: McGraw-Hill, 1976.

Faber, M.M., and A.M. Reinhardt. *Promoting Health Through Risk Reduction*. New York: Macmillan, 1982.

Farrington, John, ed. *Agricultural Biotechnology: Prospects for the Third World*. London: Overseas Development Institute, 1989.

Faux, Marian. *Childless by Choice: Choosing Childlessness in the Eighties*. New York: Anchor Press/Doubleday, 1984.

Fearon, Peter. "The Growth of Aviation in Britain." *Journal of Contemporary History* 20 (1985): 21–40.

Fichman, Martin. *Alfred Russel Wallace*. Boston: G.K. Hall & Co., 1981.

Finch, Ron. *Exporting Danger: A History of the Canadian Nuclear Energy Export Programme*. Montreal: Black Rose Books, 1986.

Finocchiaro, Maurice A., ed. *The Galileo Affair: A Documentary History*. Berkeley/Los Angeles: University of California Press, 1989.

Fischer, Claude S. *America Calling: A Social History of the Telephone to 1940*. Berkeley: University of California Press, 1992.

Fleming, Donald, and Bernard Bailyn, eds. *The Intellectual Migration: Europe and America, 1930–1960*. Cambridge, Mass.: Harvard University Press, 1969.

Flink, J.J. *The Automobile Age*. Cambridge, Mass.: MIT Press, 1988.

Forester, Tom. *High-Tech Society: The Story of the Information Technology Revolution*. Cambridge, Mass.: MIT Press, 1987.

———. ed. The Information Technology Revolution. Cambridge, Mass.: MIT Press, 1985.

———, and Perry Morrison. *Computer Ethics: Cautionary Tales and Ethical Dilemmas in Computing*. Cambridge, Mass.: MIT Press, 1990.

Forster, Christopher F., and D.A. John Wase, eds. *Environmental Biotechnology*. Chichester, England: Ellis Horwood, Ltd., 1987.

Fosler, R. Scott, et al. *Demographic Change and the American Future*. Pittsburgh: University of Pittsburgh Press, 1990.

Fox, Robert, and George Weisz, eds. *The Organization of Science and Technology in France, 1808–1914*. Cambridge, England: Cambridge University Press, 1980.

Frangsmyr, Tore, ed. *Solomon's House Revisited: The Organization and Institutionalization of Science*. Canton, Mass.: Science History Publications, 1990.

———, J.L. Heilbron, and Robin E. Rider, eds. *The Quantifying Spirit in the 18th Century*. Berkeley: University of California Press, 1990.

Fransman, Martin. *Technology and Economic Development*. Boulder: Westview Press, 1986.

Freeman, C., M. Sharp, and W. Walker, eds. *Technology and the Future of Europe*. London: Pinter Publishers, 1991.

Freeman, Michael J., and Derek H. Aldcroft, eds. *Transport in Victorian Britain*. Manchester: Manchester University Press, 1988.

Friedrichs, Gunter, and Adam Schaff, eds. *Microelectronics and Society: For Better or For Worse*. Oxford: Pergamon Press, 1982.

Galison, Peter, and Barton Bernstein. "In Any Light: Scientists and the Decision to Build the Superbomb, 1952–1954." *Historical Studies in the Physical and Biological Sciences* 19 (1989):267–347.

Galison, Peter, and Bruce Hevly, eds. *Big Science: The Growth of Large-Scale Research*. Stanford, CA: Stanford University Press, 1992.

Garson, Barbara. *The Electronic Sweatshop: How Computers are Transforming the Office of the Future into the Factory of the Past*. New York: Simon & Schuster, 1988.

Gay, Peter. *The Enlightenment: An Interpretation*. The Rise of Modern Paganism. New York: Alfred A. Knopf, 1966.

Gearhart, Clayton A. "Einstein before 1905: The Early Papers on Statistical Mechanics." *American Journal of Physics* 58 (1990): 468–480.

Giangrande, Carole. *The Nuclear North: The People, the Regions, and the Arms Race*. Toronto: Anansi, 1983.

Gieryn, Thomas F. "Distancing Science from Religion in Seventeenth- Century England." *Isis* 79 (1988): 582–593.

Gille, Bertrand, ed. *The History of Techniques*. 2 vols. New York: Gordon and Breach Science Publishers, 1986.

Gillispie, Charles C. "Etienne Bonnot, Abbe de Condillac." In vol. 3 of *Dictionary of Scientific Biography*, edited by Charles C. Gillispie. 16 vols. New York: Charles Scribner's Sons, 1971.

——. *The Montgolfier Brothers and the Invention of Aviation, 1783–1784*. Princeton: Princeton University Press, 1983.

Gingerich, Owen. "Kepler." In vol. 7 of *Dictionary of Scientific Biography*, edited by Charles C. Gillispie. 16 vols. New York: Charles Scribner's Sons, 1973.

——. *The Physical Sciences in the Twentieth Century*. New York: Scribner's, 1989.

Global Tomorrow Coalition. *The Global Ecology Handbook: What You Can Do About the Environment*. Boston: Beacon Press, 1990.

Glynn, Patrick. *Closing Pandora's Box: Arms Races, Arms Control, and the History of the Cold War*. New York: Basic Books, 1992.

Gofman, John W. *Radiation and Human Health*. San Francisco: Sierra Club Books, 1981.

Goldman, Steven L., ed. *Science, Technology, and Social Progress*. Bethlehem, PA: Lehigh University Press, 1989.

Golinski, Jan. *Science as Public Culture: Chemistry and the Enlightenment in Britain, 1760–1820*. Cambridge: Cambridge University Press, 1992.

Goodman, Anthony, and Angus McKay, eds. *The Impact of Humanism on Western Europe*. London: Longman, 1990.

Goodman, David, and Colin A. Russell, eds. *The Rise of Scientific Europe: 1500–1800*. Kent, Eng.: Hodder & Stoughton; Milton Keynes: Open University, 1991.

Goodman, Jordan, and Katrina Honeyman. *Gainful Pursuits: the Making of Industrial Europe, 1600–1914*. London: Edward Arnold, 1988.

Gordon, Scott. *The History and Philosophy of Social Science*. London and New York: Routledge, 1991.

Gorman, James. *Hazards to Your Health: The Problem of Environmental Disease*. New York: New York Academy of Sciences, 1979.

Gorman, Michael, and W.B. Carlson. "Interpreting Invention as a Cognitive Process: The Case of Alexander Graham Bell, Thomas Edison, and the Telephone." *Science, Technology and Human Values* 15 (1990): 131–164.

Goubert, Jean-Pierre. *The Conquest of Water: The Advent of Health in the Industrial Age*. Translated by Andrew Wilson. Princeton, NJ: Princeton University Press, 1989.

Gould, Stephen Jay. *The Mismeasure of Man*. New York: Norton, 1981.

Grafton, Anthony. *New Worlds, Ancient Texts: The Power of Tradition and the Shock of Discovery*. Cambridge, Mass.: Harvard University Press, 1992.

Graham, Loren R. "Concerns About Science and Attempts to Regulate Inquiry." *Daedalus* (Spring 1978): 1–23.

———. *Science in Russia and the Soviet Union: A Short History*. New York/Cambridge: Cambridge University Press, 1992.

Grant, Edward. *Physical Science in the Middle Ages*. New York: John Wiley, 1971.

Graubard, Stephen R. *The Artificial Intelligence Debate*. Cambridge, Mass.: MIT Press, 1988.

Greene, Mott T. *Natural Knowledge in Preclassical Antiquity*. Baltimore: Johns Hopkins University Press, 1992.

Greengrass, Mark, ed. *Conquest and Coalescence: The Shaping of the State in Early Modern Europe*. London: Edward Arnold, 1991.

Griffin, Keith. *Alternative Strategies for Economic Development*. London: Macmillan, 1989.

Grindle, Merilee S., and John W. Thomas. *Public Choices and Policy Change: The Political Economy of Reform in Developing Countries*. Baltimore: Johns Hopkins University Press, 1991.

Grodzins, Morton, and Eugene Rabinowitch. *The Atomic Age: Scientists in National and World Affairs. Articles from the "Bulletin of the Atomic Scientists" 1945–1962*. New York: Simon & Schuster, 1963.

Guerlac, Henry. *Antoine-Laurent Lavoisier: Chemist and Revolutionary*. New York: Charles Scribner's Sons, 1975.

Gupta, Avijit. *Ecology and Development in the Third World*. London and New York: Routledge, 1988.

Haas, Violet, and Carolyn Perrucci, eds. *Women in Scientific and Engineering Professions*. Ann Arbor: University of Michigan Press, 1984.

Hall, A. Rupert. *The Revolution in Science: 1500–1750*. London: Longman, 1983.

Hall, Marie Boas. *Promoting Experimental Learning: Experiment and the Royal Society, 1660–1727*. New York: Cambridge University Press, 1991.

———. "Robert Boyle." In vol. 2 of *Dictionary of Scientific Biography*, edited by Charles C. Gillispie. 16 vols. New York: Charles Scribner's Sons, 1970.

Hallion, Richard P. *Rise of the Fighter Aircraft, 1914–1918*. Annapolis: Nautical and Aviation, 1984.

Hamlett, Patrick W. *Understanding Technological Politics*. Englewood Cliffs, NJ: Prentice Hall, 1992.

Hankins, Thomas L. *Science and the Enlightenment*. Cambridge: Cambridge University Press, 1985.

Hanson, Bruce. "Evaluating Appropriate Technology in Practice." *Journal of Contemporary Asia* 19, no.1 (1989): 33–47.

Harris, Dianna K. *Dictionary of Gerontology*. Westport, CT: Greenwood Press, 1988.

Harrison, J.F.C. *The Common People of Great Britain: a History from the Norman Conquest to the Present*. Bloomington: Indiana University Press, 1985.

Harrison, Paul. *The Third Revolution: Environment, Population and a Sustainable World*. London: I.B. Tauris, 1992.

Hart, Clive. *The Prehistory of Flight*. Berkeley: University of California Press, 1985.

Hartcup, Guy, and T.E. Allibone. *Cockcroft and the Atom*. Bristol: Adam Hilger, 1984.

Harthill, M., ed. *Hazardous Waste Management: In Whose Backyard?* New York: Westview, 1984.

al-Hassan, Ahmad Y., and Donald R. Hill. *Islamic Technology*. Cambridge, England: Cambridge University Press, 1986.

Hatfield, Gary. "Metaphysics and the new science." In *Reappraisals of the Scientific Revolution*, edited by David C. Lindberg and Robert S, Westman. Cambridge: Cambridge University Press, 1990.

Heilbron, J.L. *The Dilemmas of an Upright Man: Max Planck as Spokesman for German Science*. Berkeley and Los Angeles: University of California Press, 1986.

———. "The Measure of Enlightenment." In *The Quantifying Spirit in the 18th Century*, edited by Tore Frangsmyr, J.L. Heilbron, and Robin E. Rider. Berkeley: University of California Press, 1990.

Heiser, Charles B., Jr. *Seed to Civilization: The Story of Food*. New ed. Cambridge, Mass.: Harvard University Press, 1990.

Henderson, W.O. *The Industrialization of Europe: 1780–1914*. London: 1969.

Herbert, Nick. *Quantum Reality: Beyond the New Physics*. New York: Anchor, 1987.

Herken, Gregg. *Cardinal Choices: Presidential Science Advising from the Atomic Bomb to SDI*. New York: Oxford University Press, 1992.

Herman, Robin. *Fusion: The Search for Endless Energy*. Cambridge, England: Cambridge University Press, 1990.

Hesse, Mary. "Francis Bacon." In vol. 1 of *Dictionary of Scientific Biography*, edited by Charles C. Gillispie. 16 vols. New York: Charles Scribner's Sons, 1970.

Higgins, I.J., D. J. Best, and J. Jones, eds. *Biotechnology: Principles and Applications*. Oxford: Blackwell Scientific Publications, 1985.

Hilgartner, Stephen, and Dorothy Nelkin. "Communication Controversies over Dietary Risks." *Science, Technology and Human Values* 12 (Summer/Fall 1987): 41–47.

Hill, Donald R. *A History of Engineering in Classical and Medieval Times*. La Salle, Ill.: Open Court, 1984.

Hoddesdon, L. "The emergence of basic research in the Bell Telephone system, 1875-1915." *Technology and Culture* 22 (1981): 512–544.

Hodge, M.J.S., and David Kohn. "The Immediate Origins of Natural Selection." In *The Darwinian Heritage*, edited by David Kohn. Princeton NJ: Princeton University Press, 1985.

Hodges, Andrew. *Alan Turing: the Enigma*. New York: Touchstone, 1984.

Hodges, Henry. *Technology in the Ancient World*. New York: Alfred A. Knopf, 1974.

Hoffman, Lance J., ed. *Computers and Privacy in the Next Decade*. New York: Academic Press, 1980.

Hoffmann, Banesh. *Relativity and its Roots*. New York: W.H. Freeman, 1983.

Hohenberg, P.M. and L.H. Lees. *The Making of Urban Europe, 1000-1950*. Cambridge, Mass.: Harvard University Press, 1985.

Holmes, F.L. "Justus von Liebig." In vol. 8 of *Dictionary of Scientific Biography*, edited by Charles C. Gillispie. 16 vols. New York: Charles Scribner's Sons, 1973.

——. *Lavoisier and the Chemistry of Life: An Exploration of Scientific Creativity*. Madison: University of Wisconsin Press, 1985.

Holmyard, E.J. *Alchemy*. London: Penguin Books, 1968.

Holton, Gerald. *Thematic Origins of Scientific Thought: Kepler to Einstein*. Rev. ed. Cambridge, Mass.: Harvard University Press, 1988.

Homer-Dixon, Thomas F., Jeffrey H. Boutwell, and George W. Rathjens. "Environmental Change and Violent Conflict." *Scientific American* 268 No.2 (February 1993): 38–45.

Horton, E.J., and W.D. Compton. "Technological Trends in Automobiles." *Science* 225 (1984): 587–593.

Huber, Peter W. "Pathological Science in Court." *Daedalus* (Fall 1990): 97–118.

Hudson, Kenneth. *The Archaeology of the Consumer Society: the Second Industrial Revolution in Britain*. Cranbury, NJ: Fairleigh Dickinson University Press, 1983.

Hughes, Thomas P. *American Genesis: A Century of Invention and Technological Enthusiasm, 1870–1970*. New York: Viking, 1989.

——. *Networks of Power: Electrification in Western Society, 1880–1930*. Baltimore: Johns Hopkins University Press, 1983.

Hull, David L. *Darwin & His Critics*. Cambridge, Mass.: Harvard University Press, 1973.

Hulme, Peter, and Ludmilla Jordanova, eds. *The Enlightenment and Its Shadows*. London: Routledge, 1990.

Hurley, Patrick. *Living with Nuclear Radiation*. Ann Arbor: University of Michigan Press, 1982.

Hyman, Anthony. *Charles Babbage: Pioneer of the Computer*. Princeton: Princeton University Press, 1982.

Iannone, A. Pablo, ed. *Contemporary Moral Controversies in Technology*. New York: Oxford University Press, 1987.

Ihde, Aaron J. *The Development of Modern Chemistry*. New York: Harper & Row, 1964.

Imperato, P.J., and Greg Mitchell. *Acceptable Risks*. New York: Viking, 1985.

Inose, H., et al., eds. *Science and Technology Policy Research: "What Should be Done? What Can be Done?"* Tokyo: Mita Press, 1991.

Iorio, Dominick A. *The Aristotelians of Renaissance Italy: A Philosophical Exposition.* Queenston, Ont.: Edwin Mellen Press, 1991.

Jackson, K.T. *Crabgrass Frontier: The Suburbanization of the United States.* New York: Oxford University Press, 1985.

Jacob, Margaret C. *The Cultural Meaning of the Scientific Revolution.* New York: Alfred A. Knopf, 1988.

Jakab, Peter L. *Visions of a Flying Machine: the Wright Brothers and the Process of Invention.* Washington, D.C.: Smithsonian Institution Press, 1990.

Jasanoff, Sheila. *The Fifth Estate.* Cambridge, Mass.: Harvard University Press, 1991.

——. *Risk Management and Political Culture: A Comparative Study of Science in the Policy Context.* New York: Russel Sage Foundation, 1986.

Jasper, James. *Nuclear Politics: Energy and the State in the United States, Sweden and France.* Princeton: Princeton University Press, 1990.

Jennings, Jan, ed. *Roadside America: The Automobile in Design and Culture.* Ames, IA: Iowa State University Press, 1990.

Jervis, Robert. *The Meaning of the Nuclear Revolution: Statecraft and the Prospect of Armageddon.* Ithaca: Cornell University Press, 1989.

Johannisson, Karin. "Society in Numbers: The Debate over Quantification in 18th-Century Political Economy." In *The Quantifying Spirit in the 18th Century,* edited by Tore Frangsmyr, J.L. Heilbron, and Robin E. Rider. Berkeley: University of California Press, 1990.

Jones, Greta. *Social Darwinism and English Thought: The Interaction Between Biological and Social Theory.* Brighton, England: Harvester Press, 1980.

Jones, Peter, ed. *Philosophy and Science in the Scottish Enlightenment.* Edinburgh: Donald, 1988.

Jordanova, L.J. *Lamarck.* Oxford: Oxford University Press, 1984.

Judson, Lindsay, ed. *Aristotle's "Physics": A Collection of Essays.* Oxford: Clarendon Press, 1991.

Jungk, Robert. *Brighter Than a Thousand Suns: The Story of the Men Who Made the Bomb.* New York: Harcourt, Brace & World. 1958.

Kaplan, Fred. *The Wizards of Armageddon.* 1983.

Kaufmann, Thomas DaCosta. *The Mastery of Nature: Aspects of Art, Science, and Humanism in the Renaissance.* Princeton, NJ: Princeton University Press, 1992.

Keller, Evelyn Fox. *Reflections on Gender and Science.* New Haven, Conn.: Yale University Press, 1985.

Kemp, David D. *Global Environmental Issues: A Climatological Approach.* New York: Routledge, 1990.

Kemp, Tom. *Industrialization in Nineteenth-Century Europe.* 2d ed. London and New York: Longman, 1985.

Kenney, Martin. *Biotechnology: The University/Industry Complex.* New Haven, Conn.: Yale University Press, 1986.

Kevles, Daniel J. *In the Name of Eugenics: Genetics and the Uses of Human Heredity.* Berkeley: University of California Press, 1985.

——. *The Physicists: The History of a Scientific Community in Modern America.* New York: Knopf, 1977.

——., and Leroy Hood, eds. *The Code of Codes: Scientific and Social Issues in the Human Genome Project.* Cambridge, Mass.: Harvard University Press, 1992.

King, Lester S. "Georg Ernst Stahl." In vol. 12 of *Dictionary of Scientific Biography,* edited by Charles C. Gillispie. 16 vols. New York: Charles Scribner's Sons, 1975.

Kirkup, Gill, and Laurie Smith Keller. *Inventing Women: Science, Technology and Gender.* Cambridge, England: Polity Press, 1992.

Klein, Martin J. "Albert Einstein." In vol. 4 of *Dictionary of Scientific Biography,* edited by Charles C. Gillispie. 16 vols. New York: Charles Scribner's Sons, 1971.

Kleinberg, S. Jay. *Retrieving Women's History: Changing Perceptions of the Role of Women in Politics and Society.* Providence, R.I. and Oxford: Berg Publishers/UNESCO Press, 1992.

Knight, David M. *The Age of Science: The Scientific World-View in the Nineteenth Century*. New York: Basil Blackwell, 1986.

——. *Ideas in Chemistry: A History of the Science*. London: Athlone Press; New Brunswick, NJ: Rutgers University Press, 1992.

Kohn, David, ed. *The Darwinian Heritage*. Princeton NJ: Princeton University Press, 1985.

Kottler, Malcolm Jay. "Alfred Russel Wallace, the origin of man and spiritualism." *Isis* 65 (1974): 145–192.

——. "Charles Darwin and Alfred Russel Wallace: Two Decades of Debate over Natural Selection." In *The Darwinian Heritage*, edited by David Kohn. Princeton NJ: Princeton University Press, 1985.

Kranzberg, Melvin, and Carroll W. Pursell, eds. *Technology in Western Civilization*. New York: Oxford University Press, 1967.

Kraut, Robert E., ed. *Technology and Transformation of White-Collar Work*. Hillsdale, NJ: Lawrence Erlbaum Associates, 1987.

Krimsky, Sheldon. *Biotechnics and Society: The Rise of Industrial Genetics*. New York: Praeger, 1991.

——. *Genetic Alchemy: The Social History of the Recombinant DNA Controversy*. Cambridge, Mass.: MIT Press, 1982.

Kuhn, Thomas S. *The Copernican Revolution*. Cambridge, Mass.: Harvard University Press, 1957.

——. *The Structure of Scientific Revolutions*. 2d ed. Chicago: University of Chicago Press, 1970.

Kuklick, Henrika. *The Social History of British Anthropology, 1885–1945*. Cambridge: Cambridge University Press, 1992.

Kulkarni, R. P. "Development of engineering and technology in India from 1000 B.C. to 1000 A.D." *Indian Journal of the History of Science* 22 (1987): 316–327.

Kupchella, Charles E., and Margaret C. Hyland. *Environmental Science*. 2d ed. Boston: Allyn and Bacon, 1989.

Kuznick, Peter J. *Beyond the Laboratory: Scientists as Political Activists in 1930s America*. Chicago: University of Chicago Press, 1987.

Ladou, Joseph. "Deadly Migration: Hazardous Industries Flee to the Third World." *Technology Review* 94 No. 5 (1991): 46-53.

Lakoff, Sanford. "Science Policy After the Cold War: Problems and Opportunities." *Technology in Society* 13 Nos. 1/2 (1991): 23-38.

Lane, L.A., ed. *Urban Transit: The Private Challenge to Public Transportation*. Cambridge, Mass.: Ballinger, 1984.

Larson, Edward J. *Trial and Error: The American Controversy over Creation and Evolution*. Updated edition. New York/Oxford: Oxford University Press, 1989.

Latour, Bruno. *The Pasteurization of France*. Cambridge, Mass.: Harvard University Press, 1988.

——. "A Relativistic Account of Einstein's Relativity." *Social Studies of Science* 18, no.1 (1988): 3-45.

Laudan, L. "Auguste Comte." In vol. 3 of *Dictionary of Scientific Biography*, edited by Charles C. Gillispie. 16 vols. New York: Charles Scribner's Sons, 1971.

——. *Science and Values*. Berkeley: University of California Press, 1984.

Lavoisier, Antoine-Laurent. *Elements of Chemistry*. Rpt. of 1790 edition. New York: Dover Publications, 1965.

Lecourt, Dominique. *Proletarian Science?: The Case of Lysenko*. Highlands, NJ: Humanities Press, 1977.

Lee, Ronald D., W. Brian Arthur, and Gerry Rodgers, eds. *Economics of Changing Age Distributions in Developed Countries*. Oxford: Oxford University Press, 1988.

Leicester, Henry M., and Herbert S. Klickstein. *A Source Book in Chemistry: 1400–1900*. Cambridge, Mass.: Harvard University Press, 1965.

Leiss, William. *Under Technology's Thumb*. Montreal and Kingston: McGill-Queen's University Press, 1990.

Lester, James P., ed. *Environmental Politics and Policy: Theories and Evidence*. Durham, NC: Duke University Press, 1989.

Levy, Mark R., ed. *The VCR Age*. Newbury Park, CA: Sage Publications, 1989.

Lifton, Robert Jay. *The Nazi Doctors: Medical Killing and the Psychology of Genocide*. New York: Basic Books, 1986.

Lindberg, David C. *The Beginnings of Western Science: The European Scientific Tradition in Philosophical, Religious, and Institutional Context, 600 B.C. to A.D. 1450*. Chicago: University of Chicago Press, 1992.

——, ed. *Science in the Middle Ages*. Chicago: University of Chicago Press, 1978.

——, and Robert S. Westman, eds. *Reappraisals of the Scientific Revolution*. Cambridge: Cambridge University Press, 1990.

Lindroth, Sten. "Carl Linnaeus." In vol. 8 of *Dictionary of Scientific Biography*, edited by Charles C. Gillispie. 16 vols. New York: Charles Scribner's Sons, 1973.

Lloyd, G.E.R. *Magic, Reason and Experience: Studies in the Origins and Development of Greek Science*. Cambridge: Cambridge University Press, 1979.

——. *The Revolutions of Wisdom. Studies in the Claims and Practice of Ancient Greek Science*. Berkeley and Los Angeles: University of California Press, 1987.

Logsdon, Tom. *Computers and Social Controversy*. Rockville, Md.: Computer Science Press, 1980.

Longman, Philip. *Born to Pay: The New Politics of Aging in America*. Boston: Houghton Mifflin, 1987.

Love, Lester B. "Toxic Substances Control in the 1990s. Are We Poisoning Ourselves with Low-Level Exposures?" *Annual Review of Public Health* 11 (1990): 69–88.

Lovins, Amory B., and L. Hunter Lovins. *Energy/War: Breaking the Nuclear Link*. New York: Harper Colophon, 1980.

Lucas, H., and J.R. Harris. *Ancient Egyptian Materials and Industries*. 4th ed., revised and enlarged. London: 1989.

Lucky, Robert. *Silicon Dreams: Information, Man, and Machines*. New York: St. Martin's Press, 1989.

Macdonald, Doug. *Politics of Pollution*. Toronto: McClelland & Stewart, 1991.

MacKenzie, John M., ed. *Imperialism and the Natural World*. Manchester: University of Manchester Press, 1990.

Maguire, Maria, et al. *Aging Populations: The Social Policy Implications*. Paris: OECD, 1988.

Malcolmson, Robert W. *Nuclear Fallacies: How We Have Been Misguided since Hiroshima*. Kingston and Montreal: McGill-Queen's University Press, 1985.

Mandelbaum, Michael. *The Nuclear Revolution: International Politics Before and After Hiroshima*. 1981.

Mander, Jerry. *In the Absence of the Sacred*. San Francisco: Sierra Club Books, 1991.

Mansfield, Jerry W. *The Nuclear Power Debate: A Guide to the Literature*. New York: Garland, 1984.

Marcorini, E., ed. *The History of Science and Technology: A Narrative Chronology*. New York and Oxford: Facts on File, 1988.

Marcus, Alan I., and Howard P. Segal. *Technology in America: A Brief History*. San Diego: Harcourt Brace Jovanovich, 1989.

Markides, K.S., and C.L. Cooper, eds. *Retirement in Industrialized Societies: Social, Psychological and Health Factors*. New York: John Wiley & Sons, 1987.

Markie, Peter J. *Descartes's Gambit*. Ithaca and London: Cornell University Press, 1986.

Marmor, T.R. *The Politics of Medicare*. Chicago: Aldine Publishing Co., 1973.

Martels, Z. von, ed. *Alchemy Revisited*. Leiden: E.J. Brill, 1990.

Martin, Julian. *Francis Bacon, the State, and the Reform of Natural Philosophy*. Cambridge: Cambridge University Press, 1992.

Martin, William J. *The Information Society*. London: Aslib, 1988.

Marx, Leo. "Environmental Degradation and the Ambiguous Social Role of Science and Technology." *Journal of the History of Biology* 25 (Fall 1992): 449–468.

Mathias, Peter, and John A. Davis. *The First Industrial Revolutions*. Oxford and Cambridge, Mass.: Basil Blackwell, 1990.

——, eds. *Innovation and Technology in Europe, from the 18th Century to the Present Day*. Oxford: Basil Blackwell, 1991.

Mayr, Ernst. *One Long Argument: Charles Darwin and the Genesis of Modern Evolutionary Thought*. Cambridge, Mass.: Harvard University Press, 1991.

McCormick, John. *Reclaiming Paradise: The Global Environmental Movement*. Bloomington, IN: Indiana University Press, 1989.

McCuen, Gary E., ed. *Nuclear Waste: The Biggest Clean-Up in History*. Hudson, Wisc.: G.E. McCuen Publications, 1990.

McKay, J.P. *Tramways and Trolleys: The Rise of Urban Mass Transport in Europe*. Princeton: Princeton University Press, 1976.

McKay, Paul. *Electric Empire: The Inside Story of Ontario Hydro*. Toronto: Between the Lines, 1983.

McKnight, Stephen A., ed. *Science, Pseudo-science, and Utopianism in Early Modern Thought*. Columbia: University of Missouri Press, 1992.

McKormick, John. *Acid Earth: The Global Threat of Acid Pollution*. Washington, D.C.: Earthscan, 1985.

McMullin, Ernan. "Conceptions of science in the Scientific Revolution." In *Reappraisals of the Scientific Revolution*, edited by David C. Lindberg and Robert S. Westman. Cambridge: Cambridge University Press, 1990.

——. "The Development of Philosophy of Science, 1600–1900." In *Companion to the History of Modern Science*, edited by R.C. Olby et al. London: Routledge, 1990.

——, ed. *The Social Dimensions of Science*. Notre Dame, Ind.: University of Notre Dame Press, 1992.

McNeill, William H. *The Pursuit of Power: Technology, Armed Force, and Society Since A.D. 1000*. Chicago: University of Chicago Press, 1982.

Meade, Teresa, and Mark Walker, eds. *Science, Medicine and Cultural Imperialism*. New York: St. Martin's Press, 1991.

Meadows, Jack. *The Great Scientists*. New York: Oxford University Press, 1987.

Medvedev, Grigori. *The Truth About Chernobyl*. New York: Basic Books, 1991.

Meek, Ronald L. *Social Science and the Ignoble Savage*. Cambridge: Cambridge University Press, 1976.

Melhado, Evan M. "Chemistry, Physics and the Chemical Revolution." *Isis* 76 (1985): 195–211.

——, and Tore Frangsmyr, eds. *Enlightenment Science in the Romantic Era: The Chemistry of Berzelius and Its Cultural Setting*. New York: Cambridge University Press, 1992.

Mendelsohn, Everett, ed. *Transformation and Tradition in the Sciences*. Cambridge: Cambridge University Press, 1984.

——, Merritt Roe Smith, and Peter Weingart, eds. *Science, Technology, and the Military*. 2 vols. Dordrecht/Boston: Kluwer, 1988.

Menzies, Heather. *Fast Forward and Out of Control: How Technology is Changing Your Life*. Toronto: Macmillan, 1989.

Merchant, Carolyn. *The Death of Nature: Women, Ecology, and the Scientific Revolution*. New York: Harper & Row, 1980.

——. *Ecological Revolutions: Nature, Gender, and Science in New England*. Chapel Hill/London: University of North Carolina Press, 1989.

Meyer-Thurow, G. "The industrialization of invention: A case study from the German chemical industry." *Isis* 73 (1982) 363–381.

Milbrath, Lester R. *Environmentalists: Vanguard for a New Society*. Albany: SUNY Press, 1984.

Millard, Andre. *Edison and the Business of Innovation*. Baltimore: Johns Hopkins University Press, 1990.

Miller, Arthur I. *Albert Einstein's Special Theory of Relativity: Emergence (1905) and Early Interpretation (1905–1911)*. Reading, Mass.: Addison-Wesley, 1981.

Miller, G. Tyler. *Living in the Environment: An Introduction to Environmental Science.* 5th ed. Belmont: CA: Wadsworth, 1988.

Mohnen, V.A. "The Challenge of Acid Rain." *Scientific American* 259 (1988): 30–38.

Moore, James R., ed. *History, Humanity and Evolution: Essays for John C. Greene.* New York: Cambridge University Press, 1989.

Moore, Walter. *Schrodinger: Life and Thought.* Cambridge: Cambridge University Press, 1992.

Moran, Bruce T. *Patronage and Institutions: Science, Technology and Medicine at the European Court, 1500–1750.* Rochester, NY: Boydell Press, 1991.

Morin, Alexander J. *Science Policy and Politics.* Englewood Cliffs, NJ: Prentice-Hall, 1993.

Morone, Joseph, and Edward J. Woodhouse. *Averting Catastrophe: Strategies for Regulating Risky Technologies.* Berkeley: University of California Press, 1988.

———. *The Demise of Nuclear Energy: Lessons for Democratic Control of Technology.* New Haven, Conn.: Yale University Press, 1989.

Morphet, Clive. *Galileo and Copernican Astronomy: A Scientific World View Defined.* London: Butterworths, 1977.

Morrell, J.B. "Professionalisation." In *Companion to the History of Modern Science,* edited by R.C. Olby et al. London: Routledge, 1990.

Mowery, David C., and Nathan Rosenberg. *Technology and the Pursuit of Economic Growth.* Cambridge, England: Cambridge University Press, 1989.

Mukerji, Chandra. *A Fragile Power: Scientists and the State.* Princeton NJ: Princeton University Press, 1989.

Multhauf, Robert P. *The Origins of Chemistry.* New York: Franklin Watts, 1967.

Mumford, Lewis. *The City in History.* New York: Harcourt, Brace and World, 1961.

Murdoch, John E. *Album of Science: Antiquity and the Middle Ages.* New York: Scribner's, 1984.

Musson, A.E. "Industrial motive power in the United Kingdom, 1800–1870." *Economic History Review* 29 (1976): 415–439.

Musson, A.E., and Eric Robinson. *Science and Technology in the Industrial Revolution.* 2d ed. Intro. Margaret C. Jacobs. New York: Gordon & Breach, 1989.

Nash, Roderick. *The Rights of Nature: A History of Environmental Ethics.* Madison: University of Wisconsin Press, 1989.

National Institutes of Health. *Guidelines for Research Involving Recombinant DNA Molecules.* Washington, D.C.: Government Printing Office, 1976.

Naylor, C. David, ed. *Canadian Health Care and the State: A Century of Evolution.* Montreal and Kingston: McGill-Queen's University Press, 1992.

Needham, Joseph. *The Shorter Science and Civilization in China.* Vol. 1. Cambridge: Cambridge University Press, 1978.

Negrotti, Massimo, ed. *Understanding the Artificial: On The Future Shape of Artificial Intelligence.* London: Springer-Verlag, 1991.

Nelkin, Dorothy, ed. *Controversy: Politics of Technical Decisions.* 3d ed. Newbury Park: Sage, 1992.

———. *Selling Science: How the Press Covers Science and Technology.* New York: W.H. Freeman, 1987.

———, and M.S. Brown. *Workers at Risk: Voices From the Workplace.* Chicago: University of Chicago Press, 1984.

———, and Michael Pollak. *The Atom Besieged: Extraparliamentary Dissent in France and Germany.* Cambridge, Mass.: MIT Press, 1981.

———, D. Willis, and S. Parris, eds. *A Disease of Society: Cultural and Institutional Responses to AIDS.* New York: Oxford University Press, 1991.

Nelson, D. *F.W. Taylor and the Rise of Scientific Management.* Madison: University of Wisconsin Press, 1980.

Neufeld, Michael J. "Weimar Culture and Futuristic Technology—the Rocketry and Spaceflight Fad in Germany, 1923-1933." *Technology and Culture* 31 (October 1990): 725–752.

Newman, William. "Technology and Alchemical Debate in the Late Middle Ages." *Isis* 80 (1989): 423–445.

Nicolacopoulos, Pantellis, ed. *Greek Studies in the Philosophy and History of Science*. Dordrecht: Kluwer Academic, 1990.

Nora, Simon, and Alain Minc. *The Computerization of Society*. Cambridge, Mass.: MIT Press, 1980.

Norwine, Jim, and Alfonso Gonzalez. *The Third World: States of Mind and Being*. Boston: Unwin Hyman, 1988.

Nossal, G.J.V., and Ross L. Coppel. *Reshaping Life: Key Issues in Genetic Engineering*. 2d ed. New York: Cambridge University Press, 1989.

Novak, M. *Successful Aging: The Myths, Realities and Future of Aging in Canada*. London: Penguin Books, 1985.

Nye, David E. *Electrifying America: Social Meanings of a New Technology*, 1880–1940. Cambridge, Mass.: MIT Press, 1990.

Olby, R.C., et al., eds. *Companion to the History of Modern Science*. London: Routledge, 1990.

Olby, Robert. "The Origins of Molecular Genetics." *Journal of the History of Biology* 7 (1974): 93–100.

Oldroyd, David, and Ian Langham. *The Wider Domain of Evolutionary Thought*. Dordrecht, Holland: D. Reidel, 1983.

Olsen, Steve. *Biotechnology*. Washington, D.C.: National Academy Press, 1986.

Olshansky, S. Jay, Bruce A. Carnes, and Christine K. Cassel. "The Aging of the Human Species." *Scientific American* 268 No. 4 (April 1993): 46–52.

Olson, Richard. *Science Deified and Science Defied: The Historical Significance of Science in Western Culture from the Bronze Age to the Beginnings of the Modern Era ca. 3500 B.C. to ca. A.D. 1640*. Berkeley and Los Angeles: University of California Press, 1982.

Oppenheimer, J.R. "Atomic Weapons." *Proceedings of the American Philosophical Society* 90 (January 1946): 7.

Oppenheimer, Michael, and Robert H. Boyle. *Dead Heat: the Race Against the Greenhouse Effect*. New York: Basic Books, 1990.

Outram, Dorinda. "Science and Political Ideology, 1790–1848." In *Companion to the History of Modern Science*, edited by R.C. Olby et al. London: Routledge, 1990.

Pacey, Arnold. *The Culture of Technology*. Cambridge, Mass.: MIT Press, 1983.

———. *Technology in World Civilization*. Cambridge, Mass.: MIT Press, 1990.

Paehlke, Robert, and D. Torgerson, eds. *Managing Leviathan: Environmental Politics and the Administrative State*. Lewiston, ME: Broadview Press, 1990.

Pagels, Heinz R. *Computer Culture*. New York: New York Academy of Sciences, 1984.

Pai, Anna C. *Foundations of Genetics: A Science for Society*. New York: McGraw-Hill, 1985.

Pais, Abraham. *Niels Bohr's Times: in Physics, Philosophy and Policy*. Oxford: Clarendon Press, 1991.

———. *'Subtle is the Lord...': The Science and the Life of Albert Einstein*. New York: Oxford University Press, 1982.

Park, C.C. *Acid Rain: Rhetoric and Reality*. London: Methuen, 1987.

Park, Chris. *Chernobyl: The Long Shadow*. London and New York: Routledge, 1989.

Partington, J.R. *A History of Chemistry*. Vol. 2. London: Macmillan, 1969.

———. *A Short History of Chemistry*. 3d ed. New York: Harper and Brothers, 1960.

Patterson, Walter, C. *Nuclear Power*. 2nd ed. London: Penguin, 1983.

Payne, Peter L. *Colvilles and the Scottish Steel Industry*. Oxford: Oxford University Press, 1979.

Perrin, Carleton E. "The chemical revolution." In *Companion to the History of Modern Science*, edited by R.C. Olby et al. London: Routledge, 1990.

Perrow, Charles. *Normal Accidents: Living With High-Risk Technologies*. New York: Basic Books, 1985.

Persley, Gabrielle J. *Beyond Mendel's Garden: Biotechnology in the Service of World Agriculture.* Wallingford, England: CAB International, 1990.

Pickstone, John V., ed. *Medical Innovations in Historical Perspective.* New York: St. Martin's Press, 1992.

Pochin, Edward. *Nuclear Radiation: Risk and Benefits.* New York: Oxford University Press, 1985.

Polkinghorne, J.C. *The Quantum World.* London and New York: Longman, 1984.

Porritt, J., and D. Winner. *The Coming of the Greens.* London: Fontana/Collins, 1988.

Porter, Roy. *The Enlightenment.* Basingstoke, Eng.: Macmillan, 1990.

——, ed. *Man Masters Nature: Twenty-Five Centuries of Science.* New York: George Brazilier, 1988.

——, and M. Teich, eds. *The Scientific Revolution in National Context.* Cambridge: Cambridge University Press, 1992.

Porter, Theodore M. "Natural Science and Social Theory." In *Companion to the History of Modern Science*, edited by R.C. Olby et al. London: Routledge, 1990.

Portugal, Franklin H., and Jack S. Cohen. *A Century of DNA: A History of the Discovery of the Structure and the Function of the Genetic Substance.* Cambridge, Mass.: MIT Press, 1977.

Posner, Erich. "Gerhard Domagk." In vol. 4 of *Dictionary of Scientific Biography*, edited by Charles C. Gillispie. 16 vols. New York: Charles Scribner's Sons, 1971.

Price, B.B. *Medieval Thought: An Introduction.* Oxford: Blackwell, 1992.

Pryor, John Y. *Geography, Technology, and War: Studies in the Maritime History of the Mediterranean, 649–1571.* Cambridge: Cambridge University Press, 1988.

Pyenson, Lewis. *The Young Einstein: The Advent of Relativity.* Bristol and Boston: Adam Hilger, 1985.

Rabino, Isaac. "The Impact of Activist Pressures on Recombinant DNA Research." *Science, Technology and Human Values* 16 (Winter 1991): 70–87.

Raggett, Jenny, and William Bains. *Artificial Intelligence from A to Z.* London: Chapman & Hall, 1992.

Rappaport, Rhoda. "Anne-Robert-Jacques Turgot." In vol. 13 of *Dictionary of Scientific Biography*, edited by Charles C. Gillispie. 16 vols. New York: Charles Scribner's Sons, 1976.

Rathbone-McCuan, E., and B. Havens. *North American Elders: United States and Canadian Perspectives.* Greenwood Press, 1988.

Ravetz, J.R. *Scientific Knowledge and Its Social Problems.* Oxford: Oxford University Press, 1971.

——. *The Merger of Knowledge with Power.* London: Mansell, 1990.

Redondi, Pietro. *Galileo Heretic.* Princeton: Princeton University Press, 1987.

Regens, James L., and Robert W. Rycroft. *The Acid Rain Controversy.* Pittsburgh: University of Pittsburgh Press, 1989.

Reingold, Nathan. *Science, American Style.* New Brunswick and London: Rutgers University Press, 1991.

Rhodes, Richard. *The Making of the Atomic Bomb.* New York: Simon & Schuster, 1986.

Riban, David M. *Introduction to Physical Science.* New York: McGraw- Hill, 1982.

Richards, Evelleen. *Vitamin C and Cancer: Medicine or Politics?* New York: St. Martin's Press, 1991.

Richards, Robert J. *Darwin and the Emergence of Evolutionary Theories of Mind and Behavior.* Chicago: University of Chicago Press, 1987.

Richardson, K. *The British Motor Industry, 1896–1939.* New York: 1977.

Rifkin, Jeremy. *Biosphere Politics: A Cultural Odyssey from the Middle Ages to the New Age.* New York: Harper Collins, 1991.

Rindos, D. *The Origins of Agriculture: An Evolutionary Perspective.* Orlando: Academic Press, 1984.

Roadburg, A. *Aging: Retirement, Leisure and Work in Canada.* Toronto: Methuen, 1985.

Roberts, L., P. Liss, and P. Saunders. *Power Generation and the Environment.* Oxford: Oxford University Press, 1990.

Robinson, Enders A. *Einstein's Relativity in Metaphor and Mathematics.* Englewood Cliffs, NJ: Prentice Hall, 1990.

Robinson, Eric, and A.E. Musson. *James Watt and the Steam Revolution: A Documentary History.* London: Adams & Dart, 1969.

Rochberg, F. Introduction to "The Cultures of Ancient Science: Some Historical Reflections." *Isis* 83 (1992): 547–553.

Roe, Shirley A. "Anatomia animata: the Newtonian physiology of Albrecht von Haller." In *Transformation and Tradition in the Sciences*, edited by Everett Mendelsohn. Cambridge: Cambridge University Press, 1984.

Roger, Jacques. "Georges-Louis Leclerc, Comte de Buffon." In vol. 2 of *Dictionary of Scientific Biography*, edited by Charles C. Gillispie. 16 vols. New York: Charles Scribner's Sons, 1970.

Ronan, Colin A. *The Cambridge Illustrated History of the World's Science*. Cambridge, England: Cambridge University Press, 1983.

Rosa, Jean-Jacques, ed. *The World Crisis in Social Security*. San Francisco: Institute for Contemporary Studies, 1982.

Rosen, Edward. "Nicholas Copernicus." In vol. 3 of *Dictionary of Scientific Biography*, edited by C.C. Gillispie. 16 vols. New York: Charles Scribner's Sons, 1971.

Rosenbaum, Walter A. *Environmental Politics and Policy*. Washington, D.C.: CQ Press, 1985.

Rosenberg, Michael. "The mother of invention: Evolutionary theory, territoriality, and the origins of agriculture." *American Anthropologist* 92 (1990): 399–415.

Rosencranz, A. "The acid rain controversy in Europe and North America—a political analysis." *Ambio* 15, no.1 (1986): 47–51.

Rosenthal, Debra. *At the Heart of the Bomb: The Dangerous Allure of Weapons Research*. Reading, Mass.: Addison-Wesley, 1990.

Ross, George Macdonald. "Science and Philosophy." In *Companion to the History of Modern Science*, edited by R.C. Olby et al. London: Routledge, 1990.

Rossi, Paolo. *Francis Bacon: From Magic to Science*. London: Routledge & Kegan Paul, 1968.

Rossiter, Margaret W. *Women Scientists in America: Struggles and Strategies to 1940*. Baltimore: Johns Hopkins University Press, 1982.

Roszak, Theodore. *The Cult of Information*. New York: Pantheon Books, 1986.

Rothschild, Joan. *Teaching Technology From a Feminist Perspective: A Practical Guide*. New York and Oxford: Pergamon Press, 1988.

Rouse, Joseph. *Knowledge and Power: Toward a Political Philosophy of Science*. Ithaca, NY: Cornell University Press, 1987.

Rousseau, G.S. *Enlightenment Borders: Pre- and Post-Modern Discourses: Medical, Scientific*. Manchester: Manchester University Press, 1991.

Rucker, Rudy. *The Fourth Dimension: A Guided Tour of the Higher Universes*. Boston: Houghton Mifflin, 1984.

Rude, George. *Debate on Europe: 1815–1850*. New York: Harper & Row, 1972.

Rudwick, Martin J.S. *The Great Devonian Controversy: The Shaping of Scientific Knowledge Among Gentlemanly Specialists*. Chicago: University of Chicago Press, 1985.

Ruse, Michael. *The Darwinian Paradigm: Essays on its History, Philosophy, and Religious Implications*. London: Routledge, 1989.

——. *The Darwinian Revolution*. Chicago: University of Chicago Press, 1979.

Russell, Colin A. *Science and Social Change: 1700–1900*. London: Macmillan, 1983.

Russett, Cynthia Eagle. *Sexual Science: The Victorian Construction of Womanhood*. Cambridge, Mass.: Harvard University Press, 1989.

Sallares, Robert. *The Ecology of the Ancient Greek World*. London: Duckworth, 1991.

Santillana, Giorgio de. *The Crime of Galileo*. Chicago: Phoenix Books, 1959.

Schaffer, Simon. "Newtonianism." In *Companion to the History of Modern Science*, edited by R.C. Olby et al. London: Routledge, 1990.

Schiebinger, Londa. *The Mind Has No Sex? Women in the Origins of Modern Science*. Cambridge, Mass.: Harvard University Press, 1989.

Schmandt, Jurgen, Judith Clarkson, and Hilliard Roderick. *Acid Rain and Friendly Neighbors: The Policy Dispute between Canada and the United States*. Revised ed. Durham NC: Duke University Press, 1988.

Schott, Thomas. "World Science: Globalization of Institutions and Participation." *Science, Technology, and Human Values* 18, No.2 (Spring 1993): 196–208.

Schuster, John A. "The Scientific Revolution." In *The Companion to the History of Modern Science*, edited by R.C. Olby et al. London: Routledege, 1990.

Schwartz, Joseph, and Michael McGuinness. *Einstein for Beginners*. New York: Pantheon, 1979.

Scientific American. *Managing Planet Earth*. New York: W.H. Freeman and Company, 1990.

Secord, James A. *Controversy in Victorian Geology: The Cambrian-Silurian Dispute*. Princeton, NJ: Princeton University Press, 1986.

Segre, Michael. *In the Wake of Galileo*. New Brunswick, NJ: Rutgers University Press, 1991.

Seitz, Frederick. *The Science Matrix*. New York: Springer-Verlag, 1992.

Shaiken, Harley. *Work Transformed*. New York: Holt, Rinehart and Winston, 1984.

Shapin, Steven. "Discipline and Bounding: The History and Sociology of Science as seen through the Externalism-Internalism Debate." *History of Science* 30 (December 1992): 333–369.

——, and Simon Schaffer. *Leviathan and the Air-Pump: Hobbes, Boyle and the Experimental Life*. Princeton, NJ: Princeton University Press, 1985.

Sherwin, Martin J. *A World Destroyed: Hiroshima and the Origins of the Arms Race*. New York: Vintage Books, 1987.

Shimony, Abner. "Conceptual foundations of quantum mechanics." In *The New Physics*, edited by Paul Davies. Cambridge, England: Cambridge University Press, 1989.

Shinn, T. "The genesis of French industrial research, 1880–1940." *Social Science Information* 19 (1980): 607–640.

Shor, Elizabeth Noble. "Othniel Charles Marsh." In vol. 9 of *Dictionary of Scientific Biography*, edited by Charles C. Gillispie. 16 vols. New York: Charles Scribner's Sons, 1974.

Simpkins, Diana M. "Thomas Robert Malthus." In vol. 9 of *Dictionary of Scientific Biography*, edited by Charles C. Gillispie. 16 vols. New York: Charles Scribner's Sons, 1974.

Sinclair, Bruce. "Technology on Its Toes: Late Victorian Ballets, Pageants, and Industrial Exhibitions." *In Context: History and the History of Technology*, edited by Stephen H. Cutliffe and Robert C. Post. London and Toronto: Associated University Presses, 1989.

Singer, Peter, and Deane Wells. *The Reproductive Revolution: New Ways of Making Babies*. New York and Oxford: Oxford University Press, 1984.

Singer, Sam. *Human Genetics*. 2d ed. New York: W.H. Freeman, 1985.

Siraisi, Nancy G. *Medieval & Early Renaissance Medicine: An Introduction to Knowledge and Practice*. Chicago and London: University of Chicago Press, 1990.

Sivin, Nathan. "Science and Medicine in Chinese History." In *Heritage of China: Contemporary Perspectives on Chinese Civilization*, edited by Paul S. Ropp. Berkeley: University of California Press, 1990.

Smith, Alice K. *A Peril and a Hope: The Scientists' Movement in America*, 1945–47. Chicago: University of Chicago Press, 1965.

Smith, Anthony. *The Newspaper: An International History*. London: Thames and Hudson, 1979.

Smith, Bruce L.R. *American Science Policy Since World War II*. Washington, D.C.: Brookings Institution, 1990.

Smith, Charles H., ed. *Alfred Russel Wallace: An Anthology of his Shorter Writings*. Oxford: Oxford University Press, 1991.

Smith II, George P. *The New Biology: Law, Ethics and Biotechnology*. New York and London: Plenum Press, 1989.

Smith, Robert W. *The Space Telescope: A Study of NASA, Science, Technology, and Politics*. Cambridge/ New York/Melbourne: Cambridge University Press, 1989.

Smith, Roger. "Alfred Russel Wallace: Philosopher of Nature and Man." *British Journal for the History of Science* 6 (1972): 177–199.

Sorell, Tom. *Descartes*. Oxford: Oxford University Press, 1987.

Sorensen, Knut H. "Towards a Feminized Technology? Gendered Values in the Construction of Technology." *Social Studies of Science* 22 (1992): 5–31.

Spector, Leonard. *Nuclear Ambitions: the Spread of Nuclear Weapons, 1989-1990*. Boulder: Westview Press, 1990.

Spiegel-Rosing, Ina, and Derek de Solla Price. *Science, Technology and Society: A Cross-Disciplinary Perspective*. London: SAGE, 1977.

Spielberg, Nathan, and Bryon D. Anderson. *Seven Ideas that Shook the Universe*. New York: John Wiley & Sons, 1985.

Spretnak, Charlene, and Fritjof Capra. *Green Politics*. Revised ed. Santa Fe, N.M.: Bear, 1986.

Stahl, William H. *Roman Science: Origins, Development and Influence to the Later Middle Ages*. Madison: University of Wisconsin Press, 1962.

Starr, Philip, and William Pearman. *Three Mile Island Sourcebook: Annotations of a Disaster*. New York: Garland, 1983.

Staudenmaier, John M. *Technology's Storytellers: Reweaving the Human Fabric*. Cambridge, Mass.: MIT Press, 1989.

Stent, Gunther S., ed. *The Double Helix: A Norton Critical Edition*. New York: W.W. Norton & Company, 1980.

Stewart, Larry. *The Rise of Public Science: Rhetoric, Technology, and Natural Philosophy in Newtonian Britain, 1660–1750*. New York: Cambridge University Press, 1992.

Stillman, John Maxson. *The Story of Alchemy and Early Chemistry*. New York: Dover Publications, 1960.

Stocking, George W. *Victorian Anthropology*. London: Collier Macmillan, 1987.

Stoff, Michael B., et al., eds. *The Manhattan Project: A Documentary Introduction to the Atomic Age*. Philadelphia: Temple University Press, 1991.

Storer, Norman W. *The Social System of Science*. New York: Holt, Rinehart & Winston, 1966.

Strahler, Arthur N. *Science and Earth History: the Evolution/Creation Controversy*. Buffalo: Prometheus Books, 1987.

Strassman, Paul A. *Information Payoff: The Transformation of Work in the Electronic Age*. New York: Free Press, 1985.

Sulloway, Frank J. "Darwin's conversion: the *Beagle* voyage and its aftermath." *Journal of the History of Biology* 15 (1982): 327–398.

Suzuki, David, and Peter Knudtson. *Genethics: The Ethics of Engineering Life*. Toronto: Stoddart, 1988.

Tamarin, Robert, and Ron W. Leavitt. *Principles of Genetics*. 3d ed. Dubuque, Iowa: Wm. C. Brown, 1991.

Tamny, Martin. "Atomism and the Mechanical Philosophy." In *Companion to the History of Modern Science*, edited by R.C. Olby et al. London: Routledge, 1990.

Taton, Rene, ed. *Ancient and Medieval Science*. New York: Basic Books, 1963.

Teller, Edward. *Conversations on the Dark Secrets of Physics*. New York: Plenum Press, 1991.

Thackray, Arnold, ed. *Science after '40*. Chicago: University of Chicago Press, 1992.

Thomas, John M. *Michael Faraday and the Royal Institution: The Genius of Man and Place*. Bristol: Adam Hilger, 1991.

Thompson, William B., ed. *Controlling Technology*. Buffalo: Prometheus Books, 1991.

Thurd, Robert, and John A. Hansen. *Keeping America at Work: Strategies for Employing the New Technologies*. New York: John Wiley & Sons, 1986.

Tiley, N.A. *Discovering DNA: Meditations on Genetics and a History of the Science*. New York: Van Nostrand Reinhold, 1983.

Tokar, Brian. "Exploring the new ecologies: social ecology, deep ecology and the future of Green political thought." *Alternatives* 15, no. 4 (1988): 31–43.

——. *The Green Alternative: Creating an Ecological Future*. San Pedro, CA: R. & E. Miles, 1987.

Travis, Anthony S. "Perkin's Mauve: Ancestor of the Organic Chemical Industry." *Technology and Culture* 31, No. 1 (1990): 51–82.

Turkle, Sherry. *The Second Self: Computers and the Human Spirit*. New York: Touchstone, 1985.

Upton, Arthur C. "The Biological Effects of Low-Level Ionizing Radiation." *Scientific American* 246, no. 2 (1982): 41–49.

Ure, Andrew. *Philosophy of Manufactures, or, an Exposition of the Scientific, Moral and Commercial Economy of the Factory System of Great Britain*. London: Charles Knight, 1835.

Vance, Mary A. *Nuclear Non-Proliferation: A Bibliography*. Monticello, Ill.: Vance Bibliographies, 1989.

Venturi, Franco. *Italy and the Enlightenment*. New York: New York University Press, 1972.

Vig, Norman J., and Michael E. Kraft. *Environmental Policy in the 1990s*. Washington, DC: Congressional Quarterly Press, 1990.

Ville, Simon P. *Transport and the Development of the European Economy*, 1750–1918. London: Macmillan, 1990.

Von Weiher, S. "The rise and development of electrical engineering and technology in Germany in the nineteenth century." In *Development and Diffusion of Technology*, edited by A. Okochi and H. Uchida. Tokyo: Tokyo University Press, 1980.

de Vries, J. *European Urbanization, 1500–1800*. London: Methuen, 1984.

Wade, Nicholas. *The Ultimate Experiment: Man-Made Evolution*. New and expanded ed. New York: Walker, 1979.

Wagner, Henry N., and Linda Ketchum. *Living With Radiation: the Risk, the Promise*. Baltimore: Johns Hopkins University Press, 1989.

Waites, Bernard. "Social and Human Engineering." In *Science, Technology, and Everyday Life, 1870–1950*, edited by Colin Chant. London: Routledge/Open University, 1989.

Wald, Robert M. *Space, Time, and Gravity*. 2d ed. Chicago: University of Chicago Press, 1992.

Walker, J. Samuel. *Containing the Atom: Nuclear Regulation in a Changing Environment, 1963–1971*. Berkeley: University of California Press, 1992.

——. "Reactor at the fault: the Bodega Bay nuclear plant controversy, 1958–1964. A case study in the politics of technology." *Pacific Historical Review* 59 (1990): 323–348.

Walker, Mark. *German National Socialism and the Quest for Nuclear Power, 1939–1949*. Cambridge, England: Cambridge University Press, 1989.

Wallace, Alfred Russel. *The Wonderful Century*. Westmead, England: Gregg International Publishers, 1970; reprint of 1st ed. of 1898.

——. *Studies, Scientific & Social*. 2 vols. London: Macmillan, 1900.

Wallace, Bruce. *The Search for the Gene*. Ithaca, NY: Cornell University Press, 1992.

Watson, James D. *The Double Helix*. New York: 1968.

——, and F.C. Crick [a]. "Molecular Structure of Nucleic Acids: A Structure for DNA." *Nature* 171 (April 25, 1953): 737–738.

——, and F.C. Crick [b]. "Genetical Implications of the Structure of Deoxyribonucleic Acid." *Nature* 171 (1953): 964–969.

——, et al. *Molecular Biology of the Gene*. 4th ed. Menlo Park, Calif.: Benjamin Cummings, 1987.

——, John Tooze, and David T. Kurtz. *Recombinant DNA: A Short Course*. New York: W.H. Freeman, 1983.

Weart, Spencer R. *Scientists in Power*. Cambridge, Mass.: Harvard University Press, 1979.

Webster, Andrew. *Science, Technology and Society*. New Brunswick, NJ: Rutgers University Press, 1991.

Weinberg, Nathan. *Computers in the Information Society*. Boulder CO: Westview Press, 1990.

Weisheipl, James A. *The Development of Physical Theory in the Middle Ages*. Ann Arbor: University of Michigan Press, 1971.

Weisz, George, ed. *Social Science Perspectives on Medical Ethics*. Dordrecht/Boston: Kluwer, 1990.

Weller, Robert, and Leon Bouvier. *Population: Demography and Policy*. New York: St. Martin's Press, 1981.

Wellington, J.J. *Skills and Progress in Science Education*. New York: Routledge, Chapman & Hall, 1990.

Westfall, Richard S. *The Construction of Modern Science: Mechanisms and Mechanics*. New York: Wiley, 1971.

———. *The Life of Isaac Newton*. New York: Cambridge University Press, 1993.

Wetstone, Gregory S., and Armin Rosencranz. *Acid Rain in Europe and North America: National Responses to an International Problem*. Washington, D.C. : Environmental Law Institute, 1983.

White, K.D. *Greek and Roman Technology*. London: Thames and Hudson, 1984.

Whitehead, M. *The Health Divide*. London: Penguin Books, 1988.

Wightman, W.P.D. *Science in a Renaissance Society*. London: Hutchinson, 1972.

Will, Clifford M. *Was Einstein Right?: Putting General Relativity to the Test*. New York: Basic Books, 1986.

Williams, L. Pearce. *Album of Science: The Nineteenth Century*. New York: Charles Scribner's Sons, 1978.

———, and H.J. Steffens. *The History of Science in Western Civilization*. University Press of America, 1977.

Williams, Rosalind. *Notes on the Underground: An Essay on Technology, Society, and the Imagination*. Cambridge, Mass./London: MIT Press, 1990.

Williams, Trevor I. *A Short History of Twentieth-century Technology, c.1900– c.1950*. New York: Oxford University Press, 1982.

Willoughby, Kelvin W. *Technology Choice: A Critique of the Appropriate Technology Movement*. Boulder, CO: Westview Press, 1990.

Wilson, L.G. *Charles Lyell, The Years to 1841: The Revolution in Geology*. New Haven: Yale University Press, 1972.

———. "Charles Lyell." In vol. 8 of *Dictionary of Scientific Biography*, edited by Charles C. Gillispie. 16 vols. New York: Charles Scribner's Sons, 1973.

Winch, Donald. *Malthus*. Oxford: Oxford University Press, 1987.

Winkler, Mary G., and Albert Van Helden. "Representing the Heavens: Galileo and Visual Astronomy." *Isis* 83 (1992): 195–217.

Wiseman, H., J. Vanderkop, and J. Nef. *Critical Choices: Ethics, Science and Technology*. Toronto: Thompson Educational Publishing, 1991.

Wolfe, Joan. *Making Things Happen: The Guide for Members of Volunteer Organizations*. Andover, Mass.: Brick House, 1983.

Wolfson, Richard. *Nuclear Choices: A Citizen's Guide to Nuclear Technology*. Cambridge, Mass.: MIT Press, 1991.

Wolinski, F.D., et al. "The Risk of Nursing Home Placement and Subsequent Death Among Older Adults." *Journal of Gerontology: SOCIAL SCIENCES* 47 (1992): S173–S182.

The World Almanac and Book of Facts, 1992. New York: World Almanac, 1992.

Wormald, B.H.G. *Francis Bacon: History, Politics and Science, 1561–1626*. Cambridge: Cambridge University Press, 1992.

Worster, Donald. *Nature's Economy: A History of Ecological Ideas*. Cambridge: Cambridge University Press, 1985.

Worthen, Thomas D. *The Myth of Replacement: Stars, Gods, and Order in the Universe*. Tucson: University of Arizona Press, 1991.

Wright, Susan. *Preventing a Biological Arms Race*. Cambridge, Mass.: MIT Press, 1990.

Wrigley, Chris, and John Shepherd, eds. *On the Move: Essays in Labour and Transport History Presented to Philip Bagwell*. London: Hambledon Press, 1991.

Wyman, Richard L., ed. *Global Climate Change and Life on Earth*. New York and London: Routledge, Chapman and Hall, 1991.

Yanchinski, Stephanie, ed. *Biotechnology: A Brave New World?* Cambridge, England: Lutterworth Press, 1989.

Ycas, Martynas. "Recent Trends in Health Near the Age of Retirement." *Social Security Bulletin* 50 (1987): 5–30.

Yearley, Steven. *Science, Technology and Social Change.* Boston: Unwin Hyman, 1989.

Yeo, R. "Science and Intellectual Authority in Mid-Nineteenth-Century Britain: Robert Chambers and 'Vestiges of the Natural History of Creation'" *Victorian Studies* 28 (1984): 5–31.

York, Herbert F. *The Advisors: Oppenheimer, Teller, and the Superbomb.* Stanford: Stanford University Press, 1989.

Young, David. *The Discovery of Evolution.* Cambridge: Cambridge University Press, 1993.

Young, Robert M. *Darwin's Metaphor: Nature's Place in Victorian Culture.* Cambridge: Cambridge University Press, 1985.

Ziman, John. *The Force of Knowledge: The Scientific Dimension of Society.* Cambridge: Cambridge University Press, 1976.

Index

A

Abacus, 163
Abstraction: in biology, 141; in Galileo's method, 62–63
Académie des Sciences (Paris), 51, 75
Acid precipitation, 224–233
Acid rain, 224–233
Acid surge, 228
Acupuncture, 14–15, 256
Adaptation: and creationism, 86–87; to environment, 89–92
Adelard of Bath, 15, 19
Aerodynamics, 158
Agencies, watchdog, 246–247
Agricultural revolution, 4–5
Agriculture, multiple origins of, 4
AI. *See* Intelligence, artificial
AIDS: public health and, 252
Airplanes, 157–161, 204
Alchemy, 17, 205; scope of, 42–45; symbolism in, 44–45
Alembert, Jean le Rond d', 67, 73–74
Alexandria: Library of, 11
Algebra: origins of term, 16
Alhazen, 16
Allergy, atopic, 254
Almagest, 27
Alpha rays, 205–206, 218–220
Alphabet: origins of, 6–7
Amino acids, 137–139
Atom, Bohr model of, 132–133
Anaximander, 9
Androids, 176
Anno Domini (A.D.): first use of term, 18
Antibiotics, 253
Antiquity of Man, 93
Apollo program, 160
Apple computer, 178–179
Appropriate technology.
   See Technology, appropriate
Aqueducts, Roman, 12
Arabic numerals: Hindu origins of, 15–16, 19
Archimedes, 10
Architecture, computer, 167

Arc lighting, 147
Arctic: acid precipitation in, 224–225
Argument from design, 86–87
Aristarchus, 31
Aristotle: criticized by Bacon, 60; Linnaeus on species concept of, 87; Lyceum, 10; physics of, 42–43
Arkwright, Richard, 97–99, 108
Arms race: biological dimension of, 201; in Cold War, 213; origins of modern, 204–210
Artificial selection, 189–190
Asilomar Conference, 194–198
Aspirin, 104, 253
Assembly line, 153
Astrolabe, 58
Astrology, 44–45
Astronomy: Kepler's Laws in, 40–41; links to navigation, 58
Aswan Dam, 258
Atomic bomb, 126, 203–212, 236
Atomic Energy Commission (AEC), 211
Atomic energy: international control of, 211–212
Atomic Energy of Canada Limited (AECL), 215–217
Automated Teller Machines, 183–185
Automation: Babbage on, 163; computing and, 163, 173–178; of office systems, 179
Automatons: Descartes on animals as, 171–172
Automobile, 149–157; cultural impact of, 154–157; as symbol of technology, 152–154
Avery, Oswald T., 140
Aviation: initial public response to, 157–159; civilian; 161–162; military, 160–161
Avicenna, 17

B

Babbage, Charles, 163
Baby Boom, 262, 264
Bacon, Francis, 102, 235, 266; career of, 56; on cultural role of science/technology, 57–60, 68–69; on Four Idols, 56–57; method of, 61–63
Bacon, Roger, 21

Balance, chemical, 52
Barber, Bernard, 242
Base pairs, 141–142
Beamish, R.J.: introduction of term acid rain by, 229–230
Beccaria, Cesare, 74
Becher, Johann Joachim, 49
Becquerel, Henri, 205
Bell, Alexander Graham, 103
Bell Laboratories, 166, 169
Benz, Karl, 151–152
Berg, Paul, 143
Bernard, Claude, 77
Berthollet, Claude Louis, 53, 75
Berzelius, Jons Jacob: introduction of modern chemical nomenclature by, 54; research laboratory of, 81
Beta rays, 205–206, 218–220
Big science: government funding of, 208–212; rise of, 243
Bioethics, 141, 241–247
Biogen, 193–194
Biogeography, 90–91
Biohazards: in biotechnology, 194–201; of radiation, 218–222
Biomass technology, 232–233
Biosphere, 197, 201; nuclear wastes in, 220–221; politics of, 267–269
Biotechnology, 188–201, 248, 254
Black, Joseph, 97–98
Bleriot, Louis, 159
Bohr, Niels, 132, 205–207
Boulton, Matthew, 98, 101–103, 151
Boyer, Herbert, 192–195
Boyle, Robert, 48–49
Brahe, Tycho, 35–36, 40
Brain, evolution of, 165
Braun, Werner von, 160
British Association for the Advancement of Science (BAAS), 79, 84
Broglie, Louis de, 131–132
Brownian motion: Einstein on, 119–120
Buddhism: not conducive to science, 15
Buffering of lakes, 227–228
Buffon, Georges-Louis LeClerc, Comte de, 88
Bulletin of the Atomic Scientists, 211, 245–246
Business history, 148, 151–154, 161
Butler, Samuel, 172
Byrd, Richard E., 160

C

Caloric, 52
Canada: free-trade agreement with U.S., 248; nuclear policies of, 213–217; universal health care in, 263–265; wartime research in, 208–210, 214–215
Canadian Coalition on Acid Rain, 230
Canadian Nuclear Association, 216–217
CANDU, 212–224, 231
Capek, Karel, 176
Capitalism: Scientific Revolution and, 20, 55, 58–59
Careers: in science, 85; women in scientific and engineering, 269–271
Carlyle, Thomas, 109–110
Carnot, Lazare, 75
Carson, Rachel, 236
Cartesian dualism, 88–89, 171–173
Cartography, medieval, 20
Catholic Church: Galileo's conflict with, 65–66
Causality, 135
Cavendish, Henry, 51
Celestial/terrestrial dichotomy: Aristotle on, 10; Copernicus' rejection of, 32; disproved by Newton, 41; refuted by Galileo, 39; Plato on, 28
Cellular functions: gene control of, 141
Central processing unit (CPU), 167–168, 181–182
Certainty, Cartesian, 61
Chadwick, James: discovery of neutron, 206
Chain, Ernst, 253
Chain of being, 87
Chain reaction, 206–207
Chalk River (Ontario), 215, 220
Chargaff, Erwin, 140, 143
Chargaff's rules, 140–143
Châtelet, Marquise du, 69
Chemical Revolution: concept of, 52–54
Chemical technique: Boyle on, 48–49
Chemistry: origins of modern, 42–54
Chemists' war, 204
Chemotherapy: origin of, 253
Chernobyl, 217, 221–222, 236–237, 265
China: failure of Scientific Revolution in, 23; medieval science and technology in, 13–15; pollution in, 224, 226
Chromosomes, 138–139

M

Machines: human relationship to, 162, 170–173
MacLeod, C. M., 140
Magazines, computer, 179
Magic bullet: neutron as, 206
Magnetic compass, 14, 20
Malay Archipelago: Wallace's travels to, 90–92
Malthus, Thomas, 89–90, 95, 109
Manchester Literary and Philosophical Society, 102
Manhattan Project, 204–212, 214–215, 243, 245
Markets, national: railroads and, 145–146
Marx, Karl, 108–109
Mass, relativistic, 126
Mass consumption, 105–106, 260
Mass-energy equivalence, 126–127
Mass market: automobiles in, 153–155; computers in, 179–181
Mass production, 105–106, 153–154, 259–260
Mass transit, 147–149, 155–157, 233
Mastery of nature, 266; Bacon on, 56–57, 59–60, 68–69; Enlightenment concept of, 68–69, 76; feminist perspective on, 269–270; in medieval alchemy, 46; origins of concept, 5
Materialism, 88–89, 172
Mathematization of nature: Galileo on, 64
Mauchly, John, 164
Maxwell, James Clerk, 121
Maybach, Wilhelm: gasoline carburetor of, 151
Mayow, John, 49, 52
McCarty, M., 140
McCorduck, Pamela, 169
McGill University, 81, 205
Mechanical clock, 14
Mechanical philosophy: in Boyle, 48; in Descartes, 62; in Galileo, 63–65; limitations of, 63–64; nineteenth-century critiques of, 119
Mechanical world-view, 269–270
Media, mass: acid rain debates in, 230; environmental protests in, 268; gender stereotyping in, 271; in health care controversies, 254–256; nuclear controversies in, 221–222; role of, 240, 246
Medicaid, 263–264
Medical genetics, 198–201
Medical-industrial complex, 264–265
Medicare, 263–264

Medicean stars, 37
Medicine: science/technology in, 251–256
Medicis: as Galileo's patrons, 62
Meitner, Lise, 206–207
Mendel, Gregor, 93, 137, 140, 190
Merchant, Carolyn, 269–270
Merton, Robert K., 242
Mesopotamia: origins of civilization in, 2, 5
Metabolism, inborn errors of, 199
Metaphysics: Comte on, 76–77
Metric system, 75
Michelson-Morley experiment, 122–124
Microelectronics, 162–188, 244
Microoganisms, genetics of, 141
Microprocessor, invention of, 167
Microwaves, 240
Middle Ages: use of term, 17
Military-industrial complex, 210–212, 214–215, 221–224
Mill, John Stuart, 77
Miniaturization, computer, 166–167
MITI, 168–169, 176
Model T, 153–154
Modems, 180, 188
Molecular biology, 136–143
Monge, Gaspard, 76
Montgolfier ballon, 158
Morveau, Louis Bernard Guyton de, 51, 53
Motion: Kepler's laws of, 40; uniform, 34, 36–37, 117, 121–126
Mt. St. Helens, 229
Muller, Hermann J., 218
Mu-mesons, 127
Mumford, Lewis, 112
Mutations, 92, 141, 190

N

Nader, Ralph, 236
Napoleon I, 75
National Institutes of Health (NIH), 194–198
Naturalism: in Buffon, 88; in Lyell, 89
Natural philosophy, 55, 71
Natural place: Aristotle on, 10; of four elements, 28–29; gravity and, 36
Natural selection, 172; joint discovery of, 89–94
Navigation, 58–59, 161
Nazis: nuclear program of, 207–208
Neolithic farmers, 4